A Repertoire of
Contemporary Portuguese Poetry

Portuguese Literary & Cultural Studies 7
Fall 2001

A Repertoire of Contemporary Portuguese Poetry

Center for Portuguese Studies and Culture
University of Massachusetts Dartmouth

Portuguese Literary & Cultural Studies is a multilingual interdisciplinary peer-reviewed journal published semi-annually by the Center for Portuguese Studies and Culture at the University of Massachusetts Dartmouth. The journal addresses the literatures and cultures of the diverse communities of the Portuguese-speaking world in terms of critical and theoretical approaches.

Manuscript Policy

Portuguese Literary & Cultural Studies (PLCS) welcomes submission of original and unpublished manuscripts in English, Portuguese, or Spanish appropriate to the goals of the journal. Manuscripts should be in accordance with the *MLA Style Manual and Guide to Scholarly Publishing* (latest version) with parenthetical documentation and a list of Works Cited. The author is responsible for the accuracy of all quotations, titles, names, and dates. Font and sizes as close as possible to the style of the previous issue of PLCS should be used throughout the text. All of the information must be in the same language (e.g., abstract, body of the article, bio-blurb). Updated specific guidelines for submission of manuscripts to PLCS (articles, short articles, review-essays, and reviews) are available at www.plcs.umassd.edu (please consult Guidelines). PLCS encourages submission of manuscripts in the form of an attached single MS Word file.

Subscription Information

The annual subscription (2 issues) for institutions is $80.00 and $40.00 for individuals. Single issues may also be purchased for $25.00. From outside the United States add $12.00 for shipping and handling.

Inquiries should be sent to *Portuguese Literary & Cultural Studies*, Center for Portuguese Studies and Culture, University of Massachusetts Dartmouth, Dartmouth, MA 02747 USA, or by email to: adamastororders@umassd.edu.

In Portugal, issues may be purchased at Livraria Buchholz. Please contact the bookstore to place your order. Livraria Buchholz, Rua Duque de Palmela, 4, 1250-098 Lisbon; Tel. 351-21-317-0580, E-mail: buchholz@mail.telepac.pt.

Advertising

Cover
Design: Spencer Ladd.

ISSN 1521-804X
ISBN: 1-933227-08-7
© 2008 University of Massachusetts Dartmouth

Printed by Command Print Solutions, New Bedford, MA

Table of Contents

Other Articles

Editor's Note

Victor K. Mendes

The first section of *A Repertoire of Contemporary Portuguese Poetry* encompasses nine poets as critically read by a younger generation of critics. As for some orchestras or theater companies, parts of this repertoire could be different in different circumstances, but any convincing alternative list of poets would have to overlap, at least partially, with the one presented here. Starting with authors publishing since 1961 and ending with those who debuted in the 1980s, this is a relatively cautious sequence, in the sense that it leaves for another opportunity poets with more recent publishing careers, some of them already highly acclaimed, like the winner of the 2008 Poetry Prize awarded by the Portuguese Association of Writers, Ana Luísa Amaral.

1961 was the complex year of the first books by Ruy Belo and Herberto Helder; the group *Poesia 61,* with Luiza Neto Jorge among its five members, was also launched. In brief, the modernist Fernando Pessoa's posthumous influence on twentieth-century Portuguese poets would start being seriously challenged over the following decades. The poets publishing consistently at least since the 1970s, an outstanding decade of Portuguese poetry for different generations, include Vasco Graça Moura, António Franco Alexandre, João Miguel Fernandes Jorge and Nuno Júdice. Two poets who debuted in the 1980s, Fernando Pinto do Amaral and Adília Lopes, complete this short repertorial list of nine.

Portuguese Literary & Cultural Studies 7 (2008): xiii-xiv.
© University of Massachusetts Dartmouth.

In the second section of this volume, among other articles and reviews, the two major figures of Portuguese poetry, Luís de Camões and Fernando Pessoa, are revisited. The renowned translators Landeg White, Richard Zenith and Alexis Levitin gave us this time their versions of some poems by Camões, Ruy Belo and Herberto Helder. We kindly invite you, dear reader, to return to some of these poets once in a while, in English, in Portuguese, or in both. These artists are among the most compelling that the "language of Camões" has to offer.

Articles

Splendor in the Grass: Ruy Belo and the Poetry Lesson

Pedro Serra

The poetry of Ruy Belo is the place of an impossible thanatology. His poetics, in this sense, is aware of not being able to objectify "death" as a *theme*. In his first book of poems, *Aquele Grande Rio Eufrates*, we read: "A morte é a grande palavra desse homem / não há outra que o diga a ele mesmo" ("Death is the great word of that man / there is no other that can utter him") (*Obra Poética*, Belo 1:19). The development of Belo's writing comes about by diluting the transcendence implied here, that of an existence with an entelechy, albeit nihilist. In his last book of poems, the same proposition is again recurrent, in the last verse of the poem "A fonte da Arte," written in Madrid on 24 April 1977: "O receio da morte é a fonte da arte" ("Fear of death is the source of art") (Belo 2: 297). "Death" is something as prosaic as "fear," but without the *pathos* of an ultimate destiny. The trope of the "fount" returns exhausted, since, as I am going to argue throughout this essay, Ruy Belo's poetry and poetics are located in the posterity of a Poetry whose too high level of consciousness signifies its dissolution as "fount." This is perhaps a possible measure of the poetry of Ruy Belo, which situates in a modern way—and in it there is an echo of a Hegelian lesson—Art as something posthumous. By transporting its own corpse, this poetry is highly aware of the historicity of the poetic *form*.

I propose, therefore, to think about the poetry of Ruy Belo as a function of its assignment to "Romanticism," a link which in its day was established by Joaquim Manuel Magalhães. To say that Ruy Belo's writing has a Romantic

Portuguese Literary & Cultural Studies 7 (2008): 17-27.
© University of Massachusetts Dartmouth.

genealogy is to say that it is poetry. The notion of "Romanticism" displayed by the author of *Um Pouco da Morte* is highly indebted to the Romantic legacy—the Wordsworthian one, for example—read as a poetics of nature. Very specifically, that "Romanticism" is based on the idea of poetry as a fusion of consciousness and the world. In the notional decanting on which he bases his poetology—by adding the operators "Romanticism" and "Classicism," in a gesture of broad syncretism of different aesthetic traditions—the strong tradition to which Joaquim Manuel Magalhães assigns Ruy Belo is that of a "Classical Romanticism" according to which, in a world of inalienable unbalances, the only canon of *decorum* is precisely poetry: "Herein resides the principle by which there is not, either in Ruy Belo or in the poets in whose work his poetry grows, a break with decorum, with the balance between sentiment and world and word. On the contrary, what is patent is the quest for a new equilibrium, where neither the world can be imposed on sentiment, nor sentiment on the world. It is a matter of a Romantic tradition in which the dynamics between the self and things is searching for a new pact through an initial breaking away: classical equilibrium becomes a superimposition on the path of excessive sabotage of sentiment. It was necessary to set up a renewed dialogue between the soul and the daily world, between the spirit and the materiality of the earth" (Magalhães, 148). The *happiness* of the "balance between sentiment and world and word" is Magalhães' *organon.* According to the premises stated, *being* in the world is *to be* a poet, or rather, only poets can transcend a separate "existence."

In my view, the "Romantic" reading of Ruy Belo must be reoriented. To think about Belian "Romanticism" in this sense is a good example of the validity of its importance as a "problem," according to Paul De Man in "Wordsworth and Hölderlin," an essay initially published in German in the journal *Schweizer Monatshefte* (1966) and later in English in *The Rhetoric of Romanticism* (1984). In this essay we read the following: "the problem of romanticism continues to dominate the other problems of historiography and literary criticism. The main points around which contemporary methodological and ideological arguments circle can almost always be traced directly back to the romantic heritage" (48). Thinking about the "Romanticism" of Ruy Belo thus presupposes not forgetting that his poetry, as a reverberation of the Romantic problem, also dominates "other problems of historiography and literary criticism." This means that to think about the "Romanticism" of Ruy Belo's poetry is also to think about the place it occupies in a history of contemporary Portuguese poetry, inseparable from the question of the situation of literary criticism in that same history. This argument is sufficient, I believe, to serve as the foundation of a necessary *revision* of the "consensus" there is on the importance of Belian poetics during the eighties and nineties in Portuguese poetry. This "consensus" is not the figure of something resolved, it is the indication of the search for a trope—for example, "Ruy Belo"—of this "consensus."

I shall return to Joaquim Manuel Magalhães as an example of what I seek to explain. I am focusing, quite specifically, on the reading of the poem "Esplendor na Relva" ("Splendour in the Grass") made by the author of the major essays included in the first edition of the complete works of Ruy Belo (*Obra Poética*, vols. 1 and 2, Lisbon, Presença, 1981; vol. 3 Lisbon, Presença, 1984). This poem appeared published in *Homem de Palavra(s)*, a 1970 book of poems which followed *Aquele Grande Rio Eufrates* (1961), *O Problema da Habitação* (1962) and *Boca Bilingue* (1966). It is the following sonnet (in Portuguese and in English):

Eu sei que deanie loomis não existe
mas entre as mais essa mulher caminha
e a sua evolução segue uma linha
que à imaginação pura resiste

A vida passa e em passar consiste
e embora eu não tenha a que tinha
ao começar há pouco esta minha
evocação de deanie quem desiste

na flor que dentro em breve há-de murchar?
(e aquele que no auge a não olhar
que saiba que passou e que jamais

lhe será dado ver o que ela era)
Mas em deanie prossegue a primavera
e vejo que caminha entre as mais

I know that deanie loomis does not exist
but among other women that woman walks
and her evolution follows a line
that resists pure imagination

Life passes and in passing it consists
and although I no longer have the one I had
upon beginning not long ago this my
evocation of deanie, who gives up

on the flower soon to fade?
(and he who at the blooming does not look at her
may know that she passed and that never

will it be given him to see what she was)
But in deanie spring continues
And I see that she walks among other women.

The cinematographic reference to Elia Kazan's well-known film is crossed, simultaneously, with Wordsworth's intertext. Let us now look at Joaquim Manuel Magalhães's reading, which starts exactly from the *quotational* nature of Belo's sonnet: "Wordsworth is directly invoked in the title of the poem 'Esplendor na Relva,' although that title refers to the film by Elia Kazan, who cites the ode by Wordsworth. The persistence, in memory, of life's past splendour, and the resistance, through creation, to the mortal flow of existence affirm the splendour of writing in the face of the defeat of the body and the natural visionary impulse. 'In deanie', i.e., in the creature of the imagination, in the artefact of art, 'spring persists', i.e., the mortality of the instant is fought against" (Magalhães 152).

In this paragraph the reverberation of the above mentioned *affirmative* poetology I have just summarized is evident—i.e., a poetry which signifies the *overcoming* of alterative time, of History—and which Joaquim Manuel Magalhães considers to be incarnated in Ruy Belo. Really, in any poet who is considered by the critic to be a poet: for Magalhães *being a poet* presupposes an anthropological sublimation, poetry is not really history but ontology. However, the passage invoked explicitly embodies a series of significant reading operations. Basically it extracts consequences from the "image" of Deanie Loomis as a "creature *of the* imagination" and, as such, a symbol of "art" itself, of an art that is precisely symbolic. Magalhães's poetology also distinguishes two time regimes: one which is "mortal flow," "defeat of the body" or "mortality of the instant" and another which is that of the products of the imagination—Art—as "persistence" of what has been lived, as "resistance" to mortality and, moreover, as persistence of "spring."

This second temporality is copied from "Nature," which produces identicals and identities of ontology without *crisis.* The "past" persists in the euphoriant exercising of "memory"; the act of creation, copied from what is *natural,* is identical to itself. Thus, the "splendour of writing" is the univocal expression of the "splendour of the past," commutable with the "splendour in the grass", and can be translated as the splendour of the "world." *Writing,* in this sense, is only one of the terms of the organic unit writing/world. The "image" of Deanie Loomis, following what is implied in Magalhães's argument, has a "correlative object": either the Wordsworthian quotation, or the film quotation, or else the "world" they symbolize. Be this as it may, they are the essential ontologized, which in relation to poetic diction is an inalienable *a priori.* In this poetology of Magalhães there is only nature, or naturalizations, which a poem can only represent naturally: poetic tradition—or the history of poetry—the poem or the poet, the latter modulated by a "natural visionary impulse," as we have read before.

But let us return to "Esplendor na Relva." The first verse of the sonnet refers us to the *negation* of what is named "deanie loomis," both from the *intellective* point of view—"I know that deanie loomis does not exist"—and as regards the *imaginative* faculty—"her evolution follows a line / *that resists pure imagination*" (italics mine). The first quatrain suggests to us a non-mediatized being that would be precisely "deanie loomis." However, what we also have is the sustaining of an imagistic tension, played in the otherness of Deanie Loomis with relation to the already mentioned *intellective* and *imaginative* faculties, and the "referential" imperative, represented by the second and third lines: "but among other women that woman walks / and her evolution follows a line," The adversative introduces that way of not existing—non-mediatized by reason or by the imagination; and let us also focus on the fact that the deictic "that" and the verbs of movement "walks" and "follows," as well as the word "woman," establish an axis of redundancy that forces the (paradoxical) suggestion of a *sensitive* mediation of what is named "deanie loomis." The effect is, moreover, intensified by an important segment of the second line: "among other women." Thus, an ontological equivalence is suggested between "other women" and "woman," something like a contiguity of *loci*: that of those "existing" and that of "deanie loomis [who] does not exist."

Let us return to this second line, a truly important one since with it the poem comes to an end, although it introduces a revealing variant. Before, however, I would call attention to the fact that Joaquim Manuel Magalhães's reading disregards a great part of the poem. The second verse is not even involved in his exegesis. The same occurs with the first tercet and the first line of the second tercet. Actually, in my opinion, what is most interesting in the poem is completely overlooked. It is a "sonnet," as I have been saying, a "classic" form, as we know, precisely based on *decorum*, on "harmony" according to the canon of its historical cultivators. The equation, thematically established by Magalhães, between "Deanie Loomis" and "artefact of art," could be that of this very sonnet as a "natural" form which, as such, can be read as a place of the *decorous* reciprocity of the terms of that equation. For Magalhães, "Deanie Loomis" exists as a natural object, that is, as an artistic artefact or poem. Thus, "Deanie Loomis," "artefact of art" or "poem" are *literally* such objects.

Rather than a "decorous" form, or the practice of formal decorum, what occurs in this sonnet—the same as in others by Ruy Belo, moreover—is the figure of what is "indecorous." Does the balance between "sentiment," "world," and "word" appear in it, as we read implicitly in Magalhães? This appearance, let us say, would be something like its consideration as "object" that was not a made thing: it would be something perfect. Here, I avail myself of a proposition by Ruy Belo to counteract this *happiness*: "a perfeição [tamanha perfeição] é coisa de mortos" ("perfection [such perfection] is a thing of the dead") (1: 18). In reality, it is actually Ruy Belo himself who contradicts this balance. The exercise of the sonnet, for the author of *Boca Bilingue*, can be assimilated to the repetitive nature of the forms of literary culture. In other words, the sonnet is, in Ruy Belo, one of his "incorrigible cultural allusions" (1: 11). In this sense I turn to a passage of the preface to the second edition of *Aquele Grande Rio Eufrates*: "If, for example, the sonnet only appeared in his third book, it was because he could no longer resist the inevitable temptation of that form which, for nothing less than fifteen long years, he practiced with the hidden and obstinate nature of a vice" (1:16). If this trope of *vice* refers us to anything at all, it is to the vicious circle of the return to the forms of cultural tradition, which strip the poetic *dictum* of a unitary expressive agency. This imperative of cultural allusion in Ruy Bello is concomitant with his broadening of the repository of canonized forms of the modernist *ethos*, in the posterity of which the poet is situated.

This idea of the imposition of a form such as the sonnet, apparently, would shape its de-historicization. However, reading *this* sonnet attentively, we see that what it does is precisely deny its naturalness and, by synecdoche, the naturalness of the tradition of the forms. And this because it revokes different essential places of that lyrical tradition. One of these is, very significantly, the dogma of a "psychological" unity that would organize and unify the poem. Really, the lyrical subject introduces self-consciousness as (if it were) another, otherness as that consciousness, specifically in the second verse: "and although I no longer have the one [life] I had / upon beginning not long ago this my / evocation of deanie." See, first, how Ruy Belo focuses the development of the poem on the very act of writing: the lyrical self is, in this sense, conditioned by the impossibility of making the moment of the writing of the poem coincide with its temporality as a subject. The subject affirms itself as not identical to itself precisely as the subject that is writing, that starts from the "singular" event which is "to begin" an evocation, or "to begin" to write a sonnet. However, it is precisely in this singular moment when the imposition of the "sonnet" as recurrence of the naturalized tradition is historicized: this sonnet does not repeat the sonnet as a commonplace of tradition (or tradition as a commonplace); it repeats the sonnet as difference, it launches it into difference precisely because it inscribes it in a metamorphic, subjective structure.

The overdetermination of the unstable subjective over the objective means that the "sonnet" of tradition does not appear *in this* sonnet. On the contrary, it denies this form as permanence or (poetic) foundation. Really, and if we return to Ruy Belo's reflections on his hidden practice of the sonnet, what we can read in that place is the exhaustion of this form as a poetic essential. The irresistible "temptation" of the sonnet leads us not so much to the imposition of a poetic foundation as to a poetics whose exhausted forms can be *revised* as historical forms. Like Elia Kazan's film or Wordsworth's poem, the sonnet, in "Esplendor Na Relva," is a reference that revokes its organicity. Furthermore, this revocation, in Ruy Belo's poetic work, follows two roads 1) the commutation of the very form "poem" in favour of the form "book," as Osvaldo Manuel Silvestre has proposed (10-11); 2) the commutation of a poetical canon dominated by the short poem in favour of the long poem.

All this, evidently, has consequences for the reading of the image of "Deanie Loomis." I argued earlier that, following the interpretation of Joaquim Manuel Magalhães, "Deanie Loomis" would be a symbol: Art as Nature or identity with itself. This reading goes through the following passage stated by the critic: "In Deanie, that is, in the creature of the imagination, in the artefact of art." See how he uses the preposition "in," suggesting both "Deanie" and the "artefact of art" as (ontologically) stable places. Whatever the "natural" object supposed by the image of Deanie Loomis as Magalhães conceives her—I am thinking above all of a poetic tradition as nature—what, as I have said, this way of reading implies is the priority of the natural object over this image.

Here I follow Paul de Man's important essay entitled "Intentional Structure of the Romantic Image," also included in *The Rhetoric of Romanticism* (1-17). Starting from the well-known place of Hölderlin's poetry—"Worte, wie Blumen, entstehn" from "Brot und Wein"—De Man shows how the way in which nature "gives origin" does not coincide with the way in which the word does. Let us read the following passage, concerning, precisely, the images that seek to express this coincidence: "This type of imagery is grounded in the intrinsic ontological primacy of the object, and its growth and development are determined by this inclination. We saw that this movement is essentially paradoxical and condemned in advance to failure. There can be flowers that 'are' and poetic words that 'originate,' but no poetic words that 'originate' as if they 'were'" (7).

For Magalhães, a Deanie Loomis as "creature of the imagination" presupposes, by its attributes of "persistence," "resistance" and "per[sistence] *of spring*," having been generated as a natural object. It presupposes an Art, a poetic word, which would give origin like Nature. A Poetry that would have given origin like Nature, however, *forgets* the following "[I]t is in the essence of language to be capable of origination, but of never achieving the absolute identity with itself that exists in the natural object. Poetic language can do nothing but originate anew over and over again; it is always constitutive, able to posit regardless of presence but, by the same token, unable to give a foundation to what it posits except as an intent of consciousness" (6). "Deanie Loomis," for Magalhães, would be that identity with itself: the "artefact of art" as essence, or the "splendour of writing" indiscernible from the "splendour in the grass."

Nature is called up by the poem in "but in deanie spring continues" and, even before this penultimate line in the second tercet, in the first line of the first tercet, which continues a sentence started in the second quatrain: "who gives up / on the flower soon to fade?" The immediate antecedent is the "evocation of deanie," and this contiguity added to the later reference to "spring" contributes to the assimilation of "deanie" to the "flower" itself. This assimilation is further reinforced in the lines between brackets "(and he who at the blooming does not look at her / may know that she passed and that never / will it be given him to see what *she* was)." This "she" that I have italicized can refer to "Deanie Loomis" as well as to "flower." The lack of deictic determination in these lines, moreover, also affects "he who at the blooming" in which "at the blooming" can be either an attribute of "he" or of "Deanie Loomis" or of "flower." This "blooming" is also an indeterminate reference; it can refer to the "moment" of the imminence of the end of the "flower" as well as to the changeable condition of the subject which we read in the second verse and, in my opinion, the "he" can refer to both the subject and, with some leeway, to a reader, for example, Joaquim Manuel Magalhães or myself.

And even to Ruy Belo himself as reader of his poem. Indeed, the poet has left us some very brief but fundamental considerations, which from here on will influence my reading of the sonnet. They are the following: "It must be noted that *Splendor in the Grass* shows the precise moment when Natalie Wood, a wonderful actress, who in the film plays the delicate and fresh figure of Deanie Loomis, brilliantly directed by Elia Kazan, attempts in vain to comment in class an extract from a poem by Wordsworth on the fleetingness of life and the need, as a condition for happiness, to pick the flower at the very instant when it blooms" (Belo 1: 137). First, it must be stressed that this reflection leads the reading back to another scenario of poetry: the class, the poetry lesson, the commentary on poetry, obviously without annulling the scene of the writing referred to before, given by the subject of the poem, aware of the evocative act and of the temporality that breaks the unity of the evocation. What is important in this new scenario of reading that Ruy Belo's commentary proposes is not so much the eudemonistic content of the Wordsworthian *carpe diem*, as the *vacuousness of commenting on an extract of a poem in class*.

It might be said that a negative dialectic determines this scenario. The "happiness" taught by the poem is contradicted by the inconsequential nature of its mediation by the commentary in class. In some way, Ruy Belo's sonnet places us before the repetition of that scene of a Deanie Loomis trying, in vain, to comment a poem by Wordsworth. Joaquim Manuel Magalhães seems to overcome this vacuousness. He would be, shall we say, a student situated "at the blooming" as the poem itself says. Magalhães *looked* and *saw* the poem as the affirming of the "splendor of writing," of Art as negation, of alterative temporal negativity. The *splendore*, the intense brightness, the intense brilliance prevails over a *gaze* that would be sensitive. Allegedly outside of History—because it would deny it—this *looking* has no place, nor time, nor enunciation, nor intertext. Art is no longer a trope of the posthumous, but an appearance, a presence, in the poem.

Magalhães not only seems to *see* "Deanie Loomis" but seems to *see* as "Deanie Loomis," a "delicate a fresh figure." However, my argument is that Magalhães says he sees that which the poem itself represents to us as not being visible. A poem on *seeing* is, in this sense, a poem on the end of *giving* poetry to be *seen*. It is Ruy Belo who says it to us: Deanie Loomis tries *in vain* to comment in class an extract from a poem by Wordsworth. Let us return again to the sonnet. The "blooming" that has to be "looked at"—and quite possibly the place from which it must be "looked at"—is the irrepresentable moment in which blossoming and fading are commutable, the "instant" which, and I follow Magalhães, has as attribute "mortality." In the sonnet we have this "instant" given by the "flower soon to fade"; in Ruy Belo's above mentioned reading, in turn, we have implied that "instant" in the passage "to pick the flower at the very instant it blooms." The ontology of the "flower" here supposed has been denied any trait of stability. To postulate the "mortality" of the "flower"—or of Nature—is to understand it also as history, to denaturalize it. If, as a natural object, that "flower" is diluted as a stable form, then it cannot be represented or sustain any ontological priority over the "word." It is like a word, that is, it is created from nothing, being deprived of permanence.

All this has very little to do with Nature structured as "balance between sentiment and world and word," or with a poetics of something like the "natural visionary impulse" and it does have a lot to do with a poetology highly conscious of its "incorrigible cultural allusions." The precedence is not that of Nature, but that of Art. In the preface of *Transporte no Tempo* Ruy Belo tells us: "I give words a little like how trees give fruit, although in a not very natural, and even anti-natural way, since poetry, being a form of culture, represents an alteration, a deviation and even violence exercised on nature" (2:11). The exhaustion of the "world" and that of "art" itself are in "Esplendor na Relva" in the first line of the second verse: "Life passes and in passing consists," a line whose redundancy, aphoristic style and aporetic *literality* returns mortality to us as a metaphor of "life," and "life" as a figure of the stagnant process of metaphorization.

One should not be surprised by a "golden key" whose *pathos* is subrogated by the fact of being the repetition of the second line of the first verse, although with a significant variant: "and I see that she walks among other women." We have seen above how the irruption of a subject in the poem that does not project on it a stable psychological unity is performed, precisely, by its self-assumption as a writing subject. This is not the only case of a break in the lyrical representation in Ruy Belo's poetry. The writing subject that is always the other—i.e., mortal—is a dimension of the temporality of the "poem," an alterative process that never manages to coincide with itself. How, then, can this "golden key" be understood? It is not the place of the autotelic imperative that would make this final place serve as a closing place for the poem. What the "golden key" does is repeat as a difference an impossible originating beginning, bending to an impossible end. The line "and I see that she walks among other women" refers us to an "image"—Deanie Loomis—which has an *aesthetic* translation. It is *visible*, although it may not be referable nor have origin in the world of "life." What he says he has seen is that the image—Deanie Loomis—exists without a correlative object, it is pure mediation. When all is said and done, he sees that the image is image, transport of the non-existence of the object. Deanie Loomis's spring is the (im)possible representation of mortality, this being the condition of all representation.

Works Cited

Belo, Ruy. *Obra Poética*. Vols. 1-2. Ed. J. M. Magalhães. Lisboa: Editorial Presença, 1981.

———. *Obra Poética*. Vol. 3. Ed. J. M. Magalhães. Lisboa: Editorial Presença, 1984.

De Man, Paul. *The Rhetoric of Romanticism*. New York: Columbia UP, 1984.

Magalhães, Joaquim Manuel. "Ruy Belo." *Um Pouco da Morte*. Lisboa, Presença, 1989. 145-174. Reproduz os dois posfácios publicados pelo autor em Belo, 1981.

Silvestre, Osvaldo Manuel. "Introdução." Ruy Belo, *Boca Bilingue*. Lisboa: Editorial Presença, 1997. 7-20.

Note: This essay was originally published in Portuguese as "'Esplendor na Relva.' Ruy Belo e a Lição da Poesia." *Inimigo Rumor* 15 (2003): 115-128.

Pedro Serra is Associate Professor of Portuguese Literature at the University of Salamanca. He is the translator into Portuguese of the seminal work, *Orientalism*, by Edward Saïd. His most recent book is *Um Intelectual na Fobolândia: Estudos Sobre o Ensaísmo de Fidelino de Figueiredo* (Coimbra: Angelus Novus, 2004). E-mail: pergs@usal.es

Time in Ruy Belo's Poetry: Three Preliminary Aspects*

Victor K. Mendes

Abstract. Taking as its point of departure the argument that Jorge de Sena failed productively in his attempt to overcome Fernando Pessoa, and that Ruy Belo—trying to emulate Pessoa but at the same time writing quite different poetry—emerges as Pessoa's worthy successor, this article proposes a brief analysis of three preliminary aspects of temporality as a contribution to a broader study of time in Ruy Belo's poetry: *i*, time as a condition of possibility; *ii*, the paradoxical time after death; and *iii*, the temporal sense of the poem's ending.

In the rich history of his country's twentieth-century poetry, Ruy Belo is the worthy successor to the great Fernando Pessoa and may be considered, within an intentionally restricted national lyric repertoire, the second Portuguese poet of the century. From the critical point of view, however, Ruy Belo is still awaiting his own equivalent of Eduardo Lourenço's *Pessoa Revisitado:* Belo's Lourenço belongs to the realm of the future. Let us therefore put an abrupt end to this reductive paragraph, with its concern for the poet's complete works, in order to focus on a relatively secure point of time. For time is precisely what it is all about.

Other poets have dealt in a more radical fashion with the making of their genealogy; and, as we cannot analytically ignore after the second Harold Bloom, this is a foundational assumption of the modern poet's self-

Portuguese Literary & Cultural Studies 7 (2008): 29-42.

affirmation.[1] In his ill-fated anxiety to overcome Pessoa, Jorge de Sena fell prey to the shortcomings of the theoretical dialectics that inform that very goal of overcoming.[2] And his was the case of the most explicit and bravest effort to confront Pessoa and fail in the process, even while leaving behind a remarkable poetic output. There were, of course, other similar attempts, but in terms of an explicit confrontation Sena subsumes them all.

Ruy Belo attempted to imitate Pessoa and, despite himself, produced poetry that was substantially different from Pessoa's. In another art form, we may be reminded of how Brahms the composer of the First Symphony related to Beethoven of the Ninth: these are imitations that make all the difference. We do not find in Belo the structural lucidity of Pessoa's prose in verse, but we encounter in it *another space* and, above all, *another time.* Some prevalent critical approaches to Belo tend to label him as an epigone to Modernism (which often means to Pessoa) or wrap him up in the miseries and anachronisms of the Portuguese literary-historical narrative of the 1960s and 1970s, in this way revealing their own share of analytic distress. These miseries and anachronisms are of little help in reading Belo's poetry in the context of the twenty-first-century republic of letters; in other words, in making it contemporary. My contribution to such an undertaking is to show how Belo inscribes in the temporality of his verses a stage in the history of how the Portuguese became hedonists, and does so—much better than Pessoa—regardless of the thematic sadness suffusing so many of his poems.[3]

In the following paragraphs, I will offer a brief preliminary analysis of three aspects of time in Belo's poetry. The poet is faced with the difficult problem of the co-existence, within the poetic text, of contradictory stances. In this regard, the most relevant factor is without a doubt the author's belonging, on the crucial issue of how to cope with life, to the party of Catholicism as well as, simultaneously and in an overt contradiction, to the party of the critics of Catholicism and, even more amply, of Christianity: "I belonged to the Western Church," we read in his 1973 poem "Sobre um simples significante" (On a Simple Signifier). This is the most intense contradiction of Belo's poetry, and it is of religious nature, as was the case, in an altogether different context, of Camões's epic (as pointed out by Almeida Garrett in *Travels in My Homeland*). Unlike what happens in Sena, Belo's inscription of this discrepancy in time fortunately does not beget a set of rules that confine temporality to a dialectical version of history. In Belo's terms, the distension of his contradiction is called a *transport in time* (as in the title of his 1973 book), and it may well be read as an umbrella title for the whole of his poetry. The increasing secularization of time in Belo's poetry, even as it occurs, for example, in the context of the Christian Christmas calendar, evades the untenability of Pessoa's design for a return to pagan temporality.

Let us focus then, first of all, on time as the condition of possibility. In the opening lines of "Viagem à volta de uma laranja" (Journey Around an Orange) from *Todos os Poemas* (311-12), the reader is once again transported into the obsessively reiterated atmosphere of "the end of the day," which is a Western atmosphere par excellence—signifying, in other instances, the end of an era or the end of a world—and which, in Belo, now and again appears *prima facie* as vested with the meaning of the end of time.[4] The poem emits crystal-clear messages about referential delusions or facile reprocessing of the word "orange" in other poets and poems: Belo's orange is not an orange, just as the journey around this orange is not a journey at all. Let us have a look at the poem's syntactic pattern:

> Laranja de cultura uma laranja só possível
>
> depois de vista a vida morta na pintura
>
> às mãos dos que tiveram nela uma razão de ser
>
> e cingiram a emoção à disciplinada dimensão da tela
>
> Laranja negação da natureza
>
> puro fruto sem fruto e sem função
>
> desafio insolente à iminente podridão
>
> que merecem as coisas que mais vivem
>
> Laranja que não morre enquanto mata sede ou fome
>
> que morre exactamente na medida em que vive
>
> e cuja vida é viver apenas
>
> laranja só redonda e amarela
>
> coisa gratuita imagem do poema

The alliterative pattern (Laranja..., Laranja..., Laranja...), of such structural importance in the construction of Belo's poetry, does not in this case imply a mimetic repetition or a performativity of the orange, but rather a peculiar version of the transcendental notion of the orange, which I will attempt to describe. A scrutiny of the conditions of possibility for Belo's orange brings us to the question of time. In the lines "Laranja de cultura uma laranja só possível / depois de vista a vida morta na pintura" (The orange of culture an orange made possible only / after a dead life painting has been seen), the temporal adverb "depois" (after) posits two moments inherent to the temporality required by the orange, whatever "the orange" may mean (to register here the disclaimer of any word's always unstable semantic import). What this orange suggests is a micro-narrative principle resting on at least two moments that are aligned as follows in the linear time of analysis: *i*, the orange is seen represented in a still-life painting; *ii*, as a consequence of *i*, the orange is made possible. What happens, then, from one moment to the next, that makes the orange possible, "only possible" in Belo's terms? The answer to this question, in the context of the poem, requires a consideration of, in the first place, the art of painting, along with the hands that paint in order to make sense, and the discipline of this art of emotional restraint, and secondly, the act of looking at painting or, more precisely, of having seen an orange painted in a picture. Art synthesizes the opposition between life and death, as in the expression "a vida morta na pintura" (dead/still life in painting); art benefits from the privilege, so dear to Belo's poems, to amplify extraordinarily the implications of the pictorial genre of still life (in Portuguese, "natureza morta," or dead nature).

This anti-Aristotelian explanation is well known to us and has its origin in some of Oscar Wilde's maxims about art and life or in the work of the outstanding art historian Ernst Gombrich.[5] The traditional antagonism between nature and culture is resolved in favor of the latter; nevertheless, this denial of nature in the "fruto sem fruto" (fruit without fruit) is unstable. Art as challenge and aggressiveness is refuted by time through an unannounced shift of register that is such a recurrent surprise of this poetry.[6] The temporal adjective is "iminente" (imminent), imminence being one of Belo's major poetic paranoias, which in "Viagem à volta de uma laranja" takes on the form of death or "podridão" (rottenness). Only for a while does the orange deny the course of time.

The orange that "mata sede e fome" (that, in a literal translation, "kills" hunger and thirst) cannot be the *painted orange,* the precondition of the other orange. The orange that is eaten becomes part of the cycle of metamorphosis by means of death. In other passages of the text, the poet occupies the place of the orange in time.[7] Between the orange as the "imagem do poema" (image of the poem) and the *thing* this image represents, what remains to be elucidated is the relationship of the image that the poem also is to death itself. Do poems die? Do painted oranges die? Is the imminence of the highest degree of "rottenness" exclusively on the side of the orange that "*kills* hunger or thirst" (my italics)? In the terms of the poem—and these are the only terms we have at our disposal—the relationship between the image of the poem and death is not clarified, so the issue whether the painted orange, or in other words art, entails an effective suspension of time is filed away as a matter that defies resolution. The image of the poem is, according to Belo, a "coisa gratuita" (gratuitous thing), which means a thing divested of being necessary in time. Metaphors inlaid in verses, such as "o vento, esse terrível tempo" (wind, that terrible weather/time), which appears to surrender to a rhyme effect the generally positive status of "wind" in Belo's poetic syntax, have to be distinguished clearly from the inverted space-time coordinates of expressions like "praias que há no tempo" (beaches that exist in time). Time does and does not allow itself to be subsumed by space.[8]

By comparison, the presumed rule of poetics mandating that one dirties "as mãos com os problemas do seu tempo" (one's hands with the problems of one's time) from the "Breve programa para uma iniciação ao canto" (Brief Program for an Initiation to Singing), hardly represents more than a repetition of a topos in which sociological analysis takes over a substantial share of poetry. Nonetheless, in Belo's works poetic thought on time asserts itself vigorously as a reversal of the linear time inherent to the notion of progress. Witness, for instance, the following fragment of "Meditação montana" (Mountainous Meditation):

> aviões impossíveis mais reais do que os reais
>
> perfeitos pássaros provindos da cessante condição
>
> ó aviões antecessores das aves
>
> palavras vindas de étimos das quais os étimos dimanam
>
> movimento de mãos produtoras das próprias produções
>
> umas mãos que ao mover-se movimentam
>
> criaturas que incríveis criam coisas suas criadoras
>
> aves imitação dos imitados aviões
>
> natureza nascida onde visivelmente nasce a vida
>
> aviões aos quais a ave deve o voo
>
> (324)

If one perseveres in the good critical creed according to which texts are the best purveyors of associations for their own reading, a reward awaits a couple of lines below in this same poem, when the author writes about the "verdade apenas vista nos jogos verbais" (truth to be seen only when playing with words). The much-quoted Nietzschean and Wittgensteinean cognitive vision that informs both Belo's poetry and my own reading invalidates the charge that Ruy Belo is unable to escape the distress of being an heir to Pessoa's Álvaro de Campos.

Let us have a look at the standard version of the history of progress. Birds preceded airplanes, airplanes emulated birds. In this poem, however, airplanes come before birds. In a more abstract formulation, effects can produce causes; if we were to look for an illustration of this claim in Belo's poetry, the very particular case of God (who in time changes into a god) may be read as the cause of man, but in Belo's terms it is man who can be read as the cause of God. In a necessary aside, let us note that the prevailing point of view in Belo's poetry is manifestly male, and that as such it recalls, by means of a displacement, the representation of modern Man still on display at the Natural History Museum in Washington, DC: a 1970s white-collar male worker with his grey suit, tie, and black briefcase. Belo's figure of "man" would certainly benefit from being read as gendered, given the prominent role played by this figure in his writing; such a reading would also be justified by the fact that Belo shares with Pessoa an idea of poetry with gnoseological claims.[9]

To return to Belo's verbal games, being more than mere play with time they allow the poet access to what he calls the truth, whatever this may be, and it is definitely consubstantiated by many different assertions in the text. One of Belo's repeated truths takes the shape of A *comes after* B, and B *causes* A. Let us collect the objects corresponding to this scheme that have been mentioned so far: the natural orange (A) and the painted orange (B); birds (A) and airplanes (B). The works of art (technics, *techné*) precede and produce nature.

Let us move now to a second aspect of temporality: the paradoxical time after death which, for Belo, is not configured as a liberation from death through salvation. In "Na morte de Georges Braque" (On the Death of Georges Braque), technologies give back to the world the dimension of times past. Braque is one of the artist heroes whose funeral Belo stages in his poetry. And the funerals in *Todos os Poemas* are many, allowing us also to regard this poetry, even in statistical terms, as an obituary. At this point, the most difficult critical task is to produce a satisfactory explanation as to the kind of psychological reward one can derive from so many obituaries including, interestingly enough, a *self-obituary* (more on which soon). The poem on Braque poses several pertinent problems related to the issue of time in Belo's poetry, most prominent among them the problem of time after death. What is this particular time like?

> Foi através dum título inserido num jornal alheio
>
> no metro por acaso de viés olhado
>
> que eu soube que saíste da velhice
>
> para entrar não se sabe bem onde
>
> mas decerto na terra dentro em pouco
>
> (314)

We know that in Belo's anthropology of death the dead get buried and that the poet has dedicated unforgettable verses to the act of burying. The exit from time, the exit from "velhice" (old age), leads to an indefinite space, "não se sabe bem onde" (who knows where). As we shall see, Belo's poetry as a whole presents a number of postmortem fictionalizations. Braque's death presents an opportunity for art and for Belo's affiliation with modernity. Braque is a hero of that "feroz luta" (fierce struggle) against art envisaged as mimesis of life, "pra que a arte deixasse de reproduzir a vida" (so that art may cease reproducing life). Regarding the question posed above, about the relationship between death and the orange that is the image of the poem, the poem on Braque gives us a helpful clue: "Fica o mais importante a obra essa pegada / do homem que passou por esta praia / e que mesmo que saia alguma coisa fica da passagem" (The most important things remain the work the footprint / of the man who walked across this beach / and even if it vanishes / something is left from the passage). Here we are again in the realm in which trust needs to be deposited on the side of the poem and not in the experiment one may wish to perform, of leaving footprints in the sand, noticing their disappearance, and investigating that *something* that remains. Thus Belo may also be presumed to suggest that, in spite of death, something is left of the "laranja imagem do poema" (orange image of the poem). This is a minimalist version of art's time after death, which secures the permanence of the poem's orange. However, this kind of permanence is itself fragile and shows no sign of the tension between time and eternity that pervades, for instance, Milton's poem "On Time."

Let us return to the question of technique and time. Braque becomes here the generic modernist hero:

Tu e os teus amigos dos princípios deste século
de máquinas de técnicas de pressa de vertigem
devolveram ao mundo o seu passado
e reduziram a distância entre nós e a nossa origem
(314-15)

The modernist accomplishment is an exploit directly related to time. To paraphrase quickly what Belo tells us, there was a time when the world was deprived of its past. Then, resorting to machines and techniques, Braque and his friends restored the past to the world. Thus, through a contraction of time—that is the implied corollary—we have come closer to our past. Or, to put it differently, the present has expanded, as many other lines suggest; for example, "essas mulheres mortas mas contemporâneas" (those women who are dead and yet contemporary) (331).[10]

Let us look now at Belo's self-obituary. This fictionalization of the poet's own death can help us reread the obituaries he has written for others, be it men, women, animals ("Requiem for a Dog") or fruit (e. g., the orange). In the poem "Elogio de Maria Teresa" (In Praise of Maria Teresa), the poet is speaking from beyond death:

Contigo fui cruel no dia-a-dia
mais que mulher tu és já hoje a minha única viúva
Não posso dar-te mais do que te dou
Este molhado olhar de homem que morre
e se comove ao ver-te assim tão subitamente
(332)

The polarization between life and death reappears here in one of the most striking settings in the whole of Belo's work; the poet situates himself in the time after his own death, which he implicitly stages. His relationship with his wife, Maria Teresa, is described as the opposite of goodness, in an expiatory mood, while his acknowledged cruelty belongs grammatically to the past: "fui" (I was). In the present, however, nothing better awaits in the realm of the conjugal relationship; hence the shocking statement: "tu *és* já hoje a minha única viúva" (you *are* already today my only widow; my italics). The separation that follows places the poet beyond death; it is thus that, after committing *this* act of poetic cruelty, the poet removes himself from his beloved by way of dying. This is an exceedingly rough game, even if one keeps present the awareness of verses being nothing but verses. What are the stakes here?

Within the temporal economy of the poem, Belo attempts to buy time. I am using the expression "to buy time" in the sense Richard K. Fenn ascribes to it, that is, as a possibility to experience, in a reasonably harmless way, as is the case of poetry, certain emotions related to a situation that threatens to annihilate the subject.[11] The contrast between the life of "dia-a-dia" (everyday) and the implicit life beyond death has a female victim, on whom a poetic gift is bestowed in the form of the alliteration "molhado olhar de homem que morre" (wet look of a man who dies). As we know, in Belo's work the man who dies is the man who *chooses* to die. The poet's venturing into death reaps symbolic gains. The complete experience of death remains, for the time being, protected in the dimension of an indefinite future time: "o que é preciso é que não doa muito / Depois que me escondam na terra como uma vergonha" (all one needs is that it doesn't hurt much / and then may I be buried under like a shame) (251). The anxiety of time is retrospective; it comes from a future death, and thus is experienced by a subject who has already lived in a *bought time.* One can hardly think of a better function for poetry as a *transport in time.*

In *Homem de Palavra(s)* (A Man of His Word[s]), the poet also conceives of himself in a postmortem time. Let us read "Cólofon ou epitáfio" (Colophon or Epitaph):

Trinta dias tem o mês

e muitas horas o dia

todo o tempo se lhe ia

em polir o seu poema

a melhor coisa que fez

ele próprio coisa feita

ruy belo portugalês

Não seria mau rapaz

quem tão ao comprido jaz

ruy belo, era uma vez (264)

The fictionalization of his own death allows the poet to buy time in order to cope with the real and unknown term of his life. The speaker of the line "ruy belo era uma vez" (once upon a time there was ruy belo) cannot be anyone other than the poet, who, for that very reason, writes his self-epitaph lightly. The present that can be read as the absence of time only becomes manifest in the line in which Ruy Belo is mentioned as being dead. In Portuguese, the verb "jazer" (to lie, to rest) is associated with being buried. This benign experience of a post-burial state makes possible for the poet the analepsis of his poetics: akin to the Horatian *labor limae,* his is a poetry produced by a *techné* that has consumed hours, days and months of his life. Two kinds of time are presupposed in this poetry: the time of writing and the time of forming and polishing; it is the latter that devours time itself. In this thematization of time, there is no place for a deliberate choice of an *emploi du temps;* Belo's time wears away in a poetic activity whose doctrine is diametrically opposed to Jorge de Sena's writing of "versos sem arte" (artless poetry). The poet's self-fashioning as "portugalês" evokes a Ruy Belo who is both old and ancient, even as it points to the Latin term *portucalense* and the construction of an outspoken, loyal character like that of the medieval Portuguese hero Egas Moniz. This brief poem and the others in Belo's collected poems, *Todos os Poemas,* that belong to the same family recall an episode in Francis Ford Coppola's 1983 film *Rumble Fish,* in which the central character, in a compensatory move, dreams of his own death and of the death of those surrounding him.

Belo's poetry requires a rhetoric of temporality for strategic reasons. The tension at the origin of this need results, as we have seen, from the main contradiction that permeates *Todos os Poemas;* we shall call it religious for short. Instead of the Nietzschean death of God, in this poetry we see God metamorphosing into a *god in language.* Belo needs time to accommodate his thorny distinctions: the poet of 1961, the poet of 1973, and so forth. The notion of a time understood as a historical or generational period proves of little help here, although vast resources can be mobilized by a critical reader collecting pertinent references from poems like "Odeio este tempo detergente" (I Hate This Detergent Time) or the much-quoted "Nós os vencidos do catolicismo" (We, the Losers of Catholicism).

The third aspect of time in Belo's poetry that I will touch upon is mostly implicit in his writing, but it may be discerned in the concluding lines of a number of his poems. This brief essay is not the appropriate place to expound on the theory of poetic endings; besides, this has already been done, and well done, by Barbara Herrnstein Smith in *Poetic Closure*.[12] How then does Belo write his own version of *La commedia è finita?* We should note that the endings of poems represent a priori a *mise-en-abyme* of that other problem, seemingly of vaster proportions but at the same time unverifiable: the end of life. In "Algumas proposições sobre um certo João Miguel" (Some Propositions About a Certain João Miguel), Belo mentions a poet, possibly a literary descendant of his: "suspeito que o poeta meu amigo / seja criptomonárquico e se não / tiro a questão a limpo é para não estragar tão promissora / carreira literária não há muito começada" (I suspect my friend the poet / is a cryptomonarchist and I only don't / make it clear so as not to damage his promising / literary career of such recent vintage). Here is what else happens to João Miguel in Belo's poem:

> O joão miguel quer qualquer coisa para os sapatos
>
> o joão miguel agora quer falar para o porto
>
> só para ouvir talvez a voz da margarida
>
> O joão miguel quer-me cá a mim parecer
>
> não saber bem ao certo já aquilo que quer
>
> [...]
>
> O joão miguel encontra finalmente a graxa
>
> e assim finda o poema escrito no invólucro da caixa
>
> onde levo os sapatos acabados de comprar
>
> (340-41)

The character of João Miguel inherits, in this poem, the shape of the contradiction that configures Belo's structural distribution of time: from "agora" (now) A to "agora" B, *now* serves as the sign of change.[13] Other characters in the poem also join this family of figures that want one thing now and then another, or who are supposed to talk about something and then talk about something else. This is what happens with the writer Vitorino Nemésio (appearing on TV), who instead of speaking of Christ speaks of the Neolithic (precisely a time when there was no Christianity yet). Another character, TV news presenter Henrique Mendes, "quando diz que vai falar de paz / fala de guerra" (when he says he'll be talking about peace / he talks about war").

Following this succession of exchanges that make up the poem, João

Miguel finds that "something" he was looking for, which turns out to be shoe polish. The poem owes its existence to an interruption in a succession of moments ("agora," "agora," "agora") in the present of what João Miguel wants and the finding of the object of his search. The beginning and the end of the poem associate João Miguel's shoes with the new shoes bought by Ruy Belo himself. The conclusion of the poem, "e assim finda o poema" (and so the poem comes to an end), marks a time of self-reference. An analogous procedure is on display in the narrative "Poema de Natal" (Christmas Poem), where the nineteenth-century writer and historian Alexandre Herculano turns up: "O Herculano entre outras coisas sabia distinguir os tempos / sabia o que num tempo é distinto de outro tempo" (Herculano knew among other things how to distinguish times / he knew what makes one time different from another time). The time of the poem's closure, once again self-referential, is imprisoned in a cyclical time that returns year after year, and the poet's words betray no sign of progress: "nem talvez tenha já a convicção de quem anualmente / escreve pontual se não contente o seu poema de natal" (perhaps I've even lost the conviction of the one who every year / writes punctually if not in joy his christmas poem). In "Versos que vou escrevendo" (Verses I Keep Writing) (346-48), one of Belo's poems in which the banality of everyday life meets the poet's art, we come across characters already familiar to the readers of this essay: João Miguel and Maria Teresa. They hike up a hill while the poet stays in the car, reading in his newspaper about, among other topics, "a escritora agustina e a jornalista albertina" (the writer agustina and the journalist albertina). The poem's ending injects it into the referential time of the present and into the action controlled by the poet: "Deixo o jornal porque voltou a juventude / e por aqui me fico que mais querem fiz aquilo que pude" (I put the newspaper aside because youth has returned / that's all for now what else do you want from me I've done what I could). With this distinction marked between himself, on the one hand, and, on the other, the younger João Miguel (a distinguished poet since the 1970s) and Belo's wife Maria Teresa, Ruy Belo stages his own identity as that of the resigned protagonist of the end. *Consummatum est.*

* An earlier version of this article appeared in Portuguese in *Inimigo Rumor* 15 (2003). This reincarnation in English has benefited vastly from the input of Anna M. Klobucka and Maria Antónia Amarante.

Notes

[1] In a long interview for an "In Depth" segment of C-Span 2's *Book TV* program, which aired on May 4, 2003, Bloom described the three main phases of his scholarship. Very summarily, the first phase was concerned with English poetry, the second with the theory of influence, and in the third stage of his work Bloom assumed the role of a popular critic. I thus refer to the "second Harold Bloom" as the author of such critical masterpieces as *The Anxiety of Influence* and *A Map of Misreading*. The first and the second Bloom are certainly among the small number of the most decisive literary critics and theorists of the twentieth century.

[2] I develop this argument fully in my article "Fernando Pessoa e Jorge de Sena, segundo este último," *Colóquio/Letras* 147-148 (1998). 132-49.

[3] I am drawing here on the concept of hedonism as explored by Benjamin Wiker in *Moral Darwinism: How We Became Hedonists*. Downers Grove, IL: InterVarsity Press, 2002.

[4] All quotations of Belo's poetry are taken from the volume *Todos os Poemas*. Lisboa: Assírio & Alvim, 2000.

[5] In her very practical essay "Stevens and Keats's 'To Autumn'," Helen Vendler recapitulates for poetry what Gombrich had proposed for painting: artists do not reproduce what they see but instead produce amalgams of preexisting representations. See Frank Lentricchia and Andrew Dubois, eds. *Close Reading*. Durham and London: Duke UP, 2003. 156-174.

[6] Belo defends the proposition that writing is tantamount to aggression in the text "Breve programa para uma iniciação ao canto" (in *Transporte no Tempo*).

[7] As in the following verse, further down in "Viagem à volta duma laranja": "A noite vem não serei nada em breve" (The night comes I will be nothing soon) (311).

[8] W. V. O. Quine made the following lapidary reference, in his decisive style, to the analysis of time in the context of Zeno's paradoxes: "a treatment of time as spacelike" (*Word and Object*. Cambridge, MA: The MIT Press, 1967. 172). In Belo's poetry, time in not treated as spacelike, but as that which makes it possible for space to exist and encompasses it. Stanley Fish's observation, in *Doing What Comes Naturally* (Oxford: Clarendon Press, 1989), that "New Critical practice spacializes time" (268-69) is worth evoking in this context. Fish confronts us with the concept of modern or modernist analysis that reduces time to space, thus allowing for a unified vision of time. In Ruy Belo, no such unified vision blocks discontinuous temporality, but thematic criticism of his work—invested as it is in the content of time as a theme—is methodologically unable to move beyond making note of the essence of time through its examples, remaining blind to what I am calling the grammar of time in Belo's text.

[9]. Entirely absent at this point from the critical literature on Belo's poetry, the strategy of gender analysis could take as one of its critical clues Barbara Johnson's chapter on "Gender and Poetry: Charles Baudelaire and Marceline Desbordes-Valmore" in her book *The Feminist Difference*. Cambridge, MA: Harvard UP, 1998.

[10] One of the most consequential formulations of the expansion of the present, coupled with a critique of transcendental assumptions, may be found in the work of Hans Ulrich Gumbrecht. His "A Farewell to Interpretation" is particularly worth mentioning in this context, although it is in some ways a popularizing account of Gumbrecht's strongest insights on the subject of time and poetry, which are articulated in "Rhythm and Meaning." Both essays are included in the volume *Materialities of Communication* edited by Hans Ulrich Gumbrecht and Karl Ludwig Pfeiffer and translated by William Whobrey (Stanford: Stanford UP, 1994).

[11] See his *Time Exposure: The Personal Experience of Time in Secular Societies.* Oxford: Oxford UP, 2001.

[12] *Poetic Closure: A Study of How Poems End.* Chicago: The University of Chicago Press, 1968.

[13]. It would be a highly promising vein of analysis to read João Miguel Fernandes Jorge's poetry as a response to Ruy Belo's. For example, Fernandes Jorge's writing evidences a recovery of certain notions that had been rejected by Belo. A symptomatic case is Belo's critique of the term "pátria" (fatherland), for which he substitutes "país" (country), a word that recurs often in his texts. Fernandes Jorge returns to "pátria," thus marking his difference from his predecessor: the only anthology of Belo's poetry, published in 1973, is entitled *País Possível* (Possible Country), while Fernandes Jorge's own anthology, released in 2002, carries the title *A Pequena Pátria* (The Little Fatherland).

Victor K. Mendes is Associate Professor and Director of Graduate Studies in the Department of Portuguese at the University of Massachusetts Dartmouth. E-mail: vmendes@umassd.edu

"The Poet Is Not a Faker": Herberto Helder and the Myth of Poetry

António Ladeira

Abstract. In this essay I primarily intend to provide the American public with an introduction to the poetry of Herberto Helder. I first comment on aspects of Helder's reception. My central task, however, will be a summarized description of the main "thematic" manifestations of *Poesia Toda*, in articulation with the myth of poetry as it is represented in Helder's work. My contention is that his literary universe operates as a particular mythicization of the poetic process (through representations of the "poetic subject," the figure of "the poet," the figure of the critic, the idea of inspiration, etc.) whose study is essential for the understanding of Helder's poetry. I will address the different dimensions of this mythicization—the most important of which is the quality of "sublimity." Finally, I will comparatively address aspects of the work of Helder and Pessoa, focusing on their respective constructions of the myth of poetry.

The poet is a faker
He fakes so completely
That he fakes the pain
He is actually feeling.
—Fernando Pessoa, *Autopsychography*[1]

Man is often vainglorious about his contempt of glory.
—Saint Augustine, *Confessions*

Portuguese Literary & Cultural Studies 7 (2008): 43-72.
© University of Massachusetts Dartmouth.

> Love for poetry has always been found among us. It is one, or, rather, it is the only cult that we have been officiating for centuries, with passion and more or less guaranteed success […]. All our modernity has lived until today off of this invention of Poetry as Myth.
>
> —Eduardo Lourenço, "Da Poesia Como Mito"[2]

A country of poets?

Many citizens of Portugal have a difficult relationship with a vastly popular, intriguing reputation: "Portugal is," allegedly, "a country of poets." What particularly concerns the Portuguese about this idea is the fact that poets are commonly regarded as daydreamers who lack a sense of pragmatism. A possible source for this reputation is the famous eighteenth-century "black legend," which also attributes to the Portuguese a tendency to nostalgic meditation, melancholic reserve or masochistic self-commiseration.

In reality, more books of poetry are annually written, published and purchased in Portugal than in most European countries. Similar to Spaniards and Latin Americans, the Portuguese reward their favorite writers—particularly their poets—with considerable acclaim and public reverence. Poetry readings are popular social events. In sharp contrast with North American children, for instance, their Portuguese counterparts are raised in a significantly more "writer-friendly" environment. A popular representation of our most celebrated poet, Luís de Camões, shows him as a fierce street brawler and a passionate seducer of courtly ladies. A famous schoolbook's illustration portrays him at the exact moment of a terrible shipwreck; he swims with one hand, away from the sinking ship, while clutching in his other hand—held up high and away from the waves' reach—his most precious possession: the manuscript of *The Lusiads*. Highly romanticized, heroic legends such as these are part of our national folklore.

In Portugal, despite relatively high illiteracy rates (and even higher functional illiteracy rates) literature in general has a widespread, popular, democratic prestige—if an elitist readership—and poetry holds an even stronger appeal. In other words, the Portuguese are loyal admirers of their poets, even though they are not necessarily "actual" readers of their works. Members of the Portuguese middle class are commonly zealous buyers of books—particularly those that are recommended by a community of "official" critics. Yet these books—in what, sociologically, constitutes a very intriguing behavior—often remain unread, yet proudly on display in many a living room bookcase.

The most popular writers move about in their public lives—actively participating in media events—displaying an unusual combination of mass appeal and elitism. They are revered by a large segment of the public while often exhibiting a certain disdainful aloofness towards the applause of this same public. Frequently—either out of vanity or out of humbleness—they resent the insistent inquiries of literary supplements, the obligation to participate in book promotions and, particularly, what they interpret as the intrusiveness of literary journalists and of the public in general. In this inaccessibility lies part of their charm as "literary celebrities." This strange love affair between author and public is as much a product of the authors' concept of "literature" as of the nation's notion of "author."

In our Portuguese literary world a very romantic "aura," suggestive of mysterious, powerful, literary powers, accompanies the "legend" of some of our most revered authors, such as Camões, Pessoa, or Camilo Pessanha. The average American—who, by far, does not have such a close relationship with his poets—may have difficulty understanding just how "mainstream" and/or "mundane" literary matters can be in Portugal. For example: *Jornal de Letras, Artes & Ideas*, a so called "cultural" or "literary" publication that often includes relevant scholarly articles, is as omnipresent in newspaper stands and kiosks around the country as any major national news periodical; writers are frequent guests on talk shows and other popular TV programs; and recently, in the Portuguese Parliament, a controversial national debate ensued following the exclusion of a popular poet from a literary anthology.[3]

I believe that there is a fascinating relationship—which I do not intend to explore in this essay—between this literary "star system" and what Ramalho Santos, referring to Pessoa, calls "poetic arrogance" (*Santos* 115). The contemporary idea of textual, literary "arrogance" and the concept of extra-textual, "literary," "enigmatic," "charismatic," personality, appear to have been (though posthumously) inaugurated by Pessoa.[4] Santos says that Pessoa's poetry is the expression of "this exceptionalist poetics, which singles out the poet as far superior to common humanity and so becomes a biting commentary on the status quo [...]" (*Santos* 148).

Who is Herberto Helder? Herberto Helder is widely considered one of the most important poets since Fernando Pessoa, if not the most important. Some critics have recently begun to include him among Europe's best contemporary poets. He was born in 1930 in the Madeira Islands, Portugal. In 1958 he published his first book of poetry, *O Amor em Visita.* In 1973 he published the first of four editions of his (practically) complete anthology of poetry—*Poesia Toda*.[5]

Herberto Helder is also an author virtually unknown to the American poetry reading public. No samples of the author's work are available, with the exception of a few poems and short stories, translated by Richard Zenith and Alexis Levitin, that very recently began circulating on the Internet.[6] There are only a few poems in print available to the English-speaking public; these were included in an anthology of Portuguese poetry published in England in 1978 (Macedo). In the rest of the world, with the exceptions of Brazil, Spain and France, Herberto Helder is either a completely ignored author or is relegated to the status of an exotic and harmless curiosity. In Portugal, Helder is still vastly unknown to the majority of our population, although his name recognition has been steadily growing among the most active members of the reading public. One may argue that, as things now stand, he is the most popular of our non-mainstream[7] writers and the least known of our quasi-canonical poets.

In this essay I primarily intend to provide the American public with an introduction to the poetry of Herberto Helder. I first comment on aspects of Helder's reception. My central task, however, will be a summarized description of the main "thematic" manifestations of *Poesia Toda*,[8] in articulation with the myth of poetry as it is represented in Helder's work. My contention is that his literary universe operates as a particular mythicization of the poetic process (through representations of the "poetic subject,"[9] the figure of "the poet," the figure of the critic, the idea of inspiration, etc.) whose study is essential for the understanding of Helder's poetry. I will address the different dimensions of this mythicization—the most important of which is the quality of "sublimity." Finally, I will comparatively address aspects of the work of Helder and Pessoa, focusing on their respective constructions of the myth of poetry.

The reception

> It is thus a [critical] move drenched in humility, although it is often performed with righteousness: those other fellows may be interested in displaying their inge-nuity, but I am simply a servant of the text and wish only to make it more avail-able to its readers (who happen also to be my readers).
> (Fish 353)

The history of the reception of Herberto Helder is a very peculiar one, to say the least. For the past fifteen years or so, a number of critics have expressed positions that are, at best, contradictory. On the one hand, Helder is regarded as one of the most important writers post-*Orpheu* (or Post-Pessoa)—Portuguese poetry, if not the most important. On the other hand, scholarly studies on Helder are perceived as scarce, timid, or insufficiently productive. Many critics have already referred to this contradiction. And the "contradiction" itself is one of the most frequent critical topics. As far back as 1983, the critic Frias Martins said that "it is not surprising that HH [*sic*] is recognized as one of the most important poets of the Portuguese language and, simultaneously, as one of the least studied" (19).

In 1995, in an article titled "Como Falar de Herberto Helder" ["How to Speak About Herberto Helder"], Eduardo do Prado Coelho wrote:

> In part, of course, due to the very high quality of this poetry, but also due to the halo of silence with which the author surrounds it [...], the truth is that both readers and critics feel a kind of panic or terror in speaking or writing about Herberto Helder. Maybe the problem resides in this "about." The poetry of Herberto Helder excludes us from any position of arrogance or haughtiness in relation to the text. The result of this confessed humiliation is a type of aphasia. Could we solve the question by saying that one writes "in departure from Herberto Helder," or rather, "along with Herberto Helder," by engaging in an uncertain shoulder-to-shoulder struggle with the author, in a collaborative writing effort that is necessarily asymmetrical? (12)

Six years later Manuel de Freitas said:

> I wish to suggest that not only the author of *A Colher na Boca* is one of the greatest living poets, but I wish also to remind [the reader] that we are before a difficult poet—as much as for the surprising splendor of his verbal art, as for his cultural attitude or, still, for the castrating silence to which he seems to condemn the critics. (17)

Academically, the landscape is also relatively uneventful: as far as I know only four doctoral dissertations and six masters theses have been devoted predominantly to Helder.[10] Relevant studies, however, were conducted by Américo António Lindeza Diogo (*Texto, Metáfora, Metáfora do Texto*) and by Joaquim Manuel Magalhães (*Os Dois Crepúsculos, Um Pouco da Morte, Rima*

Pobre). Juliet Perkins adapted her doctoral dissertation and published it under the title *The Feminine in the Poetry of Herberto Helder*. Maria Lucia Dal Farra published a book version of her own doctoral dissertation, *A Alquimia da Linguagem*. More recently, Silvina Rodrigues Lopes, who had previously written articles about Helder, published a book exclusively devoted to the poetry of this author: *A Inocência do Devir*. Manuel de Freitas authored a stimulating study about a book that was "banned" from Helder's bibliography by the author himself: *Uma Espécie de Crime*.[11]

The scholarship—with a few honorable exceptions—has always been either too timid or too encomiastic and, at times, too "a-critically" encomiastic. Criticism on Helder frequently appears to lack independence and to be exceedingly respectful of (and too "compliant with") the author's trademark position of open hostility and non-cooperation with the academic "establishment" and the community of critics. Many of the texts that proclaim themselves analyses of Helder's poetry often turn out to be little more than tearful homages to the author. In other words, critics have contributed to rigidifying the myths, to thickening the mystifications and to cultivating the prejudices instead of dispelling them. Few critics have attempted to do what, in my opinion, needs to be attempted: a kind of reading that would contribute to the dismantling of the esoteric reputation that surrounds his works so that freer, less fearful, less apologetic—and ultimately, more consequential—studies may come forth.

Critics in general—and perhaps Portuguese critics in particular—are fascinated by "difficult" authors, especially by authors who proudly cultivate their own "difficulty."[12] It is certainly tempting to say that, similar to Herberto Helder himself, his critics have openly valued an "unreadability" that, as critics, they were supposed to challenge:

No promise of happiness is offered by the poetry of Herberto Helder. No safety zone, no identifiable time, no participation in a sentimental community—or in a "sensus communis," as Kant would say—assure us of the comfort of textual smoothness: in its place, only the inexpressible, the infinite of a language that creates the retraction of any representational dimension, the incessant dislocation towards an area of shade that makes us feels like expatriates. Poetry such as this speaks a demoniacal idiom—it is some kind of absolute force. (Guerreiro 48R)

Concerning Helder's work, Silvina Rodrigues Lopes stated that:

Every time we read a poem we face the impossible: poetry is the most terrible of all arts, and the most innocent, since it offers us proximity to the state of fire. To that which is close we cannot get closer without risk and, yet, without our approaching it the poem would not exist for us. Maybe our approximation should be a ritual in which the offerings are words drunk with meanings and danger. Maybe we should be silent and choose instead words whose rumor becomes the brief breath of the wind. (11)

Fernando Pinto do Amaral confessed that:

The initial shock, the feverish surprise, that happy terror that hits us as we are invaded by the words of Herberto Helder cause in us a paralysis perhaps similar to the one we feel before the sudden revelation of someone's unknown beauty: we believe that it is impossible, that a benevolent God must have invented that dream. Later, as we find out that it is true, we still do not know what to say or what to do [with the poems]—for the fear of jumping into the unknown is great [...]. We may call him difficult, hermetic, obscure, but that obscurity is the obscurity of someone who protects his mysteries to better illuminate them from the inside. As for us, before such an intense and different light, maybe we are simply blind. (134-137)

The American critic Stanley Fish has made some illuminating observations about what he calls the stance of "aggressive humility" that is characteristic of some contemporary reading strategies. Referring to these types of excessively "self-effacing" literary analyses, Fish suggests that they are a reflection of the crisis now affecting the discipline. I am not claiming that the type of criticism mentioned by Fish is necessarily illuminated by the perspectives displayed by the three important critics quoted above whose work I respect; yet their positions, in this particular case, are representative of a long-lived and stubborn trend that is particularly concerning as it appears to inhibit *other* kinds of scholarship, namely, less overly cautious, more revealing, more muscular perspectives on the author's work:

Indeed, by a logic peculiar to the institution [of criticism], one of the standard ways of practicing literary criticism is to announce that you are avoiding it. This is so because at the heart of the institution is the wish to deny that its activities have any consequences. The critic is taught to think of himself as a transmitter of the best that had been thought and said by others, and his greatest fear is that he will stand charged of having substituted his own meanings for the meanings of which he is supposedly the guardian. (Fish 355)

António Guerreiro and others have spoken about the "retraction" or disappearance of the "representational function of language" (48R). This type of radical position—so common ten years ago—still has many followers among today's critics. This is among other, popular, critical positions that defend the combination of the dissolution of a "referential project" in poetry with the diminishing presence of "meaning" or "legibility." In turn, this crisis of "meaning" is associated with the melancholic disappearance, the dramatic dissolution or the fragmentation of the literary self or of the "subject in crisis" (Guimarães 6). This idea is in agreement with the generally accepted principles of Modernism and still appears to be among the most popular characteristics of the movement as it has been interpreted by many critics. This belief may have, in part, legitimated some positions of passive resignation toward what is perceived as the inscrutability of the literary text. Nevertheless, some recent works have led me to believe that some critics could be slowly moving towards facing the strong probability (as I see it) of this poetry being about a lot more—or a lot less—than the "absence of meaning" or the "dissolution of the poetic subject."

In defense of themes

One of the ways by which we may attempt to gain "access" to this poetry (as much as one can ever be granted entry into as dense a universe as this) is by analyzing certain recurring motifs. I prefer the unpopular word "theme,"[13] whereas others have used the terms "patterns of recurrence," "repetitions", or "main thematic" obsessions. To my knowledge, the fact that Helder *himself* makes reference to his "lexical" obsessions has never been discussed by critics. Commenting on *Apresentação do Rosto*, Helder said that "certain obsessions (even lexical ones) became clear to me during the writing of this book" ("Os Jovens Escritores" 11). In this book—which he calls a novelized autobiography—he mentions, for example, the importance of his "central themes" (44).

Joaquim Manuel Magalhães took note of these lexical recurrences and went so far as to call them "themes:"

These themes—of the "mother," "childhood," the "feminine," "woman," "love," "God," "language," "poetry"—are always a *leit motiv.* They are the ground from which variations depart, the repetitions, the conceptually baroque formalization of his style. (*Um Pouco da Morte* 127)

Nevertheless, some critics have expressed disagreement about the use of the word "theme" and, implicitly in my opinion, have manifested their disapproval of thematic readings:

[C]ertain motifs like the "child," "the mother," and the "body" are emptied of all "thematic" density—as Américo António Lindeza Diogo attests, in Helder "the correlation with the real is confessedly of a non-metonymical kind—inscribing instead the self-referential, and in all respects 'sublime,' of Poetry and of the Poet." (Silvestre 617)

In her 2003 book, *A Inocência do Devir*, Silvina Rodrigues Lopes seems to have changed—in important ways—her previous position. In her 1990 article entitled "A Imagem Ardente"—Lopes did not place any major emphasis on thematic recurrences, her essay being, in a sense, mostly a dissertation on the difficulties of interpreting Helder's book *Última Ciência*. It was a description of Helder's poetry based on its inapproachability. She asserted that, in the face of his poetry, as many have claimed before and since, "perhaps we should remain silent" (11). However, in her 2003 book—whose back cover announces the intention to "emphasize certain thematic nodes"—one may say that Lopes engages in a "thematic" reading of Helder's poetry without fully assuming the "philosophical" implications of her new approach. Apparently, she now believes that some attention should be paid to patterns, repetitions and to the constitution of a "very concentrated vocabulary," some "hallucinating" and "contagious" semantic *nuclei* such as "corporeity," "terror," "power," and "action" (*A Inocência* 64). Yet, just as she did in 1990, she still defends the incomprehensibility of texts:

[T]he poem shuts itself to the devastating curiosity, to the way it is cryptic, and its key does not open, rather, it closes—[the poem] closes itself [to scrutiny, to curiosity] as a tomb, sealed, absolutely non-desecratable, a memory stone, an epitaph. (*A Inocência* 91)

This is one of the instances where I believe Lopes's reading is least interesting. One cannot read into things while simultaneously lecturing the reader about the unreadability of things. After studying, analyzing, and moving toward deciphering Helder's patterns and recurrences she warns the reader that (true? good?) poems are immune to the "devastating curiosity" of those who interpret them—a statement that clearly excludes her own critical curiosity from the company of the *other*, "harmful," "devastating," curiosities. (But who decides which curiosities are "devastating" and which are "edifying"? Which are "legitimate" and which are "illicit"?)

This particular reading by Lopes exemplifies one of the most disappointing aspects of some contemporary styles of criticism. She appears to be playing a double game of "non-committal commitment" concerning her job of reading texts. The subtitle of Lopes's book reads "essay *from / departing from* the work of Herberto Helder" instead of, more conventionally, "essay *about / toward* the work of Herberto Helder" (5). She claims to attempt "approximations" ("A Imagem Ardente" 11) to a particular text instead of "interpretations." Hence, to critically read a text in this way is the safest act one may engage in since the critic did not really commit to any particular position to begin with; the critic removes himself / herself from all forms of liability. When faced with an objection, the critic can always go back to the original statement, take shelter in its ambivalence, and negate that he / she ever said what he / she, in fact, did say. To read a text is simultaneously "consequential" and "inconsequential," "meaningful" and "meaningless," "possible" and "impossible." Fish concludes his argument by saying that regardless of what critics claim to be doing, to interpret texts is all they can do since "interpretation is the only game in town" (355).

"Children," "the dead," "God"

> Who, if I cried, would hear me among the angelic
>
> orders? And even if one of them suddenly
>
> pressed me against his heart, I should fade in the strength of his stronger existence.
>
> For Beauty's nothing
>
> but beginning of Terror we're still just able to bear,
>
> and why we adore it so is because it serenely
>
> disdains to destroy us.
>
> (Rilke 21)

Openly opposing a type of reading that professes to "reveal"—by claiming an affiliation with a different mode of criticism—Lopes says, for example, that in a poem that mentions the word "childhoodhouse"[14] one should not attempt to see the "simple memory of an individual's childhood" (*A Inocência* 87). The original poem by Helder reads:

> I play, I swear.
>
> It was a childhoodhouse.
>
> I know how it was an insane house.
>
> I would stick my hands in the water: I would fall asleep,
>
> I would re-remember.
>
> Mirrors would crack against our youth. (*Poesia Toda* 99)

I obviously agree with Lopes when she claims that one cannot—by decree—declare the reading of such verses to be valid *exclusively* when made to signify someone's memory of his or her childhood; nevertheless, conversely, I vehemently protest against the prohibition of reading the reference to "childhood" or "childhoodhouse" *in this way*. The reader's evocation of a semantic "family" that includes "child," "children" or "childhood"—triggered by the word "childhoodhouse"—should authorize the interpretation of that moment in the poem as "someone's fond memories of childhood," despite the fact that we are dealing with Helder's fiercely "self-referential" poetry—as critics have been reminding us for over forty years.

Since the highly suggestive passage containing the word "childhoodhouse" also contains elements—as often happens in the case of Helder—that connote "emotion," "freedom", and "nostalgia" for a lost state of purity or "innocence," which may cause the reader to experience the flashing remembrance of moments of his or her own childhood, then why should the reader not be allowed to interpret the passage as, precisely, "an individual's fond memories of childhood"? Obviously, one's interpretation cannot go beyond these very succinct, abstract, and rarefied *vignettes* of life (and by "life" I simply mean the textual "life" that *mimics* aspects of our human, general, extra-textual, "life"). In this type of reading—which I am proposing and to which Lopes objects— the images of the poem may constitute the memories of a very vaguely and sparsely characterized literary entity—a "quasi-character" who is disappointingly anonymous, who did not merit physical descriptions, whose place of residence is not known, etc.—but who, nevertheless, "exists" literarily and can be recognized as, to say the least, the representation of a (although problematically) "human individual." Critics lack legitimacy to go farther than this; yet one has already gone far enough: as a consequence of this reading, it now appears to be less "blasphemous" to associate these *flashes* of familiarity with the referential world. Conversely, it seems to me that it is only fair that the critics who so desire be given the prerogative *not* to interpret the passage that contains the word "childhoodhouse" in a thematic manner. (Nevertheless, I honestly do not know what one may say about "childhoodhouse" if this word—or the semantic series to which it belongs: "child," "childhood," "house," "childhood's house"—is considered to be beyond the category "theme." I also do not know what to call the act of producing comments about a poem that is believed to be beyond "interpretation").

"Self-referentiality" is, without a doubt, an overwhelming presence in the poetry of Herberto Helder; nevertheless, I am persuaded that in his work (as in other self-referential works) "self-referentiality" is necessarily a relative term, particularly from a reader's perspective. "Reference" is the reader's only key to open up texts or, at least, his only way to look for glimpses of what the text may "hold." (Or still—if we prefer to believe that texts do not "hold" meanings—'reference' is the only basis through which texts trigger—in the reader's mind—some of those elusive, mysterious, 'meaningful' moments of literary 'recognition' or *deja vu*: where did I 'live' this before?) The reader is more than entitled to read "actual, real, extra-literary, referential child" when she reads the word "child"; in fact, readers cannot avoid reading "actual child" in the word "child." Readers of self-referential texts do not read "self-referentially." Readers only know how to read "referentially" (and, ultimately, even writers can only write "referentially"). When asked about the autobiographical overtones in his book of short stories, *Os Passos em Volta*, Helder stated: "No work of art of some seriousness can stop referring to life, as it cannot avoid being an invention" ("Não Há Verdadeira Honestidade Sem Alguma Originalidade" 11).

In *Poesia Toda*, the theme "children" shares many obvious traits with conventional, empirical, palpable, "cultural," children and with the image that, in our culturally shaped, Western "experiences," we have of children: e.g., the close relationship with "innocence," with "purity," with the "mystery" of a developing rationality, the freshness of "non-rational" and "non-moral" perspectives, etc. Besides yielding to these and other possible associations, Helder's "children" appear to be open doors to the supernatural. They display connections with the world of the "dead," with which these "children" communicate as if they were their peers and as if they spoke their language. From these relationships these "children" draw their strength. Many years ago, Helder offered a journalist the following rhetorical advice:

> Talk to a child. S/he will tell you amazing, mysterious, simple things. Some time ago, a child told me: "you are green, I am orange." What do you say about this? S/he was a normal child, without any theories about reality or language. Is it unintelligible myself being green and the child being orange? It is. But I comprehend it. Those who do not please go away. ("Os Jovens Escritores Vão Sabendo" 10)

Quite autobiographically, Helder appears to have transformed some of his real life experiences into literature and the proof is in these verses: "If it is a child, she says: I am orange. / Children of thought. / I am yellow" (*Poesia Toda* 590). This powerful and terrifying kind of "child" is a constitutive part of this poetic universe:

> Looking at themselves in mirrors,
> as night moves further, children appear with the horror
> of their candor, children that are fundamental, big,
> watchful children—
> singing, thinking, madly sleeping. (*Poesia Toda* 65)

"The dead" is one theme associated with supernatural terror and enigmatic knowledge. The poetic subject often mentions how the dead bring "salvation" and "redemption" to the living. The suspicion that the dead—a theme that in Helder has comforting, positive, connotations—interfere and collaborate in the lives of the living is more than just curiously common in *Poesia Toda*—it is a defining recurrence in this poetic universe:

> I try... to look straight ahead
> with all the inspiration of my past, and try to stay
> at the level of the dead, in the vast and splendid
> territory of their nobility—to receive that kind of indestructible
> strength [...]. (*Poesia Toda* 53)

It can be argued that the living—as much as living "humans" can be "presented," represented in this "inhuman" poetry—are portrayed in the anthology as sharing many traits with the dead. Conversely, "the dead" display undeniable characteristics of the living. The conventional gap between the world of the dead and the world of the living is eliminated. Both worlds share a strong magical dimension. The dead are commonly represented as "allies," as "helpers" of the living:

> I have heard that the dead breathe with transformed lights
> their eyes are as blind as blood.
> this one ran away from me, terrified.
> the dead must be pure.
> I have heard that they breathe.
> they run across the dew, and then
> they lay down. They help the living.
> They are sweet equivalencies, lights, pure ideas. (*Poesia Toda* 58)

In a sense, and understandably so, God is the most important theme in *Poesia Toda*. The presence of God is seen as a threat to the poet both in *Poesia Toda* and in Helder's other books: "God hunts me with his radiant spear" (*Poesia Toda* 361); "God attacks me..." (*Poesia Toda* 378). Scenes of confrontation between the poetic subject and God are far from being occasional. This cosmic rivalry is, nevertheless, not a balanced one. The poet does not see himself as God's equal—since he secretly knows that God cannot be defeated—but he appoints himself God's permanent challenger.[15] The poetic subject manifests here—as in many of his other books—significant Satanic traits that recall to us the visionary writing as practiced by Lautreamont, Rimbaud, Milton or Blake.

> Basic children turn me into a raging rose
> and they throw it
> against the mouth of God. (*Poesia Toda* 133)

In a sense—just like in some representations of Satan, Prometheus, or some of the other Titans—the poet is a damned creature, a monster who masochistically basks in the power of his own impotence and despair: "sadness, sadness—the youngest power of all" (*Poesia Toda* 35); "I only know that it was the strength of sadness or the strength of my life's joy" (*Poesia Toda* 35). The poet goes so far as announcing: "I speak the demonic idiom" (*Poesia*

Toda 549). The world in which the poet lives is an alternate version of God's world, a world of the poet's own creation; it is a fantastic territory where the poet is the shepherd and the provider of his fantastic creatures—"children," "mother," "the dead," etc. The power of the poet derives, in part, from the power of his creatures and of his creations. These "powers" are to be used against God through the utterance of the poetic word; or rather, these "powers" *are* the poetic word. Poetry is, therefore, the fittest weapon to be used against the greatest possible enemy—the one that cannot be defeated:

> It is necessary that God free himself from my fabulous gifts [as a poet].
> [It is necessary] that he does not lose himself in my fabulous
> Irony [of my poetic word]. (*Poesia Toda* 135)

In these "scenes of poetic battle" the subject has moments in which he explicitly fantasizes about God's elimination. (God has a double identity in *Poesia Toda*: at times he / she also appears as an ally of the poet, a silent accomplice of the world and of the word). Once again, the extreme power of the poetic word (here referred to as "beauty") is shown to be capable of defeating God:

> And he dies and passes from one day to the other.
> he inspires the days, he transports the days
> to the middle of eternity, and God enhances
> the bitter beauty of those days
> until God is destroyed by the extreme exercise
> of beauty. (*Poesia Toda* 123)

Another passage seems to present a similar scenario. We are before another scene in which a jubilant poet defeats a vulnerable God: "I knock at the door with my furious jubilation […] / God does not know [it] and he smiles, crushed / against the human wall […]"(*Poesia Toda* 107).

These three Helderian themes—three among many more that are possible in *Poesia Toda*—have one thing is common. They possess an undeniable dimension of sublimity—which, historically, has been in close association with supernatural representations (Voller 17). These three themes—which, in this particular case, may also be seen as three "characters" inside a very special "narrative" or "story:" "children," "the dead," and "God"—are essential elements in Helder's project of attaining the sublime, precisely through fantastic *scenes* such as the ones conveyed by the excerpts that I have commented on above. From Longinus's and Burke's classical interpretations of the literary sublime (respectively, *On the Sublime* and *Philosophical Enquiry*) we have learned that "terror" is a key element in causing the reader to "experience" the sublime, to the extent that the sublime can be expressed or experienced in literature:

> Whatever is fitted in any sort to excite the ideas of pain, and danger, that is to say, whatever is in any sort terrible, or is conversant about terrible objects, or operates in a manner analogous to terror, is a source of the sublime; that is, it is productive of the strongest emotion which the mind is capable of feeling. (Burke, qtd. in Voller 15)

This cultivation of the sublime was clearly illustrated, during the nineteenth century, by the Romantic Anglo-American Gothic novel. Helder's relationship with God reminds one of a Burkean terror based on threat and domination. The intense, paralyzing emotion—experienced by the subject and, differently, by the reader (or, differently still, by the critic)—is attained through the representation of a power so vastly overwhelming and unmatched by our own that it appears to be life threatening: "nothing is so terrible as the wrath of infinite Power" (Dennis, in Voller 18):

> We love what is beautiful for submitting to us, for being less than we are; we react with dread and awe to what is sublime because of its appearing greater than we are, for being *more*, and making us acknowledge its power. (Ferguson 8-9)

The tremendous appeal of Helder's images—which resides in their sublimity—may also be due to the indefiniteness, ambiguity or shapelessness of the objects presented. According to Burke, the sublime nature of an object may be caused by "the terrible uncertainty of the thing described" (in Letzring 21). In a sense, in my thematic readings I have tried to describe UFO-like, shape-changing, moving objects that I have called "themes" (which are like "static" pictures), and which I have presented in the context of what I would like to call "scenes" or "key scenes" (which are "dynamic," suggestive of movement, like very short films). This does not mean—and here lies the crux of my disagreement with the critical views that I have described earlier—that these objects are "unknowable" and that these "scenes" are beyond description. I believe that we, as critics, should "be allowed" to set limits to their obscurity and indefiniteness; and, more importantly, the setting of these limits appears to me to be not only legitimate ethically but also—theoretically, critically—quite *legitimate* within the boundaries of a fair, respectful, healthy relationship with the text at hand. My contention is that these supernatural objects are absolutely (surprisingly) consistent and, particularly, "recognizable," "readable" (sometimes even "relatable," as in the case of "childhoodhouse" and its semantic family) despite their complex elusiveness and fleetingness or, rather, in their complex elusiveness and fleetingness.

On poetry

A particular mythicization of poetry is at work in *Poesia Toda*. Helder's idea of poetry has a strong affiliation with Romanticism's own insofar as it implies, for instance, the concept of the poet as the privileged recipient of mysterious words dictated by inspiration. Such an understanding of poetry is inseparable from the—Modernist—myth of the critic as intruder, the critic as enemy of the poet, the critic as exploiter of the poet's work. The critic who envies the poet's relationship with the transcendental. (A myth that is, nowadays, strangely cultivated by critics themselves, as noted earlier by Fish.) Helder delegitimates the critical act, which is, to him, incorrigibly illicit or, at least, inherently suspect. Critical commentary is always an act of violence committed upon the literary work:

> The poem is centered in itself, monstrously solitary?
>
> It is not in a hurry, it can wait to be taken out of its isolation, it possesses enough expansive forces, take it out of there. Yet, either you take it whole, with its center in its center, and harnessed all around as a living body or you do not take a thing from it, not even a fragment. And what one often does do is smuggle pieces of it: we remove the wrong part of it, we transfer it to the wrong part of ourselves, towards some wrong place: Philosophy, Morals, Politics, Psychoanalysis, Linguistics, Symbology, Literature. Where is its body and where is its life and its integrity? Where is the solitude of its voice? Because it is mandatory to say this: few people [few readers, few critics] possess pure ears. Or clean hands. To read a poem is to be capable of making it, of re-making it. ("As Turvações da Inocência" 30)

Helder's poetry has very explicit metapoetic and intra-textual dimensions. For example, an entire volume of the anthology constitutes a response to Helder's own reception in a somewhat codified manner—though recognizably against the backdrop of the "evil" world of critics ("Antropofagias"). Writing elsewhere about "Antropofagias," the author states that the text was written with the intention of "confusing" the reader/critic. Some texts have an "untamed intention of denying" (*Photomaton & Vox* 134) and of "de-studying" (*Photomaton & Vox* 135). This affirmation could very well mean that, since critics abusively claim to be able to interpret (or "study") his works, he will undo ("resist," "destroy," "destroy by resisting") what they do or threaten to do. By "de-studying" (what today we, loosely, call "deconstructing") their studies, he will neutralize the dangers of their interpretation.

The author has repeatedly claimed that he is not "modern"—evidently confirming his modernity by the radicalism of his provocative affirmation. In the following passage he is showing an obvious nostalgia for Romantic, pre-modern times. As he denounces the enemies of the poet—which are also, naturally, his own enemies—the excerpt provides us with a Poetics. Helder places himself in opposition to the world we live in, one in which "God," "Poetry," and "Inspiration" are dead or made irrelevant; a world in which poets have been, for all practical purposes, expelled from the Republic, as Plato advocated:

> Meanwhile they all turned to: the death of God;
> the sovereignty of culture, of history and the daily life;
> *inspiration* is over, that fulminating alliance between experience and consciousness.
> That which is not searched but found is over, that which is magically and arduously and profoundly found, that is over.
> This is not the time to praise poets that declare: we are not modern,
> [...]
> What a bunch! They don't even know where and when they live. Expel them from the Republic. ("A Propósito de *Photomaton & Vox*" 94, my italics)

The author's notion of "the poet" is acutely ethical, moral, religious. The poet is someone who has a momentous mission to follow, or, as he suggests, someone who is assigned a "literary adventure" from which he should not deviate regardless of the hardships he may face. A poet's duty is to be impervious to praise or disapproval—while keeping his mind set on his all-important mission. Success, in particular, can be dangerous. These ideas (very frequent in this poetry) are extremely important for a characterization of Helder's mythicization of poetry. There are very strict codes of conduct by which "true poets" need to abide:

A conscious artist should know that prestige is harmful. One should be available to disappoint those who trusted us. Disappointing them is guaranteeing the movement. The confidence that others have in us is entirely theirs. What concerns us is another kind of confidence. The fact that we are irreplaceable in our adventure and that no one will pursue it for us. ("Os Cinco Livros que Até Hoje Publiquei" 14)

An extremely clear and consistent panel of principles rises to the surface as we read the preface to a book of poetry by António José Forte; in it Helder implies that the Romantic tradition is the only "legitimate" literary tradition, once again confirming his problematic (and, as I mentioned earlier, very "modern") relationship with the concept of Modernism: "Like all true poetry, it possesses only its own tradition, [which is] the Romantic tradition [...]. All true poetry is founded in its own difficulty, and success resides, not in the dissolution of the difficulty, but in making it efficiently manifest" ("Nota Inútil" n.p.). Writing about another Portuguese poet, Edmundo de Bettencourt, Helder praises the fact that, at some point in his life, Bettencourt stopped writing when he felt that Portuguese society—then under the New State dictatorship—no longer offered him conditions to preserve his integrity as a poet. Helder praises the fact that Bettencourt was being faithful to his own mission. He lived "untouched, inside his own adventure" ("Relance Sobre a Poesia de Edmundo de Bettencourt" 15). Elsewhere he mentioned that writing is "a struggle against the world, in defense of a *purity* that the world does not recognize [...]" ("Não Há Verdadeira Honestidade" 12, my italics).

He views his own poetic mission as a moral responsibility, yet he claims that the radical nature of the act of writing poetry is such that it goes beyond "moral responsibility" (*Apresentação do Rosto* 44). Writing is "an act of cruel religiosity, a kind of extremely intelligent expiation of the obscure crime of not having died" (*Apresentação do Rosto* 44). Precisely like religious language, poetry is the only language capable of rescuing the poet from a condemnation to "death":

Humbly I weave my grateful words
Over the beautiful ferocity
of your flesh, I raise my cup,
I listen to the hidden rumor of the fountain.
Humbly I dissipate the solitude, I accept your calling of sperm,

I deserve poetry.
—Humbly I say no to death. (*Poesia Toda* 18)[16]

I believe that this Modernist / late-Romantic religious view of poetry (and of the poet's mission) is, in its brilliant excess, not just unique in post-*Orpheu* poetry but in Portuguese literature. Helder's originality lies in the conciliation of these two, apparently incompatible, affiliations: Romanticism and Modernism; the meeting of both movements, this in-between point, is exactly the place— or the non-place—where some of the great visionaries have thrived.

Beyond Pessoa

Few times have Fernando Pessoa and Herberto Helder appeared in the same sentence in a critical text. Very few comparative observations on the two authors were ever published. Yet such a comparative approach may help illuminate Helder's contribution to contemporary poetry. A text by the late poet and critic Luis Miguel Nava is among the few that compare the two authors. Nava once said that, similarly to what Pessoa had represented in the time of *Orpheu*, both Ruy Belo and Herberto Helder constituted important landmarks beyond which the landscape radically changed. In different ways, both Ruy Belo and Herberto Helder represented the convergence and the maturation of a host of different tendencies that originated in previous generations (Nava 180). Joaquim Manuel Magalhães considers that, in the sixties, Helder's poetry marked a moment of renewal, just as neo-realism was failing, "with the exception of Carlos de Oliveira," and just as Surrealism was quickly becoming irrelevant, "with the exception of Cesariny" (*Um Pouco da Morte* 125). Magalhães considers that the revitalization of Portuguese poetry accomplished by Helder is comparable to that of Cesário Verde in relation to the ultra-Romantics and to the overly didactic and political tendencies of Junqueiro (*Um Pouco da Morte* 125). Among Helder's most significant "contributions" are: the use of bold, highly abstract and dense imagery; his very particular and problematic brand of self-referentiality; a lyrical perspective that is non-narratival, non-confessional, non-discursive and, apparently, divorced from traditional *pathos*. These Helderian "lessons"—whether they were applied or avoided by subsequent generations—have shaped the way people write and the way people read poetry in Portugal. Thanks in great part to Helder (but also to Pessoa) our poets of the second half of the twentieth century display much less conventional Romantic and Symbolist "residue" than they otherwise would have, while their writing feels less "traditional" than the literatures of other languages (Nava 182).

Both Helder and Pessoa lived during periods that were later considered crossroads in Portuguese letters. Both authors—in various ways, and to varying degrees—have influenced all of the generations that followed their own. In the seventies, Eduardo Prado Coelho said that, "just like previous generations wrote with / against Fernando Pessoa, this generation of the seventies writes with / against Herberto Helder" (*A Noite do Mundo* 128).

There are enormous differences between Helder's and Pessoa's views on poetry. One of Pessoa's most important achievements was the de-mythicization and de-mystification of the act of writing poetry. He proved that one could use colloquialisms "literarily," resorting to the humble materials of everyday life, without losing lyrical intensity: "It's not a dish that can be eaten cold. / I didn't make a fuss, but it was cold. / It can never be eaten cold, but it came cold" ("Oporto-Style Tripe" 180). He even invented a poet who, wrote as one of our most unlikely bards—the unsophisticated, barely literate, Alberto Caeiro, the shepherd. Pessoa granted literary dignity to the exceedingly human, to the embarrassingly human: "I have never met anyone who had gotten a licking […] and I, many times despicable, many times vile […] inexcusably dirty […] I, who many times have not had the patience to bathe" ("Poema em Linha Recta" 332).

Pessoa's poetic subject (especially in the cases of Campos and Soares) laments his thin connection with his fellow humans, his incommunicability, his existential isolation: "Make me human, oh night, make me fraternal and solicitous" ("Passagem das Horas" 279). Helder's subject is of a radically different order. His poetry pursues and celebrates the de-humanization of the poet, the isolation of the poetic subject, his incommunicability. Incomprehensibility is a triumph to poets who wish to forever remain "obscure": "My God, make me always an obscure poet" (*Os Passos em Volta* 167).

Pessoa caused Portuguese poetry to be less absolute, less Olympian, and less "literary" than ever before. Pessoa wished to implement, in a sense, literary democracy. Although he did not necessarily expect to be read and "understood" by the masses—he attempted to dismantle the myth of elitist, inspired poetry by stating that poets were artisans whose job was comparable to that of a humble and meticulous carpenter. Helder is exactly at the opposite end of the spectrum. Helder is an elitist, an aristocrat as far as his poetic materials are concerned: his images (due in part to their "readable self-referentiality") are the least likely to take part in a regular, real-life conversation and the least likely to show kinship with Pessoa's (apparently) unpretentious, non-literary, everyman sensibility.

What appears as subjective emptiness in Pessoa is equivalent to excessive, celebratory, defiant identity in Helder. Pessoa confesses: "They invoke spirits, I invoke myself and I find nothing" ("Tabacaria" 305). Helder announces: "I know / everything, everything. [...] I am of the age now—and I know everything. I say: my joy is tenebrous" (*Poesia Toda* 138). Or: "I can transform my self. / I can be higher than corruption" (*Poesia Toda* 106). Like Pessoa's, Helder's "poet" is self-obsessed. Yet Pessoa's "poetic self" appears disseminated, unsure of himself and of his place in the world. Helder's "poetic subject" proclaims—with a despair that is never "human," unlike Pessoa's, which is always "human"—his wholeness, his self-sufficiency, his grandiosity. A super-assertive, highly self-centered personality contrasts with a fragmented, multiplied or emptied subjectivity.

Eduardo Lourenço claims that Teixeira de Pascoaes (1877-1952) was our last "innocent" poet. According to Lourenço, Pascoaes was the last writer to believe in a transcendental "inspiration" that would signal an affiliation with the divine. Pessoa then marks the death of this (late Romantic) "innocence" as he sets a boundary beyond which no "innocence" is possible ("Cem Anos de Poesia Portuguesa" 203).

Helder not only "believes" in inspiration but obsessively uses the word "innocent" to refer to his condition as an "inspired" poet: "I am innocent [...] powerful / tumefied" (*Poesia Toda* 519); "I shivered as I realized how innocent I was [...] with my burned fingers and tongue" (*Poesia Toda* 554); "If you look the serpent in the eye, you feel how innocence is unfathomable and [how] terror is a lyrical shiver" (*Poesia Toda* 542). In no way am I claiming that Helder *truly* believes that "innocent" poets are possible in today's world. As an intelligent man, Herberto Helder, the citizen, knows very well—extra-literarily—that Pessoa's discovery may not be reversed. Yet, literarily, within the world of *Poesia Toda*, Helder writes *before*, or *beyond*, Pessoa's revolution.

As is well known, Pessoa once prophesized the advent of a poet who would surpass Camões in cultural (and national) importance. This poet would appear one hazy morning in the Portuguese Republic of Letters and rescue its literature from the threat of insignificance. He called this "savior" "Super-Camões," and critics have unanimously understood that Pessoa was referring to himself. One may argue that Helder is here building his own Super-Pessoa prophecy. Quite competitively—exactly according to Bloom's model—Helder writes about poetry's vocation of the "absolute" while denouncing the shortcomings of Pessoa and of some of the main poets of our modernity. He stops short of nominating himself, not necessarily Pessoa's successor, but Pessoa's "corrector":

> Names like Camilo Pessanha, Angelo de Lima, Sá-Carneiro and Fernando Pessoa will be used to indicate what degree of modernity had already been achieved among us. Yet none of them discovered in time, or did not discover correctly, or discovered so many things that he could not have discovered all things—not only that "poetry is the absolute real" but also that it is a *real absolute* and that the poem is the reality of *that absolute*. ("Relance Sobre a Poesia de Edmundo de Bettencourt" 20)

Helder's "poet" speaks beyond sincerity and insincerity. In a sense, his work constitutes a successor's—who sounds like a precursor—authoritative answer to "Autopsychography." I am not in any way claiming that Helder, the author, has *knowingly* created an answer to "Autopsychography"; yet his poetry seems to provide just such an answer. He rejects the premises behind Pessoa's poem in the sense that he does not recognize a double nature in the poet. Pessoa's poet finds himself divided between his human self (from which his "sincerity" originates) and his literary self (which summons his "insincerity"). Helder's poet lacks a "human self." He does not "lie" (or "fake") because (to him) nowhere is there a verifiable truth or empirical world that could be betrayed by his actions or from which he could deviate. One needs to be between two moral worlds in order to transgress the rules of one of them; in order to be accused of the sin of insincerity. Helder's subject does not possess this second dimension, this "real world" dimension, which frequently weighs on Pessoa's words like a nagging conscience. In Pessoa's extreme vocation towards confessionalism he sets out to reveal the deepest recesses of his "true" self—to the point of feeling the need to confess to the reader his own struggle with his own project of sincerity. Ultimately, Pessoa is so "sincere" that he confesses *even* the impossibility of attaining complete sincerity within the literary game. Obviously, this (paradoxical) game and its impossibilities are fascinating to him, and he shares his fascination with his reader in the poem "I Don't Know How to be Truly Sad":

I don't know how to be truly sad
Or how to be really happy.
No, I don't know how to be.
Might sincere souls be
Like me, without knowing it?

Before the lie of emotion
And the fiction of the soul,
I cherish the calm it gives me
To see flowers without reason
Flowers without a heart. (248)

The humanity of Helder's subject is unambiguously hybrid, subterranean, extraneous in ways that are inconceivable in Pessoa. Helder's poet displays the haughty humanity of a demigod in the same way that angels and demons share human traits with humans without being human. Either a proud super-humanity or an intensely desperate, supernatural humanity—like that of ghosts, monsters or of "the living dead." Helder's poet—though unavoidably displaying many obvious "human" characteristics—permanently operates outside the realm of real life, beyond nature and culture. His domain—the magical—is that of the non-human and that of the non-real. Helder's "poetic self" could not be more "sincere" in his coherence, in his consistency, in his self-assurance, in his divorce from the extra-literary world, in his radical fictionality.

There are no tobacco shops in these otherworldly landscapes and, if there were, their owners would certainly—frighteningly—not be smiling by the door.[17]

Notes

[1] Trans. Richard Zenith, *Fernando Pessoa & Co.* 247.

[2] My translation. Except where otherwise noted, I have translated from the Portuguese all subsequent quotes, including all excerpts from Helder's poetry, prose, and interviews, and from critical works available only in Portuguese. The following quotes either conform to the English original or to the English translation that I consulted and identified in the "List of Works Cited": Ramalho Santos, Stanley Fish, Rilke, Burke, Voller, Fergunson, Letzring.

[3] In 2002, an anthology of critical texts and poems was published under the title *O Século de Ouro*. The anthology was immediately heralded as a representative sample of the main poems and poets of the twentieth century in Portugal. The book—due to the ambitious nature of the project—had an unusually important impact beyond the community of critics and academics. Controversy surrounded it for many months, particularly because of the exclusion of some

poets that had been "considered" canonical and therefore non-excludable from anthologies of the kind. Curiously, most of the debate was not initiated by professionals of the so-called Portuguese "Republic of Letters" but by journalists and social and political commentators. A protest over the exclusion of one poet—Manuel Alegre—was made by one parliamentary group; the entire event drew considerable national media coverage and lively debate in different national venues.

4 I have no doubt that the reception of Pessoa's contemporaries contributed enormously to the shaping of the image that the poet holds for us today, affecting both his "literary" and "non-literary" personas; the critical reception, in a sense, always "creates" the author, and this is particularly true in the case of this poet. Pessoa wrote famous letters to some of the most prominent critics of his time—the letter to Casais Monteiro being the most famous example—in which he engages in extremely fantastic, radically "literary"—and rather megalomaniacal—explanations of what he describes as his heteronimical de-personalization. Thanks to the very generous reception that these letters had, and the reputation that their recipients enjoyed at the time—Pessoa's supposedly extra-literary or para-literary "explanation" of his work appears to have "haunted" every critical text that has been produced since.

5 The second, third and fourth editions of *Poesia Toda* were published, respectively, in 1981, 1990, and 1996. Assírio & Alvim was the publisher of the last three of the four editions. In each new edition, major revisions and changes were introduced by the author—to the point of causing dilemmas in the critical community as to which edition should be used when analyzing a particular poem. Since many poems were the object of considerable authorial editing, it appeared as if a "new" book was created with each new edition. The critic Maria de Fátima Marinho called this peculiar editorial habit the "aesthetics of modification" ("Uma Estética da Modificação"). In 2001, Herberto Helder further shocked his readers by announcing (or, rather, by "provocately suggesting," as is his style) that he was replacing his 436-page *Poesia Toda* by a 126-page super-condensed version of the anthology. This radical "summary" of his work was titled *Ou o Poema Contínuo*. Nevertheless, ignoring the (perceived) suggestions of the author, most critics (myself included) have continued to utilize the previous editions of the book as the scholarship on the author slowly evolves and proliferates. Ironically, an author's note in the first edition of *Poesia Toda* reads: "this edition is complete and final" (1:5).

6 During 2003, Alexis Levitin benefited from a grant from the "Arts Endowment for Poetry Translations" that allowed him to translate texts by Sophia de Mello Breyner and Herberto Helder. In the US, Levitin conducted some readings of Helder's translated poetry, namely in New York on May 22, 2003. Currently, two of Helder's short stories from *Os Passos Em Volta*—in a Richard Zenith translation—can be found in the Internet journal "The Literary Review" (www.theliteraryreview.org).

7 By "mainstream" poets I mean those who enjoy a high degree of name recognition among non-professionals (i.e., beyond the university, the community of literary critics, etc). Among these are, for example: Camões, Fernando Pessoa, Bocage, Florbela Espanca, Sophia de Mello Breyner, Eugénio de Andrade. Herberto Helder is, in my opinion, a borderline case. Yet, very soon, as I anticipate it, he may become a full-fledged "household name."

8 The anthology *Poesia Toda* will be referred to in this essay as *PT*. *PT* designates the 1996 edition unless otherwise noted.

9 By "poetic subject" I mean the textual manifestations of "lyrical subjectivity"; in other words, the instances in which "something" in the poem says "I." I consider these "instances" or "moments" to possess a particular consistency and regularity, and use the term "poetic self" to describe an "entity" that I imagine as having produced these "moments" of subjective manifestation. In the field of literary studies this category is also known as "poetic self," "lyrical self," "lyrical subject," lyrical "I," etc. Obviously, I do (as one should) acknowledge a technical difference between this literary "self" or "subject" and Herberto Helder, the man. Yet, since—pub-

licly—all the manifestations of Herberto Helder, the "extra-textual man," are still, to us the public, *textual* (in the form of interviews, notes to editors of newspapers or journals, short texts presenting a new edition of a book, etc.), I question the relevance and applicability of this distinction given the particular nature of Helder's public *persona* (which is always, for instance, distinctly "literary") and the characteristics of my own project. Therefore, at times, I do not distinguish between "author," "the poet," "poetic subject" or other "textual manifestations of subjectivity," such as the narrator in the short story "Vida e Obra de Um Poeta" in *Os Passos em Volta*. In the course of my essay, whenever a distinction between these "personas" needs to be made, I do try to clearly indicate to which "persona" I am referring.

Even though my main focus is Helder's "poetic subject" in *Poesia Toda*, I often complement my arguments by resorting to quotes by "subjects" who are not, technically, the "poetic subject" in *Poesia Toda*. These are: "Herberto Helder," the author, in interviews to newspapers; the narrator in some of Helder's short stories; or narrators in other books, such as, for example, *Photomaton & Vox*. My justification for using these different "voices" interchangeably is simple: the "voice" of the "poetic subject" in *Poesia Toda* is distinctly *present* and *recognizable* in all of these "personas"—his style, his values, his views on poetry and on the poet. Part of what I intend to accomplish in this essay is precisely to provide evidence for the relative equivalency and interchangeability of these Helderian "voices."

[10] As far as I could verify, the following is a thorough list of the academic theses produced in Portugal, Brazil, and the United Kingdom that predominantly concern Herberto Helder.

Doctoral dissertations:

Dal Farra, Maria Lúcia. *A Alquimia da Linguagem: Leitura da Cosmogonia Poética de Herberto Helder.* (Lisbon: Imprensa Nacional-Casa da Moeda, 1985);

da Silva, João Amadeu de Oliveira Carvalho. "A Poesia de Herberto Helder—Do contexto ao texto: uma palavra sagrada na noite do mundo" (U Católica Portuguesa, 2002);

Perkins, Juliet. *The Feminine in the Poetry of Herberto Helder* (London: Tamesis, 1991);

Ladeira, António. "Uma Obscura Soberania: a questão da subjectividade em *Poesia Toda* de Herberto Helder" (U of California, Santa Barbara, 1999).

Masters theses:

da Silva, João Amadeu de Oliveira Carvalho. *Os Selos de Herberto Helder* (Braga: Publicações da Faculdade de Filosofia da UCP, 1995);

Torres, Rui Manuel. "Herberto Helder, leitor de Raul Brandão: Uma leitura de *Húmus*, poema-montagem" (U of North Carolina at Chapel Hill, 1999);

Barbeitos, Diana Pimentel Penberthy de Araújo. "Estudo sobre o conceito de Reescrita em *Photomaton & Vox*" (U of Lisbon, 1999);

Daud, Roberto. "A Máquina de Letras: Um Estudo da Linguagem Poética de Herberto Helder." (U of São Paulo, 1979);

Bittencourt, Sylvia Maria C. R. "O Processo Criador de *Os Passos em Volta*: A Lei da Metamorfose" (U of São Paulo, 1978);

Silva, Nilza Maria Leal. "O Coelacanto: Uma Parábola do Homem" (Rio de Janeiro: Pontifícia Universidade Católica, 1974).

[11] The book in question is *Apresentação do Rosto*, whose only (small) edition came out in 1968 (Lisbon: Contraponto). Unexplainably, it was never republished and only very short sections of it were "recycled" and included in *Poesia Toda*. Personally, I believe that *Apresentação do Rosto* is Helder's best achievement outside of *Poesia Toda*.

[12] I am here referring to the socially perceived, "reclusive" *persona* of the writer. Helder is known for refusing to grant interviews to any Portuguese publications since the 1960s. He has rejected important literary awards and monetary prizes. In his own writings and on the few occasions when he has publicly commented on the reception of his works—he has displayed an attitude of general hostility toward the work of the critics, the publishing establishment, and the marketing of literature.

[13] I believe that I was the first critic to call attention to the importance of systematically identifying, cataloging, and studying Helderian "themes" and "recurrences." My articles of 1990, and 1997, as well as my 1999 dissertation and my 2002 analysis of "Fonte" in *O Século de Ouro* attest to this fact. Other critics had remarked upon these recurrences but had not referred to them as important "keys" for the understanding of Helder's poetic universe. I was also the first (and the only one so far, I believe) to propose the idea that, despite the diversity of the books included in *Poesia Toda* and the time span that the anthology encompasses (1958-1996), Helder's poetic subject manifests "unity," "visibility," and "consistency" instead of "fragmentation," "dissolution," "invisibility," and "inconsistency"—as most critics still assert today. I believe that a (problematically "pseudo-human") "face" visibly unfolds as one advances in the anthology. *Poesia Toda* can be seen as an "introduction to the face" or an "Apresentação do Rosto" (to evoke one of Helder's titles) of one individualized "poetic subject." I first made public reference to the consistency and self-obsession of Helder's subjectivity in my 1990 article, titled "Herberto Helder: Graça e Danação."

One of the pioneers of "thematic" perspectives seems to be Joaquim Manuel Magalhães who wrote about themes and recurrences as far back as 1989 (*Um Pouco da Morte* 125).

[14] The word in Portuguese is "casinfância."

[15] The poet's relationship with God assumes multiple forms in *Poesia Toda*. On many occasions Helder presents his own translated excerpts of Biblical texts. In the book "A Máquina de Emaranhar Paisagens," he creates a montage out of excerpts from Genesis, Revelation, as well as his own and other poets' texts.

[16] Quoted from the 1973 edition (vol. 1).

[17] "The Tobacco Shop" is the title of one of Pessoa's (viz., Álvaro de Campos's) most famous poems. The last verses read as follows:

> The man has come out of the Tobacco Shop (putting change in his pocket?)
> Ah, I know him: it's unmetaphysical Esteves.
> (The Tobacco Shop Owner has come to the door.)
> As if by divine instinct, Esteves turns around and sees me.
> He waves hello, I shout back "Hello, Esteves!" and the universe
> Falls back into place without ideals or hopes, and the Owner of the Tobacco Shop smiles.
> (Trans. Richard Zenith, *Fernando Pessoa & Co.,* 173-79.)

Works Cited

Belo, Ruy. "Poesia e Arte Poética em Herberto Helder." *Obra Poética*. Lisbon: Presença, 1984.

Burke, Edmund. *A Philosophical Enquiry Into the Origin of Our Ideas of the Sublime and Beautiful.* [1759]. Ed. J. T. Boulton. New York: Columbia UP, 1958.

Coelho, Eduardo Prado. "Como Falar de Herberto Helder?" *Público* [Lisbon] (10 June 1995): 12.

———. *A Noite do Mundo.* Lisbon: Imprensa Nacional, 1988.

Dal Farra, Maria Lúcia. *A Alquimia da Linguagem: Leitura da Cosmogonia Poética de Herberto Helder.* Lisbon: Imprensa Nacional—Casa da Moeda, 1985.

Diogo, Américo António Lindeza. *Herberto Helder: Texto, Metafóra, Metáfora do Texto*. Coimbra: Almedina, 1990.

Ferguson, Frances. *Solitude and the Sublime: Romanticism and the Aesthetics of Individuation*. New York: Routledge, 1992.

Fish, Stanley. *Is There a Text in this Class? The Authority of Interpretive Communities*. Cambridge: Harvard UP, 1980.

Freitas, Manuel de. *Uma Espécie de Crime:* Apresentação do Rosto *de Herberto Helder*. Lisbon: & Etc., 2001.

Guerreiro, António. "O Idioma Demoníaco." *Expresso* [Lisbon] (23 Feb. 1991): 48R.

Guimarães, Fernando. "A Aventura das Palavras." *Jornal de Letras, Artes & Ideias* [Lisbon] (1-14 Mar. 1983): 6.

Helder, Herberto. *O Amor em Visita*. Lisbon: Contraponto, 1958.

———. "Antropofagias." *Poesia Toda*. Lisbon: Assírio & Alvim, 1996. 319-344.

———. *Apresentação do Rosto*. Lisbon: Ulisseia, 1968.

———. "Os Cinco Livros que Até Hoje Publiquei Pouco Significam Para Mim." Interview with Fernando Ribeiro de Mello. *Jornal de Letras e Artes* [Lisbon] (27 May 1964): 15.

———. *A Colher na Boca*. Lisbon: Ática, 1961.

———. "Os Jovens Escritores Vão Sabendo que as Regras São Sempre Pessoais." Interview with Serafim Ferreira. *Jornal de Notícias* [Lisbon] (13 June 1968): 10-11.

———. "Não Há Verdadeira Honestidade sem Alguma Originalidade." Interview with Maria Augusta Seixas. *Jornal de Letras e Artes* [Lisbon] (11 Nov. 1964): 10, 12.

———. "A Não-Separabilidade." *Público* [Lisbon] (4 Dec. 1990): 31-32.

———. "Nota Inútil." Preface to *Uma Faca nos Dentes*. By António José Forte. Lisbon: & Etc., 1983. n.p.

———. *Os Passos em Volta*. Lisbon: Assírio & Alvim, 1994.

———. *Photomaton & Vox*. 3rd ed. Lisbon: Assírio & Alvim, 1995.

———. *Ou o Poema Contínuo*. Lisbon: Assírio & Alvim, 2001.

———. *Poesia Toda*. 2 Vols. Lisbon: Plátano, 1973.

———. *Poesia Toda*. Lisbon: Assírio & Alvim, 1981.

———. *Poesia Toda*. Lisbon: Assírio & Alvim, 1990.

———. *Poesia Toda*. Lisbon: Assírio & Alvim, 1996.

———. "Poeta Obscuro." *Os Passos em Volta*. Lisbon: Assírio & Alvim, 1994. 167-170.

———. "A Propósito de *Photomaton & Vox* ou de Qualquer Outro Texto do Autor." *A Phala* [Lisbon] 46 (1995): 94.

———. "Vida e Obra de um Poeta." *Os Passos em Volta*. 6th Ed. Lisbon: Assírio & Alvim, 1994. 145-151.

———. "Relance sobre a poesia de Edmundo de Bettencourt." Preface to *Poemas de Edmundo de Bettencourt*, by Edmundo de Bettencourt. Lisbon: Portugália, 1963. xi-xxxii.

———. "As Turvações da Inocência." Self-interview. *Público* [Lisbon] (4 Dec. 1990): 29-31.

———. *Última Ciência*. Lisbon: Assírio & Alvim, 1988.

Ladeira, António. "Fonte." *O Século de Ouro: Antologia Crítica da Poesia Portuguesa do Século XX*. Ed. Osvaldo Manuel Silvestre and Pedro Serra. Lisbon: Cotovia, 2002. 550-566.

———. "Herberto Helder: Graça e Danação." *Diário de Notícias* [Lisbon] (2 June 1990): 7.

———. "Sentido e Soberania em *Poesia Toda* de Herberto Helder." *Os Sentidos e o Sentido:*

Homenageando Jacinto do Prado Coelho. Ed. Ana Hatherly e Silvina Rodrigues Lopes. Lisbon: Edições Cosmos, 1997. 387-99.

————. "Uma Obscura Soberania: a questão da subjectividade em *Poesia Toda* de Herberto Helder." Diss. U of California at Santa Barbara, 1999.

Letzring, Monica. *The Adamastor Episode and Eighteenth Century: Aesthetic Theory of the Sublime in England.* Lisbon: Comissão Executiva do Quarto Centenário da Publicação de *Os Lusíadas,* 1973.

Lind, Georg Rudolf. *Estudos sobre Fernando Pessoa.* Lisbon: Imprensa Nacional-Casa da Moeda, 1981.

Longinus, Cassius. *On the Sublime.* Trans. James Arendt and John M. Crossett. New York: E. Mellen, 1985.

Lopes, Silvina Rodrigues. "A Imagem Ardente, Leitura de *Última Ciência* de Herberto Helder." *Aprendizagem do Incerto.* Lisbon: Litoral, 1990. 11-20.

————. *A Inocência do Devir.* Lisbon: Vendaval, 2003.

Lourenço, Eduardo. "Cem Anos de Poesia Portuguesa." *A Phala* [Lisbon] Special Ed. (1988): 202-207.

————. "Da Poesia Como Mito." *Jornal de Letras, Artes & Ideias.* [Lisbon] (22 Jan. 2003): 12.

Macedo, Helder and Ernesto Melo e Castro, eds. *Contemporary Portuguese Poetry.* Manchester: Carcanet, 1978.

Marinho, Maria de Fatima. "*Poesia Toda* de Herberto Helder: Para uma Estética da Modificação." *Herberto Helder: A Obra e o Homem.* Lisbon: Arcádia, 1982. 245-49.

Martins, Manuel Frias. *Herberto Helder: Um Silêncio de Bronze.* Lisbon: Horizonte, 1983.

Magalhães, Joaquim Manuel. *Os Dois Crepúsculos: Sobre Poesia Portuguesa Actual e Outras Crónicas.* Lisbon: A Regra do Jogo, 1981.

————. "Herberto Helder: 'Do Mundo': A dualidade e os mistérios." *Rima Pobre.* [Lisbon?]: n.p., 1999. 126-145.

————. "Herberto Helder." *Um Pouco da Morte.* Lisbon: Presença, 1989. 125-136

Nava, Luis Miguel. "Num País Dado a Celebrações Póstumas." *A Phala* [Lisbon] Special ed. (1988): 180-182.

Perkins, Juliet. *The Feminine in the Poetry of Herberto Helder.* London: Tamesis, 1991.

Pessoa, Fernando. "Autopsychography." *Fernando Pessoa & Co.* Trans. Richard Zenith. New York: Grove, 1998. 247.

————. "I Don't Know How to be Truly Sad." *Fernando Pessoa & Co.* Trans. Richard Zenith. New York: Grove, 1998. 248.

————. "Oporto-Style Tripe." *Fernando Pessoa & Co.* Trans. Richard Zenith. New York: Grove, 1998. 180.

————. "Passagem das Horas." *Poemas Escolhidos.* Lisbon: Ulisseia, 1984. 276-295.

————. "Poema em Linha Recta." *Poemas Escolhidos.* Lisbon: Ulisseia. 1984. 332-333.

————. "Tabacaria." *Poemas Escolhidos.* Lisbon: Ulisseia, 1984. 308-311.

————. "The Tobacco Shop." *Fernando Pessoa & Co.* Trans. Richard Zenith. New York: Grove, 1998. 173-179.

Pinto do Amaral, Fernando. "Herberto Helder: O Texto Sonâmbulo." *A Phala* [Lisbon] Special ed. (1988): 134-37.

Rilke, Rainer Maria. *Duino Elegies.* Trans. J. B. Leishman and Stephen Spender. New York: W. W. Norton, 1939.

Santos, Maria Irene Ramalho. *Atlantic Poets: Fernando Pessoa's Turn in Anglo American Modernism.* Hanover: UP of New England, 2003.

Silvestre, Osvaldo Manuel e Pedro Serra, ed. *Século de Ouro: Antologia Crítica da Poesia Portuguesa do Século XX.* Braga: Angelus Novus & Cotovia, 2002.

Voller, Jack G. *The Supernatural Sublime: The Metaphysics of Terror in Anglo-American Romanticism.* Dekalb: Northern Illinois UP, 1994.

António Ladeira is currently Associate Professor of Portuguese and Spanish at Texas Tech University, where he serves as the Coordinator of the Portuguese Program. He was a lecturer in Portuguese and Lusophone literatures at Yale University (1997-2002). He holds a Ph.D. in Hispanic Languages and Literatures from the University of California at Santa Barbara (1999). His dissertation is on poetic subjectivity in Herberto Helder. He has a "Licenciatura" in Portuguese Studies from Universidade Nova de Lisboa (1992). He has published articles on twentieth-century Lusophone literature in *Século de Ouro: Antologia Crítica da Poesia Portuguesa do Século XX* (Cotovia/Angelus Novus), *Crossroads* (UCLA) and *Colóquio/Letras* (Fundação Gulbenkian). His current research interests include contemporary Luso-Brazilian poetry and fiction and Portuguese-American literature. He has also published two books of his own poetry. Email: antonio.ladeira@ttu.edu

Estilo e ficção autoral n'*Os Passos em Volta*, de Herberto Helder

Sílvia Oliveira

Resumo. *Os Passos em Volta* de Herberto Helder, publicado pela primeira vez em 1963, é o único volume de contos numa obra predominantemente poética. Os contos deste volume têm sido sistematicamente interpretados biograficamente (estabelecendo uma unidade de autor textual e empírico); e funcionalmente (cumprindo estes textos em prosa a função de clarificar a poesia de Herberto). Através da releitura de três dos mais citados contos do volume, "Estilo," "Teoria das Cores," e "Poeta Obscuro," discuto que a categoria do narrador nestes textos cria ficções de autor, em vez de reflectir uma entidade extratextual. O princípio estrutural d'*Os Passos em Volta* é a compulsão para a narrativa. O modo discursivo por excelência destes contos é o irónico. Eu sugiro que estes dois factores inviabilizam as estratégias de leitura monológicas atrás mencionadas.

Herberto Helder fez de 1968 um local de peregrinação. Na sua monumental história pessoal, o fracasso de 1968 instituiu-se como início em maturidade de uma poética radicada na inevitabilidade do dizer e do fazer poéticos. Abandonando progressivamente a escrita em prosa, ou relegando-a definitivamente para as colecções de "textos indigentes" (como *Photomaton & Vox*), Herberto Helder manteve *Os Passos em Volta*, desde a primeira edição em 1963 num estatuto especial, não incorporando estes textos no corpus que desde 1981 leva o título de *Poesia Toda*. Pretendo neste trabalho retomar a

Portuguese Literary & Cultural Studies 7 (2008): 73-85.

questão talvez já cansada, mas em todo o caso ainda não resolvida, do lugar d'*Os Passos em Volta* na economia de *Poesia Toda*, tradicionalmente secundarizado. Para isso tomo como estratégia a releitura de três contos, "Estilo," "Poeta Obscuro," "Teoria das Cores," tornados locais de peregrinação (súmulas de sentido) da poesia de Herberto: quero dizer, da obra poética e do autor. Sugiro que, sob os auspícios da ironia, o estilo é uma ficção da mesma forma que 1968 é uma ficção, e ambos são produtos de uma muito premente compulsão para a narrativa. Este encadeamento leva-nos à questão problemática da identificação n'*Os Passos em Volta* de uma figura única de autor, à interpretação biografista e interna à obra poética de Herberto Helder, condicionadas as duas por uma (muito modernista) subordinação da prosa à poesia.

I.

Fala-se de Herberto Helder por aproximações, circumlocuções, metáforas, repetições, numa metodologia que revela simultaneamente respeito pela complexidade da sua poética e um sentimento de impotência explicativa. Fala-se da "exegese" de Herberto Helder, tomando a parte pelo todo, (con)fundindo o homem com a obra. No entanto, tal aproximação exegética é antes de mais tropológica, porque se radica no reconhecimento da subversão do sentido da palavra, extensível à linguagem que "organiza" o universo. O "homem irónico" de certos textos d'*Os Passos em Volta*, o "decrifador irreverente da matéria enigmática" (Dal Farra 18), é o garante da arquitectura textual fundada naquele que é o tropo dos tropos: a ironia (de Man, *Aesthetic* 179).

No seu diálogo com o interlocutor silencioso do conto "Estilo," o primeiro conto do livro, o homem irónico apresenta-se como o sistematizador da vida entendida "como um acontecimento excessivo": "Vejamos: o estilo é um modo subtil de transferir a confusão e a violência da vida para o plano mental de uma unidade de significação" (9). Para exemplificar a sua teoria, o homem irónico alude à história do médico que lhe receitou remédios para a loucura, e à do homem velho que, apesar de não ter já muito que esperar da vida, não prescindia do amor, e então amava as flores. Conta também como ele alcança o seu estilo "estudando matemática e ouvindo um pouco de música" e como "as crianças enlouquecem em coisas de poesia." A compulsão para a narrativa torna-se dessa forma ela mesma expressão da impossibilidade de ordenação lógica do discurso que resultaria na resolução racional do caos. Note-se como as narrativas aparecem aqui transcritas nos seus elementos mínimos de significação, pondo em destaque o seu carácter exemplar.

A sobreposição da micronarrativa à narrativa (como um palimpsesto que revelasse todas as camadas subjacentes) obedece a uma lógica da linguagem poética e, simultaneamente a uma lógica aparentada da escrita automática (sem o elemento aleatório). As duas caracterizam-se por uma manipulação económica do discurso (do que resulta uma tendência para a contenção narrativa), mas também se associam a um discurso psíquico que n'*Os Passos em Volta* aparece em diversas ocasiões: em diálogos e monólogos suscitados por uma qualquer vivência da sensibilidade inteligente, mediada em diversas ocasiões pela loucura (melhor será dizer: pela possibilidade dela): "a loucura, a tenebrosa e maravilhosa loucura... Enfim, não seria isso mais nobre, digamos, mais conforme ao grande segredo da nossa humanidade? Talvez o senhor seja mais inteligente do que eu" (12).

Afirmar a vigência da ironia, o tropo dos tropos, neste texto e em todos os textos deste autor pode ser uma leitura perigosa no sentido que Schlegel lhe atribui ao defini-la como "permanente parábase" (Miller 60). Se um texto irónico instaura a suprema incompreensibilidade, a permanente suspensão do sentido ou brecha na ilusão dramática, aquilo que Hegel, criticando Schlegel, definiu como "infinita negatividade absoluta," o leitor encontra-se num impasse irresolúvel, depara-se com uma aporia. A impossibilidade de resolução dialéctica é na verdade a asserção da irredutibilidade do signo, ou o que o nosso ironista apelida de "abstracção," uma operação intelectual de redução de tópicos que permite ordenar (momentaneamente) o caos. A ironia final do texto talvez resida na invocação constante e mágica do estilo como artimanha, princípio de composição poética e existencial:

> Consegui um estilo. Aplico-o à noite, quando acordo às quatro da madrugada. É simples: quando acordo aterrorizado, vendo as grandes sombras incompreensíveis erguerem-se no meio do quarto... Às vezes uso o processo de esvaziar as palavras... Pego numa palavra fundamental: Amor, Doença, Medo, Morte, Metamorfose. Digo-a baixo vinte vezes. Já nada significa. É um modo de alcançar o estilo. (11)

O estilo, a palavra submetida à lei da ironia, seria então a fórmula mágica performativa, não aquilo que dá a conhecer, que descreve, mas aquilo que faz acontecer. E é este carácter mágico que pode estabelecer uma barreira a certos leitores, porque "there is no way to know, for sure, whether the revelation is a true one, or only a semblance" (Miller 72). Porque acreditam no seu valor mágico, as crianças "enlouquecem em coisas de poesia." O que separa o ironista da criança é a necessidade de controlar o "volume impossível" das coisas da vida; mas o que separa o ironista do seu interlocutor é que este necessita de escapar à submissão e à lei da ironia, "está demasiado na posse de um estilo," e talvez aí resida a sua inteligência.

Como fica claro no conto "Estilo," o autor recorre ao esvaziamento das palavras, diríamos de forma compulsiva, com vista a chegar a uma paradoxal realidade pre-linguística. O falhanço de 1968 (que o poeta decretara como o ano em que se dedicaria ao silêncio) revela-se uma feliz confirmação do estilo, e legitima a união entre linguagem (poética) e consciência, desta feita reconstruídas.

A ironia aparece intimamente ligada a um conceito também composicional em Herberto Helder: a metamorfose. O conto "Teoria das Cores" é exemplar— e tem sido lido como exemplo—da lógica alquímica subjacente ao acto criativo artístico. O pintor, mais do que o filósofo, é intérprete do princípio transcendente com o qual o homem comunica através da arte. Este conto expõe uma teoria da representação realista que se articula com o texto "(A Paisagem É um Ponto de Vista)" de *Photomaton & Vox*. É de realçar o parentesco etimológico de "teoria" e "ponto de vista" (tal como "teorema" noutro conto): *theōrīa* significa em Grego contemplação, especulação, vista, sendo o *theōrós* o espectador. Nos dois textos trata-se da representação da realidade como resultado de um ponto de vista, e postula-se a verticalidade da relação espectador-real em oposição à relação horizontal das poéticas reflexivas (aristotélicas e platónicas). A verticalidade do ponto de vista é entendida como a que mais fielmente representa o real (a paisagem) por ser a única capaz de o contemplar através de várias perspectivas. Herberto Helder ensaia assim nestes textos uma poética do realismo que decorre não só da constante auto-reflexão da prática artística, mas que pretende ser igualmente uma tomada de posição na polémica que desde os anos 40 opunha neo-realistas, presencistas e surrealistas.

O pintor de "Teoria das Cores" depara-se com um fenómeno de progressiva modificação da realidade enquanto a contempla. A questão que se lhe coloca é a de traduzir essa mesma realidade para o quadro respeitando a sua natureza mutável. A cor preta que se desenvolve e alastra desde o interior do peixe no aquário, sobrepondo-se à sua cor vermelha é a "insídia do real" que abre "um abismo na primitiva fidelidade do pintor" (23), obrigado dessa forma a questionar o real para poder representá-lo fielmente:

Ao meditar sobre as razões da mudança exactamente quando assentava na sua fidelidade, o pintor supôs que o peixe, efectuando um número de mágica, mostrava que existia apenas uma lei abrangendo tanto o mundo das coisas como o da imaginação. Era a lei da metamorfose.

Compreendida esta espécie de fidelidade, o artista pintou um peixe amarelo.

Da concepção aristotélica do estilo como instrumento passamos para uma concepção do estilo como código de representação do real inseparável de uma acção personificadora: a função expressiva da obra de arte não é inteligível em última instância se não for atribuível a um autor, isto é, não pode por exemplo sustentar-se como um fenómeno natural (produzido pela natureza). Através do protocolo conceptual da repetição, o estilo cria a consistência necessária tanto à construcção como ao reconhecimento de uma figura de autor que se comunica através da obra. A projecção dessa figura de autor permite que a identificação de um determinado estilo acompanhe o reconhecimento do autor, assim envolvido na rede traumática de influências criativas/criadoras.[1]

Existem ainda paralelos interessantes a desenvolver em relação à teorização herbertiana do estilo. Recordo que é nos anos 60 que Lacan, influenciado pelos surrealistas, define o real em termos de trauma. Igualmente Andy Warhol na mesma altura serve-se do esquema repetitivo imagético para revelar o automatismo da produção. O estilo de Warhol aproxima-se da teoria herbertiana que temos vindo a debater: "the more you look at the exact same thing, the more the meaning goes away, and the better and emptier you feel."[2] A actividade de esvaziar as palavras tem o paralelo na perda ou dispersão do sentido nas imagens de Warhol. Ambas actividades só são possíveis, no entanto, por obra de ironia, já que o sentido não se dissolve na repetição, mas chama a atenção para a materialidade daquilo que facilmente passa por essência (a palavra, a imagem). Nestes casos, o sentido deriva da repetição. Os dois seguem assim os passos de Nietzsche quando escrevia repetidamente (compulsivamente) "Got ist Tot" para demonstrar que Deus é ausência, que o princípio da transcendência é o princípio da ausência.

Essa é a estratégia (de salvação) do narrador que no conto "Poeta Obscuro" traça a lápis na parede em frente da cama a frase "Meu Deus, faz com que eu seja sempre um poeta obscuro"(167). A inscrição da frase não tem o valor de lei, trata-se do mesmo intuito com que Nietzsche escreveu

"Deus é morte/Deus está morto," um intuito de clarificação: "Acerca da frase—'Meu Deus, faz com que eu seja sempre um poeta obscuro.'—julgo haver alguma coisa a explicar."

Osvaldo Silvestre lê este conto como "um metatexto do projecto da (neo)vanguarda, para quem o imperativo do novo se impõe ao poeta" (114). A invocação da transcedência, bem como do modo poético nos vocábulos "Deus" e "obscuro," e a sua materialização na parede do quarto garantem a sua existência. A lógica negativa que perspectiva a incomunicabilidade passa pela materialização da palavra e do seu poder criativo quando o poeta a escreve no papel: "O poema que se escreve—longo texto fluindo, denso e venenoso, a imitar a substância ao mesmo tempo vivificante e corruptora do sangue—não é sequer uma oferta dirigida a Deus. É a ironia, onde desliza a arma da nossa obscuridade" ("Poeta Obscuro" 169). O poema consegue o vazio que Deus habita (Diogo 150).

É neste ponto que Silvestre situa o drama das neovanguardas: "a pulsão regressiva da vanguarda coexiste com o projecto racionalista de controlo absoluto do material" (114), acompanhando uma subjectividade triunfante não por se reduzir a uma humanidade sem Deus mas ao se elevar ela mesma à divindade: "De modo que é um extraordinário triunfo tomar o papel entre duas mãos sábias e rasgá-lo aos bocadinhos, sorrindo" ("Poeta Obscuro" 169).

Em diversos momentos surpreendemos nestes contos um sorriso irónico do homem em situações de auto-reflexão que abrem para a clarificação, geralmente decorrentes de uma situação extrema de adversidade (material, física ou intelectual). É também o sorriso do louco que se junta à galeria de filósofos ironistas, poetas, bêbedos que populam estes textos que, como eles, obedece à lei dialógica básica de sempre questionar toda a asserção. A ironia como método tem em Kierkegaard o seu cultor ético por excelência. Para este filósofo, a ironia não é apenas um momento de negatividade necessário (Hegel), mas representa o início da subjectividade. Como sintetiza Lee Capel na sua Introdução à tradução inglesa da obra do filósofo dinamarquês, *The Concept of Irony: with constant reference to Socrates,* "to comprehend this much of the ideal significance of the irony is to grasp its meaning as *contradiction* (ambiguity), its structure as *dialectical,* its medium the *language of reflection,* its style *antithetical,* and its aim *self-discovery*" (32).

O momento aporético de negatividade evidenciado na atitude confrontacional em diversos contos d'*Os Passos em Volta* coloca o autor "na parte da história melancólica do modernismo tardio":

> …propõe-se, na lógica das vanguardas, como "avanço" conquanto possuído pela lentidão do tardo-modernismo…por outro [lado], ela [a obra] não deixa de desejar o salto extra-histórico que a reconduzisse àquele lugar por que grande parte da vanguarda anseia: o mito. (Silvestre 111)

Por "modernismo tardio" entende Merquior o "desengajamento progressivo dos principais elementos da poética modernista: o mito da imagem romântica, a política da recusa e redenção e a "participação nas trevas" (12). E se identificamos em Herberto Helder grande parte da gramática do Surrealismo, a confluência do modernismo tardio com a lógica das vanguardas resultou numa fuga à escola contrapondo-se a ela uma solidão autoral ou uma mitologia pessoal (Diogo 75).

II.

Solidão autoral ou mitologia pessoal indicam uma instância intra-literária, formada no texto ou na obra, de maior impacto em textos líricos, isto é, naqueles textos que expõem uma experiência fundada num Eu. A poesia encontra-se assim no centro da experiência literária como a forma que mais claramente afirma a especificidade do domínio do literário (Culler 162). Para Culler, a relação do discurso literário com o discurso quotidiano é, nesta lógica, uma de correspondência através da qual o leitor procede à naturalização do primeiro. Esse processo de naturalização será, por sua vez, a actividade da leitura que assenta na identificação de vários momentos ou níveis de verosimilhança. Uma das formas de naturalizar a ficção reside na identificação de narradores (Culler 200) estabelecendo redes de significação extratextuais. Esta é a problemática de que me ocupo em seguida.

Os contos d'*Os Passos em Volta* participam do mesmo movimento de escrita em prosa continuado em *Retrato em Movimento* (1967), *Apresentação do Rosto* (1968), *Vocação Animal* (1971), que engloba também os textos de *Photomaton & Vox* (1979) e que progressivamente se situaram em paralelo ao corpus canonizado de *Poesia Toda*. A proximidade entre estes textos, subordinando-os no entanto à matriz lírica, favorece uma coesão textual que passa por uma coesão da instância enunciativa. Assim se explica o favorecimento nos contos d'*Os Passos em Volta* da vertente intimista e da interpretação biografista que perpetuam aquela subordinação.

Nas leituras habitualmente feitas d'*Os Passos em Volta*, todas as instâncias de enunciação dos contos confluem irresistivelmente numa figura autoral

(Herberto Helder) que legitima não só os textos individuais mas a obra no seu conjunto. Isto equivale a afirmar que os vários narradores que identificamos nos contos d'*Os Passos em Volta* são ficções de um mesmo autor empírico, e também que são eles mesmos transmutações desse autor empírico. O modo interpretativo aplicado a *Os Passos em Volta* revela-se assim o biográfico, o que institui a intencionalidade autorial como o garante do sentido último dos textos. Tal análise tende, "naturalmente," a relegar para um plano secundário as zonas de ambiguidade discursiva que, ensinaram os New Critics, revelam a falácia da intencionalidade autorial como fonte credível de sentido.

Chamo agora a atenção para uma esperada coincidência. No mesmo ano em que Roland Barthes proclamava a morte do Autor (1968), Herberto Helder prometia-se ao silêncio. Parecendo que coincidiam os ânimos destrutivos, eles encontravam-se na verdade em campos bastantes distantes. A mudança de paradigma, verificada nos estudos literários desde os trabalhos de Hans Robert Jauss e da Escola de Constança concentrando-se na recepção literária, influenciou definitivamente a tese que Barthes proclamou na famosa frase: "la naissance du lecteur doit se payer de la mort de l'Auteur" (495). Mais interessado em investigar relações de poder instituídas através do discurso, Foucault um ano depois falava da "função autor" como "característica do modo de existência, de circulação e de funcionamento de alguns discursos no interior de uma sociedade" (Gusmão 486). Entre a noção da morte crítica do Autor (Barthes) e a historicização da figura do Autor (Foucault) há em comum nos dois uma análise que abala a concepção unitária e imutável tradicional daquele como guardião do sentido da obra. As duas teorias na verdade podem ler-se de forma complementar com outros ataques da época à concentração de sentido/poder numa figura (nomeadamente ataques políticos). No entanto, o decreto de Barthes abalou estruturas que não podem ser destruídas, como provam os discursos de minorias que sempre se aprestam a recuperar a figura do Autor, ainda que recusem um modo autoritário de garante do sentido. Aliás, o manifesto "La Mort de L'Auteur," não se aplica necessariamente ao próprio Barthes (neste texto figura tutelar assaz autoritária), podendo quando muito historicizar-se a sua função. A razão para este aparente paradoxo reside na impossibilidade de fazer desaparecer as posições de sujeito: ascendendo da morte do Autor, poderá o leitor substituir o autor textual?

Pretendo agora articular estas questões com a obra de Herberto Helder. As várias referências ao silêncio que percorrem principalmente as suas primeiras obras têm de ser entendidas no contexto de uma poética da modernidade na qual o sujeito vive na (e através da) linguagem a dramática cisão entre consciência e mundo. Impotência e impostura, qualidades trágicas da linguagem poética, passam a significar uma vivência em crise e a falência do sujeito. É assim que autores como Baudelaire resolvem triunfantemente a vida na obra, e analogamente, outros como Rimbaud abandonam a literatura. A vivência de um modernismo tardio, no qual o sujeito se encontra definitivamente desiludido de todas as aventuras humanas mas ainda não desistente (o que lhe garante uma réstia de esperança), permite que Herberto Helder viva conscientemente a sua condição aporética: "Devo ainda falar e falar, depois de 1968, o ano em que—finalmente!—me prometi ao silêncio? 1968 foi a minha melhor descoberta, e também um ano que me custou quase a respiração. Pois parece ser necessário que fale" (*Photomaton* 43). Ao evidente fracasso do decreto (vivido como uma descoberta) corresponde a necessidade de o narrar, a expressão da aporia só podendo ser feita pelo poeta capaz de expressar a ambiguidade da sua condição. A ironia torna-se assim no modo principal de Herberto Helder por ser o único ponto de vista que não apreende o sentido numa única direcção.

1968, que não resultou no silêncio do autor, não pode senão ser entendido como uma referência ficcional cuja verificabilidade não nos é possível averiguar. Sigo Paul De Man na consideração que a ilusão de referencialidade é em si uma ficção (e não uma representação factual de uma figura) que adquire um certo grau de produtividade referencial (*The Rhetoric of Romanticism* 69). De Man desconfia da existência do género autobiográfico que se institui em oposição à ficção com base numa estrutura verificável de referências externas ao texto. Sugere que o momento autobiográfico aparece como uma figura da leitura na qual os dois sujeitos envolvidos (o autor *do* texto e o autor *no* texto que partilham o mesmo nome) se determinam um ao outro por mútua substituição reflexiva (70). Para De Man, um texto no qual o autor declara ser o sujeito do seu próprio entendimento (autobiografia) não difere funcionalmente de quando um sujeito reclama a autoria de determinada obra; nos dois casos estamos perante uma série de substituições especulares de autoria.

Em nenhum texto de Herberto Helder esta especularidade é explicitada por via do nome: nunca o nome do autor aparece gravado em outros lugares além da primeira página. Há no entanto todo um conjunto de características que nos permitem falar de uma consciência de autor exterior à obra; essas características constituem o autor como editor da sua própria obra. Neste momento recorro ao trabalho de Helena Buescu na sua análise da instância do autor na obra *The Alexandria Quartet* de Lawrence Durrell. Defende Buescu que:

> ...ou aceitamos a autoria como gesto meramente extratextual e por isso sempre intrusivo e (no sentido repressivo do termo) autoritário...ou aceitamos a autoria como *lugar de fronteira e cruzamento* entre o que classificamos...como o extratextual e o intratextual, e reconhecemos na estrutura composicional desta obra um efeito do autor textual que não se confunde aqui, em nenhum momento, com os vários narradores dos quatro romances em questão. (32)

Embora não se referindo ao caso de Herberto Helder, parece-me que esta citação nos pode elucidar em duas problemáticas essenciais. A primeira prende-se com o acto de leitura e interpretação ("aceitamos a autoria"). A segunda prende-se com o facto de o efeito do autor textual da obra herbertiana se potencializar virtualmente em todos os seus narradores.

Parece ficar claro da citação de Helena Buescu que o papel atribuído ao leitor (chamemos-lhe empírico) será o de validar a autoria ou zelar pela verificabilidade das referências do autor. Aceitando a autoria ou o entendimento hipotético da autoria como "gesto meramente extratextual," o leitor não põe em causa a validade da entidade "autor." Já a segunda questão parece levantar mais problemas: o efeito do autor textual (tal como o deparamos nas anotações extratextuais como os prefácios) "não se confunde aqui, em nenhum momento, com os vários narradores dos quatro romances em questão." Está implicado na negativa "em nenhum momento" que o carácter autónomo dos narradores dos quatro romances se radica na ficcionalidade de cada um deles que não lembra nunca (não faz efeito de) o autor extratextual que o leitor deverá aceitar enquanto autoritário ou não.

Não pretendendo debater a questão do efeito de autor na obra-prima de Durell, transfiro esta problemática para Herberto Helder em cuja obra esta questão é certamente mais complexa. Logo à partida o autor textual, chamemos-lhe Herberto Helder (ou o poeta), compila em livro (*Photomaton & Vox*) as intervenções críticas que o referenciam como autor de toda a obra até então publicada; encontramos ainda momentos autobiográficos, isto é, narrativas especulares nas quais existe auto-referência a um sujeito ("eu") sem no entanto existir um envio a uma assinatura. O efeito de autor parece ligar-se intimamente ao discurso em primeira pessoa, a um sujeito de experiências identificáveis como pertencendo à mesma pessoa, à menção de certos dados de referência ao mundo real e à biografia do homem empírico que se imiscuiria na biografia do autor textual. Se o papel do leitor consiste em validar a autoria destes textos, uma tarefa que lhe cabe é de verificar os dados biográficos. Assim fez, por exemplo, Fátima Marinho ao comprovar os testes psicofisiológicos no Serviço de Psiquiatria do Hospital de Santa Maria em Lisboa em 1964 a que o autor faz referência num texto de *Photomaton*: "Mandaram-me fazer um electro-encefalograma para ver como ia o meu ritmo alfa" ("[os diálogos]" 31). No entanto, se aceitarmos que o papel do leitor se poderá expandir em determinados casos para além da aceitação do efeito (mais ou menos autoritário) do autor, o que equivale a delegar-lhe em certa medida características autorais na atribuição de sentido, aproximamo-nos da leitura que eu pretendo sugerir dos contos d'*Os Passos em Volta*.

Como é sabido, são variadas as estratégias que geram um sentido de unificação neste livro: a imagem global do movimento cíclico nos contos estrategicamente distribuídos; a primeira pessoa da enunciação na maioria dos contos que é sujeito e narrador de uma experiência de vida; a escassez de personagens; recurso à narrativa exemplar que projecta um narrador evidenciando todas as características tradicionais de autoridade; auto-referência do narrador como poeta ao seu ofício (invocando o autor de *Poesia Toda*). Vemos que, ao contrário do que foi dito acerca dos quatro romances de Lawrence Durell, o efeito autoral n'*Os Passos em Volta* confunde-se com e implica-se em cada um dos narradores sem, ao mesmo tempo, o fazer explicitamente. Porque o efeito de real nestes contos é problemático, os mecanismos de naturalização da narrativa não permitem estabelecer um sentido certo quanto à unidade de efeito de autor. Dever-se-á talvez falar de efeitos de autor sem abandonar a possibilidade da sua confluência num único—isto é, não submetendo *a priori* o texto à tirania do único.

Sugiro que ao potencializar simultaneamente quer um efeito único de autor quer efeitos múltiplos (correspondendo, por exemplo, a diferentes experiências de vida), as instâncias autorais nesta obra sublinham a sua ficcionalidade através do impulso para a narrativa, facto que desde logo deve precaver o leitor crítico a evitar leituras monológicas d'*Os Passos em Volta* quer de teor biográfico quer de teor pedagógico ou explicativo da poesia de Herberto Helder.

Tal atitude ou disponibilidade por parte do leitor certamente viabiliza um espaço para *Os Passos em Volta* não subordinado à exegese de *Poesia Toda* (centro, totalidade) mas, na designação de Túa Blesa, em gravitação descentrada que aponta não para a unidade de textos mas para uma "(com)unidade" (Blesa 147). Seguindo esta leitura, *Os Passos em Volta* não obedece a uma lógica temporal que o estabelece como variante em prosa de *Poesia Toda* mas como unidade-(com)unidade em equidistância descentralizada desta. No fundo, trata-se de interpretar o modelo herbertiano da circularidade enquanto modelo espacial e não temporal, isto é, como metáfora composicional da sua escrita e não metáfora para a interpretação da sua obra.

Notas

[1]Herberto Helder é certamente, depois de Fernando Pessoa, o mais significativo "poeta forte" português envolvido na rede de influências, ao que não é alheia a sua atitude anti-fraternidade comunitária (a comunidade das letras), e gerando a esperada angústia nos poetas aspirantes a uma voz autónoma, um estilo. Leia-se a este respeito a comovente e angustiada carta aberta de Joaquim Manuel Magalhães a Herberto Helder: "...quando cheguei às 'Musas Cegas' deixei de saber o que fazer com as palavras. Você não devia existir" (129-133).

[2] Citado em Foster 103.

Obras Citadas

Barthes, Roland. "La Mort de L'Auteur." *Manteia*: 1968. *Roland Barthes: Oeuvres Complètes*. Vol. 2. 1966-1973. Paris: Seuil, 1994. 491-95.

Blesa, Túa. *Logofagias. Los trazos del silencio*. Zaragoza: Departamento de Linguistica General e Hispánica, 1998.

Buescu, Helena Carvalhão. *Em Busca do Autor Perdido. Histórias, Concepções, Teorias*. Lisboa: Cosmos, 1998.

Capel, Lee M. Introdução, tradução e notas. *The Concept of Irony. With Constant Reference to Socrates*. Søren Kierkegaard. New York: Harper & Row, 1965. 7-41.

Culler, Jonathan. *Structuralist Poetics. Structuralism, Linguistics and The Study of Literature*. Ithaca, New York: Cornell UP, 1975.

Dal Farra, Maria Lúcia. *A alquimia da linguagem. Leitura da cosmogonia poética de Herberto Helder*. Lisboa: INCM, 1986.

De Man, Paul. *Aesthetic Ideology*. Minneapolis: U of Minnesota P, 1996.

———. *The Rhetoric of Romanticism*. New York: Columbia UP, 1984.

Diogo, Américo Anónio Lindeza. *Herberto Helder: texto, metáfora, metáfora do texto*. Coimbra: Livraria Almedina, 1990.

Foster, Hal. *The Return of the Real: The Avant-Garde at The End of the Century*. Cambridge, MA: MIT Press, 1996.

Gusmão, Manuel. "Autor." *Biblos*. Vol 1. Lisboa: Verbo, 1995.

Helder, Herberto. *Os Passos em Volta*. Lisboa: Assírio & Alvim, 1997.

————. "Poeta Obscuro." *Os Passos em Volta*. Lisboa: Assírio & Alvim, 1994. 167-70.

————. *Photomaton & Vox*. Lisboa: Assírio & Alvim, 1987.

Magalhães, Joaquim Manuel. *Os dois crepúsculos. Sobre poesia portuguesa actual e outras crónicas*. Lisboa: A Regra do Jogo, 1981.

Marinho, Maria de Fátima. *Herberto Helder. A obra e o homem*. Lisboa: Editora Arcádia, 1982.

Merquior, José Guilherme. "O significado do pós-modernismo." *Colóquio/Letras* 52 (1979): 5-15.

Miller, Hillis. "Friedrich Schlegel and the Anti-Ekphrastic Tradition." Ed. Michael Clark. *Revenge of the Aesthetic. The Place of Literature in Theory Today*. Berkeley, Los Angeles: U of California P, 2000.

Silvestre, Osvaldo. "Da nova música à *musica perennis*: aporias tardo-modernistas em Adorno e Herberto Helder." *Zentral Park. Revista de teoria e crítica*. 1, (1999): 109-16.

Sílvia Oliveira é licenciada em Estudos Portugueses e Franceses pela Universidade do Porto; doutorada em Estudos Portugueses pela Universidade da California, Santa Barbara (2004) com a tese: *Tendências do conto português nos anos 60: José Cardoso Pires, Maria Judite de Carvalho, Herberto Helder*. É actualmente professora assistente de literatura portuguesa e espanhola na Universidade de Purdue, Indiana. De momento os seus estudos centram-se na poesia portuguesa e espanhola de mulheres, com particular enfoque na poesia galega contemporânea. O seu último artigo, 'Enterrando vivos': especulações em torno de *O Estadio do Espello* de María do Cebreiro," foi publicado em *Lectora: Revista del Centre Dona I Literatura*. Universitat de Barcelona (2003). E-mail: soliveir@purdue.edu

The Insurgent Body Poetic of Luiza Neto Jorge

Anna M. Klobucka

Abstract. The rigorously inventive lyric of Luiza Neto Jorge (1939-1989), one of the most distinctive voices in Portuguese poetry since the 1960s, cultivates as its substantive and instrumental fulcrum a consistent emphasis on gendered corporeality. Neto Jorge's textualization of the body (particularly of the sexual body) gives substance to the complex discursive reflection on the gendered construction of cognition and experience that takes place in her poetry. At the same time, the poet's attentiveness to the physicality of language—manifest in her adroit use of deconstructive wordplay and precisely engineered syntax—brings into focus the reciprocal permeability of linguistic (and therefore also social) and corporeal matter.

One of the most distinctive voices in Portuguese poetry since the 1960s, at the time of her death in 1989 Luiza Neto Jorge left behind a body of work as compact as it is intensely and rigorously inventive. According to Luís Miguel Nava, in an essay published shortly after Neto Jorge's untimely passing, it is precisely "pela forma como em tão exíguas proporções pôde atingir uma das mais intensas fulgurações do que se fez na sua época" that her poetic legacy "deverá desde já ser posta a par da de um Camilo Pessanha ou da de um Mário de Sá-Carneiro" (49). Her work relies on an intimately woven discursive alliance between an acutely inquisitive and contestatory existential

Portuguese Literary & Cultural Studies 7 (2008): 87-108.

outlook, a distinctive rhetoric in which the vocabulary of passion and violence and an overarching drive toward the deconstruction of verbal matter are harnessed into morphologically and syntactically precise articulations—hers is a "gramática … que explode sem se desarticular" (Cabral Martins 41)—and, last but not least, a consistent emphasis on corporeality, situating the body (the body that is always both gendered and sexed) as the privileged vantage point of the poet's lyric *Weltanschauung*. It is particularly this latter aspect—recognized but generally undertheorized in the majority of critical comments on Neto Jorge's poetry—that emerges as her perhaps most distinctive legacy, at the same time anchoring her firmly in the still largely unwritten history of the specifically female and feminist lineage in modern Portuguese poetry.[1] Contrary to Maria Teresa Horta, her *Poesia 61* companion and the future member of the Three Marias collective, Neto Jorge was never in danger of being classified by the critics of her work as a "feminista, apenas"[2]; on the other hand, however, only very recently has she begun to be addressed as a poet whose work's feminist scope did not need to be tiptoed around or, put more bluntly, swept under the carpet of critical validation.[3]

Having debuted in 1960 with the volume *A Noite Vertebrada*, Neto Jorge came into the public spotlight as a member of the group of young poets whose joint publication, in 1961, of five individual brochures assembled under the common title of *Poesia 61* earned them at the time the collective status of a new generational vanguard in Portuguese poetry, a designation that the protagonists themselves both guardedly claimed and self-consciously questioned. In an extensive interview published in the "Vida Literária" supplement of *Diário de Lisboa* on 25 May 1961, the five poets—Neto Jorge, Casimiro de Brito, Fiama Hasse Pais Brandão, Gastão Cruz, and Maria Teresa Horta—described themselves as a group whose coming together, while clearly not arbitrary, should not, at the same time, be viewed as predetermined by a well-defined common artistic program.[4] In her characteristically concise and blunt contribution to the interview, Neto Jorge was ironically dismissive of the hypothetical perception of *Poesia 61* as a distinctive poetic movement:

> Isto de 5 pessoas se reunirem e publicarem, em conjunto, 5 folhetos de poesia, e o próprio título–*Poesia 61*–pode fazer surgir, nos espíritos mais impermeáveis à inércia, qualquer ideia de "movimento" (parece que já há tempos não há nenhum!). Bem, eu acho que, acima de tudo, há entre nós afinidades que só indirectamente têm a ver com a poesia! (14)

Although nearly each of the five statements that compose the collective interview expresses some form of distantiation from the notion of programmatic unity that might be postulated to exist among the poets, Neto Jorge's reply is unique in not counterbalancing her dismissal with a compensatory declaration of an identifiably aesthetic affinity with her companions in *Poesia 61*.[5] In her further comments on modern Portuguese poetry, she looks instead towards surrealism as the one bona fide poetic movement (without quotation marks) that may be hoped to continue to inspire the Portuguese cultural milieu, although such inspiration is seen as desirable also for reasons "only indirectly having to do with poetry"

> Parece-me que, entre nós, o surrealismo ainda terá a sua razão de ser—como total destruição de cânones bafientos, como reacção a um ambiente social rígido. Depois será talvez mais fácil, mais possível, a total reconstrução, formas e ideias novas. (14)

Neto Jorge's indebtedness to surrealist aesthetics has been registered with some regularity in the (relatively few) published critical accounts of her work.[6] In the present context, it is worth noting that the primary function of the surrealist intervention in the Portuguese reality of the early 1960s was expressed, by Neto Jorge, as a revolutionary overthrow of stale and rigid structures, of social and political as well as intellectual and aesthetic frameworks. Concomitantly, her inaugural volume of poetry, *A Noite Vertebrada*, adopted as its leading motif the rhetoric of spatial and temporal immobility destabilized by breaking loose into a freer, more fluid and unpredictable time and space. One such escapee is the speaker of the long prose poem, "Subitamente vamos pela rua":

> Saí de casa ontem. Vou correr mundo, vou matar-me. Emancipada da noite, livre indoloridamente, minha angústia despediu-se, lambeu-me as mãos. (31)[7]

The enslaving night from which the speaker frees herself may be read here as an extension of the "unchanging night" featured in the initial sequence of the volume, "5 poemas para a noite invariável." The first of the five poems belongs to the prehistory of the emancipation, the alliterative monotony of its repetitive affirmations barely prefiguring the rebellious violence to come (23):

Posso estar aqui
eu posso estar aqui perfeitamente pobre
um círio me acendi espora aguda
o vento ritmo negro assassinou-o
… … … … … … … … . .
que eu posso estar aqui perfeitamente pedra
insone
e um longo segredo impessoal
bordando a minha solidão

The fact that Neto Jorge's "unchanging night" is also the "vertebrate night" of the volume's title indicates, however, the escape route by which this perfectly inert (if also insomniac and latently rebellious) woman-stone is able to become, somewhat later in Neto Jorge's oeuvre, the raging, anarchic woman-goat of "Metamorfose" (64-65). For the time being—that is, by the fifth poem in the sequence—the lyric body lets her hair down, so to speak ("Degrenho cada minuto calmo— / basta de tranças imóveis dobadas sobre mim") and offers an amorous welcome to the newly unpredictable world she has endeavored to bring into existence (26):

e agonio-me de perigos escondidos
a terra imprevista sob a terra
o mar imprevisto sobre o mar

Beijo as espáduas do espaço
desfeito

This deconstruction—and the attendant corporealization—of established space are followed, in both *A Noite Vertebrada* and *Quarta Dimensão*, by further inquiries into topographic and temporal frameworks of consciousness. "Porque ficou oceânico / o escasso momento de nós?" (28) asks the poem "Introdução ao tempo" (*A Noite Vertebrada*), while "Quarta dimensão" and "Exame" (both in *Quarta Dimensão*) revisit the pedagogical origins of received knowledges:

Decerto que é isso que o senhor me diz
ao princípio é mundo

ao princípio é deus
ao princípio é homem
ao princípio é fim
("Exame" 51)

In a characteristic move toward qualifying particularization of abstract models, this lesson is then immediately put into perspective by its recipient's self-aware apprehension of her own gendered body and of its place in the scheme of things proposed above:

Passam aviões o céu está vermelho
que será de mim
… … … … · ·
Uma mulher nua
perdição do homem
ao princípio é ela
e depois sou eu

It is, in fact, in "Exame" that the construction and transmission of knowledge are presented as dialogic social practices carried out by human agents and profoundly shaped by their respective, mutual (mis)perceptions, which in turn are rooted in often unacknowledged preexisting patterns of representation; the male examiner and the female examinee examine and categorize each other as they progress, in a ritualistic dance of pedagogical validation, through the dense web of "a ciência inteira casqueando ideias / puzzles legiões de ideias / que são novas velhas" (50):

Pode
pode sentar-se senhora

Eu não sou senhora eu não sou menina
sem olhos sem ouvidos fala
… … … … … … … · ·

Sento-me
evidentemente
circunspectamente

> irremediavelmente
> senhor professor doutor
>
> Eu não sou senhor professor doutor
> minha não-senhora minha não-menina
> e se estou de pé é ilusão de óptica
> eu estou sentado todos nós sentados
> isto é não rígidos não equilibrados

The professor's egalitarian claims are, however, contradicted by the student's ironic awareness of their asymmetrical relationship and by the weight of her inescapably bodily presence among the snatches of knowledge exchanged and scrutinized in the examining room ("não vale a pena dizer que me sinto / homogéneo átomo / como um voo sem asas"). In the end, it is the recognition of the professor's authority as also, at least in one respect, physical that produces the long-sought release when the honorific "senhor professor doutor" becomes reduced to a single syllabic particle, which happens to be the requisite inaugural morpheme of intellectual inquiry, "se" ["if"]—and when, at that point, the examiner promptly declares the exam finished:

> senhor professor doutor
> senhor professor
> senhor
> se
>
> Já passa da hora (53)

As "Exame," among other poems, demonstrates and as António Guerreiro rightly noted in his review of the poet's last, posthumously published volume *A Lume* (1989), Neto Jorge favored an understanding of the poetic process as a move toward materialization and solidification, never toward sublimation (21-C). This predilection may help explain her success both in assimilating the surrealist legacy and in escaping the peril of perpetuating some of its more cliched formulas and facile venues of expression. It is the emphasis on the physicality of language, approached as the first cause and ultimately the exclusive medium of poetry that, according to Joaquim Manuel Magalhães, allowed Neto Jorge to surpass the potentially deleterious temptations of surrealist ideation and diction: her poems "propõem-nos uma nova intenção verbal, construída na distribuição sintáctica inesperada e calculada nos versos, aliada a uma pontuação que é muito mais prosódica, do que, como no caso dos surrealistas, psicológica" (208). For Neto Jorge, as for Mallarmé, poems are made of words, and illumination lies in grammar: in language's own rules and in their corresponding misrule, in the careful arrangement and agglutination of morphemes, lexemes and clauses and in their no less careful—if often also exuberantly violent—demolition.[8]

A particularly illustrative example of the poet's finely plotted progress that takes the physicality of language as the point of departure toward a revisionary upheaval of abstract categories imposing orderliness and proper conduct upon the material world—including, in particular, the world of human bodies, male and female—may be found in the sequence "As revoluções da matéria," first published in the volume *O seu a seu tempo* (1966). The wordplay on which the titles of the five poems in the sequence rely ("A esferidade: a ferocidade," "A condutibilidade: a contabilidade," and so on) carries over into the at first epigrammatic intimations of more serious signifying upsets to come:

A ESFERIDADE: A FEROCIDADE
qualidade perigosa a de alguns
sólidos quando perdidos se viram
para nós (116)

The double meaning on which the effect of the poem hinges ("se viram" may be read both as "saw themselves" and "turn") forces the reader to view the solidly spherical objects it evokes as endowed with a sudden self-consciousness of their volatility—and, at the same time, to see him/herself as dangerously implicated in the scenario of the objects' release, in the manner of Rilke's imperative punchline in "Archaïscher Torso Apollos" ("Du mußt dein Leben ändern" [You must change your life]). The extent of this implication becomes fully realized in the last two poems of the sequence, when Neto Jorge's ingenious permutations of material states—gaseous, fluid and solid—are applied to human objects of scrutiny. The male addressee of "A sublimação: a sublime acção" fulfills the promise of the poem's title in his flight through the atmosphere, ecstatic but also overshadowed by a menacing, if implicit, recollection of Icarus, "como um espelho / a aproximar-se do sol" (119):

Sem passares pelos líquidos
sais do teu sólido
e corres directamente,
saindo de cima do solo.
Não desces àquela cave
onde estão os oceanos
e os juramentos líquidos.

The association of sublimity—as well as of sublimation—with maleness is a notion well entrenched in Western culture, along with its corresponding and contrasting classification of "the beautiful" as female, to follow the terminology of Edmund Burke's influential *Philosophical Enquiry into the Origin of Our Ideas of the Sublime and Beautiful* (1757). As Christine Battersby notes, Burke "seems to have deliberately adopted the language of sexual power to explain the psychological thrill that comes from the sublime … . . By contrast, the 'beautiful,'—small, smooth, delicate and graceful—is claimed to be what men (= males) love in the opposite sex" (74-75). Carried over into the realm of artistic, and particularly literary, creativity, this attribution is what ends up anchoring Jean-Jacques Rousseau's peremptory (and often evoked) dismissal of any claim to greatness on the part of women writers: "the celestial fire that emblazens and ignites the soul, the inspiration that consumes and devours … these sublime ecstasies that reside in the depths of heart are always lacking in women's writing" (qtd. in Battersby 36). Neto Jorge's critical engagement with the concept of sublimity—an important reference in Surrealism's neo-Romantic configurations of aesthetics and ideology—resurfaces with some regularity in her work.[9] In the present context, it is worth noting that the poet's gloss on the elemental symbolism of maleness, which privileges "direct" transcendence from the solid into the gaseous realms of sublimity, is *not* followed by a poem reinforcing the association of femaleness with fluidity, implicit in the differential characterization traced in "A sublimação: a sublime acção." Such a step—at once acknowledging and potentially undermining the stereotype—could have led the poet along a path parallel to that laid out by Luce Irigaray in her essay "La 'mécanique' des fluides" ["The 'Mechanics' of Fluids"], where the French philosopher has linked the implicit association of fluids with femininity to their cultural unrepresentability within prevailing philosophical models of ontology, which privilege the self-identical unity of the solid. In her words, "Solid mechanics and rationality have maintained a relationship of very long standing, one against which fluids have never stopped arguing" (113). As Toril Moi has claimed, however, in this particular essay Irigaray's strategy of specular mimicry of patriarchal discourse "seems to fail entirely as a political device … . due to her figuring of fluidity as a *positive alternative* to the depreciating scopophilic constructions of the patriarchs": "When the quotation marks, so to speak, are no longer apparent, Irigaray falls into the very essentialist trap of defining woman that she set out to avoid" (142, original emphasis).[10]

It is precisely the threat of essentialist reiteration and reification of sexual identity that Neto Jorge skirts by following the poem "A sublimação: a sublime acção" with the final installment of her "revolutions of matter," "A divisibilidade: a visibilidade a dois." The poem's wonderfully synthetic title homes in on the crucial insight that any symbolic meaning attributable to male and female bodies needs to be predicated on the following recognition: the signs "man" and "woman" signify only insofar as they report to each other across the semantic divide that separates them in any referential system. If, in Gayatri Spivak's epigrammatic formulation, "the discourse of man is in the metaphor of woman" (169), the woman's feminine identity is also conceivable *as such* only in a relational sense, as the site of the difference between itself and the male (a.k.a., "universal") paradigm of selfhood. Sexual identity derives from sexual difference in the same fashion that Saussure's notion of pure difference creates the conditions for the emergence of linguistic value (Grosz 209). So, too, in Neto Jorge's "A divisibilidade: a visibilidade a dois" (120):

> A mulher divide-se em gestos particulares
> o homem divide-se também. Se o átomo é
> divisível só o poeta o diz.
> … … … … … … … … … … … .
> A divisibilidade da luz aclara os mistérios.
> A mulher tem filhos. Descobrem-se
> partículas soltas um dedo mínimo
> o peso menos pesado da balança
> um cabelo eloquente em desagregação.

Neto Jorge's insistence on "divisibility" (of humankind into male and female, resulting in a "visibility for two," as well as of each living entity within itself) is further qualified by her description of female identity as an agglomeration of "loose particles" and characteristically tempered by an ironic double (or triple) take brought on by a reiterated enjambment (the poem dividing within and against itself):

> Dois homens são duas divisões de uma
> casa que já foi um animal de costas
> para o seu pólo mágico.

This equivocal, self-dividing woman-house-animal, at once prone on her back and with her back turned against her hypothetical "magic pole" is a recurrent presence in Neto Jorge's poetry, fulfilling the likewise double and likewise contradictory postulate of feminist theory and politics in the 1970s and beyond: on the one hand, in Julia Kristeva's famous words, "la femme, ce n'est jamais ça"; on the other, according to Hélène Cixous, "Il faut que la femme se mette au texte" (39). Or, to quote Neto Jorge's own, equally concise formulation registered, toward the end of her life, in one of her most indelibly memorable poems, "Minibiografia":

> Diferente me concebo e só do avesso
> O formato mulher se me acomoda. (254)

The insistence on the view of femininity—as well as masculinity—as a "format," a kind of layout or template for the production of psychological and social meanings that attach themselves to human bodies, was already the leading theme in "Os Corpos Vestidos," the longest sequence in Neto Jorge's third volume of poems, *Terra Imóvel* (1964). The organization of the sequence proceeds from the recognition of what Elizabeth Grosz calls "an essential internal condition of human bodies," their "organic openness to cultural completion": "Part of their own 'nature' is an organic or ontological 'incompleteness' or lack of finality, an amenability to social completion, social ordering and organization" (xi). Thus, the opening texts of "Os Corpos Vestidos" offer a progressive charting of male and female coming into gendered signification, from "Homem / não escoado ainda / pelas costuras das ruas / e dos fatos" (60) through (presumably) the same man who "enquanto corpo vestido / seca descora ao sol" (61) to the powerful, quasi-Ovidian "Metamorfose" (64-65), in which the woman, previously shown as an "espaço / habituado a fêmea" (63) that lives buried in man's shadow, becomes a raging, rebellious she-goat:

> A mulher se transformou cabra
> ritual de emigração
> em resposta à raiz
> constante das árvores
> ao grande silêncio
> empastado nas letras
> de imprensa

The animal disguise serves here as a "ritual de emigração," an escape valve permitting a release from the oppressively stagnated status quo and a starting point in the quest for an "outra genealogia" (the title of another sequence of poems by Neto Jorge, included in *O Seu a Seu Tempo*). In the poem's conclusion, the goat's "resurrection" to femininity is envisioned, but it is presented merely as a *parenthetic* afterthought, a postscript both laconic and hypothetical to the earthshaking workings of "Metamorfose":

> (Quando a cabra
> voltar mulher–
> –ressureição)

Thus, the gradual "dressing" of male and female bodies in patterns of recognizable signification is interrupted by the metamorphic and contrarian instability claimed by the woman-goat. Her disruptive (non-)identity may be viewed as prefiguring such later presences in Neto Jorge's poetry as the Ur-Woman addressed in the thirteenth segment of her sprawling, often densely cryptic, pseudo-epic sequence *19 Recantos* (1969): the woman ("Ila, irmã de Ilo o mundo, a minha irmã") is imagined as a "repouso vasto enfurecido / [...] / da cintura irrompendo como de um jardim / para uma espécie de corpo inenarrável" (194). In "Os Corpos Vestidos," the woman-goat's irruption marks a pivotal point within the sequence: it is with "Metamorfose" that Neto Jorge's attention turns away from the scrutiny of bodies as surfaces to be inscribed with socially readable meanings—from the relatively commonplace view of the body as a blank page—to an exploration of corporeal figurations endowed with the degree of dynamic autonomy that places them far beyond facile intelligibility. The culmination of that poetic investigation may be found in the much-quoted "O corpo insurrecto" (79-80), in which the eroticized body is revealed as a dynamic and evolving universe unto itself, akin to Deleuze and Guattari's conceptualization of the body as "a discontinuous, nontotalizable series of processes, organs, flows, energies, corporeal substances and incorporeal events, speeds and durations" (Grosz 164):

> Ainda antes que pegue
> aos cinco sentidos a chama,
> por um aceso acesso
> da imaginação
> ateiam-se à cama
> ou a sítio algures,
> terra de ninguém,
> (quem desliza é o espaço
> para o corpo que vem),
>
> labaredas tais
> que, lume, crepitam
> nos ciclos mais extremos,
> nas réstias mais íntimas,
> as glândulas, esponjas
> que os corpos apoiam,
> zonas aquáticas
> onde os órgãos boiam.

The at once precise and savage, non-teleological archaeology of the (sexual) body undertaken in "O corpo insurrecto" is carried to its logical extreme by the next poem in the sequence: "Exorcismo" (81) concentrates on corporeal fluids and on the ultimate challenge they present to the mind's desire for controlling dominance over bodily matter. As Grosz comments,

> [Body fluids] affront a subject's aspiration toward autonomy and self-identity. They attest to a certain irreducible "dirt" or disgust, a horror of the unknown or the unspecifiable that permeates, lurks, lingers, and at times leaks out of the body, a testimony of the fraudulence or impossibility of the "clean" and "proper." [...] They are engulfing, difficult to be rid of; any separation from them is not a matter of certainty, as it may be in the case of solids. Body fluids flow, they seep, they infiltrate; their control is a matter of vigilance, never guaranteed. In this sense, they betray a certain irreducible materiality; they assert the priority of the body over subjectivity; they demonstrate the

limits of subjectivity in the body, the irreducible specificity of particular bodies. (194)

Neto Jorge's approach to the question emphasizes precisely the uncontainable and unspecifiable permeability of the body as seen through the prism of the fluids that it produces, exchanges and discharges—while at the same time, as the poem's title indicates, foregrounding the controlling impulse toward the separation of the dirty and the profane from the clean and the sacred that the "problem" of bodily fluids has historically provoked. I quote the poem in its entirety:

> o sangue o suor
> a água lustral
> o leite do sol
> retido na mama
> o sangue sangrando
> com o vinho
> o pranto o rito
> líquido o vinho
> tinto no mijo
> de deus no sangue
> descendo na urina
> subindo água
> benta no sangue
> o filtro do amor
> filtrando o suor
> um licor dividindo
> o choro do pus

The poem's conciseness and apparent playfulness—in the manner of surrealist poems-catalogues—belie the density and the complexity of its insights. Neto Jorge's deft deployment of the enjambment—a favorite device in her prosodic repertory, as has already been demonstrated on more than one occasion—endows "Exorcismo" with a kind of internal permeability: its verses are fashioned as communicating vessels through which apparently incompatible liquids flow back and forth, mixing and blending with scandalous promiscuity. Although the poem can hardly be said to be "about" the Christian Eucharist, it clearly emphasizes its own engagement with the fluid element of the sacred ritual, in which red wine is transformed into God's blood and then ingested by the faithful. While properly religious discourse tends to steer clear of examining further physiological implications of the Communion, it is the poet's prerogative to do so, as she traces the (literal) descent of the blood-wine in the urine counterbalanced by the (symbolic) ascension of the holy water in the blood. The final (but likely inconclusive) separation between another clear and noble fluid (tears) and a cloudy and disgusting one (pus) that concludes Neto Jorge's "exorcism" may be interpreted in the context of Mary Douglas's anthropological meditation on the social and psychological connotations of bodily fluids in *Purity and Danger* (1980). Douglas (following Sartre's analysis of the viscous in *Being and Nothingness*) focuses precisely on the unassailable purity of tears, which she distinguishes radically from other corporeal fluids, particularly those "related to the bodily functions of digestion and procreation" (125); it is by virtue of being exempt from productive and reproductive processes of the body that tears can be elevated to a higher symbolic status than its other, less superfluous secretions. In Neto Jorge's poem, however, the distinction is less absolute and the separation of fluids presumably provisional—the poem's flow becomes temporarily arrested, but this stoppage does not bear the marks of a strong rhetorical closure, an irrefutable punchline. Whether by the force of a religious exorcism or by the magic of a love philter, tears and pus become distinct substances, but, as the poem has already implied, both religion and love also provide ample ground for the confusion of these and other effluences of bodily matter.

Where "O corpo insurrecto" and "Exorcismo" offer a sort of microsymbolic dissection of the (undressed) body as a culmination of the cycle "Os corpos vestidos," in "As casas," another cycle of poems from the same volume (*Terra Imóvel*), domestic spaces are made to converge with female bodies to form intricate machinic connections that structure intimate functional alliances between women's existential experience and various socially situated aspects of domesticity. The poems of "As casas" form a series of exemplary tales whose protagonists are women-houses (houses behaving as women and/or women imagined as architectural formations, in the indirect manner of Neto Jorge's own metapoetic self-portrait in "Uma arquitectura" [*O Seu a Seu Tempo*]). Some of the poems evoke stereotypical figures that are easily recognizable in the context of a traditional rural or urban neighborhood community; for instance, "the shameless one" (103):

> Desta falaram os jornais diários
>
> A sem vergonha
>
> Despe-se a desoras para o amante
>
> mostra sentinas esconderijos camas negras
>
> Tem logo pela manhã
>
> roupa de baixo nas varandas

Further stock characters among "As casas" include a madwoman ("Louca como era a da esquina / recebia gente a qualquer hora" [101]) and overprotected young girls ("Podiam brincar aos domingos / Avançar um pouco pelo passeio / nunca atravessar-a-rua" [100]). Other "house poems" escape such ready identification, while consistently featuring anthropomorphized and female-gendered protagonists. Notwithstanding this constancy of their semiotic configuration, Neto Jorge's women-houses offer anything but an updated version of the traditional association of domestic space with femininity, in which both the house and the woman—or, more precisely, the woman *quoad matrem*—tend to figure, in the emblematic words of Gaston Bachelard, as "un corps d'images qui donnent à l'homme des raisons ou des illusions de stabilité" (34).[11] While Bachelard does not explicitly gender the house as feminine in this portion of his commentary on the "poetics of space," his even more succinct definition of the house as "le non-moi qui protège le moi" (24) points to such an identification, as it fails to account for the symbolic hypothesis of the human "moi" perceiving itself as coextensive with the domestic "non-moi": a cognitive predicament expressed commonly enough in the work of women writers, as Sandra Gilbert and Susan Gubar have argued in their critique of Bachelard's discussion.[12]

Neto Jorge's poetic conjugation of femininity and domesticity is, like Bachelard's, both unmistakable and indirect: the poems of "As casas" do not appear, at first glance, to have a feminist agenda or even to insist on foregrounding their gendered perspective, which is why a critic like Fernando Cabral Martins is able to dismiss the femaleness of the houses in a cursory aside: "Estas casas não são (apenas) metonímia da cidade, ou metáfora do corpo feminino, ou da infância" (40). His is a helpful misreading, however, in that it allows us to perceive the nature of Neto Jorge's strategy of displacement directed against the stereotypical metaphoric equation woman = mother = home. In addition to noting a nearly complete absence—with one significant and subversive exception—of maternal symbolism from her poetic congregation of women-houses (the presence of such a symbolism being the unspoken condition *sine qua non* of the commonplace evoked by Cabral Martins), it is important to register that the figurative conjunction between the two aspects of the compound corresponds instead to a metonymic relation of existential contiguity: the houses are women insofar as they situate and surround female bodies within the domestic enclosure; the women are houses by virtue of an identification (or of a refusal to become identified) with diverse facets of domesticity. The metonymic continuum does extend beyond the house, embracing not only the neighborhood street but also the political organism of the city, as demonstrated in particular by the somber monologue of the woman-house whose function is that of a political prison (104):

Maldita sou e me lamento
Os fantasmas circulam as caveiras
olham-me sentinelas escarram para o chão
o meu chão é de cimento armado

Incidentally, it is in this first-person lament of the prison house that we encounter Neto Jorge's only oblique reference to motherhood in the lyric space of "As Casas"; its portent stands, however, in direct contradiction to the traditional reassuring symbolism of house-as-uterus:

Nunca de madeiras tão rijas fosse feita
Sob o meu tecto espancam grávidas
nas câmaras soluçam toda a noite

Furthermore, the fact that the poem quoted above avails itself of the direct discourse—its speaker is the house-woman herself—brings into focus yet another challenge to the distinction between the (poet's) "moi" and the "non-moi" of the house that the cycle "As casas" sets out to upset. The initial discursive framework, in which the houses are evoked in the third person (with an occasional recourse to quoted direct discourse) is first destabilized by the poem number twelve, with its anxious irruption of free indirect discourse ("que não que não queria paredes / que não queria postigos frestas / clarabóias // que entrasse ou saísse o mar as marés / dos evadidos" [104]). The woman-prison's anguished monologue further blurs the distinction between the active discursive presence of the speaking subject of the cycle and the essentially passive role of its "protagonists." When, after this dramatic testimonial, the discursive "I" of the poet returns to the scene, it is to address directly the composite entity of woman-house—the "casa dúctil de cal viva" (105)—as if in an implicit recognition of its/her recent discursive emancipation.

This form of a subtly dialogic relationship, gendered in the feminine, between the poet and the object/interlocutor of her lyric discourse resurfaces on increasingly frequent occasions in Neto Jorge's later work. Its most eloquent example and, at the same time, explication may perhaps be found in the poem "A lume" from the homonymous, posthumously published last collection of the poet's writings. "A lume" begins by reexamining the asymmetric relationship between the sexes that Neto Jorge has repeatedly glossed throughout her work, among other instances in one of the poems in *19 Recantos*, where her adroit and inventive handling of the enjambment once again yields highly rewarding results:

> tal era a corrida de um homem para mim e a minha
> fuga para o lado da sua liberdade (195)

In "A lume," an almost identical asymmetric breakdown of the verse similarly reinforces the notion of male-female dissonance (a productive and not necessarily negative circumstance in Neto Jorge's agonistic universe):

> Olho-me nos olhos
> do meu gémeo
> (seus olhos nos meus
> ausentes)

The continuation of the first stanza ("e sempre vislumbro / fixo e refulgente / um lume") and the poem's further development suggest the possibility of reading "A lume" as an understated gloss on the metaphoric scenario of Baudelaire's famous sonnet "La mort des amants":

> Nos deux coeurs seront deux vastes flambeaux,
> Qui réfléchiront leurs doubles lumières
> Dans nos deux esprits, ces miroirs jumeaux. (94)

As Michael Riffaterre observes in his analysis of Baudelaire's poem, "[the] insistent variation on *two*" in the above lines indicates that "the description aims only to unfold the duality paradigm, until the duality is resolved in the next stanza by the oneness of sex ('nous échangerons un éclair unique')" (4, original emphasis). In Neto Jorge's slanted version of an analogous scene, the image of twin mirrors, male and female, reiterating *ad infinitum* the same luminous reflection, is undermined in its symmetric perfection, even as the poem introduces a compensating and stabilizing third term:

> Porém o resplendor
> no espelho alastra
> como na pupila
> a luz da Mestra

The luminous resplendence shared by the all-female coupling of "pupila" and "Mestra"—Neto Jorge's dexterity at wordplay is here once again manifest—is an image as affirmative as it is discrete in its implications.[13] The poem's closure foregrounds the grammatical gender of its key terms in a way that echoes retroactively throughout the poem, bringing out the semantic relevance of the gendered opposition between "um lume" in the first stanza and "a luz" in the final verse. This opposition may even be said to be operative in the poem's (and the volume's) title: "A lume," which evokes, in the first place, such expressions as "dar a lume" (= to publish) and "vir a lume" (= to become known, public), could also be read as an instance of an intentional "ungrammaticality," the distortion of mimetic perspective theorized by Riffaterre as central to the production of the poetic text and to the emergence of an independent network of semiotic relationships within the poem.[14] The charge of semantic relevance that the closure of Neto Jorge's poem attributes to grammatical gender provokes a consciously "incorrect" reading of the title, in which the initial "A" may emerge not as the preposition it is at the "mimetic" level, but as a definite article that transgressively *feminizes* the male gender of the noun "o lume."

Neto Jorge's revolutions of (linguistic) matter may thus, once again, be shown to coexist in a tightly woven alliance with the poet's emphasis on the (gendered) "divisibility of light" ("A divisibilidade da luz aclara os mistérios"). It is, however, a calculated, reticent emphasis, filtered through an ironically slanted viewpoint that, for all its committed intensity of insight, is profoundly mistrustful of encountering easy answers to difficult questions. In Neto Jorge's playful yet exquisitely wrought self-portrait "SO-NETO JORGE, Luiza," the poet's own physical markers of femininity are viewed through such a distancing, questioning lens that in an epigrammatic formulation evokes and takes apart an entire network of symbolic affinities: "Tenho o mênstruo escondido num reduto / onde teoricamente chega o mar" (209). Nevertheless, to acknowledge the oblique and strategically deferred intelligibility and consequent impact of some of Neto Jorge's most powerful articulations is not to say that they are destined to become any less explosive. Such is the message firmly conveyed in the closing distich of the poet's testamentary "Minibiografia," which will thus serve as the final, (in)conclusive *envoi* of these all too cursory comments on her unceasingly inspiring work (254):

> Um poema deixo, ao retardador:
> Meia palavra a bom entendedor.

Notes

[1] An indispensable recent exception is Manuel Gusmão's article "A invenção do corpo amoroso em Luiza Neto Jorge" (*Inimigo Rumor* 13 [2º semestre 2002], 163-175), which was published after the present study had already been completed. Gusmão's many illuminating insights focus precisely on the textualization of the gendered body as a centrally important aspect of Neto Jorge's poetic work. See also Maria Rosa Martelo, "Corpo, enunciação e identidade na poesia de Luiza Neto Jorge" (*Cadernos de Literatura Comparada* 2: *Identidades no feminino* [2001], 35-48).

[2] I am echoing here Horta's complaint in a 1990 interview published in the weekly *O Independente*: "as pessoas esqueceram-se de que eu tenho livros de poesia, esqueceram-se de que eu tenho determinada posição na literatura portuguesa, e passei a ser tratada como feminista, apenas" (III-7).

[3] To be sure, those dispersed references to Neto Jorge's feminist relevance that I have been able to register in recent years are for the most part tangential and indirect. Taken jointly, however, they do seem to indicate a more comprehensive change of perspective in Portuguese cultural discourse, from a generalized denial of any meaningful symbiosis between feminist commitment and literary value to an at least partial recognition that a specifically female perspective and identifiably feminist concerns occupy an important place not only in Western literary tradition at large, but also—and particularly—in the twentieth- and twenty-first-century Portuguese modernity. It is significant that such remarks have tended to appear in reviews of new collections published by women poets writing in Portugal today, most notably those, such as Ana Luiza Amaral, who openly signal their aesthetic and ideological indebtedness to feminism. On the connection between Neto Jorge and Amaral, see Osvaldo Manuel Silvestre, "Recordações da casa amarela. A poesia de Ana Luisa Amaral" (*Relâmpago* 3 [Outubro 1998], 37-57), where the author also cites earlier remarks on the affinity between the two poets by Maria Rosa Martelo and Américo António Lindeza Diogo.

[4] Regarding the publication of *Poesia 61* and its afterlife, see, in addition to the 1961 interview with the five poets in *Diário de Lisboa*, Manuel Gusmão and José Bento, "Os poetas de *Poesia 61*: dois depoimentos" (*O Tempo e o Modo* 57-58 (Fevereiro-Março 1968): 265-73; the commemorative tenth anniversary section ("Os dez anos de *Poesia 61*") in the "Vida Literária" supplement of *Diário de Lisboa*, with statements by Nelson de Matos, Fiama Hasse Pais Brandão, Eduardo Prado Coelho and Gastão Cruz (4 February 1971, 1-7); Jorge Fernandes da Silveira, *Portugal Maio de Poesia 1961* (Lisboa: IN-CM, 1986); E. M. de Melo e Castro, *As vanguardas na poesia portuguesa do séc. XX* (Lisboa: ICALP, 1980); and Manuel Frias Martins, "*Poesia 61* e Experimentalismo: A vitalidade de uma prática conjuntiva" in his *10 Anos de Poesia em Portugal 1974-1984* (Lisboa: Caminho, 1986).

[5] Only Fiama Hasse País Brandão's declaration escapes this general tendency by concentrating exclusively on a theoretical explanation of the method of composition followed by the poet in *Morfismos*, her contribution to *Poesia 61*.

[6] See, in particular, Joaquim Manuel Magalhães's commentary in *Os Dois Crepúsculos*, where the author diagnoses Neto Jorge's poetic trajectory as "uma das mais conseguidas tentativas de avançar a partir e para fora do surrealismo" (208). Manuel Gusmão takes this insight as the point of departure for his own, somewhat more extensive, investigation of the poet's "apropriação do surrealismo e a deslocação para além dele" (50). In her *O Surrealismo em Portugal*, published in 1987, Maria de Fátima Marinho pointed to Neto Jorge as "talvez um dos autores da nova geração que mais características surrealistas possui" (294). It is important to note in this context that in her ongoing activity as a professional translator, Neto Jorge rendered into Portuguese several key texts of French surrealism, including André Breton's *L'amour fou*. She is one of the two Portuguese poets featured in Penelope Rosemont's voluminous *Surrealist Women: An International Anthology* (the other is Isabel Meyrelles).

[7] All quotations from Neto Jorge's writings follow the collected *Poesia* volume, organized by Fernando Cabral Martins and published by Assírio & Alvim in 1993, four years after the poet's death.

[8] It is in this context that Magalhães draws a parallel between Neto Jorge and Dylan Thomas, two poets in whose work surrealist designs are "ultrapassados por um fingimento sabotador: é pela racionalidade da escrita, pela perseguição consciente, revelada pelo jogo sintáctico, de determinados efeitos que atingem a densidade do imaginário e da irracionalidade surreal. É o surrealismo ultrapassado pela aparência, pelo fingimento, pela outra via inesperada de iluminação: a gramática" (208).

[9] Perhaps the most interesting example of Neto Jorge's subtly gendered perspective on sublimity may be found in the complex, metapoetic "A magnólia" (originally published in *O Seu a Seu Tempo*), which culminates in a quasi-androgynous fusion between two initially distinct phenomena, "a exaltação do mínimo" and "o magnífico relâmpago / do acontecimento mestre": in the final stanza, the beautiful *and* sublime magnolia is celebrated as "um mínimo ente magnífico / desfolhando relâmpagos / sobre mim" (137).

[10] Irigaray's notion of "mimétisme" ["mimicry, play with mimesis"] as a feminist discursive strategy is explained in the following way:

> To play with mimesis is thus, for a woman, to try to recover the place of her exploitation by discourse, without allowing herself to be simply reduced to it. It means to resubmit herself—inasmuch as she is on the side of the "perceptible," of "matter"—to "ideas," in particular to ideas about herself, that are elaborated in/by a masculine logic, but so as to make "visible," by an effect of playful repetition, what was supposed to remain invisible: the cover-up of a possible operation of the feminine in language. (76)

While I do not necessarily agree with Moi's diagnosis of Irigaray's failure in realizing this strategy in "La 'mécanique' des fluides," I share the critic's caution with regard to the vulnerability of mimetic discourse to misreading and misrepresentation (vindicated, it could be argued, by her own adversarial interpretation of Irigaray); such a caution also appears to affect Neto Jorge's poetic trajectory in "As revoluções da matéria."

[11] I am alluding here to Irigaray's polemic with Lacan's *Séminaire XX* and with the latter text's insistence "that woman will be taken only *quoad matrem*. Woman comes into play in the sexual relation only as mother" (qtd. in Irigaray 102). As Irigaray comments: "That woman is 'taken only *quoad matrem*' is inscribed in the entire philosophic tradition. It is even one of the conditions of its possibility" (102).

[12] As they wrote, "for Bachelard the protective asylum of the house is clearly associated with its maternal features. […] Yet for many a woman writer these ancient associations of house and self seem mainly to have strengthened the anxiety about enclosure which she projected into her art. […] To become literally a house, after all, is to be denied the hope of that spiritual transcendence of the body which, as Simone de Beauvoir has argued, is what makes humanity distinctively human" (87-88). Gilbert and Gubar's implicit endorsement of de Beauvoir's advocacy of the "spiritual transcendence of the body" raises of course at least as many problems as it proposes to solve; for a concise summary and critique of de Beauvoir's position on this and related issues, see Gatens 51-59.

[13] It is worth noting here that Cabral Martins expresses an intense puzzlement over the poem's conclusion in his own brief analysis of "A lume": according to the critic, the last stanza emerges as an incomprehensible obstacle to interpretation, "um bloco opaco, deceptivo, solto" ("Recordação pessoal intransmissível...? *Private joke*? Recurso ao símbolo?") ("O filtro" 29). Some of the bafflement may perhaps be explained by the fact that the last line of the poem, "a luz da Mestra" in the earlier published version, appears in the collected *Poesia* volume (edited by Cabral Martins himself), through an apparent misprint, as "a lua da Mestra." I retain the former reading, not only because "light" supplies a more logical counterpart to "flame" than "moon" would, but also because, prior to its inclusion in the posthumous *A Lume*, the poem had been published while the poet was still alive in the supplement "Das Artes e das Letras" of the newspaper *O Primeiro de Janeiro* (20 de Julho 1988, 4). The only difference between the two versions of the last line in *O Primeiro de Janeiro* and *A Lume* is that Neto Jorge chose to capitalize the word "Mestra" in the revised manuscript that served as the basis for Manuel João Gomes's edition of the volume (Jorge *Lume* 78).

[14] "The ungrammaticalities spotted at the mimetic level are eventually integrated into another system. As the reader perceives what they have in common, as he becomes aware that this common trait forms them into a paradigm, and that this paradigm alters the meaning of the poem, the new function of ungrammaticalities changes their nature, and now they signify as components of a different network of relationships" (4).

Works Cited

Bachelard, Gaston. *La poétique de l'espace*. Paris: Quadrige, 1989.

Battersby, Christine. *Gender and Genius. Towards a Feminist Aesthetics*. Bloomington: Indiana UP, 1989.

Baudelaire, Charles. *Oeuvres complètes*. Paris: Robert Lafont, 1980.

Cixous, Hélène. "Le rire de la Meduse." *L'Arc* 61 (1975): 39-54.

Douglas, Mary. *Purity and Danger: An Analysis of the Concepts of Pollution and Taboo*. London: Routledge and Kegan Paul, 1980.

Gatens, Moira. *Feminism and Philosophy. Perspectives on Difference and Equality*. Bloomington: Indiana UP, 1991.

Gilbert, Sandra M., and Susan Gubar. *The Madwoman in the Attic*. New Haven: Yale UP, 1979.

Grosz, Elizabeth. *Volatile Bodies: Toward a Corporeal Feminism*. Bloomington: Indiana UP, 1994.

Guerreiro, António. "Risco e violência." *Expresso* (24 de Junho 1989): 21-C.

Gusmão, Manuel. "Luiza Neto Jorge: o som e a fúria do sentido." *Tabacaria* 2 (Inverno 1996): 48-55.

Horta, Maria Teresa. "Palavras de uma longa conversa" (entrevista). *O Independente* (29 Junho 1990): III 7-8.

Irigaray, Luce. *This Sex Which Is Not One*. Trans. Catherine Porter. Ithaca: Cornell UP, 1985.

Jorge, Luiza Neto. *A Lume*. Lisboa: Assírio e Alvim, 1989.

———. *Poesia. 1960-1989*. Org. e prefácio Fernando Cabral Martins. Lisboa: Assírio e Alvim, 1993.

Kristeva, Julia. "La femme, ce n'est jamais ça." *Tel Quel* 59 (1974): 19-24.

Magalhães, Joaquim Manuel. *Os Dois Crepúsculos*. Lisboa: A Regra do Jogo, 1981.

Marinho, Maria de Fátima. *O Surrealismo em Portugal*. Lisboa: IN-CM, 1987.

Martins, Fernando Cabral. "Para que serve a poesia? (sobre Luísa Neto Jorge)." *Vértice* 8 (Novembro de 1988): 39-44.

———. "O filtro do amor." *Relâmpago* 3 (Out. 1998): 21-29.

Moi, Toril. *Sexual/Textual Politics: Feminist Literary Theory*. London and New York: Routledge, 1988.

Nava, Luís Miguel. "Acme a ser arte. Alguns aspectos da poesia de Luiza Neto Jorge." *Colóquio/Letras* 108 (Março-Abril 1989): 48-62.

Riffaterre, Michael. *Semiotics of Poetry*. Bloomington: U Indiana P, 1978.

Rosemont, Penelope, ed. *Surrealist Women: An International Anthology*. Austin: U Texas P, 1998.

Spivak, Gayatri Chakravorty. "Displacement and the Discourse of Woman." *Displacement: Derrida and After*. Ed. Mark Krupnick. Bloomington: Indiana UP, 1983. 169-95.

Anna M. Klobucka is Professor in the Department of Portuguese at the University of Massachusetts Dartmouth. She is the co-editor of *After the Revolution: Twenty Years of Portuguese Literature 1974-1994* (Bucknell University Press, 1997) and the author of *The Portuguese Nun: Formation of a National Myth* (Bucknell, 2000; Portuguese translation from Imprensa Nacional–Casa da Moeda). She has recently co-edited (with Mark Sabine) a collection of essays on Fernando Pessoa, *Embodying Pessoa: Corporeality, Gender, Sexuality* (Toronto University Press). Her articles have appeared in *Colóquio/Letras, Luso-Brazilian Review, Portuguese Studies, Slavic and East European Journal,* and *SubStance,* among other journals. E-mail: aklobucka @umassd.edu

O sopro do sentido na poesia muda
de António Franco Alexandre

David Antunes

... skepticism's "doubt" is motivated not by (not even where it is expressed as) a (misguided) intellectual scrupulousness but by a (displaced) denial, by a self-consuming disappointment that seeks world-consuming revenge. (*Disowning Knowledge* 6)

What are the roots that clutch, what branches grow
Out of this stony rubbish? Son of man,
You cannot say, or guess, for you know only
A heap of broken images, where the sun beats,
(T. S. Eliot, *The Waste Land*)

Escrever sobre António Franco Alexandre, poeta português, nascido em Viseu em 1944, e professor de Filosofia na Universidade de Lisboa, é certamente uma tarefa difícil por três motivos de relevância desigual. Em primeiro lugar, trata-se de um poeta acerca do qual críticos portugueses influentes falam de um modo «provavelmente» superlativo. Por exemplo, Américo A. Lindeza Diogo, o crítico que, aparentemente, mais tem escrito sobre Franco Alexandre, discute com Joaquim Manuel Magalhães em *Modernismos, Pós-Modernismos, Anacronismos* (1993) acerca da propriedade ou não de se falar em "o maior poeta," em relação à literatura de um país ou a uma determinada

Portuguese Literary & Cultural Studies 7 (2008): 109-146.
© University of Massachusetts Dartmouth.

época, afirmando, a propósito de António Franco Alexandre, que "se não é o maior dos poetas dos últimos tempos, talvez seja...porque não se deve saber qual deles o é" (23) e que *Os Objectos Principais* (1979) "é...o livro de poesia pós-25 de Abril" (33). Óscar Lopes considera *Moradas 1 & 2* (1987) como sendo "provavelmente o melhor livro de poesia do decénio...com que, a nível da poesia, hoje mais se pode aprender" ("Alguns Nexos" 223).

Em segundo lugar, António Franco Alexandre cria alguma instabilidade em descrições de índole periodológica, assentes geralmente em critérios que registam homologias de interesses temáticos e de procedimentos literários. De facto, se os anos 70/80, da poesia portuguesa do século passado, são panoramicamente descritos como denunciadores de um *regresso ao sentido*— que se observa no "retorno a processos de escrita apoiados num fio condutor, isto é, menos voltados para malabarismos verbais do que para a simples afirmação de *linhas de sentido,*" na "retoma de um lirismo assumido sem complexos e de uma emocionalidade relativamente explícita, o que nos dá a ilusão de um discurso *mais sentido*" e na "exploração de áreas semânticas ligadas à fisicidade" ("O Regresso ao Sentido" 161) — então é, como se vai ver, claro que, ou esta descrição de *regresso ao sentido* pode sofrer modulações excepcionais para incluir a poesia de Franco Alexandre, ou o poeta dificilmente nela se enquadra, atendendo ao que se observa nos seus poemas, pelo menos até ao livro *Quatro Caprichos* (1999). Felizmente, tais discordâncias só podem suscitar um alargamento da extensão conceptual da expressão *regresso ao sentido*. O mesmo autor, cujas palavras acabei de transcrever, é imediato a citar um texto de Franco Alexandre, em que o poema é definido como "a sombra que ilumina / o lugar onde nada se vê" (321),[1] para acautelar o lugar deste poeta e para sustentar agora que "estas escritas, embora perseguindo a ideia de representação, se dissolvem muitas vezes numa magma de imagens onde é impossível distinguirmos as causas dos efeitos e onde a cómoda perspectiva *Sujeito / Objecto* se fluidifica até deixar de existir" ("O Regresso ao Sentido Anos 70 / 80" 161). Concordo que esta é certamente uma boa descrição do muito que se passa em muitos poemas de António Franco Alexandre, mas só com alguma flexibilidade teórica é que a percebo como uma descrição visivelmente complementar e contígua das primeiras definições de *regresso ao sentido*.

Finalmente, e este é provavelmente o motivo fundamental que determina as eventuais dificuldades e riscos ao escrever-se sobre Franco Alexandre, registe-se o modo tão perturbante como este poeta parece frustrar uma espécie de recusa do cepticismo que o leitor pretende experimentar perante qualquer texto, por mais hermético que este se considere. Esta recusa do cepticismo é proporcional à qualidade da experiência epifânica que resultou da leitura do texto e que as nossas teorias poéticas mais disponíveis enquadram conceptualmente ou resolvem nos casos mais dramáticos. O preenchimento desta condição de leitura é importante, porque sustenta a convicção feliz de que nós e os outros existimos e de que existe uma reciprocidade epistemológica decorrente dos enunciados que produzimos.

Inversamente, quando não conseguimos perceber nada ou quase nada de um texto, esta recusa infrutífera do cepticismo, que, paradoxalmente, não encontra sequer um objecto conceptualmente estável acerca do qual possa duvidar, tem como sintoma uma angústia e desânimo extremos e o subsequente desespero semântico resulta numa espécie de lesão da nossa integridade ontológica. Sistemáticas descontinuidades referenciais, sintácticas e semânticas correspondem não só a dificuldades e perplexidades interpretativas, mas também a descontinuidades mnésicas e biográficas, num sentido amplo, e estas são factores de instabilidade na construção de uma identidade do poeta e do leitor, i.e., são factores que impossibilitam a formulação fiável das tão importantes *linhas de sentido.*

O interesse e originalidade da poesia de António Franco Alexandre não se situam apenas no problema ontológico que acabo de referir, sendo esse problema apenas um efeito colateral desta poesia. Antes se afigura, desde logo, como essencial o modo como se contesta a ideia segundo a qual a importância de certas coisas deriva da invisibilidade daquilo a que, geralmente, se chama a sua essência, implicando-se, no entanto, com isso que o poeta é ou deva ser um tradutor de sinais que denunciam esse conteúdo essencial. Deste ponto de vista, o poema é avaliado em função de um delicado equilíbrio indicial que reúne no mesmo lugar da indecisão, dilema e vazio semânticos a chave destes tesouros literários. É por esta última razão que muitas pessoas pensam que o sentido da poesia não pode ser, desde logo, evidente, nem, sobretudo, sistematicamente diferido, e é também este aspecto que torna especiais as coisas e o poeta e faz dos leitores seres que, depois de tão dolorosa via-sacra e deserto hermenêuticos, recebem, mesmo que por instantes, a devida recompensa sob a forma de iluminação semântica e ganho cognitivo. Nada disto, no entanto e como já se percebeu, é realmente lisonjeiro para as coisas, o poeta e os leitores, uma vez que se demonstra que nem as coisas são suficientemente invisíveis, nem os poetas são necessariamente videntes do oculto, nem as perplexidades interpretativas dos leitores são realmente intransponíveis e decisivas. Um segundo aspecto relacionado com o anterior, que a poesia de Franco Alexandre parece interrogar, é a presunção segundo a qual existe um interesse naturalmente filosófico pelas coisas e principalmente, já se vê, pelo seu interior que, supostamente, reclama uma exposição e confere ao poeta o estatuto mais digno de filósofo. É que nesta poesia de uma "radicalidade negativa" ("Alguns Nexos" 223), como lhe chama Óscar Lopes, a dificuldade e o desespero nunca são o não se pressentir o sentido ou um sentido, ou um sopro de sentido, no intervalo de tantas descontinuidades morfológicas, sintácticas e semânticas. A crítica situação hermenêutica é o depararmo-nos com o facto de, precisamente porque pressentimos esse sentido etéreo, ser impossível formular raciocínios e proposições sintacticamente coerentes e sustentados por evidência textual suficiente que lhes credite alguma fiabilidade não especulativa. O que alguma poesia de Franco Alexandre descreve é uma espécie de impossibilidade da linguagem, algo congénita, de por ela e nela se cumprirem promessas semânticas, por parte de quem começa por enunciá-las ou sugeri-las. Este é, penso eu, um aspecto essencial porque transfere a discussão do poema de tópicos que habitualmente relacionamos com a mimese e o modo como o texto se relaciona com a realidade ou com outros textos, indiciando de forma mais ou menos evidente a sua própria leitura, para a questão, aparentemente prévia, da natureza da própria linguagem, enquanto suporte físico de uma coisa chamada poesia e do sentido. Como nos diz o poeta no poema 6 de *Moradas 1 & 2*, aquilo que resulta dos pedidos que lhe fazemos é uma "nódoa" de tinta e um "desalinho" prosódico, numa folha, que é o "tapete" das nossas relações infelizes e intempestivas, em que não podemos abrigar as nossas dúvidas e anseios:

> que queres de mim esse saber surpreso
> que o retrato de ti te não parece
> que outra razão de ser mais desejável
> ...
> a equação celeste do destino? no tapete
> fica depois a nódoa, o desalinho.
> ...
> não te respondo. não te repito. invento
> o vento que te arrasta a desabrigo. (280)

António Franco Alexandre (ao contrário de Alberto Caeiro, por exemplo) não nega o interior das coisas, antes se revolta contra a visibilidade por vezes fácil de mais, tanto do exterior como do interior, e pela materialidade violenta destas coisas na maneira como ostentam o seu estar perante o sujeito, exigindo dele a atenção e a voz, uma narrativa. Franco Alexandre ora se angustia com o mutismo obstinado das coisas ora se horroriza com a transparência e, sobretudo, com a presença do mundo e dos seus objectos, i.e., com a sua ausência de mistério e invisibilidade.

Na impossibilidade de se furtar à presença das coisas, o ofício do poeta e das palavras é então, para desespero dos leitores, ocultar aquilo que o mundo exibe e revoltar-se contra o modo como o mundo impõe essa presença. A poesia corresponde assim não tanto a um acto de criação e representação, muito menos de esclarecimento, mas sobretudo de negação e apagamento, de rasura. A poesia enuncia uma teoria do conhecimento que precisamente está consciente de que a apreensão e nomeação do objecto se constituem sempre como uma *reductio* da presença deste e um encolhimento morfológico do que, à falta de melhor expressão, chamo a sua extensão ontológica.

Se aquilo que constitui motivo de inquietação, para Franco Alexandre, é, deste ponto de vista, a persistência obstinada e irreverente de certas coisas, palavras e conteúdos mentais: "de tudo o que esqueci me inquieta / uma memória outra" (20), não é de admirar que a poesia seja, como se diz no poema de 1974, com o sugestivo título "L'Oubli," a consequência de uma espécie de exposição nefasta ao mundo e peso da memória e corresponda simultaneamente a um (infeliz) exercício de esquecimento e à enunciação explícita ou implícita de um desejo de evasão, inconsciência e conversão ou metamorfose:

ó somente não ter

mais nada que lembrar, mais palavras a arder

dentro do crânio quando as folhas crescem,

acordar em Rapallo ou Santa Bárbara

dentro de um corpo, colado, coincidente

...

acabar, desistir, fechar o ouvido ao arrastar das unhas

nas paredes, não falar outra língua

que a da madeira ardida no cimo da água, (25, 26)

Neste ensaio sobre a poesia de António Franco Alexandre, proceder-se-á, essencialmente, à demonstração desta hipótese de leitura explorando-se, necessariamente, tópicos aos quais a mesma conduz e com os quais se relaciona. Antes de mais e, como já referi, encontramos a recusa de uma poesia que permita a construção estável de uma referência, de uma presença e de uma identidade. Nesta poesia de negações e de uma *reductio* da realidade, obtém-se e acontece, não raras vezes, uma imagem inabitável do mundo, sintacticamente desordenada, cuja disposição dos objectos nem sequer obedece a uma racionalidade labiríntica, que suscitasse ou desafiasse a interpretação. Denuncia-se uma concepção do poema e da leitura como espaços de uma viagem errática, sem destino definido nem protagonistas identificáveis, por imagens aparentemente aleatórias e convocadas por estímulos vários e imponderáveis. A arbitrariedade calculada de quaisquer coordenadas corresponde, na rede semântica do poema, à perda da visibilidade e presença do sujeito lírico, dos personagens e objectos, o que coincide com o abandono, não complacente, dos leitores a uma sintaxe improvável, a citações inesperadas e associações semânticas tornadas abstractas pela implausibilidade dos elementos concretos que as formam, e resultantes, acima de tudo, de preocupações prosódicas e formais não convencionais. A sugestão de imagens e histórias, que indiciam a índole transaccionável e límbica da existência dos homens, das coisas e das suas relações, contribuem para a impossibilidade de uma definição da sua natureza e para a possibilidade do seu ocultamento e *travestimento* sistemáticos e repetidos. Mas há quase sempre, como diz Gastão Cruz a propósito de *Oásis*, um indício "do sentido outro" (180) que, tanto apazigua momentaneamente a angústia semântica do leitor, como inibe a interpretação. A imperatividade desta voz indecisa, imprecisa, subterrânea e caprichosa trai-se e coincide às vezes com a presença de momentos em que se suplica e ambiciona a perfeição e a perenidade do canto poético e de um espaço vazio, escuro e despojado em que cada um pertença a si mesmo, mesmo que isso passe pela citação das palavras do outro:

> hei-de gritar até que a eternidade
> devore a coisa vil que nos devora
> ou se apague do eterno o dia em que nasci
> ...
> finalmente partir, na manhã de ruas nítidas e frias,
> passar este deserto até às portas do mar, onde reis violentos

se alimentam de sal, aí

plantarei a árvore das minhas folhas acesas ao vento

e a cada um suavemente direi: «You belong to You:

também Tu crescerás para Tu: eis o teu nome. (394, 402)

A relevância dos tópicos alexandrinos que acabo de enunciar parece-me extrema na medida em que aquilo que Franco Alexandre propõe, no contexto da poesia portuguesa contemporânea, é uma radical redefinição do género lírico enquanto lugar que convencionalmente associamos à possibilidade de construção de um identidade enunciativa que polariza e modula uma percepção identificável do mundo, pese embora as peculiares mudanças e idiossincrasias dos diferentes textos. Em cada poema, são experimentadas possibilidades de destituir o texto de um sentido coerente e localizável e duas consequências disso são o desaparecimento do mundo dos sujeitos e dos objectos, num vórtice de sugestões semânticas (que não são propriamente polissémicas), e uma espécie de restituição da linguagem a si mesma, enquanto sistema gráfica e prosodicamente abstracto e inútil, do ponto de vista instrumental, i.e., comunicativo. A iterabilidade irrestrita dos signos e contextos linguísticos—que define a natureza da própria linguagem, como sugere Derrida[2] — suspende e impossibilita a formulação sintáctica de uma ordem promotora de uma leitura que resgatasse o *eu* e as coisas das metamorfoses a que são remetidos no texto que supostamente os nomeia e refere. Trata-se portanto, como o poeta sugestivamente implicita, através da epígrafe que lemos no seu último livro, *Uma Fábula* (2001), de adquirir aquele saber que permite explicar *how bodies are changed into different bodies* (7) ou, como o maior poeta da literatura portuguesa disse um dia, se transforma, "o amador na cousa amada."

A deflação do discurso filosófico na poesia de António Franco Alexandre não se deve tanto à convicção da sua putativa ineficácia no processo de conhecimento, mas antes à suspeita e, diria mesmo, irritação originadas pela percepção do seu sucesso, relativo ou não, na explicação do mundo e na definição de estratégias epistemológicas. A mera sugestão desta hipótese deve pelo menos colocar o leitor de sobreaviso relativamente a um entendimento glorioso do valor da poesia, como alternativa epistemológica. Na realidade, como percebemos pelo último livro de Franco Alexandre, tanto filosofia como literatura se encontram plausivelmente no mesmo plano que, embora não saibamos qual é, não é certamente cognitivo: "Já me não serve de nada a poesia, / a literária 'arte de chiar.' E quanto a pensamento: esse schelling / já me moeu o siso. Desisti de entender / a 'identidade.' Pense quem lê" (*Uma Fábula* 53).

E no entanto, no primeiro livro que o autor considera essencial para a definição da sua obra, observa-se ainda, a par do que julgo serem já as linhas de força desta poesia, a presença do persistente vocabulário filosófico que, ora sofre tratos de polé na submissão que lhe impõe o violento fazer poético, ora parece surgir como instrumento conceptual e epistemológico. Em "Sem Palavras nem Coisas," poema epónimo do livro a que pertence e onde se ouve, desde logo, Foucault, percebe-se, por exemplo, que o ofício das palavras e do pensamento se expressa pelos actos perigosos e *demónicos* de dividir, separar e escolher. Em versos como "(neste perigo mudo de escolher dividindo / o som de tiros altos em volta do corredor)" (14), "divido separo escolho, / de pé no corredor entornando os cabelos" (14), "dividindo o granito, acendo / o cenário e as pálpebras separam / os ramos dos braços" (15), "dividindo, separando, escolhendo as balas dos / projectores," (15), "deste perigo mudo de escolher / dividindo, cai no azul e alarga-se, cai / devagar, acendo / o ramo e a folha cai nos dedos" (15), observa-se uma espécie de implosão do sentido das palavras a que só resiste a percepção dos actos e operações mentais—dividir, separar, escolher—que permitem essa implosão e que, desde já, propomos como procedimentos poéticos recorrentes em Franco Alexandre. Dividir, separar e escolher são tanto estratégias da mente habituada ao rigor sintáctico do pensamento filosófico e discursivo, em geral, como actos de expansão poética ilimitada, no sentido que Riffaterre dá ao conceito de expansão[3] e, possivelmente, o seu interesse reside no facto de estes dois aspectos coincidirem no mesmo texto e ser impossível distingui-los. Aliás, na intersecção destes dois modos de dividir, separar e escolher considere-se, ainda que de um modo figurativo, a violência inerente a cada um destes actos. Daí que, na realidade, a única coisa que se lhes pode furtar seja aquilo que é objecto do amor que "perdura" no que se divide e separa:

> sem tempo para escolher, separar,
> dividir, perdura de repente dentro das asas,
> vê, perdura na minúcia dos pulsos,
> o que amaste perdura, não tem tempo
> para se perder,
> palavras que dividam, vê, coisas que te separem. (18)

A enunciação sistemática das estratégias que parecem permitir a produção do texto elide possibilidades de abordagem ou identificação surrealistas e considerações acerca de uma arbitrariedade não controlada. De facto, o texto progride numa encenação de si mesmo e representa-se a si mesmo e às suas possibilidades enquanto suporte e resultado dos actos de dividir separar e escolher, a partir de uma matriz lexical identificável, relativamente reduzida e nada abstracta. Como se diz em *Oásis* (1992), de um modo que, metonimicamente, cria uma identificação entre texto e realidade, e um espaço, a floresta, que se pode percorrer e onde nos podemos perder e perder coisas ou pessoas:

> Dessa experiência, que combinara a estranheza das coisas muito próximas
>
> e o ar franco dos desaparecidos […]—sem perder
>
> a perfeita coesão de todas as partes do espaço—nasceu
>
> a certeza que a simples realidade contém o aberto de todas as
>
> ramagens, que sobrepostas e enlaçadas, são o chão sucessivo da floresta. (401)

Sejam quais forem as estratégias de produção textual de Franco Alexandre, o seu propósito não é nunca o de sugerir um núcleo semântico suficientemente forte, sustentado eventualmente por "uma temática obsessiva ou muito específica," que permita a definição de uma "ideia forte para esta poesia" (*O Mosaico Fluido* 108). Pelo contrário, e como temos vindo a sugerir, o movimento é sempre o de uma recusa de que as palavras possam, de alguma forma, esclarecer ou representar a realidade, como se a poesia fosse uma vingança em relação ao modo visível como o mundo se apresenta e se manifesta na suposta ligação entre o mundo e as palavras. Mais do que uma recusa, diria que se trata de uma espécie de trabalho de Penélope em que, no entanto, a quantidade de tecido que se desfaz é superior à que se elabora, como se o único fundamento do pouco que se tece fosse o muito que, depois ou no mesmo instante, se pode destecer. É interessante notar por exemplo, ainda em *Sem Palavras Nem Coisas* e a propósito do que se acabou de dizer, o diálogo que se estabelece entre dois poemas: "Minhas Pequenas Dúvidas, E A Guerra" e "As Coisas Justamente." Aquilo que, desde logo, se observa, quando os dois poemas se lêem como um só, é que o modo como as coisas "nos rodeiam" e "nos penetram" (43) encontra evidente paralelo no *modus operandi* das dúvidas de "Minhas Pequenas Dúvidas":

1
minhas pequenas dúvidas estabelecem
habitação violenta. furam pelos ossos,
espalham os dedos em volta, os caules
aquecidos do vento, roem
lentamente os pátios inertes,
instalam a dobra azul dos cotovelos,
resistem. […] mexem
os dedos na gaveta,…
minhas pequenas dúvidas multiplicam os dentes,…
furam pelos dedos, as vísceras
intensas do vento, estabelecem
cotovelos completos.
   têm
a violência constante dos ossos
resistem, dobram lentamente
a trela das estrelas, ferem as vísceras
inertes do silêncio. (31-32)

Considere-se agora o poema "As Coisas Justamente":

1
as coisas justamente dilaceram
o verniz da violência, o sebo
prematuro das coxas, junto
ao resistente pêlo das mulheres.
…vão perfurando
o céu que por palavras se fez boca…
batem no mundo com suor inútil…
as coisas como nascem assim cobrem
a face prematura, o olho
eréctil da manhã…
as coisas justamente nos contemplam
& sorriem.

2
nos rodeiam. ameaçando

a tempestade fria dos arbustos, o pêlo
inclinado do gesso
a mansidão ardente das madeiras...
roem de sangue a melancia imóvel
chamam o tempo ao tempo e acordam,
terríveis, do fulgor das chamas...
vigiam o rumor
atento dos anéis
batem, perfuram, disseminam
o peso da neblina, penetram...
invadem o silêncio, e nas palavras
têm reinado imóvel.
nos rodeiam, nos pesam,
nos demoram.
devoram na cabeça a mão mais dura. (41-44)

Seria portanto fácil, mas relativamente ingénuo, supor simplesmente que
"minhas pequenas dúvidas" são o legítimo antídoto para as coisas e seus
métodos invasores, para a presença, mas isso não parece ser plausível se
entendermos a dúvida como método filosófico ancilar e provisório da busca da
verdade e, portanto, de um sentido. De facto, as dúvidas são também elas
objecto da disrupção poética e não apenas o seu agente provisório e metódico
relativamente à violência impositiva das coisas. A armadura bélica, que estas
dúvidas parecem proporcionar, dispersa-se, anulando-se na sua dedicação mais
do que hiperbólica e não metódica, no sentido de não selectiva e desordenada.
O sujeito que duvida é elidido por uma espécie de autonomia não deliberativa
e precipitada que as dúvidas adquirem, mas que as esgota. É talvez por isso que
o momento do seu adormecimento, cansaço e desaparecimento coincide com
o momento da exposição pornográfica do corpo e das coisas:

minhas pequenas dúvidas cansadas
adormecem num bolso, e estamos nus.
        abraço-te
devagarinho, com as costas dos ossos,
dobrando os cotovelos na gaveta...
minhas pequenas
        dúvidas, minhas trelas miúdas,

> sufocam numa névoa de granadas...
> dói-me na mão direita
> uma falta de dedos, uma falta
> de rios.
>   pornograficamente
> adormecemos. (36-37)

No entanto, percebe-se que é, quando a guerra das dúvidas termina e somos iludidos só pela aparente visibilidade dos corpos e das coisas, que se consegue a preclusão absoluta do sentido, e se coarcta, de certo modo, o dogmatismo irreverente das dúvidas que, por outro lado, não são senão tão ditatoriais quanto as outras coisas. Isto acontece não porque o poema termine nos versos que acabei de citar, mas porque a pornografia é essencialmente motivo de reacções somáticas e não semânticas. A pornografia é um *medium* que dilui os corpos e os sentidos, uma vez que opera por sinédoque e localiza numa parte a irrelevância do todo, (amputando?) despromovendo as outras partes para a categoria do meramente acessório, cobrindo-as com uma sombra.

As coisas parecem ser, assim, mais resistentes e recalcitrantes do que o autismo e o cepticismo de que, aparentemente, o poeta se protege relativamente a elas, à sua existência e ao que, por prosopopeia, lhe ditam. As coisas conseguem (só podem) habitar a forma sedutora dos instrumentos que são utilizados para nos furtar à sua presença, i.e., nós próprios, enquanto dotados de vontade, as dúvidas, a linguagem e próprio silêncio. É uma espécie de metamorfose não em função do amor que nos têm, mas em virtude da indiferença e ódio que lhes manifestamos e da sua existência frágil, mas inevitável e necessária: "frágeis as coisas justamente duram / instantes só: o tempo / de queimar-se" (44). As coisas, como se diz no final do poema "As Coisas Justamente," são, além disto, o último refúgio dos deuses mortos, os mais hábeis em disfarces e metamorfoses, e nada dados a manifestações epifânicas, mesmo vivos:

> nos convidam e traem. dos olhos nos retiram
> o olhar que nos cederam.
> violentas e precisas dilaceram
> o céu que por palavras as fez boca
> intensamente falam

até poder surgir. então se calam.

justamente não cedem: perscrutam

a sombra do silêncio. e vigiam

do imóvel pêlo os deuses que suplicam

detrás das coisas justamente, mortos. (47)

Se é nas palavras que as coisas têm "o seu reinado imóvel," então é mais ou menos claro que o modo da sua consumpção terá de ser também um modo verbal e que o cepticismo não pode já ser expresso numa e pela dúvida, mas pela recusa, por uma retracção, eventualmente obstinada e arbitrária. O poema é o lugar dessa consumpção e dessa recusa céptica e cega do sentido evidente e transparente.

Entenda-se, deste ponto de vista, que a tão perturbante questão da dirisão do sentido na poesia de António Franco Alexandre, que muitos críticos assinalam,[4] é, antes de mais, um efeito de uma perplexidade pela avassaladora presença das coisas e dos objectos e, sobretudo, por uma espécie de insolente reclamação que fazem do poeta e assalto que perpetram à linguagem. Não julgo por isso que a questão essencial seja uma espécie de incorporação das coisas ou dos objectos pelo poeta e, mesmo admitindo que isso acontece num livro como *Objectos Principais,* como sugere Américo Lindeza Diogo, creio apenas que esse é um estado transitório da relação entre as coisas e o poeta. O fim último é, como sustentarei, a dissolução pela e na linguagem quer do poeta quer das coisas. Trata-se de fazer do poema uma espécie de enunciação muda, o vestígio gráfico de um sem número de conseguidas ausências e poder dizer: "o poema traz consigo um fresco calor escuro / é um pouco cão, miserável e mudo" (239). Não me parece que exista qualquer melancolia nestas palavras, apenas a convicção de que já se restitui a linguagem à sua condição de mera coisa sem significado. Pelo exercício da poesia, descobre-se que a linguagem existe enquanto evidência material cega e muda. Como contraprova do cepticismo, a linguagem remete, no entanto, para uma recusa e um vazio.

Os poemas de *Os Objectos Principais* (1979) desiludem a possível expectativa de registo lírico e confessional, que eventualmente se adivinha e suspeita no qualificativo "principais" do título. *Os Objectos Principais* denotam assim a falência de uma crença em ícones modernos e ou pós-modernos e, por extensão, a descrença em narrativas totalizadoras e definidoras de um *zeitgeist.* Assinala-se por inteiro a disponibilidade ancilar do sujeito, que julgo identificar-se como um "Legatário Universal," um dos títulos de uma série de poemas deste livro, para receber uma herança hiperbólica e insuportável de textos e coisas já feitas.

De facto, os objectos de *Os Objectos Principais* não são principais para o *eu*, porque não se percebe exactamente quem é o *eu*, não são certamente objectos de uma operação electiva que justificasse a sua caracterização de principais e, por isso, dificilmente podem ser entendidos como principais para alguém. Eles são principais sobretudo no sentido de primeiros, i.e., prévios à linguagem e ao sujeito que os nomeia. São principais na medida em que são absolutamente incaracterísticos, do ponto de vista do valor, e portanto assumem uma autonomia colectiva indistinta que os faz presentes e principais de um modo absoluto, não sujeitos a hierarquias e igualmente disponíveis à linguagem. Como simplesmente existem, verifica-se, na e pela linguagem de que dependem para se fazer notar, a virtualidade de os referir num complexo de contextos lexicais e semânticos e relações materiais tão improváveis que perdem a possibilidade de individuação, não podendo por isso ser tomados como objectos de eleição relacionáveis com um temperamento lírico particular, ou metonímias evidentes de uma realidade outra que não se pretendesse referir. Como Américo Lindeza Diogo diz em *Modernismos Pós-Modernismos, Anacronismos*, a existência destes objectos verifica-se na vastidão informe e o facto de serem principais não torna a sua "co-ocorrência com camiões, armazéns, museus, gavetas" (34) paradoxal, acentuando pelo contrário a sua disponibilidade irrestrita e existência colectiva.

Mais do que sujeito de preferências, o poeta é, então, o que recebe, e não o que incorpora, de forma quase indiscriminada. Recebe-se portanto também o que não se pediu, aquilo em que não se crê e considera-se interrogativamente a possibilidade de serem conjugados os elementos de uma realidade tão disseminada e pulverizada pela linguagem.

Abrindo com uma epígrafe de Wittgenstein nas *Investigações Filosóficas*, parágrafo 38, em que se associa o acto de nomear ao do baptismo de um objecto, *Os Objectos Principais* é, por um lado, um livro sobre o modo de nomear as coisas, quer dizer, de infelizmente não conseguir esgotá-las pelas palavras, "a série das palavras (seja qual for a intensidade / dos seus nomes, como as razões que nos vestem / de grandes corolas) não esgota nunca os seus objectos," (113)—e, por outro, é também uma obra onde surgem interrogações constantes acerca da plausibilidade e possibilidade de existência hermenêutica em paisagens e contextos de relações semânticas e materiais tão difusos, enigmáticos e insensatos. Na segunda epígrafe, de Lévi-Strauss a propósito dos Wotjobaluk, diz-se que "a vida de um morcego é uma vida de homem" e, no primeiro poema de *Os Objectos Principais*, ficamos a saber que "o rumo / dos grandes navios japoneses à entrada da doca" depende destas estranhas "questões ignorantes":

> poderemos, um dia, amar estas vitrinas
>
> como quem ama uma ideia imperdoável ou uma
>
> breve hesitação dos condutores
>
> a meio do percurso? quero dizer,
>
> estaremos vivos para o desbotar destas
>
> folhas de plástico que brilham
>
> uma vez cada noite; e para
>
> o assobio das nuvens
>
> ao passar sobre a roupa? (81)

À indefinição morfológica, que o sujeito lírico adquire pela provável condição de herdeiro hiperbólico, de "Legatário Universal," correspondem uma particular dissolução ontológica desse sujeito no texto, uma constante indecisão no modo de agir e a insistente expressão de uma recusa do que se manifesta fantasmaticamente na poesia. De facto, reconhecendo-se como um recipiente informe e universal de coisas imprevisíveis, como armazém não mensurável, elide-se a possibilidade de reunir um conjunto identificável de interesses que confira uma forma definível à voz de *Os Objectos Principais* que, no entanto, acumula referências, metonímicas ou não, a fantasmas, à memória, a um passado e a outras vozes. É o que parece acontecer no poema que passo a citar e onde metaforicamente julgo poder ler-se aquilo que Harold Bloom designou por *anxiety of influence*:

> esse fantasma levantou os ladrilhos do corredor, entornando
>
> à passagem o balde de geleia azul. foi esta
>
> a primeira lembrança? ou seria
>
> violeta; violenta; violentada; verde?
>
> as nódoas do passado nunca se calam, apesar
>
> de colocadas debaixo do aparador, junto à tua
>
> cabeça maior.

ou teremos, um dia, medo
de lhe arremessar objectos grosseiros, alguma
espinha de água verde, ou azul, conforme
o ditarem as circunstâncias? receamos
o nosso destino, e o destino dos nossos
arbustos sem flor. esse fantasma
devorou as sementes, só nos resta
abatê-lo à socapa das mesas. e depois
viveremos na infâmia, no pavor e no nojo. (88)

A indecisão ou deliberada confusão acerca do espaço lírico, que se ocupa, compromete as decisões e a acção e em *Os Objectos Principais* as coisas não são na realidade feitas ou ditas. As coisas e o texto acontecem de um modo muitas vezes considerado impertinente e violento: "irrita-me transportar estas palavras, a elas / me obriga a sua mão coberta de alicates / esta é a nossa ignorância. decerto colhemos / o efeito de outras horas" (106); "estas ligeiras coisas me acontecem: o copo azul, o azul, as / tartarugas luminosas; e ainda assim a ausência / dos navios se agita nas gavetas" (107). O passado assume assim uma função inibidora, geologicamente sedimentada, e, em vez de funcionar como enquadramento conceptual fiável do presente, promove a revolta, a interrogação relativamente ao que fazer e o desejo de uma existência surda às palavras, aos sentidos e apenas sensível à lucidez de um tropel caótico:

e de repente deparamos com vastos armazéns
geológicos, como deuses que dormem:
como nos surpreende o seu triunfo! como nos pesa
o áspero rumor dos telefones! não acredito
sequer no que me diz. como
viver na dúvida insensata dos seus
variados usos? e assim
nos esquecemos pouco a pouco, frequentemente
mais jovens, mas também mais selvagens.
não conheço este campo, este vidro, esta porta. não ouço
sequer o que me diz. apenas o tropel
dos búfalos, ao fundo,
nos elucida: e então. (112)

Co-extensiva da indecisão relativamente ao que fazer e como viver—que se expressa pela formulação de desejos vagamente impossíveis ou por sugestivas interrogações: "como viver com estas minúsculas / intempéries, a régua sobre a mesa, a chuva / pendurada nos altos telégrafos da paciência?" (109) ou "como / obedecer ao requerimento das cortinas, quando / ao erguê-las a brisa avistamos o passado / de unhas redondas junto à balaustrada?" (110)—verifica-se a indeterminação relativamente aos destinatários do discurso, cuja indefinição condiciona também a configuração do *eu. Eu* e *você* (mas também *nós* e *vós*) coincidem, não hierarquizados, num mesmo plano lírico, não sendo mais possível tomá-los como índices textuais de uma coesão lírica convencional, determinada pela diferença entre sujeito lírico e destinatário e, desde logo, condicionada por expectativas semânticas mais ou menos definidas e previsíveis. Assim, é perfeitamente plausível que o poeta viva dentro de quem é o alvo do seu discurso, "vivo dentro de si, como um vulgar morcego...ardo dentro de si" (82) e que, por exemplo, num poema onde se parece partilhar o embaraço semântico do leitor, demitindo-se o poeta de uma posição privilegiada face ao que é dito, não se determine o género do destinatário recorrendo-se à alternativa o/a para assinalar essa indecisão e essa distância formal:

...creia-me: compartilho

da sua pena, da branca espuma

do seu seio mais alto, dos elevados

sentimentos que o/a atormentam. não é fácil

 contemplar em silêncio estes piões lançados 'à rapaz' no insensato convés

da sua tolerância. vêlos imóveis

custanos o preço de alagados cimentos, de acções

judiciais seguramente favoráveis.

 mas não foi essa a escolha

que a si mesmo/a tinha prometido? e o prazer

está nestas mesas nuas, neste ardor, nesta chuva. (87)

Nos sete poemas que fazem parte de "A Questão Urbana," a dispersão e dissolução dos seres e dos objectos, em virtude de uma espécie de replicação, sistematicamente diferente, das suas relações, é reduzida, penso eu, a uma única imagem, o "grés animal": "estas cidades, grés animal, as garrafas de sangue nos passeios / prenunciam devagarmente um acordar translúcido"

(97). Em "grés animal" condensam-se todas as equações e inequações possíveis entre o mundo animado e inanimado, racional e irracional. O "grés animal" é um novo ser improvável que irrompe de um cruzamento bizarro, proclama a morte dos progenitores e retém alguns dos seus predicados: "ombros de grés;" "recobertas de grés permanecem sentadas" (99). É por isso um elemento que é preciso ler e decifrar e que pode prenunciar "um acordar translúcido," "algum afastamento decisivo" ou "o ronco insuportável de uma boca." A qualidade animal do grés corresponde também a uma concepção do espaço como ser vivo, constituído por partes indeterminadas e acções aleatórias. O nomadismo, tão presente na poesia de Franco Alexandre, não pode ser assim entendido do mero ponto de vista da errância num espaço físico, com fronteiras mais ou menos definidas, mas como errância num espaço (animal) ele próprio em movimento e em mutação e, portanto, sem qualquer ponto de ancoragem ou relação com um mapa. Aliás, deste ponto de vista, pode ser uma errância que não logra qualquer movimento ou percorre seja o que for, porque o movimento espacial anula e contraria os esforços de quem percorre esse espaço. As acções deste ser vivo espacial, que se percorre e nos percorre e transporta, são narrativamente expressas, nos poemas de "A Questão Urbana," através de verbos na terceira pessoa do plural, cuja relação com um sujeito estável e exactamente determinável há muito se perdeu, como se pode observar no poema 2 da série:

2

movem nos muros, a vagina mineral das mães

adormecidas, entre os apitos trémulos do aço

e lenços verdes onde ocultam a cara. prenunciam, é certo,

algum visível afastamento das madeiras, algum

pensamento violentado, porisso as coisas permanecem sentadas

e compreensíveis, afastadas de súbito pelo vento oco. (97)

Na realidade, percebe-se que este aliterante espaço urbano, longe de conferir um enquadramento contextual e uma unidade a esta narrativa sobre objectos e vozes principais, é mais um espaço de aniquilação da identidade e do sentido ou de uma estrutura, pela hipérbole das suas virtualidades paradoxais, sendo a "animal" a mais surpreendente. A enigmática frase final de *Os Objectos Principais*—"assim em vós vos perderei, enfim" (119)—motiva possibilidades, relativamente inesgotáveis, de substituições pronominais de "vós" e "vos," inclusivamente aquelas em que "vós" e "vos" são a mesma coisa, porque, na realidade tudo se conseguirá realmente perder e tudo se perde nestes poemas, excepto a sua tão evidente manifestação enquanto manchas gráficas e sistemas prosódicos, como aliás é tão claro num enunciado como "assim em vós vos perderei, enfim."

Não são imediatamente visíveis os propósitos (talvez se trate mais de consequências) desta tão sublime, melancólica e, às vezes, irada, *ars poetica* de inibir a presença, a visibilidade e a transparência das coisas e dos corpos— "dedico-me unicamente / a uma cólera incessante, / este horror da tua transparência / desaparecerá, como as mais coisas que as palavras / tornaram invisíveis" (74)—pela iterabilidade de combinações linguísticas, através das quais essas coisas e corpos são sugeridos e diferidos para um espaço não cartografado de imprecisão contextual e de indecisão semântica.

A propósito de *Sem Palavras Nem Coisas*, diz Joaquim Manuel Magalhães que o contributo essencial de Franco Alexandre é o de nos fazer participantes de um "*requiem* urbano que nos faz ouvir, na mágoa dos corpos perdidos que nos faz partilhar, no desalento com que nos faz contemplar os objectos de um erotismo fatigado e infeliz" (*Os Dois Crepúsculos* 248-49). Mas aquilo que, na sequência do que já se disse, pretendo afirmar como de extrema relevância na poética alexandrina, é o modo tão obsessivo como se impugna o facto surpreendente e incontornável de dependermos da linguagem e do sistema de correspondências que esta pressupõe—"esta dependência imediata da linguagem / esta radical correspondência das coisas visíveis / nunca perde o poder de afectar-nos" (291). Consequência desta impugnação é uma determinada concepção do poema como objecto inútil, o que só ilusoriamente e momentaneamente poderá parecer uma convicção desinteressada ou melancólica. O poema é o lugar de uma linguagem que se furta à correspondência, onde a linguagem funciona como mera coisa composta de sons e riscos e por isso "o poema é inútil como uma criança, / que as águas afagam" (330), ou, numa formulação mais determinada, "o poema não existe" (356). O que de um poema se conhece pertence ao domínio do inexpressivo: "Digam que me conhecem, / assim mudado, a tinta permanente" e, num outro momento, o poeta diz-se vestígio bolorento do antigo bardo e a poesia uma "garatuja" do que o buraco sujo da memória dita:

Ouvi quem sou, pardo bolor sonoro
de horas perdidas no hangar, quieto

> e cego ao esplendor da natureza.
> Todas as frases vinham do passado, o sujo
> buraco da memória. E já por prova
> se fixe no papel a garatuja. (364)

Na sequência do que se está a dizer, Joaquim Manuel Magalhães refere, de forma enfática e com propriedade, "a qualidade da atenção prosódica envolvida nos poemas do autor" (*As Moradas, 1 & 2* 157) como uma das linhas de força desta poesia, o que, sem surpresa, o leva a classificar a escrita de Franco Alexandre como "fechada sobre si mesma," sujeita a uma "circularidade entre prosódia e prosódia" onde "temos sempre de aceitar as referências concretas como um ponto de partida para sequências que as enigmatizam" (158). Mas, enquanto Joaquim Manuel Magalhães, que entende este poeta, o poeta como alguém que, sem qualquer pretensão de impessoalidade, não quer contudo confessar-se, parece subsumir os dois aspectos anteriores na consideração conclusiva de que, em *Moradas 1 & 2*, "Estamos perante, por que não dizê-lo, obsessivos, obscuros poemas de amor" (159), o meu entendimento da condição prosódica e, por vezes, meramente gráfica dos poemas de Franco Alexandre relaciona-se mais com o delicado tratamento poético que o espaço e a consciência do espaço adquirem nesta poesia.

Por um lado, é como se as imagens e percepções espaciais de Franco Alexandre fossem sobretudo de natureza prosódica e como se uma das condições de transcendência do espaço fosse também de índole musical. São inúmeros os versos onde, por sinestesia, o som é objecto da visão ou afecta este sentido e não a audição, pelo que, deste ponto de vista, o privilégio que as imagens visuais adquirem em situações descritivas é substituído pela ênfase em imagens auditivas, que são vistas ou provocam uma cegueira preenchida de lucidez: "quando se vê a música então é fácil" (115); "nenhuma das nossas palavras mudará a altura / precisamente calculada do som que cega, / ninguém chorará as imaginações maliciosas e cruéis / que animam o progresso dramático, a intenção do verso" (329). Por outro, é como se o poema fosse, pela sua substância essencialmente prosódica, umas vezes, e quase estritamente gráfica, outras vezes, o espaço escuro e inabitado de sentido e de sentidos de onde é possível partir. De facto, basta a simples consideração dos títulos de algumas das suas obras—*Visitação* (1983), *Moradas 1 & 2,* "Terceiras Moradas" e *Oásis* (1992)—para ser obrigatório pensar na relevância que o espaço adquire nesta poesia.

Consideremos em primeiro lugar a tão estreita relação entre movimento, espaço e uma espécie de construção de imagem musical do espaço. A compreensão da questão espacial relaciona-se previamente, penso eu, com uma específica concepção do movimento, que Franco Alexandre sugere logo no primeiro poema de *Sem Palavras Nem Coisas,* "Universo Animal." Este poema, que é uma homenagem a Charles Olson, começa com os versos "there is a tide in a man / movendo as pálpebras da carne, a vaga / genital, sopro que as mãos debruçam / sobre a rosa dos rios…" (9). Inscreve-se assim no homem um movimento que o percorre, um ritmo pendular de fluxo e refluxo que configura uma viagem circular e ininterrupta, mas uma viagem que, em última análise, não depende de um exercício planificador da vontade e deliberação humanas. Daí que o destinatário deste poema seja o próprio movimento circular, como coisa autónoma e estruturante do próprio espaço habitado pelo sujeito: "o wheel, draw / that truth / to my house / para que a pedra se encoste contra a pedra, muro / a muro, noite sobre noite, no rumor das cidades" (9). As consequências mais visíveis deste movimento involuntário, mas constante, são a aparente descoordenação presente nas supostas descrições espaciais que se fazem nesta poesia, como se o sujeito se confrontasse sistematicamente com destinos falsos, em movimento ou não escolhidos, e uma espécie de apresentação do espaço como se fosse o espaço que percorresse o sujeito e não inversamente. Por exemplo, em "Tríptico Nómada" é a figuração das cidades de Nova Iorque, Paris e Veneza que é nómada e não propriamente o sujeito que eventualmente experimentou esses lugares. Ora, essa figuração do nomadismo das próprias cidades no interior do sujeito—que nos concede, em "Tríptico Nómada," alguns índices mínimos que convocam imagens suficientemente convencionais e neutras dessas cidades—não só torna todos os lugares visitáveis, visíveis e passíveis de sobreposição ou intersecção na mente do poeta e no poema—o lugar da sua visitação acaba por ser determinado pela caótica cartografia que o próprio poema lhes confere—como se revela sobretudo em complexas imagens musicais e gráficas a que, no entanto, não escapa um sussurro de uma história pessoal. Considere-se o poema 6 da série II, "Paris, Sumário," de "Tríptico Nómada," onde julgo serem perceptíveis grande parte dos aspectos que acabei de referir:

6

asa sem paz(aro), migrante: de empire
state no bolso azul de cheviote,
édipo duro dura, assobiando
madra-goa em chicago, bar-d(o)
e máfia.
paris, ocasional: pele da pele, e-
terna. Acaso um salto:
a dança: íris de riso, um rio. (54)

É contudo em *Visitação* que a questão da percepção e concepção musical do espaço, em detrimento de uma descrição que sugerisse um entendimento fotográfico de um determinado percurso, surge de forma mais evidente. A Parte III deste livro é composta por vinte e sete poemas que supostamente evocam uma viagem ao Brasil. Rapidamente percebemos que, se "...viajar / é ser penetrado pelo sempre presente / sentimento de coisas / precocemente duradouras" (134), então aquilo que desde logo invade o poeta, que imediatamente percepciona um tão vasto conteúdo num tão reduzido continente, "ó neste autocarro, um continente" (134), é a própria língua brasileira, enquanto expressão genuína do lugar (num certo sentido enquanto lugar) na sua tão clara diferença prosódica, lexical e sintáctica, em relação ao português padrão do poeta:

4

português quando chega compra garrafa,
compra e vende garrafa, logo
abre um barzinho no Rio.
o Brasil é uma coisa
genital...
japonês todo tem carro.
português quando chega,
já sabe do comércio
e de navio. (136)

A experiência do lugar é também uma experiência, sobretudo, mediada por referências a conhecidos textos da literatura brasileira—é o caso, por exemplo, da alusão a "No Meio do Caminho" de Carlos Drumond de Andrade, no poema 15; a *Iracema* de José de Alencar, no poema 21; a *Macunaíma* de Mário de Andrade, no poema 9 e a Jorge Amado em vários poemas. Esta tão recorrente dependência de outros textos, para uma caracterização de um determinado lugar, não só introduz particulares instabilidades na especificação do tipo de viagem que se deve supor, como toma o texto como o único espaço totalmente visitável e audível, onde felizmente, contudo, as coisas e os sentidos não são facilmente visíveis, porque sobretudo audíveis. Quer dizer, o texto constitui-se como lugar em que visitar e ver se desencontram. O poeta contraria, de certo modo, o nexo etimológico, pragmático e semântico que une visitar e ver, permitindo-se assim a acção de visitar, claramente positiva, sem que isso implique suportar a irritante visibilidade das coisas: "...não existe / coisa nenhuma que se não visite; / a pastilha do ar dá-nos o grito / certo no som, no gosto, no ruído; / já as coisas visíveis aborrecem" (277).

O tão firme percurso de negação e recusa do sentido adquire em livros como *A Pequena Face* (1983) uma autonomia que, no entanto, não dispensa a afirmação desse propósito logo no primeiro poema: "em silêncio me muro me demoro / no cálculo de rotas inexactas" (175). A indefinição e mistério da "pequena face" determinam diferentes possibilidades de consideração metonímica ou metafórica da expressão, que, muitas vezes, se afigura ser um oblíquo eufemismo da morte e, outras vezes, uma metáfora do exíguo rosto de um precursor, do poeta e até do poema, e inibe a atribuição de um sentido minimamente estável aos textos. Em poemas de metro irregular, mas geralmente breve, em que, por vezes e algo ironicamente, se evoca a forma convencionalmente assertiva do soneto, não se observa já a violência do recurso a estratégias de expansão e derivação lexical, na criação de ambientes semânticos tão improváveis que o sentido das palavras se impossibilita e cinde. Antes se acentua uma atenção a ritmos interiores ao próprio verso, marcados frequentemente por aliterações subtis, *enjambements* e rimas, internas e finais, que se percebem sempre retrospectivamente dada a sua imprevisibilidade: "a língua é vagarosa sabe / um sabor de saibro / então acontece pensar, é // uma corola, é o sol, é / um muito elementar milagre, / um favor exaltado" (223). Outras vezes, parece verificar-se o propósito de conjugar este rigor fonético e musical, que conduz o verso, com a visibilidade estritamente *grafemática* dos signos linguísticos, motivando-se, de certo modo, uma percepção mnemónica do espaço textual: "meu pouco amor de noitarder, de som / bra pequena em muramor, murmúrio, / meu corpo nu, meu cegamante" (215).

A compreensão de que, como tenho sustentado até aqui, pelo e no poema se pode chegar "ao campo aberto onde começa o escuro / passado dos sentidos" (281) não só contribui para um entendimento do poema como lugar da cegueira, da mudez e do vazio semânticos, situações de que julgo já ter dado exemplos suficientes, mas também para a consciência de que a existência nesse espaço, a que se chega por regressão e negação mnésica, só é possível se esse lugar for também o da sua transcendência.

Deste ponto de vista, a concepção do poema e da palavra, como lugar de vazio e de transcendência desse vazio, resulta, em Franco Alexandre, de uma espécie de consciência judaica do espaço. Não é por isso casual a referência e citação de poetas judaicos, em *Visitação* e *Moradas 1 & 2* e a presença constante dos *Salmos*, seja pela evocação de certos salmos, que é possível identificar com alguma certeza, seja pela recuperação de um ritmo e estrutura salmódicos. É o que penso acontecer neste poema de "Primeiras Moradas":

> estamos chamando, clamando, somos todos ouvidos
>
> para a tua boca de silêncio,
>
> poderíamos avançar se nos coubesse
>
> uma resposta, uma pergunta, a hesitação
>
> instantânea do gesto, quando armados
>
> erguemos o destino sobre as quatro paredes da terra.
>
> ...
>
> como julgas poder
>
> ficar mudo no escuro, amealhando a terra
>
> e o sopro dos ventos, como podes pensar
>
> que nos assusta o pequeno rumor da eternidade?
>
> Se nenhuma memória nos basta. Se estamos chamando, clamando,
>
> E em nossas mãos te levamos; tu nos levas. (296)

O modo como vejo esta consciência judaica do espaço corresponde a uma redescrição interior do significado da passagem e permanência no deserto e no desespero das perguntas sem resposta, que, sem abdicar do desejo pela Terra da Promessa, descobre que o lamento e a transcendência são possíveis e coincidentes, na ausência muda do Verbo e de quaisquer coordenadas. Transcender um determinado espaço denuncia, num certo sentido, a convicção última da inexistência de uma morada, de destinos e, portanto, da possibilidade de fazer coincidir no lugar, que se pretende transcender e que não é certamente um destino, todos os lugares, todas as moradas, o deserto e a Terra Prometida.

Este percurso pelo espaço ausente e árido dos sentidos, lugar de um despojamento ambicionado, mas a que corresponde também uma indefinição de um conteúdo ontológico e de um sentido teleológico da vida, assume proporções bíblicas e épicas no livro *Oásis* (1992), constituído aparentemente por um só poema.

Oásis é um poema pautado por uma estrutura em que se alterna a formulação de diferentes pedidos com a enunciação performativa e prospectiva de compromissos e promessas. Trata-se, portanto, da actualização de uma forma comum de oração, muito presente nos Salmos, por exemplo, onde coincidem a prece, a súplica, e a enunciação do propósito, resultante da aliança que entretanto se supõe ou lembra. Como, no entanto, é difícil, em *Oásis*, decidir se o sujeito que pede é o mesmo que promete, uma vez que muitas das estrofes em que se promete são delimitadas por aspas (é a voz de outro), é, pelo menos, legítimo especular que o mesmo *eu* que pede e promete corresponde, num certo sentido, a duas diferentes pessoas (ou mais), o que, não surpreendentemente, se enquadra nas consequências e efeitos ontológicos de determinados tipos de oração. Não é também fácil determinar, no contexto deste poema, a quem se pede e a quem se promete, tal como não é transparente quer o conteúdo do pedido quer a matéria da promessa, dada a extensão hiperbólica do pedido e da promessa. É como se o que fosse realmente importante fosse abstractamente pedir e prometer que, no entanto e deste ponto de vista, parecem ser actos falsos e infelizes de pedir e prometer e transformam o texto num exercício ilimitado de retórica.

Consideremos o acto de pedir, os seus eventuais destinatários e o que possivelmente se pede. Em primeiro lugar, em *Oásis*, há essencialmente dois tipos de pedido: o de se ser recebido e o de que ao *eu* seja dada qualquer coisa. São muitos os versos que começam e terminam, uma vez que um dos procedimentos formais mais utilizadas neste livro é o *enjambement*, por "recebe-me" e "dá-me" e justamente o poema começa por "recebe-me, coração espesso de sangue," (369) e termina com "...Ó dá-me, melodia, // A terra onde nasceu louvor E barro E céu / E a golfada de sangue que possua // O coração das folhas para sempre" (411). Quer dizer, enuncia-se o desejo de habitar um determinado espaço, de aí se ser recebido, e de, posteriormente, aí ser concedido algo ao poeta. Avaliar os lugares onde se quer e por quem se quer ser recebido poderá elucidar acerca dos espaços que se habitam e permitir previsões acerca do que se pretende. Além do verso já citado, temos, por exemplo: "Recebe-me // folha que o tempo dobra ao fim da tarde..." (369); "...recebe-me, alegria sem / idade de razão," (370); "recebe-nos, sangue embrulhado no papel,..." (371); "recebe-me / terra, toda imersa / no bafo da eternidade Aqui // reúne-nos em livro folha a folha / e pisa docemente nos meus sonhos / traduzidos a língua verdadeira" (383); "recebe-nos na sombra prometida" (383); "recebe-me / folha clara do ar / morada inteira" (384).

Interessantemente, em *Oásis*, a alternância entre pedidos e promessas de natureza tão abstracta, antitética e paradoxal é quebrada por versos que sugerem um errático percurso por Lisboa, sem qualquer sentido ou conexão lógica. Referem-se diferentes locais, como o "Sodré sem cais," Campolide, a Calçada do Combro, a Rua do Rosário, e portanto era como se se quisesse permitir a ilusão de que os locais, onde se pretende ser recebido, se encontram disponíveis no mundo do próprio sujeito que solicita a hospedagem. Este mundo, no entanto, parece ser vazio e branco, como sugere a referência arbitrária daqueles locais concretos e a recorrência da palavra "folha" neste poema. Em certos momentos, referem-se também outros lugares, percorridos heroicamente por Whitman nas folhas de *Leaves Of Grass*—Arizona, California, Mississippi, Louisiana—e a propensão é interpretá-los como destinos alternativos de uma existência poética. A ausência de coordenadas espaciais é de tal ordem que o sujeito, sem propósitos identificáveis, não sabe, ainda a muitas estrofes do fim de *Oásis*, quando termina ou deve terminar a viagem, "(ou será que cheguei ao fim da viagem?)" (389), como se, na realidade, fosse conduzido pelo poema e pelo espaço, mas não pela sua vontade.

Mas que viagem é realmente esta e que mundo é este? Já percebemos que o mundo é, num certo sentido, o mundo da poesia, o mundo enquanto poesia e a poesia enquanto mundo. Se assim for, então o percurso, que em *Oásis* se sugere, é um percurso por imagens poéticas disponíveis, existentes, num certo sentido, fora do sujeito e às quais o mesmo pretende aceder. É um percurso por folhas. Quer dizer, *Oásis* é um poema em que Franco Alexandre pretende definir a sua identidade poética e construi-la a partir de um vazio semântico a que, no entanto, só se chega por recusa e exposição do que nos forma enquanto voz, antes de reclamarmos a nossa identidade: "...vou correr velozmente // no aparelho da tromba luminosa, e esclarecer de vez / o nascimento, a morte, e o fim das / delicadas membranas que nos cobrem" (398).

Definir uma identidade poética ou pretender possui-la corresponde à percepção de que a identidade poética é uma coisa que não existe, i.e., é uma identidade que só existe enquanto usurpação da identidade dos outros. Essa usurpação pode disfarçar-se por um pedido ou denunciar uma aceitação sem quaisquer reservas, sem vergonha, uma identificação, uma metamorfose, uma confusão de identidades e perspectivas: "Acusador, ó companheiro já // comigo, pequena coisa, te confundes?" (57).

Ironicamente, em *Oásis*, o sujeito que solicita ser recebido é visitado, por quem aparentemente não se desejava ser recebido: "...um dia / visitou-me satã, em vestes condizentes; tratou // de mim como um igual, amavelmente. Inquéritos, já sabe, burocráticos, / enviados de além para recados, / coisas de gente boa, mas rupestre. Nós entretanto os dois // tão quietos ficamos, que nos tomam / por pedestais que esperam; depois / farão de nós os pedestais que espetam—esse é o ganho" (372-373). Quem pode ser este satã que visita o *eu* de *Oásis*, que o trata por igual e partilha o seu destino? Cesário Verde, um século antes de Franco Alexandre, insurgira-se num poema, sobre um passeio a Lisboa, que, "num recinto público e vulgar," estivesse vagamente esquecido num pilar "um épico doutrora," "Brônzeo, monumental, de proporções guerreiras" (*O Sentimento dum Ocidental*). Em *Oásis*, Franco Alexandre parece, ecoando Cesário, lamentar o destino de pedestal, de petrificada mudez e sustentação dos outros, do satã, que o visita e tem pelo menos dois nomes, Camões e Cesário Verde, e dele próprio, enquanto entidade poética que já pode ser tratada como igual. Percebe-se então que esta viagem caótica e alucinada, realizada em *Oásis,* é talvez uma viagem épica de confronto e identificação com dois poetas maiores da literatura portuguesa. Assumir e transcender o próprio lugar poético, que aqueles dois poetas permitem habitar, equivale tanto à sua citação sistemática (e, por exemplo, Camões ouve-se algumas vezes em *Oásis*), a fazer pedidos, a estabelecer pactos com este(s) diabo(s), como ao estabelecimento de alianças diferentes e ao desejo da sua derrogação definitiva, da sua expulsão: "...Fecho // a porta com selo e baba de palavras esgueiras-te / na multidão silenciosa enrodilhado de folhas sem sequer / um aceno a enxofre Cansei-te / cansaste-te de mim velha canção // vencite? nada ficará da viagem a dois pelas ruelas de lisboa" (397).

Este modo tão estranho de, tendo sido visitado (não só por Camões e Cesário), ter sido recebido e acompanhado nesta viagem ao inferno, que é aliás o único sítio poeticamente habitável é, no entanto, mais perene do que a ilusão da separação ou da vitória de uma das partes, que se suspeita nos versos que acabei de citar. É que, se é verdade que, depois da suposta separação, se diz "vou inventar o outro lado de todas estas folhas que caem" (397), os pedidos continuam, no entanto, a realizar-se: "Dá-me por esta noite a carne escura do poema / a canção junto ao muro que separa / as águas" (399) e a consciência (melancólica) de que é no poema que tudo se perde faz-se ouvir sempre: "...vejo / que neste mapa te perco, / que nesta vida, somente, te perco, no meio de cada verso" (400). Aquilo que se promete, aquilo que se vai fazer, denunciará sempre a consciência de uma dívida em relação a quem se pediram coisas, e a existência "livre, num arizona descarnado," só parece possível "com a memória destes panos que uma sombra estremece" (399). Proclamar religiosamente "...Ó seja // teu louvor no lábio do trombone, meu senhor Adonai" (406) não corresponde ao estabelecimento de uma fidelidade poética, que impeça todas as infidelidades e oblitere relacionamentos anteriores, uma vez que "— enquanto a mão direita ajeita a nota certa, a esquerda a contramão / insolente e ligeira—infiel a toda imagem—apontará, no vento, / o buraco vazio da tua face!" (407). É por isso que, mesmo que o sujeito dessa dívida já tenha sofrido várias metamorfoses e seja já parte integrante do *eu*, mesmo que não tenha nomes e seja uma "canção," continua a ser à "melodia" a quem se pede "a golfada de sangue," que anima o próprio poeta, e possui "O coração das folhas para sempre" (411). Como diz Harold Bloom de uma outra forma:

> A negação do precursor nunca é possível, já que nenhum efebo pode permitir-se ceder, mesmo que por um momento, à pulsão de morte. Com efeito, a divinação poética visa a imortalidade literal, e todo o poema pode ser definido como um evitar de uma morte possível. (118)

Se *Oásis* é um sublime exercício de ocultação e identificação poéticas, que contribuem para a definição de uma identidade, contra um vazio espaço semântico que se procurou, quase com o propósito de se transcender, então não é surpreendente que, no livro que se segue a *Oásis*, não só pela primeira vez Franco Alexandre nos queira contar histórias, como essas histórias se digam resultantes de caprichos. De facto, em *Quatro Caprichos* (1999), encontramos quatro histórias que, de imediato, estabelecem uma clara diferença com a produção poética anterior, pelo facto de serem habitadas por corpos (não diria propriamente personagens) que supostamente fazem coisas e têm uma voz. Estas histórias são: "le tiers exclu, fantasia política"—uma narrativa, na primeira pessoa, de uma só estrofe, em que dilemas e descobertas morais, políticas e ontológicas, se devem a circunstanciais escolhas espaciais—"corto viaggio sentimentale, capriccio italiano," constituído por trinta e nove pequenos poemas, onde o impulso sentimental determina a possibilidade de metamorfose irrestrita do poeta—"rosencrantz, episódio dramático," uma estrutura narrativa, de uma só estrofe, em que se arquitectam modos de dissolução dos corpos na vertigem das suas virtualidades dramáticas e da sua existência linguística—"syrinx, ficção pastoral," ficção lírica para duas vozes, um cliente e um prostituto, tipograficamente diferenciadas por duas cores: dez poemas a negro e dez poemas a azul.

Na impossibilidade óbvia de comentar minuciosamente cada uma destas histórias, torna-se, no entanto, imperativa a referência a um aspecto essencial que julgo não só constituir um núcleo de sentido comum aos poemas de *Quatro Caprichos* como também aos poemas de *Uma Fábula*, o último livro de Franco Alexandre.

Correndo o risco de ser inconsequente e estar errado, penso que uma das questões fundamentais de *Quatro Caprichos* reside no modo tão abrupto como o problema da identidade e diferença, que, em última análise, confere substância à crença na existência de mim mesmo e dos outros, é anulado pela consciência de que, no processo linguístico e poético de identificação e distinção, tudo o que nos pode acontecer são metamorfoses.

De facto, o mundo das histórias de *Quatro Caprichos* é composto por seres cuja existência intermitente se manifesta em sistemáticas descontinuidades ontológicas, não necessariamente morfológicas. Estas descontinuidades são, num certo sentido, resultantes da própria linguagem e preservadas por ela, sob a forma de registo ou rasto de uma série de transformações. O signo linguístico é uma espécie de prosopopeia ilimitada, que suplementa a morte e revela o aparecimento do mundo, sucessivos e quase simultâneos. Como tão enfaticamente se diz em "le tiers éxclu: fantasia política":

quase invisível de tão transparente! o mundo

não cessa de nascer, de aparecer e desaparecer

no meio das mais inúteis palavras, transforma-se

o corpo dos amantes nas palavras amantes inúteis,

transforma-se o corpo de B. no amor a todas

as coisas amantes amadas, e esta é

a minha certeza, a minha verdade, a minha virtude teologal. (25)

Por exemplo, as personagens do primeiro e terceiro poemas de *Quatro Caprichos* são apresentadas por iniciais, A., B. e G., W., cuja utilização não denuncia essencialmente o pudor de uma exposição lírica ou de uma revelação "biográfica," mas sobretudo, penso eu, uma amnésia, uma impossibilidade em relação à atribuição do ser. Um nome próprio tornaria eventualmente mais visível a identidade, uma inicial é a disponibilidade insignificante de um continente informe, inútil, um *grafema*, aberto a quaisquer ou nenhumas possibilidades ontológicas, sempre provisórias: "Na memória do corpo de G. havia a memória / de todas as coisas, de todos os seres" (58). Justamente G., o corpo indefinido e infinito de G.—pelo qual o director do grupo de teatro do liceu F. e treinador da equipa de basket do mesmo liceu, embora "demasiado incompetente para uma e para outra" (53), supostamente se apaixona—sucumbe, repete-se, é parasitado e renasce sistematicamente no vórtice da sua iterabilidade linguística e das suas potencialidades dramáticas. Estas virtualidades de G., do "corpo de G.," incluem representar o Hamlet e a Ofélia de *Hamlet* ao mesmo tempo e em todos os lugares; ser amado, num único acto de amor, "com o amor do Hamlet de G. e com o amor da Ofélia de G. / e com o amor de G. pelo corpo do Hamlet de G. / e com o amor de G. pelo corpo da Ofélia de G. / e com o amor de todas as pessoas humanas" (58); ser objecto do deslumbramento dos "jovens actores" que "devoram o corpo de G. 'deslumbrante'" (60) e "transformam a morte de G. no corpo de G., transformam / o corpo de G. na morte de G. no corpo / dos jovens actores" (61).

Estes instantâneos dos corpos, com uma possibilidade, ilimitada e não selectiva, de ser qualquer ser, são tão rápidos quanto o acender e apagar frenético das "luzes psico-analíticas, as radiações laser, / as esferas estroboscópicas que apagavam e acendiam" (54) nem sequer as faces ou os corpos, mas o casulo ou pele de virtualidades irrestritas e insuspeitas que os contém e alimenta, i.e., "o fantástico desenho da minha t-shirt / acabada de estrear, do bar *Solaris*" (54). No entanto, como também seria de prever, esta "*t*-shirt de fantástica fantasia" (53, itálico meu) é perdida "na lavandaria automática, entre outra roupa suja" (54), dias depois. No mundo de "rosencrantz, episódio dramático," a que pertence a história de G., não há surpresas e, portanto, não há a certeza de haver pensamentos—são as luzes que são "psico-analíticas"—uma vez que não há a consciência (surpresa) de conteúdos mentais anteriores e diferentes:[5] "Espantar não me espantava, ver agora / o corpo de G. junto ao balcão do *Solaris*, na véspera / do primeiro treino de basket, da primeira aula de teatro" (57). Na "coincidência espacial do ginásio e do palco" (60), que é o mundo inteiro, os corpos andróginos são tão ilimitados, na aprendizagem simultânea de basket e de teatro, na interpretação perfeita e deslumbrante das suas competências que, na consciência de quem os vê aparecer e desaparecer e apresenta, não causam qualquer surpresa. Os corpos valem enquanto objectos de revelações e epifanias constantes, mas sempre relativamente iguais, aparecem e desaparecem, sem restrições espaciais e temporais, apenas arquitectónicas, quer dizer, fruto de "decisões" administrativas e técnicas[6] de quem termina por nos dizer que anda a ler o clássico "Espaço, Tempo, Arquitectura" (62).

Aparentemente, tanto em "rosencrantz, episódio dramático" como em "le tiers exclu, fantasia política," as epifanias dos corpos saturados de ser, e por isso despojados de uma identidade e de uma história constituída por factos passíveis de alinhar num eixo sintagmático, contribuem para uma espécie de compensação epistemológica e ontológica do narrador do episódio e da fantasia, que se encontra inicialmente numa posição desfavorável. "Rosencrantz," o jovem inexperiente e incompetente treinador de teatro e director de basket, aproxima-se do corpo de G., "com a hesitação e com a insolência de um encenador / jovem e inexperiente" (54), realiza uma digressão "pelos palcos e arenas e estádios do mundo" (61), é aclamado e termina, "à espera de G., que mais uma vez se atrasara / em campo de ourique, na livraria desportiva" (62), proferindo displicentemente: "Dias depois, desinteressei-me do teatro" (62).

Com o "corpo de emigrante mal vestido" (17) e morada nos subúrbios, A., o narrador do primeiro capricho, embora admita que "seria diferente e fácil o curso da minha vida / se tivesse, esse dia, essa noite, virado à direita / como era norma!"(25), confessa que, exactamente porque não virou à direita, se reconhece a si mesmo em cada um dos corpos da sua história. Se tivesse voltado à direita, diz A. que:

> visitaria o mártir no museu, fechado, *des Augustins,*
> sem me reconhecer. Encontraria B.
> numa esplanada da praça Wilson,
> sem me reconhecer. Encontraria, outra vez, o homem
> suíço menos jovem, teólogo, sem me reconhecer.
> Encontraria A., o amigo talvez inocente de B.,
> sem me reconhecer. Encontraria o corpo de B.,

> encontraria a nudez do corpo de B. no meu corpo,
>
> sem me reconhecer. (25)

Ao contrário do homem todo inteiro, "aberto só na mesa final" (25), A. é uma espécie de transposição gráfica homoerótica da imagem do "mártir varado de flechas" (16), S. Sebastião, do "museu *des Augustins*." Atravessado, penetrado anatomicamente por todos os seres, cheio de cicatrizes e assinaturas e, assim, esvaziado de si mesmo, A. é um mártir de textos. (Aos olhos de A., B. pode, por isso, "transformar-se / num pedaço cortado do seu corpo emigrante, / isto é, numa víscera, um rim suplementar!" (21), ser um excerto da autobiografia de A.)

"Le tiers exclu, fantasia política" é assim uma história que, expondo alguns índices, conducentes a uma leitura autobiográfica—desde logo a identificação da inicial A. com o nome do poeta—demonstra a impossibilidade narrativa de toda a autobiografia, a sua vacuidade enquanto texto que contribui para o estabelecimento de uma entidade autónoma e coerente, i.e., "the impossibility of closure and of totalization (that is the impossibility of coming into being) of all textual systems made up of tropological substitutions" (de Man, "Autobiography" 71).

Tudo indica que, em *Quatro Caprichos*, não se acredita que o amor e a arte resgatem os seres "sem família," que povoam estes caprichos, da perda de ser, da metamorfose e do cepticismo, embora não se perceba se isto é necessariamente mau. Quer dizer, embora, como diz Américo A. Lindeza Diogo, o amor se afaste das "exigências e desapontamentos do cepticismo" (*Sem Família* 22), o contacto dos corpos faz-se pela "imaginação" e pelo toque equívoco das "línguas": "não havendo limite ao que podemos / imaginar, as bocas facilmente se tocam / e duas diferentes línguas se / respondem, con dolce violenza" (*Quatro Caprichos* 31). Como julgo poder concluir-se de "corto viaggio sentimentale, capriccio italiano," o amor realiza-se por uma espécie de inconsciência adolescente e "sem razão" (34), de distracção, de cuidado em relação ao corpo amado, do qual nada se quer, porque nada há a querer, nada se pode querer, uma vez que isso implica o seu desaparecimento, a sua redução fantasmática e destino de candidato a prosopopeia. Incompatível com a preservação da alteridade do outro, da diferença, o amor não se quer realizar e, portanto, aquilo que possivelmente morre, mesmo antes de acontecer, "há-de tudo morrer sem nunca / ter acontecido?" (36) é o desejo que se centra nos sujeitos e não pode ser liberto: "...Lembrei-me / como gritava, como havia grades contra a boca quando / gritava o lume animal" (33); "e só aconteceu o desejo do lume." Daí que, na realidade, o amor seja uma *performance* dramática de uma personagem que se monta e desmonta—"serei eu, fantasia, outro pessoa, novo / amável montale desmontável? / e tu existirás de facto, na manhã mais fria? / assim nos enganamos, nos engana / a verdade que em lume nos desata" (39)— ou se especializa na arte do travestimento, "mi travesto ancora. Vou dividido" (17), "já também desta imagem me separo" (44). Na indecisão que se joga entre ser este um amor narcísico, que não se dá porque não há ninguém a quem se dar, ou um sacrifício e artifício do desejo para preservar a existência do outro, que cria dentro de si mesmo, intocada do sentimento, localiza-se a angústia e a solidão do(s) amante(s).

Em "Syrinx, ficção pastoral," o último dos caprichos, a observância fria das leis do mercado e a imunidade sentimental salvaguardam a higiene do coração mas, como são falíveis e utilizadas como pretextos de aprendizagem poética e musical, não subtraem também, os que se envolvem no processo comercial, da metamorfose amorosa e estética, que anula as suas existências mercantilistas. Um suposto Pã, cliente heróico e presunçoso, põe anúncio no jornal "pedindo carne fresca pouco atlética / e nobres sentimentos de paixão" (64). Como seria de esperar, os seus propósitos não são apenas os do amor de ocasião e do desejo, mas os de pretender assegurar uma certeza quanto à sua existência: "E espero ao telefone que me digam / se sou feliz, real, ou simplesmente / uma espuma de cinza em muitas mãos" (64). Obtém-se a resposta de um quase Syrinx, prostituto que tem debaixo do colchão "o coração mais limpo desta terra" (65), mas que não sabe qual é o corpo com que cada dia acorda, "Acordo cada dia com um corpo / que não aquele com que me deitei" (65). Rapidamente percebemos que os objectivos de Pã não correspondem às respostas do produto e às expectativas deste. Surpreendido por ter ficado "preso à voz / não sei de quem, que me ouvia" (66), no outro lado do telefone, Pã mais surpreso fica quando descobre que o desejo e o amor rompem o cinismo do contrato, que já não tem coragem de anular, embora lhe tenha cabido um "caso problema que se droga e vende / e tem de todo errada a identidade" (74) e é capaz de lhe negar a existência e tirar tudo o que tem. De facto, Syrinx gere habilmente os seus interesses musicais e compromissos profissionais, continua a guardar "o coração em sítio seco / e fresco, e longe das palavras" (79) e a "vender, comprar, trocar, a vida toda acesa" (65), no único espaço provável tanto da inexistência de Pã como de Syrinx, "ali além das pontes." Mas a recusa de Syrinx dura apenas o tempo que a aprendizagem da plenitude do canto poético exige. Mais do que o amor de Pã é o que Pã ensina, "Já tudo te ensinei" (82), que despoja Syrynx de si, enquanto prostituto cínico e aprendiz de poeta. O novo ser estético, resultante do amplexo entre o amor, o cinismo comercial e a educação artística, parece, curiosamente, mais humano, mas sem ninguém para dialogar:

> Um sopro humano, a boca, um coração,
> me tocam e alimentam, como antes
> águas de chuva no lazer do pântano
> quando o vento passava nos pinhais;
> sou teu igual, não mais, e no meu corpo
> inteiramente novo é que perdura
> a liberdade, glória do teu canto.
> Desejo meu, em tua sede habito;
> meu mestre, escravo, amante, pois servimos
> no mesmo chão o mesmo antigo lume. (83)

Se este comentário for plausível, o que os poemas de *Quatro Caprichos* e também de uma *Uma fábula*, que a extensão de este ensaio proíbe comentar, colocam em questão é, num certo sentido, a possibilidade de se pensar o problema da identidade pessoal e da existência dos outros, na impossibilidade de ver os outros fora de mim mesmo. Para Franco Alexandre, metamorfosear-se, transformar-se e reconhecer-se múltiplo não correspondem necessariamente, penso eu, a uma ilusão de omnisciência por parte do poeta, a uma progressão para um posicionamento mais dramático do que lírico ou a uma espécie de osmose cósmica, em nome da poesia. O que se passa é a silenciosa consciência de uma solidão e de um cepticismo que irrompe da sistemática tentativa do sujeito querer acreditar que não está só e que os outros existem e lhe devolvem uma consciência da sua própria existência. Como se pode realmente ter uma certeza de si próprio se cada vez que se espera do outro uma confirmação, se espera poder dizer "tu," se reconhece que esse outro não é autónomo ou diferente e, portanto, num certo sentido, é impossível dizer "eu"? Que certeza posso ter de mim se a cada momento sinto que sou outro? Como se pode amar, realizar a vontade de amar, se o objecto do amor se reduz e apenas se deixa traduzir nas palavras de desejo de quem ama, não possuindo identidade ou sequer as marcas de um rosto?:

Não tinhas, reparei, 'identidade.' Faltarate, ou perderas,

identikit, umbigo de fabrico, carte de séjour; só ficaram

as marcas distintivas de um humano rosto, e depois

também elas se apagaram ou multiplicaram

nos humanos gestos amados, e na cegueira

do humano desejo desejado, da palavra "tu."

Como posso agora começar a falar-te? Ninguém

melhor conhece o amor, e o desprezo do amor. (*Uma Fábula* 57)

Como não pensar que a poesia seja uma fábula, uma pequena conversa privada, sem certeza de resposta e possíveis efeitos e, se assim for, como ter a certeza de que as palavras realmente possuem sentido? Talvez a certeza de existirmos e o amor não sejam compatíveis com "a serradura memorial, dísticos, lápides" (69), as palavras que apenas nos deixam habitar os textos como fantasmas e espíritos.[7]

Notas

[1] Foi utilizada a antologia *Poemas* (1996) sempre que se citaram passagens dos primeiros seis livros do poeta e de outros poemas aí reunidos inéditos ou publicados previamente. Nas indicações das obras citadas aparece, no entanto, a referência bibliográfica da primeira edição dessas obras, caso tenha havido uma, e as páginas que ocupam em *Poemas.*

[2] Em momentos pontuais deste ensaio utilizo, como meus, alguns termos empregues por Derrida no ensaio "Signature Évévenement Contexte" (1972), por exemplo, iterabilidade e *grafema.* Embora pense que a compreensão suficiente destes conceitos e os propósitos deste ensaio não exigem um comentário do léxico e dos argumentos de Derrida, cito duas passagens, que podem denotar minimamente a sua argumentação e esclarecer o significado daqueles termos: "Cette possibilité structurelle d'être sevrée du référent ou du signifié (donc de la communication et de son contexte) me paraît faire de toute marque, fût-elle orale, un graphème en général, c'est-à-dire,... la *restance* non-présente d'une marque différentielle coupée de sa prétendue 'production' ou origine" (378); "Cela ne suppose pas que la marque vaut hors contexte, mais au contraire qu'il n'y a que des contextes sans aucun centre d'ancrage absolu. Cette citationnalité, cette duplication ou duplicité, cette itérabilité de la marque n'est pas un accident ou une anomalie..."(381).

[3] Refiro-me aqui a um dos processos responsáveis pela produção do texto, segundo Riffaterre em *Sémiotique de la poésie* (1978; tradução francesa, 1983): "L'expansion transforme les constituants de la phrase matrice en formes plus complexes" (68). Riffaterre considera que a passagem da mimese à semiótica se opera por uma necessária suspensão das considerações referenciais relativamente à poesia, em virtude das agramaticalidades referenciais que o texto manifesta e que perturbam a nossa presunção de referência. Perante uma agramaticalidade, do ponto de vista mimético, verifica-se um esclarecedor impasse interpretativo que implica o abandono da convicção de que, no poema, se assiste a uma relação entre as palavras e um estado de coisas e permite a descoberta de que afinal o que se observa é uma rede semiótica de relações entre signos. Assim, o texto progride por expansão e ou conversão dos seus próprios dados

textuais, próprios ou alheios, e não por constrangimentos de natureza referencial. O poema é, última análise, um *continuum* de tautologias, paradoxos e paráfrases. São conhecidas as objecções a este modelo de criação poética e também de leitura. As mais pertinentes encontram-se em Paul De Man, em "Hipograma e Inscrição" de *A Resistência à Teoria* (1989), que assinala a confiança inabalável de Riffaterre na descoberta e decifração dos dados textuais de base que permitem a progressão do texto e, portanto, na crença das virtualidades cognitivas e epistemológicas da linguagem e da interpretação. Riffaterre parece confirmar de facto a objecção de De Man, quando numa frase infeliz diz o seguinte: "...la poésie doit défier toute interprétation, mais ce n'est qu'un défi d'un instant" (204).

⁴ Por exemplo, além dos já citados Gastão Cruz e F. Pinto do Amaral, considere-se Óscar Lopes em *As Cifras do Tempo* em que se diz o seguinte: "Os seus poemas (e as suas *palavras* ou *nomes*) pretendem fazer sentir, não um sentido mas como que um fugaz pré-sentido, ou pré-percepção, um breve *indício de sentido*, talvez um mero (ou mesmo *nenhum*) *sopro* ou voz.... Há como que o pudor ou repugnância de tudo quanto apareça viscosamente dotado de sentido, ou como razão..." (326). Este modo de existir da linguagem poética de Franco Alexandre encontra assim, segundo Óscar Lopes, na lítotes ou subasserção o seu procedimento estilístico mais privilegiado.

⁵ Este é um argumento que D. Davidson apresenta e desenvolve em "Rational Animals," *Dialectica* 36, 1982. 318-327.

⁶ Um arquitecto é na Atenas clássica tanto um desenhador e construtor de edifícios como um administrador do teatro.

⁷ Esta nota constitui uma adenda deficiente acerca do que, entretanto, importante se passou, relacionado com António Franco Alexandre. Dois livros novos foram publicados pelo autor: *Duende* (Lisboa: Assírio & Alvim, 2002), que recebeu o Prémio de Poesia D. Dinis da Casa de Mateus, e *Aracne* (Lisboa: Assírio & Alvim, 2004). Correndo o risco de uma leitura necessariamente apressada, diria que em ambos são explorados os dois tópicos essenciais da poesia de António Franco Alexandre, depois de "Syrinx, ficção pastoral," o quarto poema de *Quatro Caprichos*, a saber: o exercício da ficção amorosa como correspondente à arte de aquisição de uma voz poética, que aproxima o poeta da lírica camoniana; a exploração do mistério da metamorfose como algo operado pela teia textual, na qual talvez se pretenda enredar o principal objecto do sentimento amoroso, i.e., o leitor: "Gregor transformou-se em barata gigante. / eu não: fiz-me aranhiço, / tão leve que uma leve brisa o faz / oscilar no seu fio de baba lisa. / Até que, contra a lei da natureza, / creio que tenho peso negativo, / e me elevo no ar se me não prendo / ao canto mais escuro desta ilha. / Quando descer à teia derradeira / não se verá no mundo alteração, ou só / talvez alguma mosca mais contente. / Em noites de luar, na alta esquina, / ficará a brilhar, mas sem ser vista, / a estrela que tracei como armadilha" (*Aracne* 7).

Obras Citadas

Alexandre, A. Franco. *Sem Palavras Nem Coisas.* Lisboa: Iniciativas Editoriais, 1974. *Poemas.* 7-68.

———. "Relatório Um." *Nova* 1 (1975-76). *Poemas.* 69-75.

———. *Os Objectos Principais.* Coimbra: Centelha, 1979. *Poemas.* 76-119.

———. *Visitação.* Porto: Gota de Água, 1983. *Poemas.* 121-66.

———. *A Pequena Face.* Lisboa: Assírio & Alvim, 1983. *Poemas.* 171-236.

———. "Dos Jogos De Inverno." *Poemas.* 237-70.

———. *As Moradas 1& 2.* Lisboa: Assírio & Alvim, 1987. *Poemas.* 271-342.

———. "As Terceiras Moradas." *Poemas.* 343-66.

———. *Oásis.* Lisboa: Assírio & Alvim, 1992. *Poemas.* 367-411.

———. *Poemas.* Lisboa: Assírio & Alvim, 1996.

———. *Quatro Caprichos.* Lisboa: Assírio & Alvim, 1999.

———. *Uma Fábula.* Lisboa: Assírio & Alvim, 2001.

Amaral, Fernando Pinto Do. *O Mosaico Fluido—Modernidade E Pós-Modernidade Na Poesia Portuguesa Mais Recente.* Lisboa: Assírio & Alvim, 1991.

———. "O Regresso ao Sentido Anos 70 / 80." *A Phala—Um Século De Poesia.* Lisboa: Assírio & Alvim, 1988. 159-67.

Bloom, Harold. *A Angústia da Influência—Uma Teoria Da Poesia.* Trans. Miguel Tamen. Lisboa: Cotovia, 1991.

Cavell, Stanley. *Disowning Knowledge In Six Plays Of Shakespeare.* Cambridge: Cambridge UP, 1987.

Cruz, Gastão. *A Poesia Portuguesa De Hoje.* Lisboa: Relógio de Água, 1999.

Derrida, Jacques. "Signature Événement Contexte." *Marges De La Philosophie.* Paris: Minuit, 1972. 365-93.

Diogo, Américo António Lindeza. *Modernismos, Pós-Modernismos, Anacronismos.* Lisboa: Edições Cosmos, 1993.

———. "Sem Família—Sobre *Quatro Caprichos.* De António Franco Alexandre." *Ave Azul* 4, 2000/2001. 15-31.

Lopes, Óscar. *As Cifras do Tempo.* Lisboa: Caminho, 1990.

———. "Alguns Nexos Diacrónicos Na Poesia Novecentista Portuguesa." *A Phala—Um Século De Poesia.* Lisboa: Assírio & Alvim, 1988. 208-23.

Magalhães, Joaquim Manuel. *Os Dois Crepúsculos.* Lisboa: A Regra do Jogo, Edições, 1981.

———. "António Franco Alexandre, As Moradas 1 & 2, Assírio & Alvim, Lisboa, 1987." *As Escadas Não Têm Degraus* 1. 1989. 155-61.

Man, Paul De. "Autobiography As De-Facement". *The Rhetoric Of Romanticism.* New York: Columbia UP, 1984. 67-81.

Riffaterre, Michael. *Sémiotique De La Poésie.* Trans. par Jean-Jacques Thomas. Paris: Éditions du Seuil, 1983.

David Antunes licenciou-se em Línguas e Literaturas Modernas, Estudos Portugueses, na Faculdade de Letras da Universidade Clássica de Lisboa, onde obteve também o grau de Mestre (1996) e de Doutor (2003) em Teoria da Literatura. É professor adjunto de dramaturgia no Departamento de Teatro da Escola Superior de Teatro e Cinema. Publicou vários artigos sobre poesia, filosofia e teatro; traduziu para Português *Friends Of Interpretable Objects*, de Miguel Tamen (Harvard UP, 2001) e é autor de *A Magnanimidade da Teoria* que se encontra no prelo (Assírio & Alvim, 2005). Trabalha regularmente na dramaturgia de espectáculos. Email: nevesnanet@netcabo.pt

Between Time and Heaven: The Mysterious Laws
of João Miguel Fernandes Jorge's Poetry

Carlos Veloso

Abstract. The poetry of João Miguel Fernandes Jorge is a continuous attempt to grasp the spirit of the place: a poem is what is retained by the poet after his travels around the world. Avoiding the trap of simply describing his journeys, the poet creates images that reshape historical and geographic realities, that is to say, in his own poems he goes beyond his mere physical presence in a place to find the mysterious laws of poetry. In his poems, he builds homes for the gods so that they will strengthen his words and images. Since the gods know the mysteries that poets want to translate into poetry, the poet follows them, enters the deep sea, searches among ruins, overhears enigmatic dialogues, and travels around the world like an ancient oarsman.

Sometimes we read a poem and are astonished by its clarity, its familiar tone, by the straightforward logic that pervades it. There is a four-line poem by the Portuguese poet João Miguel Fernandes Jorge (born in 1943) that seems to follow this *raison d'être*:

"Where would you like to die?"
"In Venice, like Pound."

And now how can I write a poem
after this story?

Portuguese Literary & Cultural Studies 7 (2008): 147-71.

The dialogue appears so trivial that we are not immediately aware that it hides a much more profound question: how can we choose the place of our death? Is death something we choose, like we choose a poet from the bookcase to read at night? Is death a catalogue that we can use to choose a place to die, so that we may answer "in Lisbon," like Pessoa, "in New York," like Whitman, or at "Field Place, Sussex," like Shelley? The singularity of this poem is that a place is the place of poetry and that the death of Pound enhances Venice as a place. Who is supposed to be the chronicler of such a trivial wish? An anonymous passerby who aspires to be eternally connected to Venice and poetry? The answer most certainly is: the poet himself. The poet is the ghostlike being whose function it is to overhear the dialogues hovering about him. Sometimes we have the impression, as we have in this case, that the inquiry coincides with the poem—what is the point of knowing how to start a poem when the poem is already written? The poem is half-written as soon as the poet eavesdrops on a conversation, or when he has a conversation with someone he does not bother to identify. These beginnings or starting points are the crucial elements of Fernandes Jorge's *ars poetica,* and so the poem revolves around names, places, and more or less cryptic stories.

The cryptic tone of this poem is conveyed by its title: "Antonello." Another name. Antonello, a famous Italian painter (1430-1479), was not from Venice. Neither was Pound. Antonello, however, did not die in Venice. What mysterious law is the word "Antonello" supposed to reveal? One thing is certain: the mystery of the title matches the subject matter of the poem. For now we have to divine the spirit that connects these bodies or parts. Antonello was from Massina, in Sicily. Pound was from Hailey, Idaho. Fernandes Jorge is from Bombarral, Portugal. There are two important places that link these three figures: Venice, on the one hand, and the poem whose title is "Antonello." The Italian painter spent some years in Venice and influenced the development of Venetian painting. Pound died in that Italian city, adding his poetic *persona* to that already mythical place. As for the Portuguese poet, he tries to overcome his belatedness by uniting his name and poetry both with those two monumental figures and with the history of Venice. Antonello impressed the Venetians with his artistic virtuosity, by creating forms with color rather than with the usual lines. Fernandes Jorge tries to grasp or evoke the place enriched by the painter and the American poet. His virtue lies in his poem and the fact that he seemed to be in the right place at the right time. In this sense, "Where would you like to die? / In Venice, like

Pound" is for him what "In the room women come and go / talking about Michelangelo" was for Eliot. Like Eliot, he was there to capture the dialogue or invent more or less frivolous characters, that is to say, to impress by means of his poetic virtuosity. If Eliot imitated Laforgue, Fernandes Jorge imitates the spirit of the place.

As a poem as short as "Antonello" shows, Fernandes Jorge's oeuvre is a sort of poetic palimpsest, to the extent that he assembles his work over the already trodden path of other minds. More properly, a poem is made of names and places that acquire a particular meaning because they are evoked by the poet, because it is the poet who sees everything. It is his point of view that exerts a pull on the images and reshapes historical and geographic realities. A poem is, therefore, an overlapping of figures and places; it is what is retained by the poet after his travels around the world, after avoiding the trap of simply describing his journeys. The work of the poet consists in going beyond his mere physical presence in a place. This is, furthermore, his fate, as he confesses in another poem ("Chronicle, chapter III"):

> [...] And we are nevertheless condemned
> to live forever beyond our existence
> and the mobile reasons of the kingdom.
> We are condemned
>
> as it would be useless to put up doors to contain the sea.
> ....
> We have a body and we are not body
> a soul a freedom and we are not soul
> or freedom. All of this is body soul freedom
> and what we invent discover defend.

Although Pound died in Venice, even there he too was condemned to live beyond his existence, that is to say, in poetry. Both Pound and Antonello were condemned to live in Fernandes Jorge's poetry—the latter's freedom, or fate, is to invent a situation that becomes a poem, the discovery of a place where he is able to defend the existence of a dead painter and a dead poet beyond the fact of their existence.

The poet travels and by doing that he establishes his own place. Between what is hidden to him and what he exposes, there is the place of poetry. As

Almada Negreiros affirmed, man "was condemned to Poetry. He was condemned to create his own place. His 'where.'" In effect, Fernandes Jorge's magic place, from "where" he discovers and invents, may sometimes be an anonymous hotel room, but his place par excellence is at an ordinary table in a coffee shop from where he sees uncountable solitary men who become the privileged interlocutors of his vagueness of thought. From coffee shop to coffee shop, the poet intertwines the reality of his inner nature, always in motion, always creating news and unexpected paths, with the reality he sees in front of him. Seated on a chair, he broods over his youth while he flips through a newspaper or plays with a piece of lemon peel in his fingers as he observes other customers. This Epicurean-like attitude, as it were, is one of the central elements of his poetic travels, for, as he acknowledges, "I am the one who leaves and is always / happy / only because I can put my hands on the table in a coffee shop" ("Olcott Hotel, 8").

His dreams, his inventions are, consequently, the point of view of his spirit, although it is important to point out that the oneiric part of his poetry is nothing but the amalgamation of chunks of reality. So, when the poet travels, he searches for the meaning of his displacement—everything he sees, experiences, or reads is hidden in a dream-like penumbra, as we can see in the opening dialogue in "Antonello." His task is to reconcile the banality of reality with the (imaginary or real) heroes that haunt the place he visits. It goes without saying that both this reconfiguration and the revisitation of the cultural past only occur when the poet asks himself how he can write a poem with this material. There is a daydream-like atmosphere that makes him jump from one place to another, stranger place, but the dream, the mental wandering, is deeply rooted in reality. In Fernandes Jorge's poetry, there is too much reality. I venture to say that, for him, dreams are an intrinsic part of reality, all the more so because he is able to look at his dreams from the outside or, as he says in "Twelve Nocturnes of Ceuta, 3": "I always liked to see the way dreams function." All things considered, the poem may be permeated by relatively obscure references, but there is always a hint—a word, a sentence, a name—that permits us to elaborate on it. The poem may take us to winding roads and African nights, to impossible dreams, but it always brings us back to our daily reality. It brings together geographically, culturally, and historically shadowy regions; yet, those experiences are used to test the reality of the place that the poet uses as a point of departure. This poetry superimposes matter-of-fact and mysterious elements, and that is the reason why the poet lives beyond his existence, for his poetry articulates mutations and events that go beyond his kingdom, worlds that are dispersed within his mind. We, too, are invited to discover those places, and our guides are the suggestions and the reverberations we find in the poem, that is, the "secret voice" that travels with "the boat that came from Persia / loaded with odors / and touched the ruin of the earth" ("The Place of the Well, XVII").

The boats from Persia are the sentences the poet writes, with more or less legitimacy, in the middle of the night in a hotel room. In the morning, some of those sentences may form a poem. This experience is described in poem XXV of "The Place of the Well":

When one night you told me

I was a lost soul

because I only dreamt of Autumn

leaves and the tumult of voices

from times forgotten and an echo carried me

to abandoned senses, to gloomy rooms and

to a sea of ruins

then I understood the heart of an errant

who cannot hate and goes on

after walking for days without

catching even the glimpse of the shadow of a tree, goes on

castaway

singing hurt rhymes of love.

This is Fernandes Jorge's ars poetica par excellence. It is an enigmatic dialogue between the poet and someone else, an interlocutor who frequently appears in his poems. This doppelganger does not have a name, remaining anonymously in the shadows, as if he were an invention of the poet himself, another imaginary element arising from the poem, that is to say, from the poet's wanderings. The night covers both the dreams and the echoes that take the poet to dark rooms, unusual ideas or, to use an image Fernandes Jorge often employs, to a "sea of ruins"—this sea of ruins is where the remote past meets all the voices that provide the poet with a myriad of meanings. That time was abandoned but can be revisited, was forgotten but still sends echoes that permit the poet to wander over the sea of ruins. Water and the sea are themes that pervade Fernandes Jorge's poetry, for they are a privileged "where" from which the poet contemplates and scrutinizes the remains of lost meanings. That someone tells him that he goes from gloomy rooms to a sea of ruins only makes him put on another mask: he is now a harmless wanderer who travels ceaselessly during the day, singing love songs, like a castaway on a distant, forgotten island. After all, he is the dreamer who is attracted by the melancholy sight of autumn leaves and ends up identifying himself with someone whose only and final destiny is to sing love songs. He was saved from a shipwreck only to become a component of the landscape of the poem, that is, he is another ruin in the sea, living there beyond his existence.

What we can see in the above poem is that, as in "Antonello," an apparently inconsequential dialogue is written and conceived as poetry. The poet chronicles what he sees and hears and by doing this he is, at the same time, telling the reader the way he wanted the poem to be. And we have good reasons to believe that the way he wants the poem to be is the way the poem is actually written. Its lines are conceived in remote and anonymous hotel rooms; they bring to light experiences and voices with which we are not familiar, but the clear will of the poet helps them to reach us, or, more properly, lets us know that he was in a specific place at a precise moment. Put differently, the poet wants us to see him as a witness of a particular state of mind and also to note that the mental and physical landscapes he has taken hold of can be described with a certain splendor. His ambition is to reach all places and all times and we, his readers, are included in these categories—we are the place and the time of the poem. In "By David Hockney," after a pair of lines whose meaning the poet himself considers to be lost, he interrogates: "[…] I don't know what the meaning is / of beginning a poem with these lines." Apparently, we are supposed to agree with him, all the more so because we feel we are his interlocutors. Be that as it may, this outlandish world of poetry seems to be built upon doubts. Trivial doubts, for they are the doubts that emerge from daily experience, which is the most fantastic of the ruins. That the poet hears stories and writes them in the form of legends or enigmas only adds to his stature as chronicler or, as he asserts in another poem, "the poems are flags // signaling on a map the places I have been to" ("The Knight from Amares").

Like the mythic oarsmen that used to cross the oceans from shore to shore, the poet travels in a boat to bridge past and future: "Qualified to interpret the past / the flight of the birds gives them the future. / The oarsmen had the gift of prophesy" ("Study for Oarsmen and Words"). If there is something these oarsmen/poets believe in, it is History. Each poem is a return from

History, a time made of memory and dreams. And each moment of the future is a repetition of the past. Their secret mission is to be the keepers of the treasure that is hidden in History, something that makes them go beyond History. The hymns they sing, be they about real or imaginary characters, help them to reconfigure their own history, because there is no memory without both an unreal turmoil and the awareness that the starting point for this temporal adventure is the solitary space of a hotel room. Hence, the poet is the voice of the past, but his voice is subtlety covered with a shadowy aura, precisely because it materializes from his memory—it is his memory that gives shape to the memories of his characters. As a result, the figures of the past, when seized by the memory of the poet, become a combination of nostalgia and dislocated historic vigor; consequently, memory is also the silence and the shadow of the place where the past is evoked as a sea of forgetting, as we can see in this short poem included in *By the Sea in June*:

This year the summer crossed
Lisbon. The summer was invisible.
It crossed the city and the others
it took from my body
memories of your name.

What the poetry of João Miguel Fernandes Jorge tells us about the past is that it is a time we remember but also forget. In many of his poems, we do not precisely feel the effort to recuperate the time forgotten; instead, we experience the attempt to seize the act of forgetting. This is the poet's belief in History, which makes him spend time with people for whom he is nothing more than an obscure visitor. In a poem, Fernandes Jorge makes King Pedro I of Portugal say "I am alone and I am not sure I am the king" ("Chronicle, XIII"). What we see here is the poet assuming the role of the mental chronicler of the past, in which History is inhabited by ghosts that dwell in abandoned castles. For this reason, the past is not a whole entity but only allusions lying amidst the slender, flimsy sand of History. Poetry suspends time between the vagueness of the past and the future seen as prophesy—the poet has, therefore, to be the apprentice, the "disciple of the time that will never / come back" ("There was a Time in which they went through the Streets of the City"), while he is fully aware that he will end up joining the vagueness of time in a tomb. But the atemporal confusion of historical memories paradoxically coincides with the passing of time: the faces the poet sees and describes cannot but make him anticipate the centuries that will come and that will turn them into shadows in the past that had been their future. This anticipation, or prophecy, provides the act of remembering with a tone of purity when he describes castles, churches, streets and plazas in old villages, that is, images of a past dead to the present time, a time overthrown by the annoying sound of the pinball machines that will become the ruins of the future. The past is brought to the present by the act of writing the poem, but only birds, small lizards, and beetles subsist in the rocks that were once its glory.

This brings to mind an idea the Italian essayist Roberto Calasso has recently stated, according to which this sort of debt to the ancient world is like a spell that frustrates our ambition to seize the whole of the past. What really oppresses us, something that also especially oppressed Hölderlin, is the notion that the past will never belong to us in its entirety. That is the spell of the past that keeps haunting our relation with kings, angels, and gods. Because of this spell, gods disappeared from literature, but this disappearance, however, contributes to the history of literature: "the gods are fugitive guests of literature. They cross it with the trail of their names and are soon gone. Every time the writer sets down a word, he must fight to win them back." For a certain time, it was not easy to see the gods—but they are around us, although in different forms, as if they chose to let us think they had abandoned us. How can we be certain that the gods are still among us? How can we recognize them? I am convinced that modern mythology can better be grasped in poetry, not as a mere ornamentation, but as the stuff of literature itself. The way Fernandes Jorge invites the gods to his poetic universe has to do with his motivation to apprehend the hidden meanings of History, as well as with his relation with the past: "a god will one day / amplify what we are / with harmony and eternal peace and reward" ("Mozart / Alicia de Larrocha"). This god (or ensemble of gods) is coming, as is noticed by Calasso and by those who read modern poetry. In truth, the gods never left us, but now they "are no longer made up of just one family, however complicated, residing in their vast homes on the slopes of a single mountain. No, now they are multitudes, a teaming crowd in an endless metropolis. […] The power of their stories is still at work." Poems are the gods' new homes, and they are there to help poets to defeat their enemies, just as the gods used to protect kings before blood-spattered battles. Now they amplify the poet's words as they used to bless the king's sword. And, since gods know the mysteries poets want to translate into poetry, the poet follows them, enters the deep sea, searches among ruins, travels around the world like an ancient oars-man, overhears enigmatic dialogues, and is willing to merge several layers of temporal dimensions into one, to go beyond himself, to be somehow more human, like the mythical mariners who have the privilege to know "what happens / in heaven and on earth" ("Ida Lupino by Carla Bley, 11").

The poet, therefore, puts the gods into the world—they may be traveling incognito in the world, like the poet, but they are scattered across poetry, for poems are the place of their epiphanies, i.e., they are the point of view of heaven. Up to a certain point, the plasticity of the poem coincides with the nature of god to the extent that in both there is a mystery, a dramatic igno-rance of the circumstances of human and divine existence. In a certain poem, Fernandes Jorge talks about she-goats and a tempest, about Muslims offended by beauty and the vastness of the universe contained in a synagogue, and then he distances himself from the poem, assuming the point of view of the gods to say that "god is not pleased with this story" ("In Tomar"). As a consequence, the poem may be "an indignation of the gods," because what really matters is "the magnificent ship between obscure faith and invention." Calasso alludes to a "mnemonic wave" along which the gods manifest themselves. In Fernandes Jorge's case, this wave is the journey to a past inhabited by gods:

> By god by the god of Cister that God that explodes
>
> by the window is not hiding from you anymore
>
> he navigated with you at night through paths and
>
> dreams. ("Ruy Belo")

This god is capable of being wild and exploding, but he is also the silent guide of the poet (or the poetic doppelganger, his interlocutor) through remote landscapes and eerie places. God provides the poet with a destiny and the willingness to live the stories of the dreams. Put differently, the poet becomes the "angel of melancholy" who writes about men, the sun, fire, the stars, rivers, water and the sea, in order to preserve in his poems those ele-ments that constitute the adventure of the gods.

The poet lives between the laws of the earth and the order of the gods. A poem may be the earthly sign that confirms that the nature of the poet will never be similar to the gods, but it is also, without any doubt, a robe in which the gods can wrap themselves. A poem cannot aspire to become a god, but it is thanks to the poem that the gods acknowledge their own perennial nature, something that is inevitably linked with their sense of immortality. Here is a poem called "Wooden Sculpture from the Sixteenth Century":

The father, the son, missing only the holy spirit,

maybe for this reason this Trinity in the museum of Angra

emits most passionately an aura of the divine Nazarene.

The father cradles the son and we can almost hear their conversation

in a church near the sea—immense is the light in the Jewish

Port, the blue of its narrow bay, those who travel far

from their homeland disappear. In the houses, fires are lit. The

ancient place, its rocks so beloved that the eye

always comes to rest on them—those who travel afar

return no more. Death deserves the son, transmitted by

the father: this is the life that leads to the other life. The ash

deserves the opposite, the reward for a

much tattered body: the spirit is absent,

it was stolen. What remains is the belief in blood and in martyrdom,

it remains the soul; and holding his son's hand beyond his death

is the hand of the father, ripping through the gold and green of his robe.

I see no difference between that and other hand that holds, not

the punished hand of the son, but a mighty glove. Humiliated and

distraught; martyrdom and blood are not worth the brief hour of his

time; light, not blood among wounds and pain and

the lost eyes of human suffering; see the plurality

of the world; light, not fire is the keeper of the heart of nature.

The holy ghost is absent and this fact cripples the Trinity—the ghost may be missing from the sculpture seen in the Museum in Angra do Heroísmo, in the Azores, but the spirit is undoubtedly present throughout not only the poem but also in the passionate expression of the Nazarene. Again, the poet himself is another kind of spirit that almost hears this most private of conversations, the one the father holds with the son in a Catholic church near the sea (the poet's strongest ally, as we know), close to the Jewish port—it is from this place that those who have to leave depart, those who will not return. As the father transmits death to the son, which puts him beyond death, those who head off are going to die only to live a different life. That is the immortality of the gods and the near immortality of the poet. That is the reward for his dispersed, lacerated body. Although the spirit is not present, its function is performed by the soul, which is a ritualized belief in blood and martyrdom. Hence, the hand that links this life with the other world beyond life breaks through an intense and prodigious blend of gold and green. Yet, that hand also merges with the myriads of hands that are both humiliated and distressed. In the end, time is light, pain and human agony, but it is the experience of absence that permits the plurality of the world, the creation of poetry whose nature is the light the poet/god gathers around the world.

The death of the spirit, or the death of God, is the beginning of a new future, because the gods always return, albeit in different forms and wearing new masks. Their light is always accidental:

> […] First
> they announced the death of god—and
> god let himself die. Then
> they killed the king—and the king let himself
> be killed.
> Tomorrow
> what will happen to the blue of the sky and the blue of the sea?
> There will be always someone who sings
> someone who dies in a different manner. ("October, Fall 1993")

It is as if God died to sacrifice himself for poetry, so that the blue of the sea may be always sung. When someone disappears, the blue of the sky becomes brighter, the angels radiate with light, and at night the golden flames of the candles accentuate the bleak color of dead things. After the death of God and the king, the poet acquires an absolute freedom to bring them back in different forms. The multitude of gods revolves around poems, they manifestly contradict each other—by evoking them with his poetic universe, the poet makes them simulate the creation of the world. In this regard, the death of God is, as Calasso believes, like the death of Orpheus, "the primordial scene of all literature."

There is always a world beyond this world as well as signs the poet tries to come to terms with, by setting the poem among obscure ruins. His ideal is to give meaning to the exact place where his trip begins. He realizes he is what he is, but he is also what he is not; he gives life to the amorphous reality he finds in the most inconspicuous places, but he also has to fight with the instinct of death, the feeling of disappearance that constantly haunts the meaning of the poems. Every now and then, the poem does not restrain him from appropriating someone else's mind, as when he thinks he is a boy who works in the fish market and imagines he is an insect, describing in a clear way the curve of his flight: "he flies the flight of the insect, the sudden noise, the safe / meaning of the trip […] / Time becomes the spiral flight in the space" ("Ribeira Grande Market"). This is, indeed, a very significant feature in Fernandes Jorge's poetry—the assimilation of the poet to a different body, with a new form, always trying to find a privileged interlocutor. Maybe this is not really different from Friedrich Schlegel's idea that the gods now have different forms. In his seminal essay "Dialogue on Poetry," the German thinker stated that "man, in reaching out time and again beyond himself to seek and find the complement of his innermost being in the depths of another, is certain to return ever to himself." In Fernandes Jorge's poem, this projection of the self is achieved within a certain vagueness, for the poet cannot identify the person he talks with, or, if he can, he simply refuses to do that. Thus, complete integration is never accomplished because, as Schlegel points out, "absolute perfection exists only in death." Fernandes Jorge's poetic persona is in the neighborhood of this perfection, for instance, when he admits his belatedness and sees "Achilles crying your death" ("In Miss Bradbury Tavern").

When the poet seeks absolute communion with the ideal "you"—"But your name during this entire day is my name. And / I don't want any other" ("Pedro")—he may be, to use Schlegel's terminology, giving a new form to the sublime. He seems to aspire to the creative metamorphosis that Schlegel coined as the "symmetry of contradictions." In a certain poem the person he sees as his doppelganger may have been a handsome man with an expressive appearance, while in another the figure that calls his attention is nothing more than a mere silhouette half-hidden in a corner of a bar. But times have changed and so the forms of the gods have also been modified. One thing is certain: now, more than ever, the gods are closer to men, at least to poets, than they have ever been. It is as if the spirits that used to exist in statues and sculptures are now free to run wild in the world. And the poet tries to figure out the laws that govern their movement, something that is crucial for him to maintain a certain "poetic sobriety," as is the case with "Over the Highest Shadow":

> I saw him, seated two tables away from mine
> in a coffee shop on Avenida de Roma. Dark, very

dark complexion, very straight hair,
finely cut, with
a dark gray suit and a purplishblue sweater
he read with the unmindful attention of someone
who burns the halfhour before a
date, for which he fixed

a blue and brown tie to
his pale gray shirt.
Dressed in this way by Battista Moroni
he left. He was short, broadshouldered.

I did not hesitate. For him I drank my hurried,
much too burnt coffee; and I smoked what remained of my
cigar. I was also in a hurry
because I had quickly burnt the days of my fire.

That man, whoever he was, I saw him
at the forbidden limits of this land
upon the ruins of authority and throne. Without
greeting anyone as he walked

he was the dark shadow that looks much like the solitary
bull that runs away through the mountains of the city.

Again, the site of the apparition is a coffee shop, an anonymous place along a famous avenue in Lisbon. This time, the figure that is the origin and the end of the poem is portrayed with all the details available to the poet (face, hair, suit, shirt, tie). This encounter seems to occur in an idle, timeless setting that even allows the poet to identify the designer of the man's suit. If anything, the poet wants us to be quite familiar with the physical traits of the man. There is, however, something that separates the poet from the individual he describes: while the man reads aimlessly, the poet admits that he is in a hurry, that throughout his entire life he has been running. His life is running out. The appearance of the man instigates a series of thoughts in the poet's mind. Ironically, the one who is in a hurry is the one who stays there brooding over his life. But who is this mysterious being disguised as a common soul who dwells in an old city? Why was he at the forbidden limits of the earth, assuming a human form, upon the ruins of an unspecified throne? As a black shadow, absolutely indifferent to human beings, he was the mythical bull whose spirit dwells in the highest and darkest paths of the polis. For a brief moment, though, the poem was able to describe him, to outline his bodily form, probably because he was allowed (or allowed himself) to go beyond his outward appearance and place himself above the highest shadow.

In the poem above, the poet tried to be worthy of the greatness of the moment that soon would vanish from his eyes. "All thinking is a divining," wrote Schlegel, and added that "he who could understand his age […] would understand the earth and the sun." This is, indeed, the kind of mythology that underscores Fernandes Jorge's poetry, a poetry that is transparent to the eye although enveloped in an aura of mystery. The "you" in his poems, be he a king or a man of the working class who is trying to catch a bus to Cais do Sodré, in Lisbon, gives him license to set his impressions in motion, talking about this character as if we all knew one another, as if we had to remember a history that we had already forgotten or, more precisely, as if we were familiar both with the earth and the sun. Be that as it may, the poem is written so that the image of these semi-physical, semi-ethereal beings can be preserved. Yet, the poem also aims to preserve the physical image of the poet and his body that lies in a hotel room and begins a sort of movement or expedition towards his memory and his past. He does not hesitate to imagine himself looking at his former self. He sees himself in the reflection of a window in a train, although he is fully aware of the passing of time, and that the flame of his life is quickly vanishing. In "The Fake," the poet concedes that he knows what shadow and light are, but that he is not really capable of realizing what the soul and the body are:

> […] At that
> moment I looked at myself in a mirror, with a thick
> frame, a solitary mirror in which any face
> can be contemplated forever—my
> face seemed repugnant to me; pale, even
> vile, covered by a dust of anger, short
> and very spiky hair: the eyes could barely
> be seen—there was something evil

that bit my own heart, with a whisper. And
that gave me pleasure [...].

In this poem, a true self-portrait with a mirror, or a double self-portrait, soul and body are a single entity. The poet is incapable of portraying himself without resorting to a negative kind of pleasure, noting that his image cannot be contemplated forever in the mirror. It is as if, for only a short moment, the soul allowed the body to be seen, which his heart experienced as a calm, subtle reward.

What this and other incomplete self-portraits make clear is the absolute inexistence of a perfect image. There is always a kind of noise that impedes the image from being shown in its full splendor. Like the gods, the poet cannot be totally seen, his existence goes beyond the image reflected in the mirror. What the poet observes when he sees himself for an ephemeral moment in the mirror are intimations of his own death, visions of death. For him, death is a slow business; it is the condition of History, of heroes—the death of the latter is the death of the poet, although the death of heroes, brought by oarsmen from distant regions, fuels the poems the poet is willing to devote to the mythical past. Above all, death is for him being alone, among tourists, in a plaza, seated at a silent table, sipping coffee, looking at a blind musician without actually seeing him, mentally wandering from flower to flower in the nearby garden. This is the way his body is reminiscent of ancient monuments covered with sand. Now his body is his boat, his weather vane, his guide: "I continue the navigation descending the absolute / the miracle to have a body and gods" ("Two Pages From London, IX"); his body takes over everything: "Towers, labyrinths, boats / everything was the undulating body. As for me, I / no longer existed" ("Twelve Nocturnes of Ceuta, Four"). This empowerment of the body allows it to be loaded with a cargo of thousands of images and dreams that will transform it into a succession of new and distant bodies, that is to say, of new and different poems.

The symbiosis of the body of the poet (or the body of poetry) with the images he grasps is sometimes so intense and vivid that the poet looks at himself and what he sees is a boat, a beach, a sea. These are indeed aspects extremely crucial for the movement of the poet between different temporal and geographic categories. The sea is like an incommensurable plastic object sustained by ruins, and the blue of the water is the ideal mirror for the poet. What he sees when he looks at this mirror is his body scattered amidst a heap of ruins—roots of trees, empty bottles, the arm of a doll, or even a David Hume book with the knave of hearts as a bookmark; this type of maritime ruins is the complement of the ruins the poet sees in old castles, convents, fortresses, cathedrals, and palaces. With one foot on the ground and the other in the sea, the poet can configure the poem as a mirage of forts, boats, and kingdoms. His temporal dimension coincides with the existence of the mythical boat, the boat he relies on to show him the way:

> I cannot think but about the boat
>
> that is going to take me away.
>
> It is necessary that it leaves quickly
>
> white, crossing the Tagus.
>
> ……………………………
>
> I
>
> Seated here,
>
> a bottle and a glass on
>
> the marble, iron table,
>
> I drink
>
> to a quay, a sun, a river
>
> to the white ship
>
> that is going to take me away.
>
> ("Seaweeds and Blue Sea")

In Fernandes Jorge's poetry, sooner or later the reader discovers a boat that is ready to leave.

The mythical sea, with birds, sun, boats, and beaches, is an archetype of a real or invented childhood spent in the southern seas. This archetype evolved and is now the solitary place of the poet. The sea is now a sea of images, an attempt to redeem the present time but also to comfort the navigator who once built his kingdom in the middle of undulating dunes. Again, we remember what Fernandes Jorge makes King Pedro I say: "I am alone and I am not sure I am the king" ("Chronicle, XIII"). The whiteness of memory is counterbalanced by the blue of the present time, and June seems to be the bluest month for the poet, when his sight can reach the vastness of the blue horizon. As Fernandes Jorge writes apropos some photos of Jorge Molder, "blue is burdened with the paths of time, even with those that stay forever in the world of shadows." The abundance of blue contains the circular totality of heaven and sea. Let it be said in passing that in the sea all the boats are beautiful, each seascape with boats is a powerful element of the transfiguration of the poet's self, seduced by the juxtaposition of water and color. The sea provides the poet with the intimate light that breeds his silence and solitude so that he can imagine the noise and bewilderment of some legendary quay, with white smoke and the smell of fish. Blueness is what makes him pay special attention, in his imagination, to the hands and arms of the oarsmen, who, with their instruments, plough the seas, following the invisible path that leads them to the time of the poet, bringing to him the sea of Herodotus. Most of all, blue is the color of his dreams—in this indeterminate space, the poet is able to go on with his obscure kind of existence, adding more mystery to his mysterious journeys.

By and large, the aim of the trips is to give the poet the opportunity to confirm his dreams, it is a kind of repetition of his experience inside the labyrinth of images. The paradox, however, is that the repetition distorts the original image, because the idea of not knowing one's destiny is more likely to lead us to beauty. The poem "Things of the Countryside and Some Pictures" may shed some light about this idea:

> He walked aimlessly.
> He crossed the woods.
> The foggy weather allowed him
> to wander. He did not need
> to go to any place.
> He walked aimlessly
> he lost himself in the fields
> in the water of the night.

What mysterious appeal lies in the water of the night, what kind of fog is this that impels the poet to travel to its heart? About a century ago, Marcel Proust tried to answer a similar question in his essay "Poetry, or the Mysterious Laws." Like Schlegel, who affirmed that both nature and poetry were ruled by sacred mysteries, Proust was convinced that the starting point of the sacred act of poetry, as he defined it, was the private, isolated space of a room. How "sacred and dizzying" the task of the poet is, to use Proust's words, is shown by the wanderer of the poem above when he tells us of his experience in the foggy night. Without knowing exactly what he is looking for, or what the object of his attention is going to be, the poet gazes both into the night and into himself, waiting for the specific instant when the "tide uncovers the ancient quay" ("The Place of the Well, VI"). This is one of the "exalted moments" Proust talks about. To feel them is to live through the mysterious laws of poetry, or the sacred nature of beauty. When the poet shows us his own place of creation, when he admits that poetry is the interpretation of the past and the future, when he intertwines several strata of time, when he goes beyond himself to reunite his being with the prophets of History, when he describes the new forms of the gods, when he looks at the sea and realizes that what he sees in the blue immensity is his own dreamt-of image, when he does all of this, the poet lets us have a glimpse of the magnified image of his mysterious laws.

Fernandes Jorge's poetry is filled with evocations of mysterious walks through imaginary landscapes, through the extraordinary scenes and the historic worlds imagined by the poet. Each poem is a palimpsest of epochs, figures, states of mind, and other displaced elements. For that reason, it is not surprising that sometimes both the poem and the landscape evoked by it need to be disentangled: "One face came in the evening and asked for your help / to solve the landscape, / confused conglomeration of rough elements" ("Scott Burton"). It goes without saying that this person who inquired about the meaning of the visual scenery is not identified, adding, thus, one more ingredient to the puzzle and the mystery of the poem. But, as was eloquently stated by Antero de Quental, probably the most eloquent of the Portuguese philosophers, "the ultimate mystery of man needs only be *felt*, for it is the self-same mystery of God." This perception may explain the tendency of Fernandes Jorge's poetry to be more familiar with allusions than with categorical assertions, with inexplicable instincts rather than with symbolic missions, with light rather than psychology. The future of the poet is unpredictable, and that is his best legacy to poetry. More than a century ago, Antero summed up this effect of journeying through the mysterious imaginary: "This is the crepuscular empire of feeling, the world of mystery. Holy and blessed mystery. We need only a small light in the distance to see *where* we are going. *How* we will go is the unpredictable aspect of the journey, the drama, the life—it is the soul's sublime surprise." There are always other worlds on the other side of time, dream, and History: there are boats, suns, and seas, there are ineffable lights that guide the poet in his journey, for the other guides that for centuries were sent to the earth from the heavens have also been lost in time. The gods are now part of the vagueness of the poet's destiny, they are part of the poet's sublime surprise, i.e., they flee over and in the poem.

The gods' new forms make them perform new tasks, but also make them assume new masks. They may even revolve around us in the guise of artists. The luminosity Fernandes Jorge sees in Mark Rothko, for example, puts the painter on the same level as other divine entities. "Rothko's Brown and Grey Series" is a group of eight poems freely inspired by the work of the American painter, with Morton Feldman's musical piece *Rothko Chapel* as a complement. The poet looks at the abstract paintings through a representational perspective, associating them with an ordinary and daily context—"in the middle of the music it is difficult / to stand the light of the coffee" (2)—paying close attention to the visual details of his familiar world as a form of appreciation of the musical work. This is unquestionably one of the most eclectic meditations on abstract painting ever written, because it matches abstraction with trivial aspects and objects, such as pink pants, red fish, gray birds, horses and riders, knives, stars, trees, theatres and wars. Rothko's fields of color are here rendered as chunks of dialogues, small thoughts and impressions, and the large-scale paintings become short, almost pointillist poems, with the sense of the tragic and the sublime conveyed by rhymes of love or dreams, or a dialogue with a fisherman near the Nile, as if the poet wanted to pay homage to the painter by grounding his work in unambiguously lived experiences. To put it differently, Fernandes Jorge looks at Rothko's art and establishes direct associations with his immediate visual experience—"the sad heroes / […] / cut their fingers with a kitchen knife" (5); as he forms his poetic imagination, he acknowledges that his poetic universe is as infinite as abstract painting, and can be stimulated by the nourishment of other worlds and artistic minds. Feldman's *Rothko Chapel* was itself a brilliant attempt to translate the painter's stasis into music, and its presence in the poem indicates that the poet also takes notice of other heroes through a process of mediation. In this regard, Feldman is the angel, the messenger of the gods. It was Feldman who said that in order to experience Rothko, one has to find a way out of his abstraction. "The total rhythm of the paintings as Rothko arranged them created an unbroken continuity," Feldman said. But, to create the piece, he "felt that the music called for a series of highly contrasted merging sections. I envisioned an immobile procession not unlike the friezes on Greek temples." More drastic than Feldman, Fernandes Jorge goes beyond Rothko's immobility: on a mountain, he says, the ice "changes direction / verses and prose / horse and horseman" (4), because, while someone has a brown and gray heart, "the body is under the domain of the body" (6).

In the short afterword to *The Stealer of Water*, published in 1981, Fernandes Jorge clearly acknowledges the intense mystery of his poems: "each line is the enumeration of my own evidence. I do not feel responsible for them, but I also know that I cannot ignore them. [...] I am surrounded by a developing kind of truth that has to do with error. [...] I live in the error of those truths; I live in its limits—I shed light on it, I ignore it, I develop it inside my time, I turn it into my subjectivity. [...] my poems know something that I am ignorant of." What this means is that his poetic universe is made of doubts, that is, some indeterminate aspects that do not allow us to immediately identify a given sequence of words. Let us look closely at the first lines of a poem called "The Last":

A painter should never speak because words
are not his field.
What trivial doubts can you do? Doubts.
Let's take, for example, an untidy room
the need to shave and coffee waiting
books everywhere
newspapers from the weekend
the wrinkled pajamas
the rain hitting the windows.

The enigmatic sentence "What trivial doubts can you do?," originally written in English, is the center of this intimate landscape. The poet hesitates, he cannot decide what he should do, he is torn between action and inaction, between his inner motion and the weather outside. His mind is filled with doubts: he lives among them, sees them in his own face, in the coffee cup, scattered among the books and newspapers. As for the painter, the poet is absolutely certain he must remain silent. Words are for poets, and we know that Antonello and Rothko, and also Clyfford Still and Vieira da Silva, among the many others that turn up in Fernandes Jorge's poetry, do not speak in this poetry, because the poet speaks for them—he is the one who is qualified to expand on their doubts. Painters and musicians, as well as princes and seamen, cannot be confounded with the voice of the poet, the one who puts them into his subjectivity. They are like messy newspapers the poet uses to enliven his art. What is utterly astonishing is that some of the lines of this same poem, "The Last," were included, with slight changes, in a text of art criticism on the photographer Jorge Molder (in *Landscape with Many Figures*). According to this account, the trivial doubts associated with the objects of our daily life only lead to other doubts, to many more doubts. Mystery leads to more mystery. This is nothing but "the shadow of a dream. But I know that what I am saying is not an explanation for the photographs of Jorge Molder." The critic does not explain. What about the poet? Does he explain? Probably not, because a poem only amplifies the act of seeing, not the actual object. Knowing that the perfect image is an ideal, the poet interrogates the image he sees, and this becomes his own evidence, his own reality, his own doubts. To come to the point, his own myth.

Permeated by doubts, poetry is for Fernandes Jorge what mythology was for the ancients. This new mythology comes forward from the ruins that sustain the poet's atemporal sea, from the stories and legends that he overhears in his journey to the daily dreams that help him to divine the point of view of the gods. Moreover, this mythology makes his spirit explode in all directions, from land to sea, from earthly to heavenly time. The remote past is alive again and is mixed up with the chaotic remains of present time, with books and pajamas in an obscure room. Besides, the past is a kind of oracle that shows the poet multiple paths to happiness. That is the reason he writes poems based on legends, avoiding putting them into an emotional nutshell, because the sublime quality of this mythology cannot be contained in emotional glass-cases. The "arabesque of imagination," as Schlegel puts it, is the point of origin of poetry that transports us to "the original chaos of human nature, for which I know as yet no more beautiful symbol than the motley throng of the ancient gods." This horde of ancient gods has now new forms, and they manifest themselves in ways that the poet, a messenger between them and his pagan world, wants to apprehend, all the more so because of his wish to create images of them. If his poems do not have gods and heroes, if there is nothing to mediate between his mysterious imagination and what simply is in the world, then the poet is nothing more than the guardian of a mere discrepancy, of the same void that used to lock the gods within decrepit libraries and onto disintegrating pedestals. When the poet succeeds, however, the reward for him is to be in the company of the real gods: "He wanted to be a god just like the other gods, without mercy. / He deserved the coffee he drank; a simple pleasure between / heaven and sea" ("A Crime Between Várzea and Candelária").

The poetry Fernandes Jorge writes has a voice that speaks, but it also has gods who watch over what is said. Occasionally, these three entities are so entangled that the triangulation of the I, the Self, and the Divine cannot be understood except as a manifestation of the immortality of the poet. His body, as well as his spirit, incessantly shifts from poem to places and mental attitudes. The ambiguity of poetry is also the ambiguity of the role of the poet as the gods' courier, wandering from different temporal dimensions to divine dimensions, as we can see in the poem "Fajã Grande":

> I read in Francisco Pimentel Gomes about the
> forty-one fortified areas on Flores
> and Corvo islands. Many were no more than guard
> houses; small forts, batteries, watch-posts, most of them are now
> piles of stones. Next follows the list of
> commanders-in-chief, captains and sergeants, and a bit
> of the tale that connected them to the islands.
> In Fajanzinha, before we arrive at the church,
> just after the small plaza, there is an
> ochre-painted house, with a window hovering about the floor,
> the exterior stairs made of stone.
> At Fajã Grande. The streams tumble down the
> cliffs. They form with the land of Fajã and the sea
> a circular body. Families follow the natural
> movement, creating and destroying themselves: variation,
> instant, mobility: along the hazy
> path and the green darkness, in another century
> and in this one, a fleet boy is the messenger.
> He ran along the difficult foot-path, bringing from the port
> the news of someone who managed to return
> from the not-so-distant America. He receives a silver piece
> for the good news, the messenger who seems constant
> and eternal in his agile run between time
> and heaven. His callused hand accepts the steaming
> mug of coffee, poorly made from toasted fava beans.

The poem begins with the ruins, so old that some of the fortresses now only exist in history books. What is left, a pile of stones, is the remains of what was once there. There are also the military men who served there, and the poet almost yields to a narration of their stories, their tales. He flees over the old village, Fajanzinha, and sees a church, a plaza, and a house. Surrounding the old village, mountains, the sea, and brooks form a circular body. So far, the voice of the poet is indistinguishable from the voice of the divine being who knows and sees everything. The mythological voice suddenly breaks through, enlightening us about the biological movement of families that are like poems—some are built over the ruins of others, and that constitutes the history of their existence, their ephemeral life. But out of the darkness comes the herald who, like the poet when he tells us the story of this poem, brings the news from one century to the other. Between the Azores and the mythic American lands there is the sea, the privileged element of the poet. And the courier is paid twice for being what he is: a silver coin for his mythical journey and a cup of coffee made from fava beans for his earthly task. Both the rewards and the poem invigorate him, encouraging him to continue on as the eternal, light-heeled messenger between time and heaven. After all, he is a being surrounded by a type of wall that will not perish, and his story is not going to be told by any Francisco Pimentel Gomes simply because his story is the poem, which includes both the past and the historian.

In his ceaseless journeys between time and heaven, the poet also communicates with dead heroes, thus bringing them to the life that is poetry. He has his own dead people to remember, and he sees them in the streets and in the churches, as well as in his memory. His relation with the literary dead is somehow painful on account of the bliss he once shared with them. "The Place of the Well, VII" is a good illustration of this relationship:

IKAPOS. The bookstore; the pine cones and pomegranates painted
on the desk lamp, the milky white glass globe of the ceiling
the portraits of Seferis, Kavafy, Elytis, the
surrealist poet Engonopoulos
the most beloved editions Eliot, Rilke, Lorca

and the dark image of Lello, in Oporto, Guimarães,
Hyperion
when I had a publishing house I left among the books
some photographed faces Sophia, Sena, Agustina, Cesariny
Belo, Cinatti

I lost some of those shadows, others I brought
along; a painful estate; the books
I wanted them, in the verses more beauty
and not the filthy and little left-wing politics or the snotty realistic
prose; that loss

cost me the feeling of treason
the scheming of someone who used my name and yours;
the sentences, in Greek, the variations on a Mexican theme by
Cernuda, I see them
inhabiting the pleated robe of wisdom.

These are the literary myths of the poet, which will acquire a new form, for they are part of the life of this poem. What is remarkably important is the idea that, in reality, some of these writers are still alive (e.g., Sophia de Mello Breyner, Agustina Bessa-Luís, Mário Cesariny), which means that, when their names are inserted into the poet's universe, they become invested with new forms; they also become eerie beings, mysterious gods, or shadows. This literary heritage cannot but be a painful, heavy weight—when the poem travels from place to place, from poem to poem, some of the literary relics are left behind while others are carried in his baggage.

History, as well as poetry, has many actors, many witnesses, and Fernandes Jorge uses them to conjure up a certain theatricality, which is another name for the ordered delirium of his memory. When he visits shadowy regions, establishing dialogues with sacred beings half-hidden in the past and behind artistic masks, assuming his role of messenger between sea and myth, time and heaven, the poet crafts poems as eternal miscellany of different eras. Therefore, someone who is seen, still in a coffee shop, in a modern city may be confounded with a "librarian of Alexandria copying *The Laws*, / written by Plato on little wax boards" ("Fed Up With the Others and the World"); on other occasion, Dionysus is seen singing a hymn in the Azorean landscape. The sight of an ordinary person evokes mythical activities and places, and memories of remote, mythological beings are transposed to the present time. There are commonplace activities that endure for centuries, without being lost or forgotten, and this poetry is a physical process that permeates the mystery that bridges different times and different heroes. With the help of the boat of imagination, "time run away from one century to the / other century" ("Twelve Nocturnes of Ceuta,

1"). Each place reminds the poet of another place, each face brings back the memory of another person, real or imagined, who, at a certain moment, came across the poet. Above all, each seascape is a reminiscence of the dreamt life of the poet on his distant, imaginary Olympus. Every moment is an eternal new beginning, an eternal repetition, for "I turn the streets of / Bairro Alto into roads full of caravans leading to the // ports of Syria, to the Persian Gulf, to the sea of Eritrea" ("Actus Tragicus, 21"). And we are here, traveling with him, following his random itinerary, dreaming his dream within a dream, seeing him weaving his immortal plots. His mysteries will be illuminated by the same gods that conceived them: the always absent and always present spirits of poetry.

Works Cited

Alamada Negreiros, José Maria de. "Poesia e Criação" ["Poetry and Creation"]. *Obras Completas*. Vol. 6. Lisbon: Imprensa Nacional/Casa da Moeda, 1993.

Calasso, Roberto. *Literature and the Gods*. Trans. Tim Parks. New York: Knopf, 2001.

Feldman, Morton. *Give My Regards to Eighth Street: Collected Writings*. Cambridge: Exact Change, 2000.

Fernandes Jorge, João Miguel. *Obra Poética*. Vol. 4. Lisbon: Presença, 1991.

———. *Direito de Mentir* [*The Right to Lie*]. Lisbon: Arcádia, 1978.

———. *À Beira do Mar de Junho* [*By the Sea in June*]. Lisbon: Regra do Jogo, 1982.

———. *O Regresso dos Remadores* [*The Return of the Oarsmen*]. Lisbon: Presença, 1982.

———. *Paisagem com Muitas Figuras* [*Landscape With Many Figures*]. Lisbon: Assírio e Alvim, 1984.

———. *O Barco Vazio* [*The Empty Boat*]. Lisbon: Presença, 1994.

———. *Não é Certo Este Dizer* [*This Way of Saying is not Certain*]. Lisbon: Presença, 1997.

———. *O Lugar do Poço* [*The Place of the Well*]. Lisbon: Relógio d'Água, 1997.

———. *Bellis Azorica*. Lisbon: Relógio d'Água, 1999.

Proust, Marcel. "Poetry, or the Mysterious Laws." *Against Sainte-Beuve and Other Essays*. Trans. John Sturrock. New York: Penguin, 1988.

Quental, Antero de. "The Feeling of Immortality." *The Feeling of Immortality: Selected Writings*. Trans. Richard Zenith. Dublin: Mermaid Turbulence, 1998.

Schlegel, Friedrich. "Dialogue on Poetry." *Dialogue on Poetry and Literary Aphorisms*. Trans. Ernst Behler and Roman Struc. University Park, PA and London: Pennsylvania State UP, 1968.

Carlos Veloso received his B.A. in English and German Languages and Literatures from the University of Lisbon, where he also earned an M.A. in Literary Theory. He is currently a Lecturer at New York University, where he concluded a Ph.D. in the Department of Comparative Literature (2008). He is now doing research in the fields of aesthetics, the history of architecture, and contemporary literature. E-mail: cv14@is8.nyu.edu

Nuno Júdice: arte poética com melancolia

Ida Ferreira Alves

Resumo. Neste artigo desenvolve-se reflexão sobre a poesia portuguesa contemporânea, com destaque para o trabalho poético de Nuno Júdice, além de algumas referências à sua produção ensaística. A melancolia em sua escrita como resultado do questionamento sobre o sujeito, a linguagem, o mundo e o lugar da poesia na sociedade contemporânea, num tempo reconhecido como *pós-moderno*.

"Quem canta," perguntaram as sibilas, "quem canta com voz divina / entre ruínas?"
(Nuno Júdice, *A Noção de Poema*)

Há muito acompanhamos, entre surpreendidos e assustados, as transformações que a política mundial—definida por uma minoria economicamente poderosa—vem provocando em todo o mundo. Tais transformações incidem diretamente sobre as culturas nacionais e as formas de recepção, compreensão e debate dos temas que circunscrevem a nossa existência cotidiana. A discussão, desde meados da década de setenta, sobre uma *pós-modernidade* se fortalece, sob essa perspectiva, a partir do questionamento sobre a contemporaneidade globalizada, sem utopias, num mal-estar existencial que advém da contraposição entre desejos diversos e a impossibilidade de realizá-los tanto no nível coletivo (nas áreas político-econômica e sociocultural) quanto no nível pessoal (em relação às experiências diversas do sujeito).

Portuguese Literary & Cultural Studies 7 (2008): 173-83.

Especialmente em relação à literatura, pergunta-se com muita freqüência, de forma por vezes polêmica, para onde caminham os estudos literários e qual o papel ou contribuição do literário na sociedade atual, em face de realidades tão díspares. Sabemos bem como, a partir dos anos 50, verificou-se a expansão de uma cultura de massa que desejava dar conta do mundo e estar presente na vida diária por meio dos discursos banalizantes veiculados principalmente pela televisão, rádio, jornais e revistas (hoje há que se pensar também na Internet como veículo de comunicação), os quais são pródigos em criar heróis e simular um poder quase divino de omnipresença e ubiqüidade. Em decorrência desse quadro, a produção literária respondeu ao movimento caleidoscópico da contemporaneidade com uma textualidade muito consciente do confronto com a mídia, procurando igualmente uma inserção mais forte no mercado de consumo. Isso, muitas vezes, significou a produção de obras pouco preocupadas com o nível estético e mais interessadas em atingir uma parcela significativa de público, com a defesa de que o fundamental é comunicar.[1]

Também a escrita poética refletiu essa crise e essa demanda, questionando de forma cada vez mais crítica suas possibilidades de existência e interferência sociocultural. Sempre desafiadoramente nos limites, ou contra eles, considerada freqüentemente escrita da subjetividade, sem utilidade específica, a poesia parece estar, neste tempo tão visivelmente pragmático, condenada ao desaparecimento. Como a palavra poética pode competir com a *mass-media* e o poderio tecnológico? Como se fazer ouvir na agitação consumista das grandes metrópoles? Como enfrentar os sistemas político-econômicos que vêm redefinindo as fronteiras do mundo atual num movimento de indiferenciação das culturas? Como atrair o homem comum, em meio ao turbilhão da vida, para a leitura ou audição de poesia? No entanto, apesar de tantas dificuldades, os poetas não se calam e a produção poética mundial se mantém como uma estratégia de resistência por meio da qual o homem ainda se pode pensar com autonomia, questionando o mundo e a linguagem, reagindo às barreiras impostas pelos múltiplos processos de massificação. Por isso, os poetas continuam a dizer que é fundamental demonstrar que a palavra poética tem uma função importante: ser o espaço livre da reflexão de tudo que importa ao homem, afirmando sua dignidade existencial, num tempo marcado pela descrença, distopias, negatividade e banalização da vida.[2]

É fato que a poesia, na paisagem contemporânea de supremacia do tecnológico e do materialismo, é um discurso desvalorizado socialmente, desvalorização, aliás, que tem uma longa história. Porém, até meados do século XX, o poeta gozava de um certo reconhecimento "burocrático" em alguns meios sociais, com presença pública mais visível e, por vezes, razoavelmente respeitada. Nas últimas décadas, sob o ponto de vista de "consumo," presença e reconhecimento, a poesia foi sendo relegada a uma posição bastante secundária e isso se pode comprovar, sem pretensões estatísticas, com a simples verificação do espaço que a mídia lhe tem dado, ou pela quantidade de leitores que a ela se dedicam com fidelidade. No entanto, os poetas continuam a produzir e a encontrar os seus leitores entre aqueles que não seguem as regras de mercado.

No panorama cultural português, é interessante observar a vitalidade que a produção de poesia mantém, como confirma o crítico António Guerreiro: "E o que é um facto é que se continua a editar muita poesia em Portugal, e ela continua a ter um grande peso na instituição literária (ao contrário do que se passa noutros países da Europa, onde se tornou um domínio quase esotérico)."[3] Sem dúvida, a literatura portuguesa do século XX tem uma plêiade de nomes que atingiram uma realização poética bastante superior sob vários aspectos. Entre esses nomes, destacamos Nuno Júdice como uma das mais representativas vozes poéticas da contemporaneidade, com uma escrita que tensiona os limites (limites?) entre modernismo e pós-modernismo, configurando o que poderíamos nomear de uma *poética da melancolia.*

Nascido em 1949, em Mexilhoeira Grande (Algarve), era um jovem nos anos setenta e, ao longo de trinta anos, construiu vasta obra literária das mais reconhecidas[4] em Portugal, com predomínio da poesia sobre a prosa, também algum teatro, e importantes incursões pela crítica literária, representativa de seu magistério universitário (é professor de literatura na Universidade Nova de Lisboa), além de presença assídua como cronista ou crítico em diversos jornais e revistas portugueses e não só. Sua obra nos possibilita discutir de forma imediata uma *teorização da escrita e da leitura* na poesia portuguesa mais recente, uma vez que, desde o seu primeiro livro, *A Noção de Poema* (1972), preocupa-se sobremaneira com a realização do poema e a compreensão do "ato poético," questionando o sujeito lírico e sua existência no texto e no mundo. Em 1991, publicou *Obra Poética*, reunindo seus livros de poesia editados de 1972 a 1985. Em 2000 voltou a publicar o conjunto de sua obra poética, *Poesia Reunida (1967-2000),* incluindo um poema de 1967 e um texto de prosa poética, de 1970. Com regularidade, vem publicando outros livros de poesia, intercalando-os com obras narrativas e ensaísticas.

O tom dessa poesia é freqüentemente pessimista; no entanto, essa afirmação deve ser relativizada porque, de fato, não é seu tom único, e sim expressão variável de diferentes sujeitos poéticos que vão aparecendo na cena do poema, representando um "drama em gente" a falar da condição humana no mundo contemporâneo, em meio a ruínas e fragmentos da memória. Escrita perpassada de ironia, transita de forma crítica pela tradição poética ocidental, muitas vezes enfrentando a melancolia com um breve sorriso de quem sabe que o canto se faz de ficções e que é, apesar de sua desilusão, uma janela aberta, mirando o horizonte para além das ruínas deste mundo.

Essa melancolia, por vezes dramaticamente exposta, é provocada, principalmente, pela evocação da morte e pela certeza de que o tempo tudo corrói, sobretudo em nossa realidade urbana globalizada na qual dominam a desilusão, a descrença, a dissolução rápida de todos os valores. Visão disfórica provocada, é certo, pelos fatos que marcaram o século XX como um tempo especial de degradação da vivência humana, sob o constante risco de aniquilamento total. Degradação que atingiu também a linguagem da Arte em tempos pós-modernos, sempre que esta se submeteu aos discursos do consumismo imediato com seus paraísos artificiais e a banalidade dos sentidos. Em depoimento sobre "O Lugar da Poesia,"[5] Nuno Júdice destacou a gradativa perda da potencialidade dos discursos oral e escrito atuais frente à massificação e simplificação dominantes nos diferentes veículos de comunicação. Para ele, "a poesia funciona como o discursos depositário da memória da palavra como mundo pleno de uma significação inteira [...]." Portanto, a sua poesia, ao mesmo tempo que diz essa perda profunda do contato original com a linguagem que guardava o sentido da presença humana no mundo, um canto elegíaco, é ainda uma forma de insitir na oposição a esse movimento de esquecimento e indiferenciação.

Também as reflexões estéticas que Nuno Júdice desenvolve, como ensaísta e crítico literário, confirmam a imagem do poeta que logo se configura para o leitor de sua poesia: um teorizador da linguagem poética e um pesquisador dos seus limites e processos imagéticos. Obras como *O Processo Poético* (1992) e *Máscaras do Poema* (1998) nos fazem refletir sobre a constituição do discurso da poesia, a especificidade de sua linguagem, as relações produtivas entre escrita e leitura, as condições atuais de produção de poesia e a ação de resistência que pode exercer em relação à homogeneização cultural dominante, para além da abordagem analítica da escrita dos diferentes poetas ou de momentos literários específicos com os quais dialoga freqüentemente em sua poética.

Desde os seus primeiros livros de poesia desenvolvem-se as indagações metapoéticas e a discussão filosófica sobre o ser, a linguagem, a poesia e seu lugar no mundo. Por isso, evidencia-se em sua obra uma reflexão contínua sobre a escrita e a leitura, ações que instalam o sujeito na sua Língua para nomeação e criação de mundos. O poético torna-se igualmente um lugar ímpar da linguagem, pois é nele que todos os discursos sobre o ser, o mundo e a própria linguagem estão em tensão crítica. Muitos dos poemas de Nuno Júdice discutem exatamente a distância entre as palavras e "as realidades do mundo," preenchendo essa lacuna com a "invenção de imagens," a estabelecer um outro espaço só percorrido no poema. Nesse sentido, a experiência poética é um exercício solitário em busca de algo não nomeável e o poeta "um escultor do movimento. Fere, / com a pedra do instante, o que passa a caminho da eternidade; / suspende o gesto que sonha o céu; e fixa, na dureza da noite, / o bater de asas, o azul, a sábia interrupção da morte" ("Teoria Geral Sentimento" 136).

Sua poesia ao falar constantemente de mudanças (no sujeito, na natureza, no texto), fala igualmente das perdas diversas que os sujeitos vivenciam, seja na sua *história pessoal* (o amor falhado, a nostalgia da infância, a inevitabilidade da morte, as impossibilidades do ser num tempo corrosivo), seja na *história coletiva* (o apagamento da memória comum, a indiferença à identidade cultural, a negação da história partilhada), e em relação a isso a noção de perda se amplia refletindo a crise das ideologias, a dúvida sobre o futuro, as indagações teológicas e as interrogações filosóficas, enfim a descrença de que haja alguma unidade, alguma totalidade que se possa manter na sociedade contemporânea. Sua poesia, portanto, torna-se uma "meditação sobre ruínas," título aliás de um dos seus livros, de 1995, reconhecido com o Prémio de Poesia da Associação Portuguesa de Escritores.

Essa meditação propõe o que chamamos de "análise arqueológica" no texto. O arqueólogo examina as ruínas de uma cidade e consegue recuperar uma época, a história de um povo. O antropólogo, recolhendo, por vezes, fragmentos de textos e de histórias orais, busca os elementos para recuperar uma unidade de sentido, para recompor uma história de cultura. Em poesia, esses elementos residuais são as emoções, as palavras, as imagens que, reordenadas pela lógica do poema, pela escrita e pela leitura, podem revelar o ausente, lembrar o perdido e dar a conhecer o inexistente. A arqueologia de que falamos se organiza para *re-significar* o que se encontra sem sentido.

> Às vezes, um verso transforma o modo como
> se olha para o mundo; as coisas revelam-se
> naquilo que imaginação alguma as supôs; e
> o centro desloca-se de onde estava, desde
> a origem, obrigando o pensamento a rodar
> noutra direcção. O poema, no entanto, não
> tem obrigatoriamente de dizer tudo. A sua
> essência reside no fragmento de um absoluto
> que algum deus levou consigo. Olho para
> esse vestígio da totalidade sem ver mais
> do que isso—o desperdício da antiga
> perfeição—e deixo para trás o caminho
> da ideia, a ambição teológica, o sonho do
> infinito. De que eternidade me esqueço,
> então, no fundo da estrofe? *(O Movimento do Mundo* 7)

Ao longo dos séculos o homem foi construindo uma história coletiva que estabeleceu como as grandes unidades Deus, o Sujeito e o Mundo. Na poética de Júdice, tais unidades estão fragmentadas e o que se encontram são seus vestígios espalhados pelos poemas. Caberá ao leitor a recolha desses resquícios e a tentativa de reencontrar um sentido, estabelecendo uma outra ordem de significação no nível da linguagem poética, que é, na perspectiva do poeta, um espaço capaz de *re-conhecer* a totalidade.

Em relação ao sujeito lírico, os vestígios de sua existência são os sentimentos que se espalham pelos versos: o amor, a nostalgia, a solidão, a tristeza, a melancolia, indiciando faces de uma individualidade moderna que se auto-contempla, como Narciso, e não pode mais crer na ilusão de sua imagem.

Esse sujeito é reflexo de um mundo também em fissura, principalmente num tempo como o de agora em que tudo é relativo e não há mais possibilidade de recuperar uma pseudo "idade de ouro" sem diferenças ou conflitos. O mundo fragmentado que se recolhe na poesia de Júdice é exatamente esse mundo cheio de lacunas, com os sujeitos vivendo a tensão entre o natural e o artificial, o isolamento e a multidão, a cultura e a massificação. O movimento desse mundo é o movimento automatizado e ininterrupto das pessoas nas ruas das grandes cidades, dos carros nos congestionamentos, dos retalhos de vida que se estampam nos jornais, enfim o burburinho urbano que não constitui diálogo, deixando à mostra restos que apenas lembram a presença humana na sua inteireza. A escrita poética na sua autonomia possibilita a leitura desses destroços e reconta a história do sujeito, avaliando o movimento do mundo que o formou. Assim, também se oferece como lugar de acolhimento no meio de ruínas.

O homem que falava sozinho na estação central de munique
que língua falava? Que língua falam os que se perdem assim, nos
corredores das estações de comboio, à noite, quando já nenhum
quiosque vende jornais e cafés? O homem de
munique não me pediu nada, nem tinha o ar de
quem precisasse de alguma coisa, isto é, tinha aquele ar
de quem chegou ao último estado
que é o de quem não precisa nem de si próprio. No entanto,
falou-me: numa língua sem correspondência com linguagem
alguma de entre as possíveis de exprimirem emoção
ou sentimento, limitando-se a uma sequência de sons cuja lógica
a noite contrariava. Perguntar-me-ia se eu compreendia acaso
a sua língua? Ou queria dizer-me o seu nome e de onde vinha
—àquela hora em que não estava nenhum comboio
nem para chegar nem para partir? Se me dissesse isto,
ter-lhe-ia respondido que também eu não esperava ninguém,
nem me despedia de alguém, naquele canto de uma estação
alemã; mas poderia lembrar-lhe que há encontros que só dependem
do acaso, e que não precisam de uma combinação prévia
para se realizarem.—É então que os horóscopos adquirem sentido;
e a própria vida, para além deles, dá um destino à solidão que empurra
alguém para uma estação deserta, à hora em que já não se compram
jornais nem se tomam cafés, restituindo um resto de alma ao corpo
ausente—o suficiente para que se estabeleça um diálogo, embora
ambos sejamos a sombra do outro. É que, a certas horas da noite,
ninguém pode garantir a sua própria realidade, nem quando outro
como eu próprio, testemunhou toda a solidão do mundo
arrastada num deambular de frases sem sentido numa estação morta.
(*Um Canto na Espessura do Tempo* 34)

A imagem da extrema solidão que esse poema apresenta fala dessa espécie de morte que é a ausência de diálogo e, reagindo a esse vazio social e humano, o poema é um lugar em que a linguagem se manifesta impondo o diálogo, requisitando o encontro. A melancolia desse texto evidencia que não há mais a ilusão romântica de que a poesia pode transformar o mundo, no entanto, falando da ausência compartilhada de palavras numa estação morta, afirma a idéia de que o exercício da linguagem pode transformar o sujeito, tornando-o apto a reavaliar o mundo e sua posição nele. Diz o poeta: "Por isso, ao contrário da ideia romântica da poesia como transformação do mundo, prefiro a formulação: a poesia como transformação do eu."[6]

Se procuramos demonstrar que a temática da fragmentação e da ruína está na poesia de Nuno Júdice como representação melancólica da perda de unidade do sujeito e do mundo, agora é necessário refletir que, também, no nível da enunciação ela se apresenta como uma estratégia intertextual. O que desejamos dizer é que a escrita do poeta se vale de vestígios, sinais e indícios de outros textos ou sistemas de significação (como a música, a pintura). Não há fragmentos textuais propriamente ditos, com exceção de algumas poucas epígrafes, mas um sistema complexo de citações diluído na tessitura dos poemas, que pode ser recuperado e re-significado no ato de leitura horizontal e vertical de sua poesia. Por todos os livros, os poemas apontam as marcas de outros textos que foram lidos pelo poeta ou que estão presentes no imaginário do leitor ocidental contemporâneo. Os próprios índices de seus livros apontam à superfície da obra poética de que a escrita se faz de leituras e que o poeta habita também a linguagem alheia. Como exemplos, citemos alguns títulos entre os muitos que poderiam ser destacados: *Stéphane Mallarmé; Holderlin; W.B.Yeats em Rapallo; "Ulisses," uma página; A camiliana noite; Homenagem a Blake; Penélope; O enigma de Inês; Bernardim Ribeiro; Clearly Campos (citação); A ilha de Ovídio; Virgínia Woolf; Paráfrase de C.G.R; Quadras com citações de Sartre e Shakespeare; Imitação de Propércio; Se, numa noite de Natal, a prostituta; Arte poética com citação de Hölderlin; Romance de cordel do banqueiro suicida e da cómoda D. Maria.*

O cruzamento textual deve ser compreendido como um encontro de versões de mundo, versões que são interrogadas pelo poeta e que devem interrogar o leitor, ampliando no tempo e no espaço a reflexão constante sobre a escrita poética. Assim o que se constitui também na enunciação é a necessidade, urgência de diálogo, de troca de sentidos e de imagens, para que se efetive uma "comunidade" cujo território é a experiência da Arte. Leiamse, como exemplo desse cruzamento, partes do poema "Tema com variazon":

Uma tarde, em berna, lendo ruy belo e—não sei porquê—
lembrando-me de um túmulo de uma portuguesa que foi morrer
a pisa, pus no giradiscos a "dido e eneias" do
purcell, deixando que o canto saísse pela janela
e contaminasse os campos que, nessa primavera, estavam
azuis e verdes—flores e relva—com vacas a correrem
à frente de um cão. Não havia nada a ligar a ópera
inglesa, o poeta português e a portuguesa de pisa, a não
ser a que as próprias circunstâncias de um acaso
de tarde estabeleceram; e no entanto uma imagem única
se sobrepunha a essas, a que se poderia dar o nome de poesia
se a poesia não fosse algo de abstracto numa paisagem que
nada tinha a ver com um sentimento preciso—a melancolia
de uma breve primavera entre campos e prédios, susceptível
de trazer até mim a tão vaga imagem da mulher antiga
com a música de purcell.
[...] O mistério, digo, faz-se com estes reencontros
que não têm uma explicação precisa; eles surgem de imagens
que guardamos dentro de nós, num recanto de alma,
e que um dia se abrem inesperadamente. Sei, no entanto, que
não é só o motivo pessoal da memória de um poeta, nem
a tentativa de reconstituir a figura de uma portuguesa
morta em itália, nem o canto sacrificial de dido na ópera
de purcell, que me levaram a escrever, agora, este poema. De
resto, nenhum poema terá uma razão imediata—e mesmo
aqueles que nascem de um episódio concreto depressa nos levam
para uma zona abstracta de confluências interiores
de impressões e gestos que, sem o verso, não teriam tradução.
Assim, o soldado de Giorgione sai do quadro onde o pintor
o fixou e, trazendo atrás de si o cão que, séculos depois,
afugentou as vacas do pasto de wittigkofen, pergunta-me
pelo ruy belo—sem que eu possa responder, ocupado a escrever
este poema e a tentar explicar à portuguesa enterrada
em pisa por que é que, precisamente, foi a ária de dido
numa ópera de purcell que a trouxe até junto de mim. (*As Regras da Perspectiva* 47-48)

O processo dominante de citação manifesta o desejo de manter a linguagem partilhada, apesar das diferenças e fortalece, em sua poética, o tema da comunhão possível por meio das palavras, defendendo a necessidade de guardar o humano do vazio característico dos discursos cotidianos—babel que nada partilha ou ensina. Esse desejo contrasta fortemente com o tom elegíaco e descrente que atravessa seus versos pontuados de ruínas, escolhos, restos do mundo e do sujeito, naufragados numa realidade sem sentido.

A arte poética de Nuno Júdice acentua a solidão do leitor e do poeta, personagem deambulador na cidade, mas também aponta formas de reencontrar *sentidos* no cotidiano por meio do exercício e da experiência poética. Com esse olhar ambíguo entre o vazio do mundo e a plenitude da poesia, sua escrita permite-nos também uma citação: o filme de Wim Wenders—*Der Himmel über Berlin* (*Asas do Desejo*, na versão brasileira), em que, em meio às ruínas urbanas, um velho narrador insiste com as palavras, resistindo ao tempo e à morte, enfrentando a ruína da História. Não é, afinal, o que faz o poeta ao partilhar imagens, ao buscar nossa perdida memória?

Notas

[1] Em torno dessa questão desenvolveu-se certa polêmica com a publicação da antologia *Poetas sem Qualidades* organizada por Manuel de Freitas. Lisboa: Averno, 2002. Veja-se sobre isso o nº 12, da Revista 04/2003, Lisboa: Fundação Luis Miguel Nava.

[2] Blanchot, Maurice. *Para onde vai a literatura?* In: *O livro por Vir*. Trad. Maria Regina Louro. Lisboa: Relógio d'Água, 1984, 205-234.

[3] Guerreiro, 2003, 11-18.

[4] Veja-se em Júdice, 2000, a bibliografia ativa do autor (poesia, narrativa, teatro, ensaio, além de edições críticas, antologias e traduções). Sua obra literária somava então 31 títulos. Há traduções de seus livros de poesia para diversas línguas e recebeu diversos prêmios literários.

[5] Inquérito realizado pela revista portuguesa *Relâmpago* 2, abril de 1998, com a publicação de depoimentos de oito poetas portugueses contemporâneos. O de Nuno Júdice, "A poesia, hoje, ocupa o lugar da eloqüência," encontra-se nas páginas 41-43.

[6] Inquérito publicado em *Cadernos de Serrúbia* 3, dez. 1998, 42.

Obras Citadas

Amaral, Fernando Pinto do. *O mosaico fluido—modernidade e pós-modernidade na poesia portuguesa mais recente*. Lisboa: Assírio & Alvim, 1991.

Barrento, João. *A palavra transversal—literatura e ideias no século XX.* Lisboa: Cotovia, 1996.

Blanchot, Maurice. *O livro por vir.* Lisboa: Relógio D'Água, 1984.

Compagnon, Antoine. *Os cinco paradoxos da modernidade.* Belo Horizonte: Edição da UFMG, 1996.

———. *O trabalho de citação.* Belo Horizonte: Edições UFMG, 1996.

Guerreiro, Fernando. "Alguns aspectos da poesia contemporânea." *Relâmpago* 12 (04/2003), 11-18.

Harvey, David. *Condição pós-moderna.* 7ª ed. São Paulo: Loyola, 1992.

Júdice, Nuno. *As regras da perspectiva.* Lisboa: Quetzal, 1990.

———. *Obra poética* (1972-1985). Lisboa: Quetzal, 1991.

———. *Um canto na espessura do tempo.* Lisboa: Quetzal, 1992.

———. *O processo poético.* Lisboa: Imprensa Nacional—Casa da Moeda, 1992.

———. *Meditação sobre ruínas.* Lisboa: Quetzal, 1996.

———. *O movimento do mundo.* Lisboa: Quetzal, 1996.

———. *As máscaras do poema.* Lisboa: Aríon, 1998.

———. *Poesia reunida 1967-2000.* Lisboa: Dom Quixote, 2000.

———. [resposta] "Inquérito sobre a poesia portuguesa do século XX." *Cadernos de Serrúbia* 3 (dez. 1999). Porto: Fundação Eugénio de Andrade. 41-42.

Ida Ferreira Alves é Doutora em Literatura Portuguesa pela Universidade Federal do Rio de Janeiro, professora adjunta de Literatura Portuguesa da Universidade Federal Fluminense (Niterói—Rio de Janeiro), e Vice-Coordenadora do Núcleo de Estudos de Literatura Portuguesa e Africana, no Instituto de Letras da Universidade Federal Fluminense. É também Coordenadora do Núcleo "Literatura Portuguesa" do Pólo de Pesquisa sobre Relações Luso-Brasileiras—PPRLB, com sede no Real Gabinete Português de Leitura do Rio de Janeiro. Tem-se ocupado sobretudo de estudos sobre a poesia portuguesa do século XX. Da sua produção científica, entre diversos trabalhos publicados em livros e revistas, destacam-se: "Poesia portuguesa contemporânea e a opção pela narratividade," em *Revista Alea* 3: 2; "Diálogos e confrontos na poesia portuguesa pós-60," *Revista Gragoatá* 12; "Quando cantar é cortar a língua: a poesia de Gastão Cruz e Adília Lopes," *Estéticas da crueldade.* Desenvolveu pesquisa de pós-doutoramento sobre figurações da morte nas obras poéticas de Ruy Belo e de Nuno Júdice, no âmbito de projeto de pesquisa inter-institucional *"As Máscaras de Perséfone," figurações da morte nas literaturas portuguesa e brasileira contemporâneas,* sob coordenação da Prof. Dra. Lelia Parreira Duarte, Centro de Estudos Luso-Afro-Brasileiros da Pontifícia Universidade Católica de Minas Gerais. E-mail: alberto.ida@br.inter.net ou idalves@vm.uff.br

Poesia e museologia em Vasco Graça Moura

Fernando Matos Oliveira

Resumo. Este ensaio cruza a poesia de Vasco Graça Moura (VGM) com algumas das aporias que definem a configuração museológica da contemporaneidade, aspecto particularmente relevante num autor filiado na tradição *culturalista* da poesia portuguesa de Novecentos. A cena do museu na obra de VGM oscila entre a visitação individual, marca da sua origem setecentista, e a saturação turística actual. Recorrendo ao poema intitulado "morte de paolo e francesca na livraria do louvre" procuro sobretudo mostrar como, apesar do comércio acelerado da cultura, o processo de esteticização posto em marcha pelo museu na modernidade aprisiona a poesia do autor, sujeitando toda a sua referencialidade à condição museológica.

Criatura emblemática da modernidade, o museu é hoje uma instituição florescente entre as denominadas indústrias da memória. Aquela racionalização que o universalismo de Setecentos começou por anunciar com as curiosidades da *Wunderkammer* tem sofrido notáveis transfigurações nesta passagem para o terceiro milénio. A narrativa histórica que sustenta o museu fez-se com os mesmos argumentos do progresso que levou o Renascimento ao mundo pós-industrial. O museu nasceu de idêntica vertigem temporal, da urbanização, da 'deslocação' do sujeito, enfim, da compressão espacial a que a modernidade vem submetendo o planeta por todo o lado (Walsh). O museu representa tão-só a institucionalização do passado que o presente renega

Portuguese Literary & Cultural Studies 7 (2008): 185-92.

como resto, espécie de indemnização por perdas e danos. Mas a ressonância histórica do museu concentra ainda uma outra narrativa: a da constituição autónoma dos objectos artísticos. Não por acaso, a estética nasce ao mesmo tempo que o museu moderno, por meados do século XVIII, tornando-se este o local por excelência da contemplação sensível—embora cada vez menos "desinteressada," até mesmo quanto à benevolência dos seus propósitos públicos. O museu está, pois, especialmente habilitado para despir os objectos da sua contingência histórica, tornando-os aptos para o sequestro estético. A única contingência que os define é a autoridade do lugar e a lógica da simbolização que lhes atribui as propriedades de obra de arte.

O que aqui pretendo analisar é simplesmente o modo como a poesia de Vasco Graça Moura (VGM) oscila entre a visitação individual do museu, herdeira do seu instante original, e a visitação colectiva que pauta a sua saturação turística em tempos mais recentes. Para tanto, e sem descurar a natureza museológica que envolve todo o projecto poético de VGM, limito-me sobretudo a extrair algumas implicações de uns quantos poemas que na sua obra explicitamente convocam a ida ao museu.

A perturbação da visita à casa da Arte pode, pois, começar por uns "magotes excitados" que se atravessam entre a pessoa do poeta e a contemplação de *ticiano*, título do primeiro poema. Apesar do protesto, deve notar-se que a visita é aqui já feita sob a influência protocolar da *promenade* a dois. Enquanto lugar de afectividades, o museu do poeta permite-lhe assim a entrada de mão dada com a mulher. No entanto, o constrangimento da circulação por entre a muita "gente a mais" manifesta-se num certo "desespero":

eu desespero nos museus: há sempre
gente a mais e quadros realmente
bons a menos. mas nos melhores há sempre

uma miraculosa descoberta. passeando
 no louvre, uma vez, de mãos dadas, e a custo
atravessando magotes excitados de turistas,

disse à minha mulher que estava ali, à nossa
frente, uma prova na pintura italiana
do século XVI, a evidência de que só

o ticiano se importava com as mulheres

de maneira ostensiva e radical (...). (*Poesias* 149)

Como se vê, o "desespero" perante as massas vai a par de certas discriminações qualitativas que recusam a inflação turístico-comercial da objectualidade museológica. Daí a necessidade de um procedimento distintivo do visitante culto, preocupado apenas com "quadros realmente bons." Os "bons" são-no tanto por deliberação crítica do espectador como pela sua especial aptidão sensível. Submetidos ao olhar do visitante, apenas certos quadros se propõem inesgotáveis, resistentes ao esgotamento provocado pelo interminável círculo hermenêutico. Deste modo, os quadros "bons" são aqueles que permitem "uma miraculosa descoberta," isto é, são os que aguentam o investimento aurático que se apodera do olhar no momento da contemplação da arte, sendo esta "realmente" boa.

O momento aurático do visitante tem como pré-condição o encontro individual do sujeito com a obra. Só no sossego deste encontro se permite a subjectivação do objecto e a mobilização da imaginação que o acto interpretativo pede. As condições desta percepção vêm sendo cada vez mais insustentáveis no museu-espectáculo da actualidade. O museu ideal de VGM seria, por isso mesmo, aquele que concentrasse a diversidade e a riqueza patrimonial dos grandes museus públicos com a circulação restrita das colecções privadas. A intimidade da *Kunstkammer* seria algo próximo de tal situação. É sob estas condições ideais—onde o burguês se reconcilia com o mundo através da arte—que a poesia de VGM tem preferencialmente visitado o museu, dando absoluta primazia às obras "realmente" boas. Entre estas contam-se, naturalmente, os grandes mestres da pintura, desde que fiéis à "minúcia da transcrição do real" anunciada com os *primitivos flamengos* (271). Neste Museu Imaginário entram também obras musicais, de Schubert a Mozart, desde que um nível acima do "choque pedagógico" provocado por Mick Jagger, significativamente associado a uma experiência biográfica no Novo Mundo:

"você não sabe quem é mick jagger?" disse elisa

byington travando o carro a fundo de tal

modo que estive a ponto de aprender

por choque pedagógico quem era o dito

no pára-brisas. o mundo

> das onze da noite em copacabana
> ia desabando sobre mim, arranha-céus e tudo,
> morros inclusive. eu não sabia
> do papel que para elisa, digo, para a história
> da civilização tinha tido o mick.
> "por onde que você andou?" fiquei enver-
> gonhadíssimo, porque era confessável (...). (*Poemas* 285)

Confrontado com a música de Jagger, no que diz respeito à política do gosto, o poeta tende a situar-se deliberadamente numa época bem mais antiga, por exemplo, "entre o machado / de bronze e a roda de fiar" (*Poemas* 285). No seu caso, o mais que pode acontecer em matéria de revoluções artísticas é a admissão da fotografia ao altar da contemplação estética. É que o museu, como colecção, é um somatório de objectos *e* de comentários sobre os mesmos, pelo que a arte contemporânea se vê condicionada no acesso ao espaço museológico, muito particularmente ao de VGM. Como escreve Jean-Louis Déotte a propósito das palavras de Walter Benjamin sobre o coleccionismo, "l'histoire de l'art será donc constitutive de l'art, puisque le temps est le grand artist. Les œuvres, pouvant être considérés comme le temps mis par la 'source' lumineuse pour nous parvenir, seront indissociables de la temporalité de la réception, de la multiplicité des accueils de l'œvre" (Déotte 11).

O poema que melhor explicita as aporias do estado museológico na contemporaneidade é contudo o que se intitula *morte de paolo e francesca na livraria do louvre* (*Poesias* 299-302). O título é por si só um programa diversamente cifrado. Esta livraria—convém distingui-la da biblioteca comum—leva mais longe o virtuosismo das tecnologias da reprodução, pois exagera a estilização que no interior do museu já vinha dificultando o confronto directo com as coisas. Esta mesma estilização, aliás, pode ler-se como espectacularização do objecto, que assim quase dispensa a interpretação. O visitante quase só precisa de dizer que esteve lá; a presença do objecto foi-lhe tornada presente de modo gratuito. As lâmpadas que fazem os efeitos de luz no interior do museu, como simulação aurática, estão na livraria do poema também numas "lâmpadas / que às vezes espelhavam." O museu turístico tende nestes casos para um passeio pelas montras. Os "magotes de turistas" que também aqui aparecem no início do texto são agora clientes de um museu reificado. Por experiência pessoal, sabemos que este comercializa o passado à custa de uma parafernália de efeitos que vão do livro ao *recuerdo*. Quando os protagonistas do poema entram na "pirâmide," no verso de abertura, o lugar tem com as pirâmides do Egipto uma semelhança meramente formal. No poema de VGM estamos no Louvre, tendo Paolo e Francesca de descer, como todos os turistas, "pela escada rolante."

A deslocação do museu para a livraria deste é, pois, um movimento que duplica a emancipação do material histórico para além de qualquer vestígio contingente. A livraria do museu é, digamos assim, um museu em segundo grau. Esta última radicalizou precisamente a componente crítica com que a modernidade havia instaurado a ordem do museu, exibindo agora não já o objecto, mas apenas o comentário em livro ou, então, já só a imagem dele. Nos termos de Platão, a livraria do museu exibiria sombras de sombras ou, na terminologia poética de VGM, "imagens do mundo das imagens" (*Poesias* 299). Estas imagens surgem como peças de um "labirinto" que, na acumulação da livraria, se apresenta como cadinho temporal. A livraria do museu não reproduz sequer a narrativa espacial que a disposição do museu ainda permite. É pela deslocação física dos amantes que as coisas se vão pelo menos "combinando." Esta *combinação* é uma narrativa didáctica que, na verdade, vem das Luzes anteriores à iluminação eléctrica:

> (...) sobre as mesas
> cintilavam retratos e paisagens,
> estátuas e objectos e animais,
>
> deuses da grécia, tótems da oceania,
> máscaras africanas, bronzes da ásia,
> lavores medievais, marfins e flores,
>
> as imagens do mundo das imagens
> que se iam combinando nos seus olhos
> e percorrendo os tempos lhes traziam
>
> gente da renascença e maneiristas,
> explosões do barroco, impressionismos,
> cubistas e vanguardas (...). (*Poesias* 299)

Perante a disposição dos materiais na livraria, Paolo e Francesca ensaiam diversas vezes a narração do caos. A indecisão dos amantes ao circularem na livraria vem-lhes de um estado de deriva, bem compreensível nos mortos-vivos. Por "quererem e não quererem," acabam por ficar sem saber "se queriam encontrar alguma coisa." A "perdição" de ambos no espaço da livraria faz-se precisamente num movimento entre o caos e a ordem. O desejo de ordenação é uma necessidade afim à que emana do caos da memória que confronta todo o coleccionador apaixonado. O caos diz-se com "labirinto," "dúbia fronteira," "metamorfoses," "mudanças," "sombras," "gestos incompletos." A ordem prefere a deliberação verbal, com *organizar, inquirir, entender, apropriar, soletrar, reler, perguntar.*

Mas o problema maior levanta-se quanto à ontologia dos protagonistas desta ida à livraria do Louvre. Paolo e Francesca entram na livraria pela escrita do poeta, na qualidade de fugitivos dantescos, vindos directamente do Círculo Segundo do "Inferno," tal como é descrito n'*A Divina Comédia*. A sua aventura é narrada no condicional, como sobrevivência hipotética à morte que o livro de Dante sancionara. Em rigor, os amantes de Dante chegam à livraria do museu já na condição de objectos museológicos. Apesar disso, e este é o *punctum* do poema, VGM insiste num exercício que põe à prova a mortalidade dos amantes, marcando-lhes um encontro suplementar com a vida. A vida aparece neste encontro derradeiro como uma promessa ou esboço que apenas se insinua por entre a acumulação mortuária da livraria. O caminho em direcção à vida, para fora do "labirinto" desse passado—um passado que era também o deles, pois o labirinto era o "das suas próprias voltas dentro dele"—é um trajecto que lhes exige um *abrandamento* (inteligível) dos tantos "livros e mais livros" que se mostram nas estantes. Recorde-se que estamos em pleno centro da agitação do museu-espectáculo. Daí que a coisa se faça por tentativas, vagarosas: "tentar devagar apropriar-se"; "a pouco e pouco haviam as sombras de ir-se dissipando"; "talvez (...) entrando aos poucos numa líquida ternura"; "talvez entre as palavras"; "devagar, mais devagar / ainda do que antes." Estas, enfim, algumas formas de irem "soletrando as sílabas da vida" ou de viverem minimamente as "partículas do dia," "momento a momento." A ter existido, a positividade da "líquida ternura" ter-se-ia espalhado "sem palavras," quer dizer, sem a mediação das letras. O impulso vital manifestar-se-ia sensivelmente, pelas "pontas dos dedos" ou, "feita aroma," como "bálsamo":

(...) e a luz daria

uma voz aos contornos afagados
da melodia a desprender-se dela
numa gavinha leve, numa curva,

talvez entre as palavras, ou talvez
a esgueirar-se das pálpebras, entrando
aos poucos numa líquida ternura,

aos poucos capturada pelas pontas
dos dedos, devagar, mais devagar,
ainda do que dantes, feita aroma,

ou bálsamo ou concêntricas ondinhas
do sossego a espalhar-se sem palavras,
mas soletrando as sílabas da vida (...). (*Poesias* 301)

Apesar de reiteradas tentativas, a vida entrevista pelos amantes foi "breve alegria." O fracasso do esforço resulta sobretudo da impossibilidade de o poeta VGM salvar a vida de ambos pela re-escrita de Dante. Esta diferença revela-se, mais adiante, no facto de a alegria (a vida) se consumir "nos gestos," enquanto "os ditos" (os livros) só podem aspirar à fabricação de "cinza":

(...) e lembrou-lhes um verso de repente:
"a boca me beijou todo a tremer,"
e sem ser bem assim, era isso mesmo
e o seu deslumbramento por receio
foi só breve alegria, ardeu nos gestos,
e houve amargura e cinza nos seus ditos
por quererem e não quererem. Regressaram

ao livro a que pertencem. e morreram. (*Poesias* 301-02)

Este final supõe a certeza da morte e, mais ainda, a certeza da pertença dos amantes ao livro a que "regressaram." A gramática impõe-lhes finalmente a certeza de um "pertencem." O círculo museológico acaba assim por se fechar completamente. Entre a visitação da livraria e a re-escrita, VGM jamais abandona o museu, pois a morte de Paolo Malatesta e de Francesca de Rimini teve como causa imediata, já em Dante, a leitura de um livro com os romances da Távola Redonda. A letra de VGM tomou um caso cuja origem se perde nas páginas dos livros. O próprio amor proposto pela "ternura líquida" se revela simultaneamente dádiva e ficção museológica, resultado do poder e da autoridade interpretativa do visitante compulsivo que é VGM. Fê-lo, diga-se, sabendo que nas palavras de Francesca de Rimini o livro/museu também testemunha a mortalidade:

> Quando lemos do desejado riso
> a ser beijado por tão grande amante,
> e este, que de mim seja indiviso,
> a boca me beijou todo anelante.
> Galeoto foi o livro e quem o disse:
> Nesse dia não lemos adiante. (Dante 63-65)

Obras Citadas

Dante Alighieri. *Divina Comédia*. Trans. Vasco Graça Moura. Lisboa: Círculo de Leitores, 1995.

Déotte, Jean-Louis. *Le musée, l'origine de l'esthetique*. Paris: Editions L'Harmattan, 1993.

Karp, Ivan; Lavine, Steven D. *Exhibiting Cultures: The Poetics and Politics of Museum Display*. Washington and London: Smithsonian Institution Press, 1991.

Moura, Vasco Graça. *Poemas Escolhidos*. Lisboa: Bertrand, 1996.

———. *Poesias 1997/2000*. Lisboa: Quetzal, 2000.

Walsh, Kevin. *The Representation of the Past. Museums and the Heritage in the Post-Modern World*. New York: Routledge, 1997.

Fernando Matos Oliveira é Docente da Faculdade de Letras da Universidade de Coimbra. Vem publicando artigos sobre literatura e teatro em diversas revistas. É autor dos livros *O Destino da Mimese e a Voz do Palco: O Teatro Português Moderno* (1997) e *Teatralidades: 12 Percursos pelo Território do Espectáculo* (2003). Editou uma *Antologia Poética* de António Pedro (1998), um volume com o *Teatro—Ódio de Raça* e *O Cedro Vermelho*, de Gomes de Amorim (2000, em colaboração com Maria Aparecida Ribeiro) e os *Escritos sobre Teatro*, de António Pedro (2001). E-mail: fmatos@ci.uc.pt

Os desejos a que ninguém responde

Jorge Gomes Miranda

O filósofo alemão Fichte ergue o "eu" à categoria de princípio criador do mundo, atribuindo-lhe a capacidade de propor em absoluto a realidade a partir da subjectividade ("Doutrina da Ciência" 1794). Os românticos partilham com Fichte a concepção de que o ser do homem se não cumpre neste mundo, realizando-se somente no infinito. A esta crença fundamental corresponde a conversão da estabilidade em mobilidade, do ser em devir.

A "flor azul" surgiu como símbolo do infinito. Na obra *Heinrich Von Hoterdingen*, o herói de Novalis é um jovem artista, o peregrino da flor azul. Esta é o símbolo, a infinita nostalgia pelo misterioso e irradiante fundamento da realidade que une todas as coisas.

Na poesia portuguesa contemporânea, o percurso espiritual de Fernando Pinto do Amaral (FPA) revitalizou este salto do real para quimera, simbolizado pela "flor azul."

> Desaparecendo
> de hotel em hotel, perseguia
> a nota mais azul, a única razão,
> o seu único fim. (248)

> ficarás
> nos teus jardins à minha espera,
> ó flor do século vinte regressando

Portuguese Literary & Cultural Studies 7 (2008): 193-210.
© University of Massachusetts Dartmouth.

> ao silêncio do século dezoito
> e à solidão, que é cúmplice dos mortos. (156)

> Ó vã Lisboa,
> cai sobre mim o peso dos teus sonhos,
> "quimera azul" da minha dor sem pátria. (396)

Imprevisível, rebelde, a sua poesia esboça-se num desejo de conhecer as muitas extensas zonas de mistério que nos circundam; o poeta é o companheiro oculto, o silencioso irmão de todas as coisas, havendo apenas uma única lei a que obedece: não impedir a coisa alguma o acesso à sua alma.

E, embora o poeta hoje não seja o príncipe espiritual ou o prelado laico, iniciado às verdades do mundo invisível, como o foi na Idade Romântica, a sua vocação espiritual permanece, sobremaneira num combate orientado para o futuro, mas sem tirar os olhos da materialidade do mundo.

Com efeito, a poesia de FPA, perseguindo, neste sentido, um caminho homólogo à do francês Yves Bonnefoy, encontra-se entre uma espécie de materialismo inato e um desejo sequioso de transcendência. Zona de interseção entre o mundo que se conhece, o fenomenológico e o mundo do que nos escapa; entre o que se conhece de modo lógico e o conhecido através da intuição.

Assumindo o desígnio de Francis Ponge—"O homem é um deus que se desconhece"—a escrita de FPA supera as clivagens daqueles que procuram separar as águas entre a espiritualidade e o materialismo, a profundidade e a superfície, o desejo da alma e a estrita materialidade das coisas.

O poema é, aqui, um objecto misto, partilhado e contraditório, cuja principal função ou propriedade seria de conjugar e conjurar realidades aparentemente incompatíveis: forma e sopro, visível e invisível, proximidade e lonjura, limite e ilimitado, vago e rigor, movimento e fixação.

A obra espiritual é realizada não sobre um mundo místico que implicasse um acesso a verdades escondidas, ou sequer sobre o modo religioso que supõe um sistema de relações e de ligações constantes, fixadas pela tradição e duplicadas por uma crença, mas, particularmente, sobre o modo aleatório da experiência lírica que liga por relações instáveis o sujeito àquilo que o transporta ou excede.

Seria erróneo, no entanto, conceber esta poesia como estético—filosófica, como um sonho ou devaneio. Pelo contrário, FPA não esquece que é

Cada vez mais próxima,
a indiferença natural das coisas,
a pobreza do tempo. Pelas ruas
o deserto das montras luminosas
ensina a cada sonho a herança do caos. (140)
Não há para o que resta deste mundo
nenhum jardim. O mais distante
paraíso
ficou para trás, cavaleiro
fugindo entre montanhas. (127)

Pobreza que se manifesta igualmente nos rituais mundanos que todos mais ou menos temos de cumprir. Com acutilância e auto-ironia o poeta descreve uma dessas festas onde vai desaguar o "jet-set" cultural:

Entre beijos de afecto e circunstância
ia representar o meu papel:
simpatia com um toque de distância
de modo a não parecer muito infiel

à presença dos outros seres humanos,
afinal, convidados como eu
prós frequentes rituais mundanos
do nosso Portugal tão europeu. (472)

Apesar do sujeito que fala no poema ser, tantas vezes, um personagem, uma ficção do eu, a prática da poesia implica sempre a autenticidade. Uma distância em relação aos gestos da gesticulação aprendida e assumida como própria no teatro do mundo. Neste particular, a estratégia verbal que estes poemas endereçam surge despojada de ornatos e adereços teatrais.

Muitos dos versos que FPA escreveu encerram um fundo trágico: o reconhecimento de que o infinito nunca poderia ser vivido nos confins da realidade. Daí a contradição inquieta e a nostalgia elegíaca que acompanham estes poemas.

Não surpreendendo, então, que o regresso do "eu" a que muita da nova poesia é sensível não possua já a mesma confiança ontológica, a mesma segurança na hipotética profundidade de sentido que pretende comunicar-nos.

No terceiro dos seus Quartetos, "The Dry Salvages," T. S. Eliot aponta em dois versos o que poderia ser em substância todo o progresso tacteante do conhecimento poético, ao referir que tivemos a experiência, mas perdemos o sentido, e aproximarmo-nos ao sentido restaura a experiência.

Qual, então, o caminho, ou um dos caminhos, que o poeta irá seguir?

Para continuar a sua busca espiritual e manter na linguagem alguma esperança, a poesia deverá, porventura, voltar-se mais para o rosto do outro, do que para uma paisagem cada vez mais desolada.

O "outro" surge como uma crença forte, uma espécie de fé metódica num tempo em que a dúvida metódica parece ser aplicada a tudo.

A emoção surge, assim, como conteúdo central do poema. Emoção que implica igualmente interpretação do mundo e indagação moral. A este poeta interessa-lhe em poesia a voz pessoal, não a voz original. Sendo um poeta da intimidade, procura o seu eu secreto. Trata-se de tornar presente o esquecido, voltar a conhecer...

E se, por exemplo, interrogarmos certos versos amorosos e eróticos, procurando saber o que neles há de reflexo de experiências pessoais, eles dizem-nos que a componente amorosa e erótica, as formosas mentiras do corpo têm aqui, igualmente, o valor de um símbolo, de procura em desvelar o mais profundo da essência humana. Neste particular, a poesia nunca é um espelho, mas sim um desvelamento. O poeta não procura aí reconhecer-se, mas conhecer-se.

A afirmação de um modo de ser no mundo e duma poética que se queriam indissociáveis, conduz a uma inocência respiratória: a identificação da poesia à vida e esta ao amor, que encontramos também num poeta como Paul Éluard, em cuja poesia o amor é um perpétuo delírio de quem já tudo disse, mas tudo ainda tem para dizer.

O imaginário amoroso é léxico e sintático: nomeia as coisas do mundo e mostra-se atento às suas coordenadas:

Cheguei a casa há pouco e amanhã

celebrarei contigo pla primeira vez

esse dia que alguém convencionou

ser para os namorados: eu e tu,

dois seres quase sonâmbulos,

afogados em histórias mal cicatrizadas

que extravasam ao longo de conversas

plas estradas nocturnas por onde fugimos

da vida que nos dói: velhos amores

refulgindo na tua memória,

na minha fantasia que os volta a viver

em ti, por ti, como se também eu

ressentisse na pele o sabor desses beijos

esvaindo-se no tempo, que lhes toca

ao de leve, com lábios de veludo,

e os arrasta num caudal de espectros,

de vagas silhuetas, na penumbra

que foi a minha vida até chegar a ti. (282-83)

Meditando nos versos de S. João da Cruz—"Os olhos do meu amado levo-os desenhados nas minhas entranhas"—Maria Zambrano diz-nos que não há poesia enquanto algo não fica desenhado nas entranhas; a poesia foi sempre coisa da carne, da inferioridade da carne, da interioridade da carne: das entranhas. No entanto, se aqui encontramos paixão, voracidade que destrói o corpo, há também veneração exaltada de um ideal inacessível, mas absoluto e necessário. O amor surge ao mesmo tempo como doença e vocação. Não por acaso a ideia de Agustina Bessa Luís—autora com quem o poeta dialoga no poema "No Bom Jesus do Monte"—de que a infelicidade é a mais ardente das amantes aparece nestes versos: "A Agustina / tem deveras razão, é necessário / o sofrimento." (238)

O "outro" nunca é aqui objecto de posse e de poder. Só admite comunicação. Quantas vezes se retirando para o seu mistério. A exacerbação subjectiva implica a solidão do "eu." E para enganar a solidão, o sujeito busca os alimentos terrestres, para utilizar-mos uma linguagem afim da do filósofo lituano-francês Emanuel Levinas. Fruições pelas quais tenta iludir a solidão: ler um livro, colocar um CD, falar com os amigos, uma saída nocturna a bares.

Apenas tu

irás acompanhar esse fantasma

pelo abandonado panteão

dos quartos e dos bares e dos écrans

como se ambos quisessem regressar

à solidão mais próxima dos astros. (173-74)

Os românticos, recordemo-lo, experimentavam dolorosamente a alienação das relações humanas, a destruição das antigas formas comunitárias da vida social, o isolamento do indivíduo no deserto da cidade. Numerosas são as obras que mostram e analisam o malogro da comunicação como condição universal e trágica. Na modernidade o sujeito é actor principal na história. O homem que nasce, sofre e morre. Com as suas afecções, os seus vícios, num tributo pago ao tempo e ao outro. O homem encontra-se em trânsito sobre a terra, ele próprio é lugar de passagem. Como o sujeito, a realidade é móbil e descontínua. O "flâneur" inscreve-se na economia aleatória de relações que a grande cidade permite.

Amor do fugaz e do inalcansável, quer dizer, do movimento e das suas conexões, do que nos escapa, amor de uma aspiração indefinida, eis o rosto do passeante.

A cidade é a paisagem moral da transitoridade, concentrando em si o moderno caracterizado por uma "diminuição progressiva da alma e uma dominação progressiva da matéria," nas palavras de Baudelaire.

Este autor, caracteriza ainda a urbe como o Inferno, mas reconhece-a também como fantástico lugar de conhecimento. Tornado "pintor da vida moderna" o poeta é o guia, a testemunha, o passeante e o hermeneuta. Os poemas de Fernando Pinto do Amaral presentificam esta realidade que remonta a Fichte e tem no poeta das "Flores do Mal" um dos seus personagens principais. Muitos dos poemas que o português escreveu são inspirados num tipo histórico, o "flâneur" de Baudelaire: um homem passeando sozinho pelas ruas movido pelos estímulos da grande cidade que o rodeia, a qual lê hoje como se fosse um "perverso turista acidental" (394).

A multidão é o seu domínio, como o ar é o do pássaro, como a água é o do peixe, como afirma Baudelaire.

As cidades são por excelência os lugares do anonimato, da diversidade e do encontro, três qualidades que se apreciam idealmente caminhando.

Certas vezes, as ruas preservam a ideia de que a cidade deve favorecer os encontros fortuitos; e, ainda que por instantes, as cidades abandonam a sua realidade trágica: aglomerações, subúrbios, controlados, compartimentados, concebidos para os automobilistas.

Sem mapa, aquele que vagueia continuamente—um olhar para os passantes, outro para os sítios abertos onde se pode comprar tabaco, cigarros ou uma última revista—passando do que observa ao que conjectura, chega sempre demasiado tarde ou abandona demasiado cedo o lugar dos acontecimentos. A sensação de que a perda, reverso da morte, move o tempo e a bússola dos seus passos, guiam-no. Os que caminham na rua são familiares de um estado particular de solidão, uma solidão negra pontuada de encontros como o céu nocturno é pontuado de estrelas.

Pois quem nos assegura que aquele corpo visto de longe naquele dia e àquela hora, com quem nos cruzamos sem trocar palavra e que talvez não tornemos a encontrar não era o corpo que poderia dar um rumo diferente à nossa vida? Um simples olhar curioso torna-se interesse, o interesse conduz ao sorriso, e o sorriso a outra coisa.

E como recordar mais tarde o que apenas entrevimos numa praça, à entrada do metro, a meio do caminho da nossa vida?

Na estética moderna, a memória, a fim de superar as suas limitações, tende a ser assimilada à imaginação. Enquanto a memória tradicionalmente concebida é reprodutora (evoca somente o que foi), a nova memória imaginada é criadora: desperta aquilo que também podia ter sido.

Já dizia Bernardo Soares no *Livro do Desassossego* que "exploramos as nossas sensações como grandes países desconhecidos."

"Dez elegias para o fim do milénio," ciclo inicial de "A Cinza do Último Cigarro," obra que encerra *Poesia Reunida 1990- 2000*, reactualiza esta questão. Aqui, encontramos poemas onde se indagam todas as correspondências entre o funcionamento descontínuo da memória imaginada, da leitura e das viagens. Como outros seus companheiros de geração, FPA pratica uma estratégia da memória semelhante à do melancólico. Este, segundo ao Agamben, não recorda com a intenção de evocar algo perdido, mas imagina que recorda para poder desfrutar (pelo menos privativamente: enquanto objecto de nostalgia) de uma coisa de outro modo inacessível. Daí, podermos afirmar que os livros de FPA são livros de um nostálgico, de alguém que mostra nostalgia tanto por aquilo que viveu como pelo que não viveu, que é o modo como se manifesta para Octávio Paz a melancolia neste final de milénio e início de outro. Neste sentido, e ainda parafraseando Agamben, a melancolia não seria uma atitude regressiva perante a perda do objecto de amor, mas sim a capacidade fantasmática de fazer aparecer como perdido um objecto inapropriável.

E se a modernidade se constitui como a atracção pela actualidade do presente, não é menos característica sua a tendência para se evadir desta mesma actualidade. Na primeira elegia, intitulada "Elegia de Lisboa," o poeta abre-se ao ritmo da cidade, dialoga com Cesário Verde e segue mais ou menos o trajecto que este percorreu num crepúsculo de neblina lisboeta, em "O Sentimento dum

Ocidental." A viagem exterior delimita a viagem interior. E embora a paisagem seja distinta, o sofrimento a caminho da morte que o poeta vê nos rostos é o mesmo. História, vida e literatura ainda que separadas confundem-se sempre na sua sensibilidade.

"Nas nossas ruas, ao anoitecer,"
abre-se num olhar a pena errante
de quem se ilude em passos vagarosos,
em mais um jogo incerto de cem luzes
sob este céu tão baço. Como sempre,
os mudos automóveis sobem, descem
ruas e ruas rumo a outras ruas
polvilhadas de gente que regressa
sem ter partido—insectos ondulando
ao som das lentas horas fatigadas,
rostos esfarrapados de trabalhos
inúteis como a tarde que se entrega
às doces mãos secretas do crepúsculo
vibrante no declive dos telhados
em degraus sobre o Tejo. Devagar
cola-se ao espírito a membrana escura
dos sonhos que perdi ou que pedi
há tantos anos à eternidade
e agora se dispersam na colmeia
das pequenas janelas reacesas,
no bafo das famílias indiferentes
no seu "tinir de loiças e talheres,"
suspensas de ecrãzinhos onde vêem
outras famílias e outras indiferenças
até ao infinito. As sombras crescem
quando a lua aparece e pouco a pouco
a solidão retoma os seus direitos,
devora o que ainda resta do azul
e eu vou descendo a pé, já transformado
num perverso turista acidental
e condenado a "combater em vão
o velho tédio" ocidental, em bares

> onde reagem faces conhecidas
>
> em acenos voláteis que se cruzam
>
> com esse aroma surdo e espesso e dócil
>
> das vozes que por vezes me esvaziam
>
> qualquer recordação. (393-94)

Herdeiro igualmente de um Prufrock, um Leopold Bloom ou uma Mrs. Dalloway, o personagem poemático (no qual podemos ler o próprio autor ou um qualquer de nós) deambula pela cidade recolhendo o caos de impressões e sensações provocados por ela, escutando o que de mistério e segredo ainda restam, num tempo em que só a dor parece ocultar-se por detrás da superfície, sob os rostos dos que para nós fingem olhar. Por vezes a paisagem interior aproximando-se da cantada por Eliot.

O que caminha é um "caleidoscópio dotado de consciência." E é precisamente a expansão da consciência a que Baudelaire chama o gosto do infinito, que vai viver na poesia de Cesário e, hoje, na de FPA. A alma que atravessa a vastidão do espaço até à ilimitada amplitude do horizonte, voo que atravessa as distintas paisagens das demais elegias: sobre Muzot, Sever do Vouga, na Costa del Sol, sobre Coimbra, Zurique, Porto, Viena, Braga ou o Bósforo.

A caminhada é também uma espécie de sintaxe que organiza os pensamentos, as emoções e os encontros. E uma cidade como a Lisboa descrita por este poeta pode aparecer como uma selva, um quarto, um livro que se lê à medida que se caminha.

Tal a cidade de Paris, "lida" pelo francês Jean-Christophe Bailly, Lisboa "é uma grande biblioteca, uma memória conservada pelos peões. Que estes últimos venham a desaparecer, e as coleçcões de histórias da cidade tornar-se-ão indecifráveis" (Sheringham 111).

Mas—e atendo-nos ainda à "Elegia de Lisboa," metonímia de muitas das inquietações que cruzam esta escrita—quando ao entardecer se deambula pelas ruas de Lisboa, experimenta-se (ensinou-nos a poesia que é uma elevada forma de vida) sensações, estados anímicos que pertencem ao domínio do tédio: um enervamento, uma dolência, um mal-estar, um desconforto que se manifesta e se tenta combater em bares.

> Recomeço o meu circuito,
>
> arranco e desço mais um pouco, até

à zona antigamente industrial,
aos pálidos felizes contentores
sob a penumbra imensa dos guindastes
quase irreais. Alguns amigos entram
em armazéns de espuma onde exercito
os fúteis bocejantes sentimentos,
a mais falsa alegria, a peregrina
febrícula do espírito embrulhado
em *whisky* ou nas falas transparentes
de alguém que por acaso eu poderia
talvez amar—"I'm so crazy for you!"—,
mas não há "nunca nada de ninguém,"
só esta bílis negra que me espera
á saída dos últimos lugares
acompanhando agora o rio que alastra
e se mistura à crónica euforia
de uns "tristes bebedores" que mal trauteiam
frágeis franjas de música boiando
no seu vazio que é também o meu
quando parto agarrado a um volante
e na aragem dos vidros entrabertos
saboreio um cigarro que se evola
só para ti, Lisboa. Sempre quis
pulsar ao mesmo ritmo que tu,
transpor este deserto e conseguir
em golfadas de versos libertar
o encarcerado sopro do teu peito-
— cidade atravessada de armadilhas
traindo e atraindo cada gesto
das poucas silhuetas ainda vivas
sob os pilares da ponte. Ó vã Lisboa,
cai sobre mim o peso dos teus sonhos,
"quimera azul" da minha dor sem pátria,
e entre dois semáforos suplico-te:
apaga do meu corpo o sobressalto
dos seres de carne e osso, dessa estranha
realidade apenas virtual

que me despe de todos os fantasmas
e fica projectada no silêncio
das cinco e meia, enquanto vou seguindo
a "correnteza augusta das fachadas,"
as pombalinas rectas, um cortejo
de iluminadas cinzas. Uma estrela
parece ter sorrido para mim
como se finalmente esta cidade
me confiasse a rota imperceptível
das suas ondas a perder de vista—
"marés de fel, como um sinistro mar,"
caudal por onde singro e me despeço
do sangue de quem solta, solitário,
algum suspiro em quarto derradeiro
até ser minha a cor da tua voz,
ó morte a que abandono luz e sombra,
o grito do meu nada ainda em fuga,
mas de súbito em paz entre os teus braços. (395-97)

Mas, como sucede tantas vezes, a chama que nos alenta é a mesma que nos vai consumindo: talvez pressentindo isto, a melancolia, é um estado de alma vivido pelo personagem poemático no interior dos seus versos, como num envio a essa fenomenologia da tristeza—conhecida por Acédia (título do seu primeiro livro) durante a Idade Média—, que entre nós, lembremo-lo, é caracterizada por D. Duarte, no "Leal Conselheiro," como nojo, pesar, desprazer, aborrecimento e saudade.

Depois das viagens, depois da noite, depois do desejo, junto ao frio e à melancolia, o poeta acompanha os convidados das últimas festas. E o que permanece nas mãos frias depois dos encontros mais frios são os restos da neblina que antecipa a madrugada. Fiapos de névoa que o poeta transmuta em monólogos dialogantes com esses corpos que abandonou.

O registo de apontamentos mais ou menos biográficos de encontros amorosos ou nem tanto, bem como o conjunto de actos transcendidos liricamente, procuram encontrar por entre a névoa algum sentido, por entre os beijos e as mágoas, as consequências da ilusão. A isso chamamos poesia.

As distintas histórias vividas sabem que o tempo e a fugacidade plasmam a nossa biografia, existindo por isso nestes versos uma materialidade alada que tenta justificar as ilusões diante da paisagem da desilusão: são o último olhar para uma fotografia que prendeu um gesto inicial, a dolência travestida de felicidade com que são contados os argumentos de filmes que nos poderão recompor (a esta luz leia-se o ciclo "Planos e sequências," que estilisticamente porventura procura conservar a ingenuidade dos sonhos). Em cada desencontro gravado na pele esta certeza:

> Saber recomeçar, fugir de novo,
> outra vez indefeso, vagueando
> pelos mesmos lugares, como se neles
> houvesse mais do que o mundo, uma alegria
> imediata, ardendo, ao abandono,
> entre casas e ruas vazias. Pra quê
> voltar a tudo isso? (199)

Todos os lugares, cenários e palavras convocadas nos falam duma plenitude ferida pelo tempo: um deslumbramento corporal fugidio, as marcas dessas desconhecidas que podíamos amar na discoteca nocturna, um desejo por cumprir junto a um mar que esta noite não se abre em fruto. Daí que mais do que sentimentos das ilusões desfeitas os versos cantem a consciência de que a beleza é o rosto da morte. Os fracassos, perdas inevitáveis por definição.

Com temas de sempre, com imagens de sempre, como queria Borges, procura o poeta de novo o mistério da emoção pessoal. A poesia sendo nesta obra entendida como sentimento, inteligência comovida, pensamento emocionado. A inteligência, aqui quer dizer: procurar erigir, de um modo exacto que se furta ao ênfase e ao sentimentalismo, a ficção de uma experiência de carácter individual partilhável, e que mediante ela se aceda a esse grau superior de conhecimento acerca da existência que é a emoção.

Na vida de todos os poetas chega um momento em que, depois de anos a aprender a ser poeta, deve aprender a deixar de sê-lo, quer dizer—e a ideia é de Auden—que procura advertir-nos do perigo da auto-indulgência, uma ameaça que acontece quando dedica uma parte significativa da sua vida a escrever poemas da melhor maneira possível.

Com o correr dos anos o poeta aprende alguns truques—astúcias, no sentido borgesiano—deste ofício. No entanto, apercebe-se que vai perdendo igualmente algo precioso: a liberdade e a inocência quase brutal do tempo em que se confrontava com um poema. O que fazer então?

Na convicção de que um poema não tem de ser, e de que o poema somos nós ou não é, o poeta procura ignorar o censor que se auto-impõe e que determina como tem de ser—e só o poeta interiormente pode responder a este desafio, não as vozes críticas que o cercam—um poema.

Escrever um poema é, ainda, converter-se no seu próprio interlocutor, alguém com o qual não guardamos distância, não podemos ocultar nada, de nada valendo subterfúgios hipócritas. A poesia brotando como necessidade de um poeta que de livro para livro procura definir e redefinir o seu território, uma fonte de intensidade, uma força que se tonifica procurando escapar aos territórios conhecidos. O que nos transporta ao entendimento de que a impressão digital de cada poeta encontra-se na sua poesia e no seu esforço para marcar o território da poesia do seu tempo.

Outra das características marcantes da poesia de FPA é a de ser, como a de outros seus companheiros de geração, aberta "às estridentes vozes de outro século," (405) mostrando a necessidade, muito borgesiana, de recuperar com os leitores a história literária de cada país. Daí que os versos que estabelecem esse contacto com o leitor sejam por todos reconhecidos. Também é borgesiana a idéia de que cada autor é modificado por todos os que o precederam, mas também os modifica a eles, cada poeta cria os seus precursores. Aqui, Cesário Verde, António Nobre ou Mário de Sá-Carneiro.

Em muitos momentos desta obra a figura do "flâneur" dá lugar à do "voyeur," alteração que simboliza a passagem do espaço exterior, da rua, dos passeios, para os espaços privados onde se desenrola a outra face da cidade. Para esses lugares onde a multidão se oferece em espectáculo. Já não se trata da rua onde, ao passar, os desconhecidos se exponham como um relâmpago ao escrutínio do caminhante, mas sim para os cenários que a pintura de Hooper mostrou: quartos, praças, janelas, cafés, hotéis, casinos, discotecas. Lugares onde a atenção está sempre vaga e disponível para o magma dos desejos.

No entanto, o poeta sabe que a estrela que nos ilumina, com o tempo vai deixando de nos guiar: "sóbrio *voyeur* / aprendi as razões do desencanto" (456) Percepção que nos liga ao que Walter Benjamin observou sobre o melancólico. Este, ao tomar o mundo como objecto das suas reflexões, inevitavelmente atraiçoa-o, já que transcende a aparência concreta das coisas ao interpretá-las sob a óptica da caducidade, descobrindo no seu esplendor prenúncios de morte.

Face ao sentimento de finitude e angústia pela desaparição, a poesia funda-se sobre a interrogação que as Elegias de Rilke inauguram:

Quem, se eu gritasse, me ouviria dentre as ordens
dos anjos? e mesmo que um me apertasse
de repente contra o coração: eu morreria da sua
existência mais forte. Pois o belo não é senão
o começo do terrível, que nós mal podemos ainda suportar,
e admiramo-lo tanto, porque, impassível, desdenha
destruir-nos. Todo o anjo é terrível.
E assim eu me reprimo e engulo o chamamento
dum soluçar escuro. Ai! de quem poderíamos
nós então valer-nos? Nem de anjos, nem de homens,
e os bichos perspicazes reparam já
que nós não estamos muito confiados em casa
neste mundo explicado. Resta-nos talvez
qualquer árvore na encosta, que de novo a vejamos
diariamente; resta-nos a estrada de ontem
e a fidelidade amimada dum costume,
que gostou de estar connosco, e por isso ficou e se não foi. (Rilke 193)

Questionamento sobre a possibilidade mesma do apelo e da escuta.

Esta realidade irá conduzir a uma situação em que o poeta moderno, como o afirma Philipe Jacotett exprime a angústia da ruptura entre céu e terra, do canto sem eco, da errante, do grito perdido. Num trajecto que primeiramente consiste em reconhecer-se e definir-se como mortal.

Daí, muitos dos poemas serem elegias ou aparecerem impregnados de um tom elegíaco que mais do que ser de oração fúnebre, amplie esse clamor surdo a uma meditação sobre o destino de todos nós. Procurando reencontrar no interior de si os fios que se desataram na história.

Ao mesmo tempo, que uma totalidade interior se substitui à totalidade exterior perdida. E a elegia abre à poesia o espaço de uma ética, como na "Elegia de Muzot" de FPA. Escutemos de novo:

"Quem, se eu gritar," será capaz de ouvir-me
sob o sangrento sol da tarde exausta,
agora que as palavras estão mortas

para sempre? Ninguém, até ao fim,

resgatará os sonhos de quem ousa

pedir a noite ao dia, o dia á noite,

como se esta só-vida não valesse

o peso de uma nuvem sobre os cumes

já perto do esplendor dessa ilusão

com que finjo falar a esta hora

em que desce da encosta, devagar,

um véu de sensações que mal oculta

uma cruel retórica, abraçada

por invisíveis asas que protegem

todo o sabor da solidão.

(...)

na minha nostalgia: ainda espero

um espasmo do destino que alimente

as enganosas teias deste corpo

e celebre com elas a aliança

de uma nova palavra sonolenta

quando as flores do crepúsculo, em segredo,

cintilarem ás cegas e então

a meiga meia-lua for subindo,

estremunhada e feliz, quase divina,

sobre o silêncio humano—será esse

o preço da mais trémula pergunta

a ecoar num escuro sobressalto

mas nem os anjos lhe darão resposta. (Amaral 398)

E é justamente *a morte* como limite absoluto de uma existência o motivo que condensa o universo poético de Fernando Pinto do Amaral. Segundo Freud, a nossa idéia da morte não passa de uma vaga possibilidade (consideramos a morte como uma dúvida que há que pagar à natureza) e esta possibilidade não se concretiza até que nos vemos forçados a presenciar o falecimento de alguém próximo e querido. Num comovente poema, intitulado "Por causa de uma ave," dedicado a sua mãe, o poeta conta-nos como ao chegar a uma casa de província o esqueleto dum pássaro desencadeia a recordação da morte de seu pai:

Cada vez gosto menos de saborear
o travo tão pastoso da morte, o murmúrio
secreto dos seus olhos invisíveis
dentro de mim. Porém, há pouco tempo,
passou-se um episódio que rompeu
de repente na alma todas as comportas
que fingem proteger os ópios tranquilos
a que chamamos vida. Aconteceu
depois de ter chegado a esta casa
perdida numa encosta de província
e onde venho só de longe em longe:
foi durante a limpeza da sala
que, afastando um armário, descobri
entre pequenas teias, quase envolto
num sudário de pó, ali esquecido,
na treva e no silêncio dos meses de inverno
o esqueleto de um pássaro. Entrara
pla chaminé de pedra e escorregara
até cair junto à lareira. Hoje
imagino o pavor do seu voo suicida,
poisando às cegas de móvel em móvel,
dias e dias plo escuro deserto
da sala fria, à toa, procurando
escapar ao seu naufrágio, encontrar
uma réstia de céu, até que, já sem forças,
se deixou deslizar para trás desse armário
onde morreu de sede e fome e solidão
enquanto mal batia as asas
em arremedos de frustradas fugas.
Ao ter na mão aquele resto de corpo,
os "pedacinhos de ossos," toda a quilha
do peito sustentado o arco das costelas,
as minúsculas patas quase intactas,
lembrei-me, num relance de terror,
de outros ossos maiores, os do meu pai,
a não muitas centenas de metros daqui,
num absurdo cubículo de pedra

sobre o qual está gravado um nome de família.
Apodrecem há mais de quinze anos
em sombras que serão iguais a nós
—passageiros ingénuos e translúcidos
de corpos consumidos no seu próprio lume.
Ao sentir entre os dedos o que foram asas,
vi nos últimos gestos dessa ave,
chocando com as paredes, sem saída,
o mesmo desespero esbracejante
de uma nocturna cama de hospital
onde houve um homem que lutou às cegas
no seu estertor febril e consciente,
junto à fronteira íntima, abissal,
que nem a voz transpõe. Nenhum dos gritos
pode ecoar nos meus, aqui, agora,
nesta dádiva exangue e sem destinatário,
porque toda a poesia se resume
a um calafrio embalsamado em letras,
palavras destinadas a morrer
no momento em que as páginas de um livro,
como as asas de um pássaro, os braços de um homem,
se fecharem num sono a que ninguém responde. (352-54)

Uma palavra ainda para afirmar que concordo com George Steiner quando este afirma que o labor crítico deriva de uma "dívida de amor" pelo texto que é a imagem de "um instinto primário de comunhão"; uma espécie de compromisso pessoal, muito por cima de toda a teoria, com a literatura. O crítico deve, para lá de julgar a literatura (e da arte em geral) da sua própria época, explicar que o texto se encontra sempre em relação completa e provisória com o tempo. E ser uma espécie de intermediário e guarda da obra de arte que ajuda a comunicar a experiência estética. A mediação apenas pode conseguir-se eficazmente se aquele que a exerce mantêm uma vigilante e sempre angustiada convicção da enorme distância que separa o seu próprio trabalho do da obra de que é intérprete.

Quando lemos, conjuramos a presença, o sentido profundo do texto. Por isso, ler bem é arriscar-se muito. Esta breve nota crítica sobre a poesia de Fernando Pinto do Amaral depende, naturalmente, da minha sensibilidade e entendimento sobre a sua obra, mas procurei nunca impôr qualquer grelha interpretativa; antes olhar os seus poemas como ponto de partida, capaz de me conduzir a novos núcleos de sentido e compreensão. O leitor dirá se consegui ou não escapar ao "Conselho," que FPA dá, "aos críticos do novo século," num dos poemas que recentemente publicou:

Se queres parecer inteligente,

desdenha de quem escreve coisas simples

e desconfia, desconfia sempre

dos sentimentos, das convicções.

Diz mal da tua época,

procura dar a tudo um ar difícil

e cita alguns autores que ninguém leu.

Se queres que te respeitem,

reserva a admiração e o elogio

pra certos mortos bem escolhidos,

de preferência estrangeiros,

e acima de tudo

não caias nunca na vulgaridade

de ser compreendido pelos que te lerem. (*Saudade* 35)

Obras Citadas

Amaral, Fernando Pinto. *Poesia Reunida 1990-2000*. Lisboa: Publicações D. Quixote, 2000.

———. "Conselho" Saudade 1 (2001): 35.

Fichte, Johann Gottlieb. *Fundamentos da doutrina da ciência completa*. Trans. e apresentação de Diogo Ferrer. Lisboa: Colibri, 1997.

Rilke, Rainer Maria. *Poemas As Elegias de Duíno e Sonetos a Orfeu*. Trans. Paulo Quintela. Porto: O Oiro do Dia, 1983.

Sheringham, Michael. "City Space, Mental Space, Poetic Space: Paris in Breton, Benjamin and Réda." *Parisian Fields*. Londres: Reaktion Books, 1997.

Jorge Gomes Miranda. Nasceu em 1965. Escreve regularmente sobre literatura em jornais e revistas. É autor dos seguintes livros de poesia: *O Que Nos Protege* (1995); *Portadas Abertas* (1999); *Curtas-Metragens* (2002); *A Hora Perdida* (2003); *Postos de Escuta* (2003); *Este Mundo, Sem Abrigo* (2003).

The Door Ajar: Adília Lopes and the Art of Approximation

Rachel Rothenberg

Abstract. A self-declared "pop-poetess," Adília Lopes has gained recognition in recent years in both literary and pop-cultural spheres, publishing fifteen books since 1985, contributing constantly to Portuguese periodicals and making frequent television appearances. Lopes is not only an influential contemporary poet, but a public figure whose pseudonym holds both the weight of her written work and the attributes of the persona that she has created in the public eye. Perhaps it is due to her extreme visibility in the media, her absolute candor—whether in writing poems that address her literary influences or revealing the details of her personal life on the latest permutation of reality television—that she is so often taken at face value. Much of the critical attention afforded her is aimed at her reliance upon satirical allusion, word games and shock value, as the polemic nature of her poems often outshines their actual intentions. This paper seeks to demonstrate that Lopes should not be taken lightly, that despite the initial response that Lopes's poems incite, a deliberate, ambitious voice emerges from the body of her work. Within the bounds of her poems, Adília Lopes lucidly defines her relationship to Portuguese and international literary continuities while presenting a meticulously formulated aesthetic in which instances of deferred resolution come to define a process of approximation that holds greater value than any anticipated conclusion.

To this faire tree, taking me by the hand,
You did repeat the pleasures which had past,

Portuguese Literary & Cultural Studies 7 (2008): 211-36.
© University of Massachusetts Dartmouth.

> Seeming to grieve they could no longer last.
> And with a chaste, yet loving kisse tooke leave,
> Of which sweet kisse I did it soone bereave:
> Scorning a senceless creature should possesse
> So rare a favour, so great a happinesse.
> No other kisse is could receive from me,
> For fear to give backe what it took of thee:
> So I ingratefull Creature did deceive it,
> Of that which you vouchsaft in love to leave it. (Lanyer 162-172)

As two women walk the grounds of an estate in "The Description of Cooke-ham," Renaissance poet Aemelia Lanyer presents a material syllogism in which a kiss passes from the lips of a woman to the trunk of a tree, and subsequently to the lips of her patroness. She devises a convoluted means of connection that evades actual contact, an intricate system wherein actions are implied and approached rather than committed outright. If nature can hold the same communicative properties as mathematics, then one could argue that the women kiss indirectly, the tree between them acting as a medium and interrupting the trajectory of the intended act. In assembling this construct, Lanyer highlights the most tangible aspect of the relationship it defines, its deliberate manner of navigating space. For Adília Lopes, whose poems so often hinge upon calculated manipulations of proximity and division, the delineation of nearly any relationship requires a structural component. Though fairly unlikely that "Cooke-ham" falls within the wide range of Lopes's literary influences, much of her work reflects Lanyer's use of complicated paths of logic and sequence that allow her to hold a narrative in a state of suspension rather than allowing it to advance towards completion. Lopes refuses to simplify the corporal, mythical or canonical associations that she establishes within the bounds of her poems, choosing instead to forge them with schemes of carefully staged approximations; while suggesting an attempt to bridge the gap between the poet and the relations that she approaches, be they spatial, personal or historical, Lopes counters any convergence that she ventures with a palpable sense of distance, a notable absence of any anticipated conclusion.

In the poems that appear in her first published volume, *Um Jogo Bastante Perigoso* [*A Rather Dangerous Game*], Lopes's fundamental aesthetic of approximation emerges and begins to gain definition. A poem in which her formal sensibilities are most clearly presented is one of her earliest, "Para um Vil Criminoso" ["To a Vile Criminal"], an elegant tirade delivered to a criminal who has done her, "mil maldades / e uma maldade muito grande / que não se faz" (1-3) ["a thousand wrongs / and one great wrong / that isn't done"]. Within the bounds of this poem, the many unnamed wrongs come to no better result than a fractional exponent that closes in on an unattainable sum; no amount of simple wrongs can measure up to the great wrong that is perpetually denied, and a thousand advancements will not bring the poem any closer to a final destination. She claims, "a maldade muito grande está feita / e não se faz" ["the great wrong is done / and it isn't done"], petulantly repeating her insistence that such a wrong is clearly inappropriate, and at the same time asserting that the greatest wrong is not one that can be committed but an anticipated offence that fails to come to fruition, one that can only be outlined in negative space (19-20). After questioning the criminal's regrets or lack thereof for committing these acts, or perhaps for his failure to commit them, Lopes lets the poem trail off:

> acho que essa maldade muito grande
>
> nos aproximou um do outro
>
> em vez de nos afastar
>
> mas para mim é um drôle de chemin
>
> e para ti também deve ser
>
> mas com um vil criminoso nunca se sabe (21-26)

> [I think that this great wrong
>
> brought us closer together
>
> rather than parting us
>
> but to me it is a drôle de chemin
>
> and should be to you as well
>
> but with a vile criminal one never knows]

The reader is left never knowing rather than possessing sufficient evidence to draw a logical conclusion, Lopes does not even grant the finality of punctuation. Yet while asserting the fact that the "great wrong" served only to closer approximate her to the criminal himself, she concedes that the wrong is not an event that occurs at a single point in time, but a "drôle de chemin," a "strange path" that underlies the meticulous construct of the poem.

Delineated solely by the speaker, the criminal that she speaks for, the thousand wrongs and the great wrong that remains undone, the poem is definitively contained and deliberately self-reflexive. Only within such a structure can a poet so successfully deny the reader a conclusion, and not only the reader, but the poem itself seems to await some grand gesture or great wrong that will either secure or unravel the relentless weave of its looping chain of events. By constantly returning to an act that is both unnamed and uncommitted, Lopes is able to suspend a narrative that depends upon incompletion by excluding all but the vaguest reminders of what lies beyond the boundaries of the poem, forcing the poem to define its own context. Only in brief allusions to acts that occur outside the poem's limits does she allow the strange path of narrative to reach beyond its circular course. She reproaches the criminal: "Acho que devo ter sido a pessoa / a quem fizeste mais maldades" ["I think I must have been the one / that you have wronged the most"], and later admits, "eu também sou uma vil criminosa / mas não para ti" (4-5; 13-14) ["I too am a vile criminal / but not to you"]. In the first instance she implies that the criminal has committed lesser wrongs against unidentified others; in the second, she claims that though the "you" she addresses is a vile criminal in reference to her own experience, she in turn is a vile criminal to someone else. The poem does not merely approach a simple deferred outcome, but vaguely insinuates a connection to an existing chain of events and eventualities from which it can only remain separate while it hangs rapt within its own perspective. These brief moments are loosed as though containing all the energy of centripetal force, lines that run tangential to the poem's circle; they both illuminate the precarious nature of her formal aesthetic and foreshadow the manner in which many of Lopes's later poems draw their complexity from the way that they create seemingly impenetrable forms and then allow those forms to crack.

Along with outlining the way she approaches questions of form in her first book, Lopes defines the manner in which she approximates the literary canon as well, using Luís De Camões as a reference point. "Le Bain Turc" begins with a verse that is taken directly from *Os Lusíadas*. The opening line, "Braços, pernas, sem dono e sem sentido" ["Arms, legs, without owner and without sensation"] evokes at first read the image that Camões intended, a gruesome pile of broken bodies, the carnal remains of a battle (III, 52). Yet Lopes takes Camões's antiquated tongue and makes the bodies her own, trading the bloodbath for a bathhouse, brawlers for bathers. However radical the adaptation, the transition between Camões's words and Lopes's is seamless, fluid as the interweaving skins of bathing women. Whereas in the original context, "sem dono e sem sentido" refers to a pile of dismembered limbs, in Lopes's version, the same phrase illustrates a group of bathers reclining in such close proximity that divisions between the bodies are indiscernible. Being that Lopes has remained true to Camões in failing to change "sem dono" to "sem dona," an alteration that would have allowed the limbs to agree in gender with the women they belong to, the phrase may refer not only to the ownership of the limbs but to the very ownership of the women, or even to the words themselves. Perhaps Lopes intends to call attention to the fact that men are not permitted to enter the bathhouse; both the bathing women and the poet herself are free from any masculine challenge, whether it be the claim of ownership a man might impose upon his wife, or Camões's ownership of his verse. Though the poem develops into little more than an artful description of the scene, Lopes firmly stakes her claim upon the rights to the canon, insisting that it is hers to mold. Rarely is Lopes content to simply allude to the work of her predecessors; rather than writing herself into an existing continuity of literature, she often chooses to align herself with her chosen influences by contextually altering or rewriting their words, directing the force of their voices through her own like light converging through a prism. Her body of work can be regarded as a canonic composite rather than a mere addition, its assertions deliberate and ambitious. By calling upon classical references such as Camões, Diderot, and Homer while focusing heavily on the work of women writers, both Portuguese and international, she proposes a literary continuity that can be bent to include a narrative of feminine Portuguese literature that has only recently begun to gain definition.

Though Lopes's interest in feminine poetics becomes increasingly central as her career progresses, the basic philosophy that binds her aesthetically and canonically to her relentless approximations is most lucidly presented in her second volume, *O Poeta de Pondichéry* [*The Poet of Pondichéry*], a series of poems based on a minor character in Denis Diderot's *Jacques the Fatalist*. Lopes explains in the book's preface:

> Diderot (ou quem fala por ele em *Jacques le Fateliste*) recebe um jovem que escreve versos maus e diz ao jovem que ele há-de fazer sempre maus versos. Diderot preocupa-se com a fortuna do mau poeta. Pergunta-lhe se tem pais e o que fazem. Os pais são joalheiros. Aconselha-o a partir para Pondichéry e a enriquecer lá. E a que sobretudo não publique os versos. Doze anos mais tarde o poeta volta a

encontrar-se com Diderot. Enriquiceu em Pondichéry (juntou 100 000 francos) e continua a escrever maus versos.

Porque é que o mau poeta deve ir para Pondichéry e não para outro lugar? Porque é que os seus pais são joalheiros? Porque é que juntou 100 000 francos? E porque é que passou doze anos em Pondichéry? Não sei explicar. O que me atrai é precisamente isto: Pondichéry, pais joalheiros, 100 000 francos, doze anos. (51)

[Diderot (whoever speaks for him in *Jacques the Fatalist*) receives a young man who writes bad poems and he tells the young man that he will always write bad poems. Diderot is concerned about the bad poet's fate. He asks him if he has parents and what they do. His parents are jewelers. He advises him to go to Pondichéry and to get rich there. And above all else, not to publish his poems. Twelve years later the poet returns and comes to see Diderot. He has gotten rich in Pondichéry (he saved 100,000 francs) and still writes bad poems.

Why is it that the bad poet has to go to Pondichéry and not some other place? Why are his parents jewelers? Why did he save 100,000 francs? And why did he spend twelve years in Pondichéry? I can't explain. What attracts me is just this: Pondichéry, parents who were jewelers, 100,000 francs, twelve years.]

In choosing Diderot's poet and initially reducing his character to the quantitative and circumstantial details that define his fate, she creates a context in which Diderot's determinism acts as a foil for her own formal sensibilities. Diderot came to terms with his own fatalism by conceding that although "natural law" is inalterable, composed of great chains of cause and effect that cannot be overridden, "civil law" allows for certain measures of free will. Lopes is equally aware of the givens that bind her world to its looming eventualities: the physical properties of the universe, literary predecessors, societal standards. In a practical sense, however, providing she is true to certain immutable reference points, in this case the basic facts outlined by Diderot ("Pondichéry, pais joalheiros, 100,000 francos, doze anos"), she can order the space between them as she chooses. By working within formal compositions that insist upon convoluted narrative paths, exchanging obvious solutions for calculated approximations, she is liberated rather than confined by such "fatalistic" limitations, using preexisting constructs as forms from which to deviate. Furthermore, by enforcing rather than subverting these boundaries, she is able to write poems that exist completely within their own delineations, relegating any connection to a larger chain of events to the space beyond their limits, a practice initiated in "To a Vile Criminal." In effect, Lopes is not commenting on the role of contextual relativity but redefining the role of the poet herself. She rejects the Shakespearian definition of a poet as one who lends, "to airy nothing / A local habitation and a name," one who imposes order on chaos, choosing instead to impose whatever chaos she may on a strictly ordered universe (*MND*, V.i.16-17).

As if seeking to address Lopes's initial question, "Porque é que o mau poeta deve ir para Pondichéry e não para outro lugar?" the bad poet begins the collection's third poem with what seems a simple explanation, one that Diderot himself could have prepared: "Parti para fazer fortuna / e para escrever poemas / de que eu (e Diderot) pudéssemos gostar mais" (1-3) ["I left to make my fortune / and to write poems / that I (and Diderot) would like better"]. Lopes is true to the story's physical parameters, but alters the priorities of Diderot's faithful poet by giving precedence to the poet's own evaluation of his work, reducing Diderot's opinion to a parenthetical afterthought. The character is further complicated as Lopes highlights an essential difference between her poet and Diderot's; while the original poet is content in the end to continue writing bad poems, Lopes's poet bears the weight of awareness, fully conscious of his own failings. He justifies his bad poems with a disclaimer and a metaphor, assuring, "não gosto deles / de tudo o que escrevi em Pondichéry / guardo um ou dois poemas / esses poemas são a parte visível de um iceberg / de que acho a parte submersa envergonhante" (5-9) ["I don't like them / of all I wrote in Pondichéry / I've kept one or two poems / those poems are the visible part of an iceberg / of which I find the submerged part shameful"]. A metaphor is, by definition, a poetic device that sets up a comparison between entities by means of equation, an overstated simile that never amounts to anything but a close approximation of its subject. Any metaphorical statement is a lie waiting to be uncovered, poised on the edge of dissolution; the poet can claim his poems are the visible part of an iceberg, they may temporarily exist as such in the imagination, but the image is destined to collapse, the kept poems falling back into their original forms. The poet continues however: "uma metáfora que dura muito tempo / leva a dizer disparates como este / uma metáfora permite aproximações mais vertigionosas / do que o bólide inter-galáctico" ["a metaphor that endures / brings out this sort of nonsense / a metaphor allows approximations more dizzying / than an intergalactic meteorite"], admitting that the frailties of a metaphor are precisely what allows Adília Lopes her approximations (11-14). Approximations are dizzying, precarious, and though a metaphor allows the vertigo of the "nearly," its assertions are as provisional as meteorites that disintegrate as they break the barrier of the earth's atmosphere. So the poet is correct in consenting to the fact that the metaphor "não deve durar muito tempo" ["shouldn't last too long"], because if it endures long enough to call attention to its own shortcomings, the poem's components lose their relative values, the mechanism falls apart, the connected elements of even a poetic universe reclaim their separate definitions (15). The poet realizes that in paying such close attention to metaphor he has dedicated himself to "um luxo que era um lixo" ["an extravagance that was trash"], invested in a practice that will render his efforts useless (18). Perhaps Lopes means to imply that the poet's fatal flaw is letting metaphors last too long, relying on extensions that are sure to fall short of their intentions instead of abandoning them before their failures become apparent. An image of a treasure chest supports this theory, as the poet finds inside, "um ninho de víbora / ou cotão (que é mais desolador do que víboras)" (20-21) ["a nest of vipers / or lint (which is even more alarming than vipers)"]. The lint is even more dangerous than a poisonous snake because it designates an absence rather than a presence, lacking the very substance that would allow for the temporary suspension of a complicated metaphor; this metaphor falls apart even before it can be conceived. If any metaphor is doomed to failure, the best way for a bad poet to compensate may be to construct metaphors that skip the approximations and point directly at their own limitations. In the final lines of the poem Lopes's theoretical approximations are put into practice. Whereas the poet begins the poem with a lucid statement that his reason for coming to Pondichery was to write better poems both for himself and for Diderot, he seems to approach the end of the poem with far less conviction, explaining "se escrevesse um poema sobre Diderot / escrevia os teus ossos e os teus olhos / evito escrever / e vivo como escrevo" (22-25) ["if I wrote a poem for Diderot / I'd write your bones and your eyes / I avoid writing / and live as I write"] turning his attention to an unidentified "you." If a conventional poet's aim is to order his poems in a linear manner, one that allows for resolution, then perhaps the true failure of the poet, and indeed Adília Lopes's success, is his lack of directional sensibilities, the ease with which his aims are displaced, the way in which he falls out of Diderot's neatly outlined path and into one of Lopes's approximations. If a poem for Diderot must be written with "your bones and your eyes," then the bones and eyes of a poem written for the aforementioned "you" must in turn belong to someone else, an anonymous figure that stands outside the poem. Regardless of the poem's initial objective or direction, it is not equipped with the means to maintain its course, redirecting its energy in ways that insist upon a logical leap from the reader in order to bring it to any sort of stasis. The syllogistic conclusion that the reader must extract from the closing lines, "I avoid writing / and live as I write," is that the poet avoids living. The very construct of such a statement illuminates the manner in which she does so, using approximations to evade any semblance of a conclusion, choosing a carefully orchestrated sense of lyricism over eventualities that she refuses to commit to.

Although the Pondichéry poems are essential as a means of understanding the workings of Lopes's poetry, the only sustaining connection to Diderot in her later work is thematic rather than philosophical, as the myth of the exile remains a central concept. "A Ladainha Minha" ["My Litany"] is an early version of this myth. Though most closely aligned with the Homeric depiction of Penelope, famed for the twenty years she spent waiting for Odysseus while weaving and unweaving a shroud to fend off a host of suitors, this poem can be seen as an amalgamation rather than a retelling of any one mythical narrative. Figures of other women such as Emily Dickinson, Mariana Alcoforado, and even the growing myth of the woman behind "Adília Lopes" haunt not only this poem but much of the body of her work, all sharing a certain condition of circumstantial or self-imposed exile. In "A Ladainha Minha," Lopes's litany is a tirade launched from a locked room wherein a woman voices the discontent she shares with her sisters, claiming, "Há cem anos / que bordamos / os nossos enxovais / para nenhuma boda" (1-4) ["For a hundred years / we've embroidered / our trousseaus / for no wedding"]. Once again Lopes grounds her verse in the details that define the existence of the women by locking them in their rooms, allowing them to begin stitching towards their intended marriages, and even fixing the timeline to one hundred years in the past, a concrete linear measure that lets their narrative project extend indefinitely into the future. Indeed, Lopes's women do not have to unravel their work as Penelope did; whereas Penelope's task was a means of holding time in a state of cyclical suspension until the hero could return, Lopes's women seem to realize that the fabric they embroider holds its own lack of eventualities. They are not waiting for a man to arrive so that the story can end appropriately, since their fiancés are in plain view, walking the grounds below in funeral attire. Despite the close proximity there will never be a wedding, the suspension that they live in is perpetual rather than temporary. Lopes, however, builds upon her assertion that the condition of waiting is inarguably more fruitful than any possible outcome, and counters the poem's fixed points of origin with an abundance of tears and threads that seem to thrust the poem towards a final destination as the woman rants, "eu e as minhas irmãs / choramos a nossa sorte / copiosamente a fio / dia após dia / o pavio das nossas velas / esfuma-se / as nossas lágrimas / grossos como punhos / formam uma ribeira / que corre para o nosso mar / e o nosso mar?" (23-33) ["my sisters and I / weep our fates copiously / the thread / day after day / the wicks of our candles / up in smoke / our tears / thick as fists / form a river / that runs to our sea / and our sea?"]. Conjuring an image of the mythic fates in the throes of deciding their own destinies, the women are unable to cut off the flow of tears and threads; they are not equipped with the means to tie up the loose ends of the narrative. The sisters cannot commit to a conclusion, but their tears converge and form a river that runs into the sea, creating the illusion of a linear extension of the narrative and a move towards resolution. Even so, the poem ends on uncertain terms as the river "runs to our sea / and our sea?" The repetition of the final line holds the poem to an enduring penultimate moment, the phrase echoing rather than meeting the expectation of the "and," a conjunction that should imply a grammatical connection to a closing gesture, a point beyond the sea and beyond the confines imposed by the poem. Even the punctuation allows the poem to hang in question form instead of arriving at an answer, and the only point that is cemented is Lopes's continued rejection of the denouement, her insistence that the desire to marry carries more weight than any wedding vow.

Lopes addresses the Penelope myth more directly in an untitled poem that was published eight years later in "Sete Rios Entre Campos":

1.

Penélope
é uma aranha
que faz
uma teia
a teia é a Odisseia
de Penélope

2.
Penélope está

sempre
sentada

3.
Ulisses é abstracto
Penélope é concreta
a teia é abstracta
e concreta

4.
Penélope casa-se
com Homero
Ulisses fica a ver
navios (394-395)

[1.
Penelope
is a spider
that spins
a web
the web is Penelope's
Odyssey

2.
Penelope is
always
seated

3.
Odysseus is abstract
Penelope is concrete
the web is abstract
and concrete

4.
Penelope marries Homer

Odysseus is left watching
ships]

Depicted as a spider in this poem, Penelope is shadowed by another mythical woman: Arachnae was so talented a weaver that she dared compare herself to the goddess Athena, who punished such hubris by turning her into a spider, doomed to spin in silence. In claiming that the web is in fact Penelope's "Odyssey," that her work creates the fabric of her own narrative rather than existing only as a narrative device that enables the suspension of her husband's story, Lopes allows Penelope an elevation of status as seemingly audacious as the one Arachnae might have hoped for. The act of weaving becomes an assertion of authority, and the fact that Penelope is "always seated" anchors her to her central position in this version of the myth; she takes the place of Odysseus as the primary reference point while his odyssey becomes peripheral. Continuing to write against the Homeric standard Lopes states, "Odysseus is abstract / Penelope is concrete." Homer's illustration of Penelope always remained something of an abstraction, acting more as a representation of fidelity and patience than as an actual character. Not only does Lopes relegate Odysseus to a similar state of abstraction, giving him the empty task of waiting and watching ships, she calls attention to a transition that she is making from an epic sensibility, the narrative construct upon which both Homer's *Odyssey* and "A Ladainha Minha" are built upon, to a grounded yet lyrically timeless voice. The web is both "abstract / and concrete" because Penelope's version of her story contains both the concrete structure of the original myth and the lyric aspirations of its derivative, as any allusion acts as a vessel for that to which it alludes. In the end Penelope embraces Homer rather than the long-awaited hero, joining the ranks of the storytellers instead of welcoming Odysseus home. Though a marriage to Homer seems less a romantic act than a decision to couple with her art instead of her husband, this poem does grant the reader a rare moment of resolution as Penelope manages to choose a more suitable ending to her tale.

The key to understanding Lopes's work falls somewhere between the loose ends and locked doors of "A Ladainha Minha" and the steady hands of Penelope who abandons her traditional narrative for an alternative solution, between her tendency to write within systems of abstractions that allow her to approach conclusions that she never reaches and her obsession with the concrete nature of the world's most basic facts. Despite her inclination to hold her poems in flux, Lopes exhibits a practiced awareness of the intimacy of the absolute as certain poems are stripped to their barest minimums. Even more stylistically diminished than the untitled Penelope poem is an early "autobiographical" poem:

Autobiographia sumária de Adília Lopes

Os meus gatos
gostam de brincar
com as minhas baratas (80)

[Summarial Autobiography of Adília Lopes

My cats
like to play
with my cockroaches]

If the life of Diderot's poet could be reduced to his story's most basic details, then the poet claims to live a life that amounts to only cats and cockroaches. There is the sense that if Lopes chose to let go of her approximations the reader would be left with a woman who lives out the myths that she alludes to, choosing an artistic existence that allows room only for her cats. As the voice behind her poems, in frequent media appearances and in a recent author's note, expressing the anxiety that stems from "never having had a boyfriend, a husband, children" (464), Lopes presents herself as a Dickinsonian figure. Keeping in mind that "Adília Lopes" is itself a pseudonym, a deliberately fabricated myth that is perpetrated by the representations of women in her work, it becomes increasingly difficult to separate the poet from the implications of her chosen subject matter. Her actual references to Dickinson may seem insubstantial, dropped casually rather than thoroughly explored, but the sustained influence of the American poet's cloistered life is impossible to ignore. One such reference follows:

Emily Dickinson

Mesmo que pudesse
dizer tudo
não podia dizer tudo
e é bom assim (383)

[Emily Dickinson

Even if I could
say everything
I couldn't say everything
and it's better that way][1]

Even if Lopes were capable of saying everything, of reaching the conclusions that logic demands, she would still withhold certain aspects from the reader. If the poem had thirty lines instead of three, ample space and time to disclose "everything," she would likely find a way to write around the ends that she did not care to reach. Judging from the ending that she eventually allows Penelope, it seems that what she strives most to evade is not the finality of resolution but the bleak eventualities that await women who allow themselves to come to the standard conclusions, adhering to the world's common expectations. This is a concern borrowed directly from Dickinson, who writes in poem 640,

I cannot live with You—
It would be Life—
And Life is over there—
Behind the Shelf

The Sexton keeps the Key to—
Putting up
Our Life—His Porcelain—
Like a Cup— (1-8)

Dickinson is not rejecting life in terms of her own existence but a "Life" of domestic regularity, ordered and conventional as porcelain displayed on the mantelpiece. She goes on to list a whole host of other reasons for rejecting a life with one she loves, culminating with her fear of separation in the afterlife, but the prevailing truth of the poem, the one that Lopes carries into her own poems, is that it is much easier to live beneath the weight of one's desires than to relent to the life that remains after those desires have been fulfilled. That is not to say that either poet wants to close the door completely to the idea of marriage; Lopes's women remain in a state of perpetual engagement and the last stanza of Dickinson's poem contains a veiled invitation, explaining, "So We must meet apart— / You there—I—here— / With just the Door ajar / That Oceans are…." Separated by a spatial measure that seems like oceans, by an excess of dashes between "you" and "I," the two may still "meet apart," the division implied by "apart" not completely eliminating the prospect of a meeting (45-48). The door is not shut but left ajar and the possibility of union overrides the poem's initial refusal.

Lopes borrows a similar preoccupation from Sylvia Plath, using a line from her "The Babysitters" as a preface to an untitled poem in her thirteenth book, *Florbela Espanca Espanca* [*Florbela Espanca Spanks*]. She reasserts her rejection of domestic resolution, writing:

"But I didn't know how to cook, and babies depressed me."
Sylvia Plath, "The Babysitters"

É preciso pensar
Em tudo
Dos preservativos
Às panelas
E há mesmo quem
Nos preservativos
Veja já as panelas
Pensa-se de mais
E não se pensa
De facto (416)

[It is necessary to think
Of everything
From prophylactics
To pots and pans
But one who seeing prophylactics
Sees pots and pans as well
Thinks too much
And doesn't think
In fact]

The ability to "think of everything" allows the author to separate her erotic desires from an obligation to maintain a conventional lifestyle with her lover. Lopes insinuates that seeing prophylactics, here an implication of the sexual act, should not intuitively lead the mind to pots and pans, the details of the domestic realm. Prophylactics are meant to prevent conception, and Lopes uses them to draw attention to the tangible and theoretical division between sex and marriage. The Plath poem draws similar conclusions, chronicling the decision of two sisters who escape their child-rearing duties by rowing out to a deserted island that is "Stopped and awful as a photograph of someone laughing, / But ten years dead" (175). Even the horrible suspension of a dead island where time has ceased to advance is a preferable alternative to the drudgeries of cooking and babies. Lacking even the ambiguity of a door left ajar, Plath's women are bound irrevocably by their self-inflicted exiles, asking, "What keyhole have we slipped through, what door has shut?"

Plath's words are echoed yet again in a poem from Lopes's recent book, *O Regresso de Chamilly* [*The Return of Chamilly*], a collection in which the myth of Portuguese nun Mariana Alcoforado is extended to include the return of her lover, the Marquis of Chamilly, who was the supposed recipient of the famous letters that Guilleragues penned in her name.[2] In this poem Alcoforado addresses the man whose return she once awaited:

Não quero
Ter filhos
Gosto muito
De foder
Contigo
E com outros
Mas de bebés
Não gosto
Uma vez
Por outra
Tem graça
Mas sempre
Não
Os bebés deprimem-me (459)

[I don't want
To have children
I like fucking

You
A lot
And fucking others
But babies
I don't like
Once
In a while
They're all right
But forever
No
Babies depress me]

The Alcoforado that Lopes has recreated bears so little resemblance to the voice of the original letters that she seems to be someone else entirely, a woman who has as little interest in childbirth and marital fidelity as Plath's sisters, telling Chamilly that her only remaining use for him is sexual. Lopes's enduring interest in her may have less to do with her monastic existence than with the way that Alcoforado was able to have love without the "Life" that Dickinson so readily rejected, despite the pain she suffered in abandonment. The path that could have led her past desire and into marriage disappeared with her lover and she was thus spared a standard domestic resolution. Alcoforado continues her address, proposing an alternative arrangement that better suits her needs:

Ficas no
castelo de Beja
e eu aqui
no convento
com vento
(as janelas
fecham mal
estão empenadas)
há uma passagem
subterrânea
como nos romances
que liga
castelo e convento
podemos fechá-la (31-44)

> [You stay
> at the castle of Beja
> and I here
> in the convent
> with the wind
> (the windows
> close badly
> they are warped)
> there is a subterranean
> passage
> as in novels
> that connects
> castle and convent
> we can close it]

Perhaps the reckless intensity with which Alcoforado addressed Chamilly in her letters was made possible by the fact that a life with him was never a tenable possibility, by the luxury of living with a myth instead of a man. Lopes would like to believe that if she had ever been faced with the thing she most desired, the return of her lover, Alcoforado most likely would have rejected a conventional life with him. She would have chosen instead to have separate homes, a passageway that she could open and close at her will and loose-fitting windows that held all the insinuated possibilities of Dickinson's "door ajar."

Even prior to this drastic modification of character Lopes found much to admire in Guilleragues's work. Though her sexual desires have already been fulfilled, her unanswered letters hold her life in the state of suspension that so much of Lopes's aspires to. Alcoforado writes in her second letter to Chamilly,

> I see very plainly the remedy for all my ills, and I should soon be delivered from them if I no longer loved you. But alas! What a remedy! No, I would rather suffer still more than forget you. (59)

It seems that Alcoforado is more in love with her own suffering than with the man she suffers for, or as Nietzsche wrote, "In the end one loves one's desire and not what is desired" (93). The desire to sustain a sensation rather than allowing it to pass is a sensibility that Alcoforado explains in her fifth letter as she contemplates the return of all the portraits and bracelets that Chamilly has given her, writing, "I shall enjoy all the pain of parting from them and cause you at least some chagrin" (119). Lopes complicates this moment in a poem from the first collection that the *Lettres Portugaises* [*Portuguese Letters*] inspired, *O Marquês de Chamilly (Kabale und Liebe)* [*The Marquis of Chamilly (Kabale and Liebe)*], explaining how Alcoforado,

> Tira do braço o bracelete
> Que o marquês lhe deu
> Para poder voltar a enfiar
> No braço o bracelete (93)

> [Takes from her arm the bracelet
> That the Marquis gave her
> So that she may slip the bracelet
> Back on her arm]

Whereas Alcoforado merely expressed a desire to enjoy the return of the bracelets, Lopes allows her to enjoy their receipt and return in a cyclical fashion, and the image of a bracelet that is taken on and off perpetually is a physical manifestation of the suspension that Alcoforado claims to desire.

Protected from her desires by barred windows and unanswered letters, however, Alcoforado was able to commit herself to the greatest excesses of expression, exclaiming, "amo-te perdidamente."[3] The contextual translation of this utterance is "I love you desperately," but the most literal translation of "perdidamente" is "in a manner pertaining to loss," and the implication of its use is that love is bound irrevocably to loss, whether it be the loss of the self or the loss of the loved one. Florbela Espanca paraphrases Alcoforado's words in the first stanza of her sonnet "Amar":

> Eu quero amar, amar perdidamente
> Amar só por amar: Aqui… além…
> Mais Este e Aquele, o Outro e a toda a gente
> Amar! Amar! E não amar ninguém! (134)

[I want to love, to love and lose everything
Love only to love: Here… there…
And This and That, the Other and everyone
To love! To love! And not love anyone]

Espanca capitalizes the abstract recipients of love, "This," "That," and the "Other," while refusing to love anyone or anything specific; love becomes its own ends and need not narrow its scope by focusing upon any one object. In reference to Alcoforado's predicament, the loss of a lover is inconsequential because one's love should not be measured against the response it draws; it is not subject to relativity. For Adília Lopes, however, everything is defined according to its reference points because nothing holds any objective value. In writing a poem that responds to Espanca's "Amar," Lopes systematically defines the references and relations that shape the body of her work. Justifying the title of the collection that it commences, *Florbela Espanca Espanca*, Lopes's untitled poem is a reversal of the desperate love that Espanca borrowed from Guilleragues. Rather than altering content contextually as she did when she used the verse of Camões, Lopes rewrites Espanca word by word, keeping only her diction intact. Exchanging the sonnet for free verse, love for sex and loss for discovery, Lopes writes, "Quero foder foder / achada-mente" ["I want to fuck to fuck / and find everything"]. If Espanca and Alcoforado saw love as a vehicle for loss, including the loss of one's connection to the object of that love, then Lopes defines "foder" as the very opposite of such a love, as a means of defining one's self in relation to the specific connections one makes with one's own work and with others. The body of Lopes's work, based primarily upon the velocity of intention, is written against the idea of love for its own sake, an arrow released without a target. This poem reiterates her insistence upon the fact that one's life and art exist relatively, defined by material proximities, interpersonal relationships, historical reference and canonical allusion. Lopes sets up the parameters of the revolution that this poem seeks to define by addressing all the other revolutions that might come to mind, continuing,

se esta revolução
não me deixa
foder até morrer
é porque

não é revolução
nenhuma
a revolução não se faz
nas praças
nem nos palácios
(essa é a revolução
dos fariseus) (3-14)

[if this revolution
doesn't let me
fuck until I die
it's because
it isn't a revolution
at all
the revolution
doesn't happen
in the plazas
or in the palaces
(that's the revolution
of the Pharisees)]

Lopes uses the word "revolution" four times before she reaches a definition that suits her. She insists that the revolution let her "fuck until [she dies]," implying a sexual revolution that the poem does not directly address. She then explains that the revolution does not take place in plazas or palaces, eliminating its political connotations by alluding to the Portuguese revolution of 25 April 1974, and parenthetically negates the concept of a biblical revolution by referencing the Pharisees. Instead of drawing connections, this section of the poem seeks to undo connections by introducing a concept, deciding upon the response she wants to elicit from her reader, and erasing alternatives through a system of announcement and dismissal. After cataloging these rejected associations she is able to address her own revolution:

A revolução
Faz-se na casa de banho
Da casa
Da escola

Do trabalho
A relação entre
As pessoas
Deve ser uma troca
Hoje é um relação de poder
(mesmo no foder) (15-25)
[The revolution
happens in the bathroom
of the house
at school
at work
relations between
people
should be an exchange
today it's a relation
of power
(even fucking)]

This is a revolution that is personal rather than political, having more to do with one's individual relationships to people and to society than with one's alignment with any group of revolutionaries, regardless of cause or context. Situating the revolution in the domestic realm of the bathroom and then claiming that relations between people, sexual relations included, have become power struggles, the implied conclusion is that this revolution will deal with the issues that exist between the sexes. But apt as always to work against her readers' expectations, Lopes has moved far beyond gender issues; the remainder of the poem focuses primarily on the interactions between women:

a ceifeira ceifa
contente
ceifa nos tempos livres
(semana de 24 x 7 horas já!)
a gestora avalia
a empresa
pela casa de banho
e canta

contente
porque há alegria
no trabalho
o choro da bebé
não impede a mãe
de se vir
a galinha brinca
com a raposa
eu tenho o direito
de estar triste (26-43)

[the reaper reaps
happy
she reaps in her free time
(24 hours a day and 7 days a week now!)
the manager evaluates
the company
by the state of the bathroom
and sings
happy
because there is joy
in her work
the child's cry
doesn't stop the mother
from coming
the hen plays
with the vixen
I have a right
to be sad]

This reaper is taken from the Fernando Pessoa poem that begins:

Ela canta, pobre ceifeira
Julgando-se feliz talvez (86)

She sings, poor reaper
Believing, perhaps, that she is happy

As the poem continues, Pessoa grants his reaper the dubious contentment that a lack of awareness facilitates but the true measure of her happiness is an inconsequential unknown. Lopes argues that the reaper's happiness is not merely illusory, that a woman's relationship with her work is reason enough to be content. In the context of the Lopes poem, the reaper is so engaged by her work that the boundaries between work and leisure disappear; she chooses to work in her free time and reaps of her own volition rather than out of obligation. Lopes assertion of her free will undermines Pessoa's assumption that the reaper may only be happy because she lacks the capacity to realize that she is not. By conceiving of a reaper that seeks to reform Pessoa's image, Lopes initiates a relationship with the poet that can nearly be construed as the type of power struggle that she earlier rejects. But Lopes's reaper issues no complaint; the reference to Pessoa is delivered without contempt and makes its point without effectively presenting a challenge. Furthermore, the lines that follow present women that are sufficiently content in the roles they play and the relationships they maintain; the manager inspects the bathrooms, the mother is unperturbed by the cries of her child, even the hen and the vixen are able to peacefully coexist despite their natural roles as predator and prey. Illustrating a wide variety of women, all happy in their various relationships, and then claiming that she has "a right to be sad," Lopes presents yet another incomplete syllogism. If happiness stems from the success of one's relationships, then the sadness to which Lopes feels entitled exposes her recognition of the fact that the connections she ventures fail to take hold.

Whether by conjuring the voices of her influences, alluding to mythical figures or by relying on formal and contextual devices to keep her narratives from reaching their conclusions, Lopes establishes a system of approximation that permeates her work. Yet any approximation is by definition a failure, doomed as an extended metaphor because it always falls just short of its intentions. However successful Lopes's poems are in aesthetic terms, the relationships that they define are flawed by her refusal to allow any situation its resolution. The closest she comes to marriage is engagement, to certainty, insinuation; even the allusory efforts to connect with such writers as Dickinson, Espanca, and Pessoa, though effective in establishing her position in the continuity of world literature, are intrinsically unsatisfying: any attempted dialogue with the dead is essentially a monologue, a litany to use

Lopes's own terminology. Even more indicative than her pursuit of an art that reveals its weaknesses by approximating its subjects is the requisite tension that such a pursuit creates, the rift between proposal and actualization that has become the most definitive aspect of Lopes's work.

In the Author's Note that follows "O Regresso de Chamilly," Lopes argues,

> Acho que era a Sylvia Plath que estava convencida, por volta de 1950, que para escrever romances era preciso ter amantes e fazer viagens. É um mito, isso dos amantes e das viagens. Pode-se ser feliz e escrever romances sem ter amantes e sem fazer viagens. Mais importante que amantes e viagens é ter um espaço próprio, um domínio, um território, uma casa, pelo menos um quarto com privacidade, como muito bem viu Virginia Woolf. (463)

> [I think it was Sylvia Plath that was convinced, from 1950 on, that to write novels it was necessary to have lovers and to travel. It's a myth, that about lovers and travel. One can be happy and write novels without having lovers or traveling. More important than lovers and travel is having one's own space, a dominion, a territory, a house, at the very least a room of one's own, as Virginia Woolf knew well.]

The juxtaposition of Woolf and Plath is a measure of extremes: Lopes weighs solitude against wanderlust, the word against the flesh, the art that precludes life against the life lived in pursuit of one's art. Considering the women that populate her poems, her alignment with Woolf seems an obvious stance. In rhetorical terms, however, Lopes does not judge Plath's opinion on the basis of its merits; she rejects it because the idea of needing lovers and travel in order to write "is a myth." Quick to dismiss Plath's claim, Lopes counters it with an even more established myth, the myth of the self-appointed exile, a myth that has become the foundation for so much of her work. For Lopes, to be a poet is to write within the space between the locked door and the door swung open, to situate one's art within the boundaries that these two myths designate. In the end it makes little difference which polarity holds the greater value, which myth is worth perpetrating. The choice for Lopes is no longer whether or not to approximate a myth; she has only to decide which myth to approximate.

Notes

[1] Though the poem has been translated here in the first person, English grammar does not allow for the aspect of ambiguity that is implicit in the Portuguese version. The poem could just as easily be translated in the third person, and furthermore, does not contain any indication of gender. The poem "Emily Dickinson" is in fact one half of a diptych; the other half is a poem entitled "São João da Cruz" ["Saint John of the Cross"], and is identical to "Emily Dickinson" in all aspects save the title. While I have chosen to focus here upon the allusion to Dickinson, it must be noted that Lopes is clearly addressing issues of similitude and difference, contrasting the first person with the third, the masculine with the feminine, and the sacred with the profane.

[2] *Lettres Portugaises* was originally published in 1668. Mariana Alcoforado, a young woman who was indeed a nun at the convent in Beja, was once supposed the author of these letters. Alcoforado maintains a mythical presence in Portuguese literary and cultural history, but the letters have been attributed to Guilleragues. The English quotations have been taken from the first translation of the original French, an edition that was wrongly attributed to Alcoforado herself.

[3] The original French text is, "Je vous aime éperdument" (156). The English translation reads "I love you to distraction," while the above quoted "amo-te perdidamente" is found commonly in unattributed translations from French to Portuguese.

Works Cited

Alcoforado, Mariana. *The Love Letters of a Portuguese Nun.* Trans. R. H. New York: Cassell, 1890.

Camões, Luís de. *Os Lusíadas.* Ed. Emanuel Paulo Ramos. Porto: Porto Editora, n.d.

Dickinson, Emily. *The Complete Poems of Emily Dickinson.* Ed. Thomas H. Johnson. Boston: Little, [1955].

Espanca, Florbela. *Sonetos.* Ed. Fransisco Lyon de Castro. Mem Martins: Publicações Europa-Americana, n.d.

Guilleragues. *Lettres Portugaises.* Ed. Frédéric Deloffre and Jacques Rougeot. Genève: Librairie Droz, 1972.

Lanyer, Aemilia. *The Poems of Aemilia Lanyer.* Ed. Susanne Woods. New York: Oxford UP, 1993.

Lopes, Adília. *Obra.* Lisboa: Mariposa Azul, 2000.

Nietzsche, Friedrich. *Beyond Good and Evil.* Trans. Walter Kaufmann. New York: Vintage, 1966.

Pessoa, Fernando. *Poemas de Fernando Pessoa.* Ed. Isabel Pascoal. Lisboa: Editorial Communicação, 1986.

Plath, Sylvia. *The Collected Poems.* Ed. Ted Hughes. New York: Harper Perennial, 1992.

Shakespeare, William. *The Complete Works of William Shakespeare.* Ed. William Aldis Wright. New York: Doubleday, 1936.

Rachel Rothenberg received her BA in English Literature from Tufts University in 1997. She is currently pursuing her doctorate in Portuguese and Brazilian Studies at Brown University. Email: auntconsuelo@hotmail.com

Other Articles

Love and the Empire in *Os Lusíadas*

Saúl Jiménez-Sandoval

Metida tenho a mão na consciência,
E não falo senão verdades puras
Que me ensinou a viva experiência.
—Luís Vaz de Camões

Abstract. Throughout the centuries, *Os Lusíadas* by Camões has been read as a Neoplatonic and Platonic text that follows the basic precepts of the *dolce stil nuovo*. Yet there is an inherent contradiction in this reading, for firstly, it disregards Camões great genius in reinventing the style, and secondly, it does not account for the total sexual contact between the Portuguese sailors and the nymphs on the *Ilha dos Amores*. Furthermore, it does not contextualize Camões within the historical, social, and personal framework that must have played an important part in the composition of the poem. The article's main argument is that Camões composes *Os Lusíadas* considering the dire need that Portugal has for an heir. Hence, it was necessary for the poet to downplay the Platonic and Neoplatonic traditions that influenced the *dolce stil nuovo*, in order to incite King Sebastian to seek a sexual encounter that will produce an heir.

European maritime explorations, the colonization of distant lands, and the encounter with unknown people greatly influence the notion of knowledge and writing in sixteenth-century Portugal: indeed, the sailors that encoun-

Portuguese Literary & Cultural Studies 7 (2008): 239-54.

tered distant lands and people were forced to rely on their own experience to describe and catalog what they saw. Hundreds of years of scholasticism, and a strict adherence to ancient sources of knowledge, preceded the drastic change marked by the maritime explorations. As Donald Pease states, "Instead of returning to their culture's ancient books for allegorical prefigurations, many New World explorers described what they discovered by making up words of their own (or borrowing terms from the natives)" (105). To experience the world with one's own senses, hence, becomes cornerstone of the enrichment of the self, the language, and the greater community. The poet of this period presents his own experience as the protagonist in a writing exemplifying a vision that will both certify and unveil the truth of the world. This is not to say that the personal experience of the poet will override the entire gamut of poetic tradition, for the poet will maintain a close bond with the ancient sources. Yet the poet will, nevertheless, use the ancient sources within a distinctively personal interpretation. Hence, for the sixteenth century, truth is guaranteed in the elaboration of a philosophical argument that is based on personal experience.

In a world where experience is highly valued, the senses are paramount to the acquisition of personal experience, and of the five senses, sight is privileged above all. It is within this framework that we position Luís Vaz de Camões and his epic poem *Os Lusíadas*. Camões, as a soldier with many personal experiences in foreign lands to his name, and as a man who had experienced love with women, will urge King Sebastian to "see" the body of women as the key to Portugal's future. This essential message in *Os Lusíadas* is fundamental to the continuation of the kingdom, for if King Sebastian is able to appropriately decipher the message that a woman's body contains, he will be incited to experience a sexual pleasure that will produce an heir to the throne. Camões places King Sebastian within a symbolic system of social values that must be upheld. Mainly, the king must understand, and implement, the most basic social contract: a man must choose a woman as his mate and reproduce. King Sebastian must conform to the natural law of masculine sexuality upheld by patriarchy. Love within the Portuguese empire is a social and civic responsibility, one that will grant a man a highly prestigious social standing and a vision that will lead him to the acquisition of a knowledge that transcends his own time and space.

In writing *Os Lusíadas*, Camões is conscious of the danger the kingdom faces. Without an heir from King Sebastian, the next Portuguese heirs to the

House of Aviz are Queen Catalina and Cardinal Enrique, grandmother and great uncle to the King. As Queen Catalina is no longer of child-bearing age, it is obvious that Cardinal Enrique could not legitimately produce an heir within the laws of the Catholic Church. It is outside of Portugal where the danger lies, for King Phillip II of Spain has a legitimate direct claim to the Portuguese throne as the brother to Juana —King Sebastian's mother (Oliveira Marques 307). Hence, in light of this situation, more than an epic, *Os Lusíadas* is a *sententia* that attempts to teach King Sebastian how Portugal's history is inherently related to the "good" love between a man and a woman.

King Sebastian's personality would have worried Camões. According to Mary Elizabeth Brooks, the king was educated under the strict supervision of the Jesuit Luis Gonçalves, and professed a strong religious conviction to become a soldier of Christ (9). Furthermore, António de Oliveira Marques and Brooks, as well as many other prominent historians, agree that King Sebastian had a volatile temperament, a selfish personality and a total lack of discipline (Brooks 9; Oliveira Marques 312). Additionally, King Sebastian exemplified an almost fanatical dedication to hunting and military training. Yet, what might have seemed most disturbing to Camões was his total lack of interest in women. Various historians, along with Camões's first critic Manuel Faria e Sousa, mention his complete disinterest in women. Oliveira Marques states: "He abhorred the prospect of marriage" (307). The King's lack of interest in women, coupled with an obsessive personality encouraged by ill-informed counselors, must have been factors Camões considered when writing *Os Lusíadas.*

Os Lusíadas, therefore, is born out of an attempt to prolong the independence of the only kingdom in the Iberian Peninsula to successfully defer the power of Castille. More than a celebration of past Portuguese military conquests and heroic feats, or the simple application of what has been read as Platonic and Neo-Platonic theories, *Os Lusíadas* exalts the sexual attraction the prototypical Portuguese male should feel toward the body of women. It is this sexual attraction that a man feels toward a woman that guarantees the biological continuity of Sebastian's progeny, and by metonymy, Portugal's survival. It is here, therefore, that we begin our textual analysis of the poem's most important cantos, IX and X. Within these two cantos, the entire weight of past, present, and future Portuguese history rests, for the great sacrifices endured by the sailors will be rewarded with the physical pleasures Venus orchestrates. Venus, indeed, as the maximum symbol of feminine sexuality, will be coined as the ultimate solution against any perils from Fortuna. Thus, Camões presents the body of woman as the guarantor for the history and genealogy of the Portuguese royalty and kingdom.

Very few critics have presented Venus as a driving force behind the message of *Os Lusíadas*. Indeed, Camonian criticism of the seventeenth, eighteenth, and nineteenth centuries was concentrated in reconstructing Camões's biography, or in finding the "muse" that inspired Camões's writing. Diogo de Couto, Severim de Faria, Faria e Sousa, the Visconde Juromenha, Wilheim Storck, and Theófilo Braga all conclude their studies with a name of a woman that might have served as the inspiration for Camões. Within this group, Storck and Braga, two of the most renowned nineteenth century scholars that shape Camonian criticism in the 20th century, start to read Camões exclusively through the prism of the Italian Renaissance and the basic precepts of the *dolce stil nuovo*. Based on this parameter, since Dante had been inspired by Beatrice and Petrarch had been inspired by Laura, these critics sought to find the specific name of the poet's lady-muse. This orientation in Camonian scholarship will continue throughout a major part of the twentieth century, without considering the inherent contradiction that lies in juxtaposing Platonism and Neoplatonism with *Os Lusíadas*.[1]

Two important stages in the history of literary criticism of the poem complement our present endeavor: The publication of *Lírica de Camões* in 1932 by José Maria Rodrigues and Afonso Lopes Vieira, and the more recent studies by Jorge de Sena and Helder Macedo. As we stated earlier, most of the early critics established a parameter that marked Camonian studies by reading the poem through the precepts of the Italian *dolce stil nuovo*, and by trying to compare and approximate Camões' figure to Petrarch's. Thus, the entire poetic corpus of the poet was reduced to a mere "romantic" exercise, or imitation of Petrarch. Yet Rodrigues and Vieira are the first to shun the precepts of the *dolce stil nuovo*, and introduce the concept of *sentido da realidade*. With this bold new way of reading Camões, the poem's sensual and sexual tones are directly associated with a physical relationship of the poet with a woman. This new filter for reading Camões is central to our present argument, for it was instrumental in the revision of hundreds of years of Camonian Platonic and Neoplatonic literary history. Consequently, this *sentido da realidade* resonates with the period's quest for a knowledge that is derived exclusively from experience.

The Platonic and Neoplatonic thought that had dominated Camonian criticism did not permit a poetry focused on the enjoyment of the senses, or sexual pleasure. With Rodrigues and Vieira's work, though, a new interpretative field is established with the concept of *sentido da realidade*. Although this bold form of reading Camões still has the main objective of finding the woman who inspired Camões in his writing, what is cardinal to this study is the first association of the poetry's sensuality and sexuality to a concise amorous relationship with a woman. *Os Lusíadas*, therefore, is not relegated to a mere mental exercise of a poet, but upheld as a concrete experience that influenced the vision of the poem's contents. Hence, *sentido da realidade* contradicts Platonic and Neoplatonic thought, the main sources of influence of the *dolce stil nuovo*, in that Dante and Petrarch never touched their "muses," since both Beatrice and Laura are observed from afar and always remain physically untouchable.

The recent studies by Jorge de Sena and Helder Macedo constitute the second group of critics that have shaped the vision of this study. Both Sena and Macedo point to the importance of love in the poem. In their works, the critics present Camões as the poet-philosopher who seeks to harmonize the political chaos he perceives. Yet even more important to our study is their insistence of Camões's role as Sebastian's teacher with a main lesson: Love is the philosophy that brings order to the world.[2] As Macedo states: "Love, for Camões, is a first cause, an existential process and the ultimate purpose of human quest. Through love, appetite is transformed into reason and reason into knowledge" (3). Love is the lofty ideal through which a socially viable human sexuality develops, and through which biological reproduction takes place. Sena, on the other hand, explains how the majority of critics have read Camões's poetry as a collection of "poemas de amor finos" in which the courtly lover suffers from unrequited love. According to Sena, however, the critics do not have an explanation for the explicitly sexual tones found in the poem: "Some of the most sexually explicit passages of *The Lusiads*, and one or another of the minor pieces, have always shocked the prudish" (10). Furthermore, the undeniable influences of the *dolce stil nuovo* in the poem lead the critics to read Camões vis-à-vis Petrarch:

> And, since Camões poses constantly as the lover in distress, disdained by his lady, separated from her by the great spaces of earth and time, it was quite easy [...] to view many of them as clever exercises in the Petrarchan tradition. (Sena 11)

Camonian thought, is therefore, specific to its own historical, social and personal framework, one that takes the most important literary influence of the period and transforms it to a unique expression that manifests a personal philosophical interpretation.

The use of the sun at the beginning of the poem, together with what the critics have pointed out is an insistence on the use of the verb "ver," constitute the key to the last two cantos of the poem. Canto IX is the culmination of the image of Venus, for it is in this canto that the importance of woman as the re-producer of the male identity is fully constructed. Since Canto IX is the most extensive of the cantos, constituting twenty percent of the poem, Camões must have developed this particular canto for more than aesthetic reasons.

Camões's great innovation is to have Venus organize a sexual encounter in the *Ilha dos Amores* between the sea nymphs and the returning Portuguese sailors. This encounter, a prize and reward for the tired sailors, exemplifies Rodrigues and Vieira's *sentido da realidade*, Sena's approach, and Macedo's stance. It is clear that Camões does not advocate a Platonic or Neoplatonic vision of women, for through this scene the poet clearly states that women are the base of a symbolic social order that insures the life of the patriarchy: "(Women) yield to him their natural and social value as a locus of imprints, marks, and mirage of his activity" (Irigaray 177). Women within patriarchy are the *tabula rasa* that can be imprinted in order to prolong the social value of men. Hence, Venus will typify this when she prepares, and by synecdoche becomes, the earthly paradise that will be possessed and enjoyed by the sailors. This, before any other fundamental message that might be drawn from *Os Lusíadas*, is Camões's central message.

Venus, as goddess of beauty, mother of love, mistress of the Graces and pleasures, protectoress of marriage, promoter of harmony and fertility in the couple, and goddess of childbirth, is the main figure Sebastian has to correctly "see," that is, interpret. Venus is the archetypal figure of women who not only supports patriarchy, but promotes and sustains it. Indeed, the sailors' victories have been ensured, in large part, by the intercession of Venus before Zeus. Venus, effectively, uses her body's sensuality to convince Zeus to protect the Portuguese ships from the perils of the sea and the wrath of Bacchus. It is through the power of Venus that the Portuguese have sailed safely to India, and it is through the power of Venus that the Portuguese will be rightly rewarded.

To Camões, the world that knows not the body of Venus, is a world devoid of noble ideals, vision, and community. Indeed, the attack on the rebellious world that disdains Venus, where "ninguém ama o que deve, / Senão o que sòmente mal deseja," is an attack on the "mal regida gente" (IX, 29). Consequently, Canto IX begins with the story of Acteon, a mythological figure that spurns the body of women in preference to the passion he feels for hunting. The parallel between Acteon and King Sebastian is undeniable, and the fierce onslaught by Cupid's army that ensues can be interpreted as Camões's desire to impose discipline on the King.[3] It is this rebellious world that Cupid, on Venus's petition, must subdue. Indeed, hunting makes Acteon a desocialized being, "tão austero," while its ultimate effect is the blinding of the mind and reason: "De cego na alegria bruta, insana" (IX, 26). The hunt for the wild forms does not lead to a greater knowledge, nor does their possession lead to a fruitful life. Subsequently, Acteon's obsession in the wrong type of hunting, the hunt for the "ugly" beast, leads to a disastrous conclusion: "por seguir um feio animal fero"; Acteon dies a horrific death at the mercy of his own hunting dogs (IX, 26). It is the example of this death, one that leaves no presence in the world, that frames the beginning of the Canto IX. Self-indulgence does not lead to the discovery of the "bela forma humana," but to the destruction of both reason and body.

The hunt for wild beasts that leads Acteon to his death is displaced and surpassed by the hunt for nymphs that the sailors fulfill. This hunt for nymphs, instead of causing austerity in the sailors, converts them into semi-gods that, while delighting in the body of women, are symbolically eternalized by their coupling and marriage to mythical beings. Hence, the nymphs, more than mere loci that testify to the sailor's masculinity, will be the vehicles through which the Portuguese defy an anonymous death.

The Island exemplifies a total symbiosis between the body of woman and Nature, for all the natural elements on the Island typify female characteristics. And it is here where sight, the most important of senses, is fully charged. The description of the Island begins with stunning images of trees overflowing with perfect virginal fragrant fruit, a direct simile to the body of women: "os formosos limões ali cheirando, / Estão virgíneas têtas imitando" (IX, 56). It is in this earthly paradise where Cloris, goddess of flowers, competes with Pomona, goddess of fruit, while songbirds fly and resonate with joy. This is Camões great invention, the archetypal *locus amoenus* that will serve as the background to an orgiastic sexual encounter that will celebrate the experience gained from the senses of the body.

Once all has been orchestrated, the "fortes mancebos" land on the Island with the intention of hunting wild beasts. On the Island, the initial vision of the nymphs is unclear to the sailors, and the sailors confuse the nymphs with beasts that possess fine wool and silk, "lã fina e seda" (IX, 68). Nevertheless, these sailors are able to appropriately judge and see that these "cores" are "humanas rosas" (IX, 68). Therefore, the initial hunt for wild animals, is quickly replaced with the hunt for nymphs —the accepted and appropriate "beast." Woman, as the only possible means through which the power of Fortune can be resisted, is represented as the island that must be taken and hunted, enjoyed and exalted. Indeed, the first fruits that women bear are the symbolic social stability and continuity they provide men. In the words of Lionardo, "Vencerás da fortuna a força dura" (IX, 79). What is most impressive is the description of the sexual act between nymphs and sailors, a truly unique event in the poetry of the sixteenth century:

> Oh! Que famintos beijos na floresta,
>
> E que mimoso chôro que soava!
>
> Que afagos tam suaves, que ira honesta,
>
> Que em risinhos alegres se tornava!
>
> O que mais passam na manhã e na sesta,
>
> Que Vénus com prazeres inflamava,
>
> Melhor é experimentá-lo que julgá-lo;
>
> Mas julgue-o quem não pode experimentá-lo. (IX, 83)

This explicit description of the sexual act transforms the paradise into a celebration of the pleasures of the body. Yet, this stanza does not describe the sexual act gratuitously, for it ends with a challenge to the reader: It is better to experience it than to judge it, but may he judge it, who cannot experience it. Clearly, these verses are directly written for the main reader of the poem, the King. On the other hand, the insistence on the verb "julgar," to judge, combined with the visually charged scene, are meant to provoke the reader's imagination and behavior. This scene establishes a strict social norm that demarcates the proper behavior of the masculine social subject that must learn how to read and interpret the value of women correctly. The poem is meant to incite the King to imitate not only the great models of Portuguese history, and the great feats of these sailors, but the sexual love they all personify with regard to women.

Canto X describes the fruits of an appropriate hunt. It is only after the sexual encounter that Camões mentions "honra," honor. The pleasure that Tethys and the nymphs represent, along with the promise of fame and children, constitute the initial drive that gives value to life. Male honor is expressly based on the feminine body, since patriarchy demands the possession of the substances that can prolong the masculine image—women and land. As Luce Irigaray states: "[woman's] value-invested form amounts to what man inscribes in and on its matter: that is, her body" (187). The inability of King Sebastian to possess a female body immediately positions him outside of the value-driven system he heads, one that is based on the female body. This is due to the fact that it is only through the sexual act with a woman that a man can solidify his identity. Thus, when the sailors prove themselves as worthy lovers, they witness their own fame exalted in song: "Altos varões que estão por vir ao mundo" (X, 7).

Yet sex provides the sailors with much more than a secured and respected social standing. The lovemaking scene is a necessary preparation to the acquisition of a much grander vision and knowledge. The knowledge gained from the physical encounter serves as the main key to the vision Tethys allows Vasco da Gama to access. Tethys leads da Gama to the summit of the highest point of the Island, where a great "fábrica se erguia" (IX, 87). Sex has made da Gama and his sailors worthy of ascending the mountain. This mountain, as Stephen Reckert writes, is a space par excellence that equates to knowledge, since it is the nexus between heaven and earth. The ascension to the top of the mountain, as Reckert states, "representa a unidade primordial, o Paraiso perdido (e por conquistar) onde crescia a Árvore cujo fruto, símbolo de *gnosis*, acabou por transformar-se, graças a uma intuição certeira como ingénua, em símbolo de *eros*" (191-92). Love and knowledge are fused to port a new form of seeing destiny and the future. It is the sexual encounter that will lead da Gama to the incredible knowledge that the *máquina do mundo* contains— a machine with the power to represent all times and spaces, past, present and future, that belong to Portugal. Such a vision defies both time and space, a vision provided only through the possession of the body of women. This knowledge that the *máquina do mundo* provides "é sem princípio e meta limitada" (X, 80). It is, ultimately, Camões's philosophical treatise on the entire reason for the universe, the possessor of the fifth essence, the Good.

It is here that the prophetic vision of Portugal's victories, future cities, and lands that will withstand the passing of time, is revealed. These are the future feats that are interconnected by a past genealogy of dynasties that have safe-guarded the continuation of the House of Aviz; indeed, what the reader witnesses in Cantos I-VIII. The sexual domination of the nymphs by the Portuguese make the latter worthy of a prize that is much grander than the physical, "Sapiência Suprema" (X, 80). This knowledge and information are based on the personal experience gained from the sexual act between a man and a woman. With the *máquina* the past and future are revealed, and the only missing link is the present.

Thus, women as the virtues and prizes are much more than physical enjoyment for Camões, for it is the initial physical knowledge, this *sentido da realidade*, that promises the deferral of the male figure. Venus is exalted to a mythic level within a frame of social responsibility and service to the empire, and the collective behavior of the Portuguese sailors in the *Ilha dos Amores* is presented as *the* model of masculinity, and the *only* option for King Sebastian. With the possession of the female body, the male's reproduction of his image defies death through the procreation of a son. This son, therefore, will be the testimony for self and others, and will assure a new generation of self-identity for the male seed (Irigaray, 1974, 27). This essentially economic pleasure is used by Camões as the manifestation of the male power that provides the medicine, or *phármakon*, necessary to cure King Sebastian of his disinterest in women.

The Cantos IX and X are meant to incite the king to take action. Hence, the series of imperatives that begin the poem are also reflected in its closing. While at the initial point of the poem Camões urges the King to "see" clearly, "Ponde no chão: vereis um novo exemplo / De amor dos pátrios feitos valerosos, / Em versos divulgado numerosos," the ending of the poem urges the King to appropriately evaluate its contents: "Olhai que sois (e vêde as outras gentes) / Senhor só de vassalos excelentes" (I, 9; X, 146). Sight, the primary sense that opens *Os Lusíadas*, is also the sense to conclude. In addition, the ending strongly urges the King to compare the high quality of the kingdom's people to that of those in other kingdoms. It is this last challenge that Camões poses before the king, one that would socially bind him to follow and uphold the law of his people.

The great innovation of the poetic imagination of Camões succeeds in using the *dolce stil nuovo* as a point of departure that, combined with the great breakdown of physical, mental, and epistemological spaces, presents a bold reinvention of the Platonic and Neoplatonic philosophies. It is the bustling character of the period, a period characterized by the supreme importance of an eye-witness experience, that forges the unique vision Camões presents. In the poem, the order of the world is grounded on the bodies of Venus and her nymphs, an order that clearly demarcates the sexual identity of men, an identity substantiated in the possession of the female form. Therefore, the culmination of the epic points toward the essential and centralizing philosophy of the Canto IX: Love, as a social and civic value, is the vehicle necessary for the acquisition of total knowledge *on earth*. The insistence of Camões that King Sebastian experience the body of woman as a means of obtaining total knowledge and continuing a vision long-forged through the centuries, must be attributed to the special situation that afflicted the House of Aviz. It is this specific historical need that aided Camões in his vision, along with his specific valuable experience, that provided him the material with which he reinvented the *dolce stil nuovo*—the most influential literary current of the 16th century.

I would like to express my tremendous gratitude to Ana Paula Ferreira, for all I have learned from her about literary theory and Luso-Brazilian literature, and for reading and providing helpful suggestions for improving the present article.

Notes

[1]We think of Platonism as emphasizing the feelings of love that are developed in the ascension from the material to the immaterial—an ascension through which the mind is impelled toward the search for love in the beautiful. This stance takes the beauty of material objects as a point of departure from which one ascends to the contemplation of the beauty of the human body, and ultimately to the understanding of the beauty of the good, ideas, knowledge, and absolute beauty. Most of the poets of the sixteenth century, and Camões was not an exception, were heavily influenced by this specific Platonic thought. Plato in the *Symposium* describes the ultimate goal of the ascent in the following manner: "[the] Beautiful itself, absolute, pure, unmixed, not polluted by human flesh or colors or any other great nonsense of mortality..." (59). The connection, therefore, is clear: The different stages of the material good serve to transport toward the spiritual good —the total understanding of beauty itself. This philosophical stance dictates the elimination of sexual love, since it is understood that the bodily pleasure of sex would distract the mind in its quest for knowledge. Sex, whether for pleasure or for reproduction, is here justified as the mere fulfillment of a biological need. The danger of sex lies in its power to trap the person in its physical pleasure. Hence, sexual love is too big a risk to be considered within the Platonic system.

Renaissance Neoplatonic thought, on the other hand, is heavily influenced by Plotinus and the Neoplatonists that emerged from the third to the fifth centuries. The image of woman has a central role with the Neoplatonists. The quest for beauty that stimulates the mind is focused on the specific beautiful form of beauty that is manifested in the body of a woman. It is from this specific manifestation of beauty that man will progress from the physical plane, on to the intellectual, to finally reach the spiritual. All the manifestations of beauty, as well as of goodness and truth, that are found in the world of the senses are due to an emanation—that is an irradiation—

that stems from the One or Absolute; the source of all being and goodness. The Neoplatonic lover is irresistibly drawn to the corporeal beauty of the beloved, but never in a sexual manner. The veneration of the beauty of the body is perceived as an important link that is interwoven with the fabric that maintains the spiritual beauty. At the same time, the Neoplatonist considers the beauty of the body as an essential step in the total contemplation of the Celestial Beauty of God. It is in this primary sense that Platonism and Neoplatonism heavily influence the courtly love tradition, which in turn will greatly impact the Italian *dolce stil nuovo*.

[2] There are many articles that insert *Os Lusíadas* within the same pedagogical framework as Virgil's *Aeneid*. See Cleonice Berardinelli, "Os excursos do Poeta n'*Os Lusíadas*," in *Occidente* 415 (Novembro, 1972), 246-258; Robert Clive Willis, "*Os Lusíadas* and its Neoclassical critics," in *Occidente* 415 (Novembro, 1972), 269-285; and Maria Helena da Rocha Pereira, "Conferência/Conference: Presenças da antiguidade clássica em *Os Lusíadas*," in *Revista de Letras*. Ser. Lit., vol. 25, 1985, 1-14. Some of the main studies that deal with the relationship between teacher and monarch include Allan H. Gibert, *Macchiavelli's Prince and its Forerunners: The Prince as a Typical Book de Regimine Principum* (Durham, NC: Duke University Press, 1938; reprinted New York: Barnes and Noble, 1968); and Lester Kruger Born, "The Perfect Prince: A Study in Thirteenth- and Fourteenth-Century Ideals," in *Speculum*, 3 (1928), 470-504.

[3] Countless critics, beginning with Faria e Sousa in the 17th century, have stressed the great similarities between Acteon and King Sebastian: "Se pone delante del Rey Don Sebastián, como un Bautista delante de Herodes a condenarle sus costumbres" (Faria e Sousa, 2, 54).

Works Cited

Andrews, Norwood H. Jr. "An Essay on Camões' Concept of the Epic." *Revista de letras* 3 (1962): 61-93.

Aguiar e Silva, Vitor Manuel de. "Aspectos petrarquistas da lírica de Camões." *Cuatro lecciones sobre Camoens*. Madrid: Fundación Juan March/Cátedra, 1981. 99-116.

———. *Camões: Labirintos e Fascínios*. Lisboa: Cotovia, 1994.

Albuquerque, Luis de. "Do clima em que Camões planeou *Os Lusíadas*." *Vértice* 40 (1980): 333-354.

Anderson, Robert N., III. "Epic and Intertext: What *Mensagem* Tells Us about *Os Lusiadas*." *Romance Notes* 28:1 (1987 Fall): 13-19.

Ares Montes, José. "El Portugal de Camões visto por los españoles de su tiempo." *Homenaje a Camõens: Estudios y ensayos hispano-portugueses*. Ed. Extremera Tapia, Nicolas et al. Granada: Universidad de Granada, 1980. 15-38.

Azevedo Filho, Leodegário. "Sobre o cánone lírico de Camões." *Colóquio* 99 (1987): 10-19.

Beirante, Cândido. "Dois estudos: 1. *Os Lusíadas* de Camões–circunstâncias epocais e aspectos da obra." *Estudos de Castelo Branco* 6 (Dezembro de 1980): 27-57.

Belchior, Maria de Lourdes. "Problemática religiosa na lírica de Camões." *Camoniana Californiana*. Santa Barbara: Jorge de Sena Center for Portuguese Studies, 1985. 40-55.

Berardinelli, Cleonice. "Os excursos do poeta n'*Os Lusíadas*." *Ocidente* 415 (Novembro, 1972): 246-258.

Bismut, Roger. "Camões lecteur de Jorge Manrique." *Arquivos do Centro Cultural Português* 19 (1983): 521-28.

Blasco, Pierre. "Faut-il Prendre au Serieux le 'Vieillard du Restelo'?." *Arquivos do Centro Cultural Português* 16 (1981): 143-156.

Borges Coelho, António. "3 variaçõe para o 4o. centenário da morte de Luiz Vaz de Camões." *Vértice* 40:. 436-439 (1980): 450-460.

Braga, Teófilo. "O centenário de Camões." *Ocidente* 415 (Novembro, 1972): 387-405.

———. "Libro I: Os poetas lyricos: Capitulo I: Camões e o platonismo erotico-mystico no seculo XVI." *Historia de Camões: Parte II: Eschola de Camões.* Porto: Imprensa Portugueza-Editora, 1874.

Brownlee, Marina. "The Dark Side of Myth en Camões 'Frail Bark'." *Comparative Literature Studies* 32 (1995): 176-99.

Buescu, Maria Leonor Carvalho. *Aspectos da Herança Clássica na Cultura Portuguesa.* Biblioteca Breve 33. Lisboa: Instituto de Cultura Portuguesa, 1979.

Camlong, Andre. "La Poetique de Camões dans le Chant VI des *Lusiades* ou l'Art Consommé de l'Epopée et du Raisonnement ou le Discours Poetique et Politique Humaniste." *Arquivos do Centro Cultural Português* vol. XXI, 1985, 273-312.

Camões, Luis Vaz de. *Obras completas.* Lisboa: Livraria Sá da Costa Editora, 1946. Vol. 1 & 2.

———. *Os Lusíadas.* Lisboa: Imprensa Nacional de Lisboa, 1931.

———. *Os Lusíadas.* Edited with en Introduction and Notes by Frank Pierce. Oxford: Claredon Press, 1973.

———. *Los Lusiadas.* Edición de Nicolás Extremera y José Antonio Sabio. Traducción de Benito Caldera. Madrid: Cátedra, 1986.

———. *The Lusiadas.* Edited and with an Introduction by Geoffrey Bullough. Carbondale: Southern Illinois University Press, 1963.

Carvalho, Joaquim de. "Estudos sobre as leituras filosóficas de Camões." *Estudos sobre a cultura portuguesa do século XVI.* Coimbra: Acta Universitatis Conimbrigensis, 1947.

Castro, Armando. *Camões e a Sociedade do Seu Tempo.* Lisboa: Editorial Caminho, 1980.

———. "Unidade estructural de *Os Lusíadas.*" *Estudos sobre Camões.* Lisboa: Imprensa Nacional-Casa da Moeda, 1981. 95-102.

Coelho, Jacinto do Prado. "Camões: ideologia e poesia." *Cuatro lecciones sobre Camoens.* Madrid: Fundación Juan March/Cátedra, 1981. 43-70.

———. "Camões' concept of epic poetry and myth." *Camões à la Renaissance.* Paris: Presses Universitaires de France, 1983. 57-70.

Coimbra Martins, António. "'Quem na estirpe seu se chama…'." *Arquivos do Centro Cultural Português* 16 (1981): 283-295.

Cornil, S. "Camões et la Renaissance au Portugal." *Camões à la Renaissance.* Paris: Presses Universitaires de France, 1983. 15-20.

Costa Miranda, José da. "Ainda sobre Camões e Ariosto." *Arquivos do Centro Cultural Português* 16 (1981): 777-784.

Crabbé Rocha, Clara. "Metáforas do amor ou amor-metáfora nos sonetos de Camões." *Cadernos de Literatura* 5 (1980): 46-56.

D'Alge, Carlos. *O exílio imaginário.* Lisboa: Fortaleza, 1983.

Deming, Robert H. "Love and Knowledge in the Renaissance Lyric." *Texas Studies in Literature and Language* 16 (1974): 389-410

Deswarte, Sylvie. La 'Machine du Monde': Camoens et Francisco de Holanda. A Propos de *Lus.* X, 76-91." *Arquivos do Centro Cultural Português* 16 (1981): 325-344.

Dias Agudo, Francisco. "*Os Lusíadas*: D. Sebastião e a censura." *Ocidente* 415 (Novembro, 1972): 341-351.

Dixon, Paul B. "History as Prophecy in Camões's *Os Lusíadas.*" *Luso-Brazilian Review* 22:2 (1985): 145-150.

Dores Santos, Raimunda das. "A prensença do mito em *Os Lusíadas.*" *Arquivo do Centro de Estudios Portugueses Universitários* 3 (1980): 13-24.

Duque, Alquilino. "Camoens y Pessoa: poetas del mito." *Hispanic Review* 56 (Winter 1988): 39-52.

Earle, T.F. "Autobiografia e retórica numa canção de Camões." *Arquivos do Centro Cultural Português* 23 (1987): 507-521.

Esteves Pinheiro, José Júlio. Os Tempos Verbais n'*Os Lusíadas*: Intemporalidade e anacronia." *Arquivos do Centro Cultural Português* 16 (1981): 311-323.

Faria e Sousa, Manuel. *Lusíadas de Luís de Camões.* Lisboa: Imprensa Nacional-Casa da Moeda, 1972.

Fernandes, Rogerio. "*Os Lusíadas* e a educação do príncipe." *Vértice* 40:436-439 (1980): 375-399.

Ferreira Reis, Arthur Cezar. "Camões e o mundo d'*Os Lusíadas.*" *Ocidente* 415 (1972): 259-267.

Freitas, William. *Camoens and his Epic.* Stanford: Institute of Hispanic American and Luso-Brazilian Studies, 1963.

Gentil da Silva, José. "L'Espace et l'Action des *Lusiades*: L'Histoire Exprimée par le vocabulaire." *Arquivos do Centro Cultural Português* 16 (1981) 109-117.

Hart, Thomas R. "Aspectos medievais e renacentistas d'*Os Lusíadas.*" , *Arquivos do Centro Cultural Português* 16 (1981): 51-59.

———. "The Author's Voice in *The Lusiads.*" *Hispanic Review* 44 (Winter 1976): 45-55.

———. "The Idea of History in Camões's *Lusiads.*" *Ocidente* 36 (1972): 83-97.

Leal de Matos, Maria Vitalina. "O Tempo na Poesia Camoniana." *Arquivos do Centro Cultural Português* 16 (1981): 127-142.

Lier, Henri van. "Le portugais et l'océan." *Le français dans le monde* 49 (1990) 41-46.

Lipking, Lawrence. "The Genius of the Shore: Lycidas, Adamastor, and the Poetics of Nationalism." Publications of the Modern Language Association of America" 111:2 (1996): 205-21.

Lourenço, Eduardo. "Camões et l'Europe." *Critique: Révue des Publications Françaises et étrangères* 44 (1988): 664-75.

Luzes, Pedro. "O Eros Camoniano." *Estudos sobre Camões.* Lisboa: Imprensa Nacional-Casa da Moeda, 1981. 71-84.

Pais Brandão, Frama Hasse. "A Ilha do Amor." *Estudos sobre Camões.* Lisboa: Imprensa Nacio-nal-Casa da Moeda, 1981. 111-124.

McGrady, Donald. "'Era no tempo alegre': Notes on Camoes's Use of Petrarch." *Romance Quarterly* 35:4 (1988): 443-447.

Macedo, Helder. "O braço e a mente. O poeta como herói n'*Os Lusíadas.*" *Arquivos do Centro Cultural Português* 16 (1981): 61-72.

———. *Camões e a Viagem Iniciática.* Lisboa: Morães Editores, 1980.

———. "Love as Knowledge: The Lyric Poetry of Camões." Unpublished essay. 1998.

———. "The Lusiads: Epic Celebration and Pastoral Regret." *Portuguese Studies* 6 (1990): 32-7.

Marmoto, Rita. "A figura feminina petrarquista em Camões: entre imitação e transformação." en *Lírica Camoniana: Estudos Diversos.* Lisboa: Cosmos, 1996. 49-63.

Martins Garcia, José. "A contradição fundamental d'*Os Lusíadas.*" *Camoniana Californiana.* Santa Barbara: Jorge de Sena Center for Portuguese Studies, 1985. 13-19.

Martins, Wilson. "Camões and the Super-Camões." *Ocidente* Número especial (Novembro, 1972): 39-43.

Matos, Maria Vitalina Leal de. "O tempo na poesia camoniana." *Arquivos do Centro Cultural Português* 16 (1981): 127-142.

Mimoso-Ruiz, Duarte. "Les figures mythiques feminines dans *Os Lusíadas* de Camões." *Arquivos do Centro Cultural Português* 16 (1981): 267-282.

Namorado, Egídio. "*Os Lusíadas* e os movimentos ulturais do Século XVI." *Vértice* 436-439 (1980): 434-449.

Nicolopulos, James. *The Poetics of Empire in the Indies: Prophecy and Imitation in La Araucana and Os Lusíadas.* University Park: Pennsylvania State University Press, 2000.

Ovtchrenko, Olga. "A mulher na obra camoniana." *Colóquio* 125/126 (1992): 9-13.

Pereira, Edgar. "Camões e Pessoa: Ruínas." *Minas Gerais Suplemento Literário* 23:1140 (1990): 6-7.

Pereira, Maria Helena da Rocha. "Conferencia/Conference: Presencas da Antiguidade Classica em *Os Lusiadas.*" *Revista de Letras* 25 (1985) 1-14.

Pierce, Frank. "Camões and Inês de Castro." *Ocidente* Número especial (Novembro, 1972): 123-132.

Prado Coelho, Jacinto do. "A 'Ilha dos Amores': Conjunçoes e dissonâncias." *Arquivos do Centro Cultural Português* 16 (1981): 181-189.

Probyn, Elspeth. *Sexing the Self: Gendered Positions in Cultural Studies.* London: Routledge, 1993.

Quint, David. "Voices of Resistance: The Epic Curse and Camões's Adamastor." *New World Encounters.* Ed. Stephen Greenbatt. Los Angeles: University of California Press, 1993.

Rebelo, Luis de Sousa. "Camões e o sentido da comunidade." *Vertice* 37 (1977): 544-63.

———. "O texto e o contexto num soneto de Camões." *Arquivos do Centro Cultural Português* 16 (1981): 437-446.

Reckert, Stephen. "A Ilha dos Amores (Iconografia de um arquétipo)." *Arquivos do Centro Cultural Português* 16 (1981): 191-200.

———."Significantes parciais na semióticade Camões." *Camoniana Californiana.* Santa Barbara: Jorge de Sena Center for Portuguese Studies, 1985. 56-72.

Resina Rodrigues, Maria Idalina. "O Teatro no Teatro: A Propósito de *El-Rei Seleuco* e Outros Autos Quinhentistas." *Arquivos do Centro Cultural Português* 16 (1981): 469-485.

Roche, Jean. "O vocabulário do episódio de Inês de Castro em *Os Lusíadas.*" *Ocidente* 415 (Novembro, 1972): 317-327.

Rodrigues, José Maria y Afonso Lopes Vieira. *Lírica de Camões.* Coimbra: Imprensa da Universidade, 1932.

Roig, Adrien. "L'Inês de Camões." *Arquivos do Centro Cultural Português* 16 (1981): 157-179.

Saraiva, António José. "A 'fábrica' d'*Os Lusíadas.*" Arquivos do Centro Cultural Portugues 16 (1981): 73-94.

———. *Vida Ignorada de Camões.* Lisboa: Publicações Europa-América, 1978.

Sena, Jorge de. "Camões: novas observações acerca da sua epopeia e do seu pensamento." *Ocidente* Número especial (Novembro, 1972): 3-24.

———. "Camões, the lyrical poet," *Camões: Some Poems.* London: The Menard Press, 1976.

———. *Os Lusíadas e outros estudos camonianos e da poesia peninsular do século XVI.* Lisboa: Portugália Editorial, 1970.

Sérgio, António. *Obras completas: Ensaios: Tomo IV.* Lisboa: Sá da Costa, 1972.

Sims, James H. " 'Delicious Paradise' in *Os Lusíadas* and in *Paradise Lost.*" *Ocidente.* Número especial (Novembro, 1972): 163-171.

Silva, Jose Gentil da. "L'Espace et l'action des Lusiadas: L'Histoire exprimee par le vocabulaire." *Arquivos do Centro Cultural Português* 16 (1981): 109-117.

Soares Amora, António. "Análise retrospectiva e prospectiva dos estudos camonianos em 1980." *Brotéria* 110:7 (1980): 5-18.

Souza, Ronald W. "*Os Lusíadas:* Voz poética/leitura." *Estudos Ibero-americanos* 6:1 (1980): 67-72.

Storck, Wilheim. *Vida e obras de Luís de Camões.* Lisboa: Academia Real das Ciências, 1898.

Tavani, Giuseppe. "Ainda sobre a estrutura espácio-temporal d'*Os Lusíadas.*" *Brotéria* 111:5 (1980): 359-366.

Taylor, L.C. *Luis de Camões: Epic & Lyric.* Manchester: Carcanet, 1990.

Torres, Amadeu. "A 'Ilha dos Amores' d'*Os Lusíadas* na versão de cinco poetas neolatinos: uma restituição que se impõe." *Arquivos do Centro Cultural Português* 16 (1981): 201-241.

Veríssimo, A. Pedrosa. "A realidade e o mito em *Os Lusíadas.*" *Ocidente* 415 (Novembro, 1972): 269-286.

Walker, Roger M. "Baco ou Venus? Pergunta de Camões ainda sem resposta." *Ocidente* Número especial (1972): 173-180.

Willis, Robert Clive. "*Os Lusíadas* and its Neoclassical critics." *Ocidente* 415 (1972): 269-286.

Saúl Jiménez-Sandoval is Associate Professor of Spanish and Portuguese and Graduate Studies Director of the Spanish section at California State University, Fresno. He is a graduate of the University of California, Irvine, where he finished his dissertation under the supervision of Ana Paula Ferreira and Jacobo Sefamí in 2001. His dissertation deals with the concept of community in the poetry of pre-Hispanic Mexico, Luís Vaz de Camões and Sor Juana Inés de la Cruz. His current research involves Luís Vaz de Camões and the construction of masculinity as the foreground to Fernando Pessoa's *Mensagem,* and the condemnation of war in *Piedra de sol* by Octavio Paz. E-mail: sjimenez@csufresno.edu

The Monstrous Lineage of Adamastor and His Critics

Josiah Blackmore

Abstract. This article considers the figure of Adamastor in *Os Lusíadas* and, in particular, Adamastor's status as a monster and how this becomes implicated into criticism of the poem. The article argues that Adamastor's monstrosity invests him with a special hermeneutic currency. Comments are made on monsters in literary and cultural criticism. Then, Manuel de Faria e Sousa's commentary on the Adamastor episode in his 1639 edition of *Os Lusíadas* is analyzed. In this text, Adamastor's monstrous body is key to establishing him as a contravening principle to Portuguese imperialism.

Halfway through *Os Lusíadas* and halfway through the voyage from Portugal to India that serves as the historical basis of the poem, Vasco da Gama and his fleet approach the southern tip of Africa. Known as the Cape of Storms and later as the Cape of Good Hope, or Cabo da Boa Esperança, this locale looms famously on the fabled horizon of western seafaring as a danger to those who would attempt its passage. As Gama's eastward-bound sailors draw near, a black cloud appears and roils in the darkening sky, out of which an apparition soon takes shape—suddenly, thunderously, and terrifyingly, like a storm at sea. This apparition, whose name is Adamastor, towers above the ships and berates the mariners: how dare they violate the ancient geographical and nautical boundary at which he stands guard, how dare they presume to uncover secrets of nature and the sea. Adamastor, the "eclipsing menace" as Herman Melville would call him three

Portuguese Literary & Cultural Studies 7 (2008): 255-63.
© University of Massachusetts Dartmouth.

centuries later, delivers a series of prophecies to Vasco da Gama about the fate of the Portuguese explorers to follow in his footsteps that are as historically true as they are disastrous and tragic. On questioning by Gama, Adamastor relates his own tragic story, one of military and amorous defeat. A Titan, a giant of the earth, Adamastor rose in rebellion against Neptune and fell in love with the sea goddess Thetis, only then to be deceived at the moment of an arranged tryst. As punishment for his presumption in desiring the nymph, Adamastor was transformed, eternally, into the inhospitable and rocky terrain of the cape.

Adamastor is arguably Camões's most famous poetic creation, a feat of literary invention rivaling the composition of *Os Lusíadas* itself. Manoel Correa, an early editor (1613) and commentator of the poem, remarked apropos of the introduction of Adamastor in stanza 39 of canto V that "Não tenho palauras para encarecer a linguagẽ, propriedade, & eloquentia desta octaua, que realmente faz este fingimento & Metamorphosi que vay tratando deste Cabo de Boa Esperança, vẽtagem as de Ouidio" (153r). Over time, the Adamastor episode has generated a mixture of awe and interpretive grappling that might be said to reflect Adamastor's own enigmatic nature.[1] He is, for instance, at once the anthropomorphic manifestation of the Cape of Good Hope and a nebulous, airy specter; he is fear and apprehension incarnate and an endpoint of geographic and cartographic knowledge, a numinous glimpse of "os segredos escondidos / Da natureza e do húmido elemento" (V.42.i-ii).[2] Adamastor is polysemous, an exegetical conundrum. Indeed, much of Camões's fame, both within Portugal and without, is linked to Adamastor and the polemic surrounding him. In this essay, I want first to focus on Adamastor's monstrosity, one of his principal characteristics, and argue that it is Adamastor's status as a monster that invests him with much of his hermeneutic currency. Then I will consider Manuel de Faria e Sousa's commentary on the Adamastor episode in his 1639 edition of *Os Lusíadas*, in which monstrosity underwrites broader theoretical issues relating to allegory and imperialism.

Let us begin by noting how Camões, through the voice of Vasco da Gama, describes the appearance of Adamastor:

...hũa figura
Se nos mostra no ar, robusta e válida,
De disforme e grandíssima estatura;
O rosto carregado, a barba esquálida,
Os olhos encovados, e a postura

> Medonha e má, e a cor terrena e pálida;
> Cheios de terra e crespos os cabelos,
> A boca negra, os dentes amarelos.
> Tão grande era de membros, que bem posso
> Certificar-te que este era o segundo
> De Rodes estranhíssimo Colosso... (V.39-40.i-iii)

A few stanzas later, Gama remarks that "ia por diante o monstro hor-rendo, / Dizendo nossos Fados" (V.49.i-ii), and in so doing echoes Virgil's description of Polyphemus as a "monstrum horrendum, informe, ingens" ["a monster, awful, shapeless, huge"] (*Aeneid*, III.v.657). Camões hence desig-nates Adamastor as both a "figure" and a "monster." Terry Cochran analyzes in detail the significance of *figura* as it relates to figurality, history, and dis-course in this episode, and explores these issues in the context of the nine-teenth-century polemic over Adamastor in the writings of José Agostinho de Macedo and others.[3] If, on the one hand, we might read Adamastor through the abstracting label of *figura*, we can also and equally significantly read him as a "monstro," a staple of Renaissance culture that in the poem is both an immediate, dramatic corporeality and a key metphor of Camonian poesis. Camões's designation of Adamastor as a monster, therefore, not only situates the apparition within a tradition of classical and epic monsters but also con-nects him to a contemporary critical practice of reading monsters as especially fecund cultural constructs that embody, among other things, notions of the-ology, history, science, aesthetics, and epistemology.

Perhaps one of the most interesting facts about Camões's use of "monstro" to refer to Adamastor is that this is one of only three times the word appears in *Os Lusíadas*, a poem teeming with mythological beings, penned and first read in a time when the western fascination with the East and its *mirabilia* was firmly part of the European (textual) imaginary. The history of monsters in western culture has garnered considerable critical attention in recent years, especially monsters of the Middle Ages and Renaissance. Far too complex a subject to summarize adequately here, suffice it to say for the purposes of the current argument that the plethora of monsters reported to exist at the edges of the known world or in the fabulous realms of the East sprung from many discursive practices. Writers such as Marco Polo, John Mandeville, or Gómez de Santisteban (whose *Libro del infante don Pedro de Portugal* contains pas-sages describing the kinds of monsters supposedly witnessed by Polo or

Mandeville) helped establish monsters and monstrous races in the imaginations of travelers, merchants, and explorers. There were also pamphlets and books on the teratological or medical monster (those with birth defects or deformities) as detailed in the famous treatise, *Des monstres et prodiges* (1573) by the French surgeon Ambroise Paré.[4] This latter kind of monster could include the products of unnatural couplings (such as those between humans and animals) and is, in fact, the kind of "monstros" Camões refers to in canto X in Tethys's survey of the globe to Vasco da Gama:

> Olha o reino Arracão; olha o assento
>
> De Pegu, que já monstros povoaram,
>
> Monstros filhos do feio ajuntamento
>
> Dhũa mulher e um cão, que sós se acharam.
>
> Aqui soante arame no instrumento
>
> Da gèração custumão, o que usaram
>
> Por manha da Rainha que, inventando
>
> Tal uso, deitou fora o error nefando. (X.122)

The fact that this is the only use of *monstro* apart from the reference to Adamastor prompts an unavoidable comparison between the monsters of canto X and the specter at the end of Africa. The comparison suggests that, on one level at least, Camonian monstrosity relates to genealogical or lineal descent. Recall that, on interrogation by Vasco da Gama, Adamastor recounts his own monstrous ancestry by noting that "Fui dos filhos aspérrimos da Terra, / Qual Encélado, Egeu e o Centimano" (V.51.i-ii); the names here are all of giants, with Centimano ("cem mãos") standing as the most obviously "monstrous." Camões seems to imply that Adamastor's lineage is "legitimate"—he can trace his origins back through mythology—while the eastern realm of Arakan is the site of unnatural lineage, a result of the "error nefando."[5] The claim to a legitimate (monstrous) lineage, one vindicated by the mythological histories of antiquity, allows Adamastor, in part, the privilege of his own historiographic voice. In the context of the Portuguese tradition of the *livros de linhagens* (a narrative genre that permeates the historical consciousness of *Os Lusíadas*) Adamastor's narrativization of the past is one of the discursive behaviors that arrests Gama's attention.

Yet the trait of Adamastor that most determines his monstrosity is his body. This gigantic body, which Camões takes pains to detail by describing its limbs, hair, mouth, teeth, face, and beard, is monstrous because it is excessive and, in aesthetic terms, contravenes Renaissance notions of symmetry and proportion. It erupts precipitously into view and in so doing causes Vasco da Gama to react by declaring "Que esse estupendo / Corpo, certo, me tem maravilhado!" (V.49.iii-iv). Camões's / Gama's choice of "maravilhado" is significant since he is rehearsing the trope of marvel or wonder that the encounter with monsters traditionally triggered. Adamastor's hypertrophic body occasions a temporary suspension of certainty that is the hallmark of *maravilha*. As an overwhelming moment of the embodiment of alterity, the strange, and the terrifying that not only causes wonder to Gama but subsequently to critics of the poem, Adamastor exemplifies the essence of the monstrous body as Jeffrey Jerome Cohen argues for it:

> The monstrous body is pure culture. A construct and a projection, the monster exists only to be read: the monstrum is etymologically "that which reveals," "that which warns," a glyph that seeks a hierophant. Like a letter on the page, the monster signifies something other than itself: it is always a displacement, always inhabits the gap between the time of upheaval that created it and the moment into which it is received, to be born again.... Monsters must be examined within the intricate mix of relations (social, cultural, and literary-historical) that generate them. (4-5)[6]

In this line of reasoning, Adamastor stands as a monstrous corporeality that beckons to be read within the expansionist logic of *Os Lusíadas*. Manuel de Faria e Sousa (1590-1649) does just that, and I now want to consider this critic's interpretation of Adamastor's monstrous body as a decisive moment in the critical history of the poem.

Faria e Sousa's meticulously annotated two-volume edition of *Os Lusíadas*, published in Madrid in 1639, perhaps did more for establishing the contours of interpretive practice on the poem than has been recognized to date. Following the methods of earlier commentators (such as Manoel Correa), Faria e Sousa proceeds stanza-by-stanza, and provides a translation into Castilian of each stanza along with an often verse-by-verse critical commentary.[7] He cites an impressive range of primary sources in his interpretations, and his edition contains detailed indices and word and author lists. Faria e Sousa argues for an allegorical reading of Camões's poem that foregrounds its mythological underpinnings, and in so doing becomes one of Camões's preeminent mythographers in his agenda to allegorize history through the mythological pantheon. While we might disagree with the critic's thesis that the allegorical structure of *Os Lusíadas* responds to nothing more than Camões's desire to represent the victory of the Catholic church in foreign lands, we cannot overlook the nuance of argument and detail Faria e Sousa often brings to the defense of this proposition. Whatever interpretive disagreement critics might have, Faria e Sousa's critical methodology is watertight.

One of the lengthiest disquisitions Faria e Sousa provides on any episode is on Adamastor. The critic repeatedly insists on Adamastor's monstrosity as central to his interpretation. In the religious narrative Faria e Sousa sees underlying the text, Adamastor unilaterally represents Mohammed and Islam as the enemy of Christendom. With the repeated claim that "este Gigante representa al demonio" (see, for example, 522 and 525) and that he is the head of "la torpeza Mauritana" (541),[8] Faria e Sousa points to an understanding of Adamastor that moves beyond the simple, overall allegorical reading of the poem. For, as he inscribes Mohammed into the universe of *Os Lusíadas* through Adamastor, Faria e Sousa invests him with a theoretical importance as an expansionist negativity, a dark embodiment of the tenets of imperialism. Adamastor appears in the pages of the *Lvsiadas comentadas* as a body and a force that impede the smooth (re-)mapping of the world according to a Christian cosmology. He threatens to unmap the world into diabolical chaos as a countermap of Christian imperialism. Adamastor's phantasmal and monstrous body arises from the tip of Africa as the cartographic principle, demonically inflected, driving expansionist movement.

Faria e Sousa builds this reading of the monster by construing Africa as solely and exclusively the seat of Islam, a gesture that effectively wipes Africa clean of its non-Islamic cultures, with which Portuguese colonists had been familiar for over two centuries. Underneath the apocalyptic identification of Adamastor as the "segundo Lucifer; porque muchos dixeron, que Mahoma era el Antechristo" (541), there also lies an awareness of a more immediate, historically present threat, namely, the fear of Islamic imperialism and, by extension, of Turkish resistance to Portuguese overseas colonies. This "estupenda fabula" (539), an embodiment of Mohammed and consequently of "toda la Morisma" (573), realizes his danger by mobilizing a Moorish "navegación," a term that for Faria e Sousa encompasses the idea of both a European itinerancy through the collective movement of ships and the overall exercise of imperial power. This inimical *navegación* recognizes that the Moors also possess a cartographic imperative in that they are just as capable as the Portuguese of traveling across water and plotting and conquering parcels of space into which they will inscribe their infernal belief. The cartographic power Adamastor darkly wields is symbolized by Faria e Sousa's reading of his body as partitioned and dispersed throughout the globe, a kind of anatomization that recalls Adamastor's own physiological, monstrously formed body:

> es tambien propio de la gente Mahometana que possee (i posseìa màs entonces) grandissimos miembros de todas las partes del mundo a la sazon descubiertas, no solo en toda la Africa, i en las dos Asias, sinò que en Europa posseyeron mucho... (541)

Adamastor's limbs stretch to the four corners of the globe in a totalizing gesture that encompasses and touches all points of the *orbis terrarum*. Adamastor's monstrous limbs enable him to act as a diabolic mapmaker since he can insidiously reach the ends of the earth. His body parts throw the spiritual cosmos out of order and emplot the coordinates of sacrilege. In other words, these body parts are a deforming presence across Camonian world-space that obstruct the cosmic harmony that is so dramatically negotiated by the gods and instantiated by imperialist action in every canto of *Os Lusíadas*.

In conclusion, I would like to consider Faria e Sousa's reflection on monstrosity as it relates to his own exegetical enterprise. At the outset of his comments on the Adamastor episode, he writes:

> Pondrème aqui a componer una monstruosa nota de monstruos, para que me tēgan por monstro [*sic*] de erudicion? Hagalo quien tuviere essa codicia, que yo con actos vio[l]entos no quiero mostrarme ciente: porque en este lugar basta dezir, que monstruo es aquello que en la forma de su genero es desproporcionada, irregular, sin medida, qual el Poeta pintò este Gigante […]. I este aqui era monstruo en mala forma, i en desproporcion... i en prometer sucessos monstruosos, cõ una mõstruosa passion vengativa […]. (535)

The monster and the monstrous may turn the critic himself into a monster, as Faria e Sousa lightheartedly suggests, but in so doing acknowledges an inbuilt reciprocity between monsters and exegesis. Perhaps not a little slyly does Faria e Sousa disavow an overly ambitious erudition as an "acto violento," only then to present a de facto apologia of monsters in the form of his lengthy critical commentary. Adamastor's monstrous self, transformed in Ovidian fashion into the Cape of Good Hope, embodies but one discrete moment of the dynamic of change and metamorphosis pulsing through *Os Lusíadas* as history, myth, and hermeneutics shape the geographical and ideological *oikumene* of expansion. Faria e Sousa ultimately stands as one of Camões's most influential mythographers since he establishes *Os Lusíadas* itself as a mythos, a decisive, foundational moment in the Iberian cultural archive. The poem, like myth, is a narrative repeatedly told and from which beginnings emanate. The complex hermeneutic dimension of Adamastor is possibly the greatest discovery recorded by Faria e Sousa, the progenitor of a critical tradition that finds in the "monstro horrendo" a source of renewed polemic and controversy on the Portuguese expansionist imagining of Africa.

Notes

[1] For most critics, the Adamastor episode comprises stanzas 37 to 60 of canto V, that is, from the appearance of the cloud out of which Adamastor emerges to his final, anguished cry and his disappearance. For José Benoliel, the episode extends to stanza 70. To my knowledge, Benoliel is the only scholar to argue for an Arabic source for the Adamastor episode, which he finds in the "Conto do Pescador" of the *Thousand and One Nights.*

[2] Citations of *Os Lusíadas* are from the edition of Emanuel Paulo Ramos.

[3] See Cochran, chapters 4 and 5. Cochran's argument, in part, proposes that Camões himself is a figure that "becomes at the same time the bearer of Portuguese culture and paradigmatic for the relationship between culture and state that literary and national history presuppose" (121). Cochran further argues that "the disjuncture between the historical and the figural, between experience and its idealization, come to a head in the looming figure of Adamastor" (139). Additionally, *figura* may be a synonym here for "map," which would support Faria e Sousa's cartographic reading of Adamastor's body (see below). In his study of cartographic literature in early modern Spanish empire, Ricardo Padrón notes that Cortés uses "figura" in reference to territorial representations (93).

[4] For studies on monsters in the Portuguese context, see Costa, Gil, and Vieira.

[5] In this third *Década da Ásia*, which certainly served as Camões's source for the lore about Arakan, João de Barros elaborates on the "pouo de Pegú" and what the poet would call the "error nefando": "Porem quanto á maneyra de sua religiam, templos, sacẹrdótes, grandeza de jdolos & cerimonias de seus sacrificios, vso de comer toda inmudicia, & torpeza de trazer cascauẹes soldados no instrumento da gẹraçam....Donde se póde crer ser verdade o que elles contam *que* aquella tẹrra se pouoou do ajuntamẽto de hum cam & hũa molher: pois que no aucto do ajuntamẽto delles querem jmitar os cães, por que quem o jmita delle deue pr, proçeder. E a história desta sua gẹraçam, ẹ que vindo tẹr á cósta daquelle reyno Pegú que entam ẹram tẹrras hermas hum junco da China com tormenta se perdeo, de que sómente escapou hũa molher & hum cam, com o qual ella teue copula de que ouue filhos que depois os ouuerã della, com que a tẹrra se veo a multiplicar, & por nam degenerarem do pay jnuentáram os cascauẹes....Outros dizem que esta tẹrra & a de Arracam foy pouoáda de degradados, & que o vso dos cascauẹes foy remẹdio contra aquelle nefando peccado contra natura" (66r).

[6] Cohen's well-written and persuasive essay is requisite reading for any scholar interested in the interpretation of monsters. One of its many strengths is the applicability of the ideas pre-

sented to a wide range of monsters, both notionally and historically.

[7] Also see Flasche for comments on Faria e Sousa's scholarly method.

[8] References to Faria e Sousa's text are by column number.

Works Cited

Barros, João de. *Ásia… Dos feitos que os Portugueses fizeram no descobrimento e conquista dos mares e terras do Oriente. Terceira Década.* Lisbon: Imprensa Nacional-Casa da Moeda, 1992.

Benoliel, José. *Episodio do gigante Adamastor: Lusiadas, canto v, est. XXXVII-LXX. Estudo critico.* Lisbon: Imprensa Nacional, 1898.

Camões, Luís de. *Os Lusíadas.* Ed. Emanuel Paulo Ramos. Porto: Porto Editora, 1990.

———. *Os Lvsiadas do grande Lvis de Camoens. Principe da poesia heroica….* Ed. Manoel Correa. Lisbon: Pedro Crasbeeck, 1613.

———. *Lvsiadas de Lvis de Camoens, principe de los poetas de España….Comentadas por Manvel de Faria i Sousa, Cavallero de la Orden de Christo, i de la Casa Real.* Vol. 1. Madrid: Ivan Sanchez, 1639.

Cochran, Terry. *Twilight of the Literary: Figures of Thought in the Age of Print.* Cambridge: Harvard UP, 2001.

Cohen, Jeffrey Jerome. "Monster Culture (Seven Theses)." *Monster Theory: Reading Culture.* Ed. Jeffrey Jerome Cohen. Minneapolis: U of Minnesota P, 1996. 3-25.

Costa, P. Fontes da. "Between Fact and Fiction: Narratives of Monsters in Eighteenth-Century Portugal." *Portuguese Studies* 20 (2004): 63-72.

Flasche, Hans. "O método de comentar de Manuel de Faria e Sousa (contributo para a interpretação d' *Os Lusíadas*)." *Actas da I Reunião Internacional de Camonistas.* Lisbon: Comissão Executiva do IV Centenário da Publicação de "Os Lusíadas," 1973. 135-73.

Gil, José. *Monstros.* Lisbon: Quetzal, 1994.

Padrón, Ricardo. *The Spacious Word: Cartography, Literature, and Empire in Early Modern Spain.* Chicago: U of Chicago P, 2004.

Paré, Ambroise. *Des monstres et prodiges.* Ed. Jean Céard. Geneva: Droz, 1971.

Santisteban, Gómez de. *Libro del infante don Pedro de Portugal.* Ed. Francis M. Rogers. Lisbon: Minerva, 1962.

Vieira, Yara Frateschi. "O médico e o monstro: sobre a evolução do discurso teratológico em Portugal, do século XVI ao XVIII." *Arquivos do Centro Cultural Português* 25 (1988): 461-82.

Virgil. *Eclogues. Georgics. Aeneid* 1-6. Loeb Classical Library 63. Cambridge: Harvard UP, 1935.

Josiah Blackmore is Professor in the Department of Spanish and Portuguese at the University of Toronto. He is author of *Manifest Perdition: Shipwreck Narrative and the Disruption of Empire* (Minnesota, 2002) and co-editor of *Queer Iberia: Sexualities, Cultures, and Crossings from the Middle Ages to the Renaissance* (Duke, 1999). This article is part of a book in progress on Africa and Africans in Portuguese expansionist texts of the fifteenth and sixteenth centuries. Email: j.blackmore@utoronto.ca

Einstein e Pessoa

Kenneth Krabbenhoft

Resumo. Em Fernando Pessoa, o poeta e o pensador, reuniram-se o espírito não-conformista e a sede de perceber verdades universais, que o impulsionaram ao longo da sua vida a estudar as correntes mais novas do pensamento científico da sua época. O que lhe interessava não era tanto o progresso da ciência em si mas as consequências dos últimos achados científicos para a sociedade em que vivia, tanto na ética como na política, tanto na arte como nas relações íntimas dos indivíduos. No seu caso, o de um homem dedicado corpo e alma à criação poética, a ciência era uma fonte de revelações que, em conjunto com o seu génio particular, ajudavam-no a aprofundar a compreensão (ou pelo menos a confirmação) da sua própria arte, além de sugerir possibilidades e caminhos a serem explorados. Este ensaio examina uma faceta do tópico—a teoria restrita da relatividade—da heteronímia. Os textos que apoiam o argumento são de três tipos: 1. livros pertencentes à biblioteca particular do poeta, hoje conservada na Casa Fernando Pessoa em Lisboa; 2. o espólio literário do poeta, isto é manuscritos não publicados conservados na Biblioteca Nacional de Portugal; e 3. as obras publicadas de Fernando Pessoa ortónimo e heterónimo.

Introdução

O espírito não-conformista e a sede de perceber verdades universais impulsionaram Fernando Pessoa ao longo da sua vida a estudar as correntes mais recentes do pensamento científico da sua época. O que lhe interessava

Portuguese Literary & Cultural Studies 7 (2008): 265-81.

não era tanto o progresso da ciência em si mas as consequências dos últimos avanços científicos para a sociedade e a cultura em que vivia. No seu caso, o de um homem dedicado de corpo e alma à criação poética, a ciência era uma fonte de revelações que, em conjunto com o seu génio particular, ajudavam-no a aprofundar a sua compreensão da arte, além de sugerir possibilidades e caminhos a serem explorados.

Este ensaio examina dois achados importantes do início do século XX europeu: nas ciências, a teoria restrita da relatividade de Albert Einstein, e na poesia, a heteronímia de Fernando Pessoa, que no seu aspecto teórico reflecte premissas enunciadas por Einstein e depois estendidas por pensadores como Henri Bergson à filosofia. Os textos que apoiam o argumento são de três tipos: 1. livros pertencentes à biblioteca particular do poeta guardada na Casa Fernando Pessoa em Lisboa; 2. o espólio literário do poeta conservado pela Biblioteca Nacional de Portugal; e 3. certas obras publicadas de Fernando Pessoa ortónimo e heterónimo. Os livros da primeira categoria interessam não só pelo seu conteúdo mas também pelos sublinhados, sinais marginais, e pelos comentários que Pessoa escreveu à mão nos seus exemplares. Uma coisa é constatar, por exemplo, que Pessoa possuiu um exemplar de *Initiation aux théories d'Einstein* do físico francês Gaston Moch, outra coisa é saber quais eram as linhas e os parágrafos que chamaram a atenção do poeta, informação que tem implicações importantes para o estudo do fenómeno heteronímico.

Einstein e a teoria da relatividade

Albert Einstein tinha apenas 27 anos quando publicou o esboço inicial da teoria restrita da relatividade, o primeiro dos achados que lhe dariam renome sem igual na história das ciências.[1] Não foi a "estreia" do jovem físico na prestigiosa revista *Annalen der Physik*, pois anteriormente (embora no mesmo ano de 1905) tinha publicado estudos sobre o movimento molecular e o carácter físico da luz: o primeiro ensaio explicou de uma forma original o chamado "movimento Browning" e o outro, a natureza material da luz. O terceiro estudo na série descreve a teoria restrita da relatividade, geralmente considerada o avanço mais importante na física desde os *Principia mathematica* de Isaac Newton (1687). Einstein mostrou que a velocidade da luz é constante em todo e qualquer campo de referência: portanto, se se admite que as leis naturais também se mantêm constantes dentro de um campo em movimento, o tempo e o movimento serão forçosamente relativos com respeito a uma pessoa que os observa de outro campo. Como consequência dessa teoria, Einstein descobriu a fórmula que expressa a equivalência da matéria e da energia, a conhecidíssima E = mc^2, que apareceu num quarto estudo do mesmo ano. Em 1916, uma década mais tarde, Einstein deu ao público a sua segunda teoria relativista, a teoria generalizada da relatividade, que define a gravidade não como uma força inalterável mas como uma distorção do *continuum* do espaço e do tempo criada pela presença da massa de corpos físicos dentro do *continuum*.[2]

A primeira das duas teorias relativistas é a que mais relevância tem para o estudo da heteronímia, por ser aquela que mais facilmente se aplica à problemática do perspectivismo literário e da voz poética. Para melhor explicá-la, cita-se a a obra *Space and Time in Contemporary Physics* do professor vienense Moritz Schlick, publicada em tradução inglesa em 1920— a edição citada por Pessoa numa lista de leituras, embora não conste no inventário da sua biblioteca (Pina Coelho 155). Schlick concentra-se no problema que surge quando se nega a objectividade física *a priori* ao tempo e ao espaço: resolve-o propondo que a única maneira de compreender a realidade é tomar em conta a teoria da relatividade e como, de acordo com ela, os objectos, o espaço e o tempo juntos formam uma realidade física unificada (65-66).

Schlick afirma que é fácil aceitar as leis da mecânica clássica de Newton, porque concordam com a experiência quotidiana:

> It is a matter of everyday experience that all mechanical events take place in a system which is moving uniformly and rectilinearly (e.g. in a moving ship or train) exactly in the same way as in a system which is at rest relatively to the earth. But for the inevitable occurrence of jerks and rocking… an observer enclosed in a moving air-ship or train could in no wise establish that his vehicle was moving. (10)

A novidade da teoria restrita da relatividade é que nega um valor absoluto a esses mesmos "eventos mecânicos":

> The length of a rod, the duration of an event, are not absolute quantities, as was always assumed in physics before the advent of Einstein, but are dependent on the state of motion of the co-ordinate system in which they are measured. The methods which are at our disposal for measuring distances and times yield different values in systems which are in motion relatively to one another. (13)

Para ilustrar a teoria, Schlick oferece o famoso exemplo dos quatro relógios. Imaginemo-los instalados em comboios diferentes, digamos K¢ e K (o que segue é uma tradução mais ou menos literal; para os que não conhecem a prova, é útil deitar mão de lápis e papel). Em K¢ há dois relógios, A¢ e B¢; os relógios A e B no comboio K estão na mesma posição com respeito aos seus semelhantes no outro comboio. K¢ viaja a uma velocidade q em relação a K, em direcção A Æ B. Suponhamos que um observador em K olha pela janela no momento exacto em que K¢, ao ultrapassar K, alcança exactamente a mesma velocidade. Nesse instante, o observador no comboio K vê que o relógio A, montado na parede ao seu lado, dá as 12:00 horas, e que o relógio A¢ que enxerga através da janela do comboio K¢ também dá as 12:00 (o mesmo para B¢ e B). Às 12:00 em ponto A¢ e A emitem raios de luz. A luz de A¢ alcança o relógio B, reflectida do relógio A, quando ele marca as 12:00 e um segundo. Mas o relógio B¢, porque está no comboio K¢, neste momento já viajou uma distância q e haverá viajado um pouco mais antes de receber a luz de A, reflectida de A¢. Para o observador no combio K, portanto, a luz precisa de mais do que um segundo para ir de A¢ a B¢. O mesmo observador verá que a luz, reflectida de B¢ a A¢, tomará *menos* de um segundo para alcançar A¢, porque em relação a ele, A¢ viaja em direcção *à luz* (15). O observador no comboio K concluirá que a luz toma mais tempo em ir de A¢ a B¢ do que de B¢ a A¢, mas o seu parceiro no K¢, imóvel com respeito a A¢ e B¢, não verá nenhuma diferença porque *dentro do sistema K¢* a luz vai à mesma velocidade nas duas direcções. Portanto dois eventos da mesma duração no sistema K¢ são de duas durações diferentes quando medidos no sistema K. O tempo é relativo ao sistema em que é medido, e não só o tempo: também a largura dos corpos materiais varia, recolhendo-se na direção do movimento relativa ao observador imóvel a um valor determinado pela fórmula do físico holandês Hendrik Lorenz: $a = \div 1 - q^2/c^2$ em que a = a largura do objecto medida desde um sistema imóvel com referência a ele, q = a velocidade do sistema com relação ao sistema imóvel e c = a velocidade da luz. (16-17) Os que utilizaram a fórmula de Lorentz para matar o tédio das aulas de colégio a calcular a contracção de um lápis em movimento sabem que o efeito é quase nulo a qualquer velocidade que não se aproxime da da luz.

A conclusão de Schlick pode fazer as vezes de uma justificação físico-epistemológica (no sentido metafórico, claro) da poética heteronímica: a fim de contas, se se toma em conta a relatividade é ainda possível to indicate identically the *same* set of facts by means of *various* systems of judgments; and consequently there can be various theories in which the criterion of truth is equally well satisfied, and which then do equal justice to the observed facts, and lead to the same predictions. *They are merely different systems of symbols, which are allocated to the same objective reality.* (86, sublinhado do autor)

O aspecto material, as consequências físicas da teoria restrita da relatividade não interessavam a Pessoa: para ele, o importante eram sempre as implicações epistemológicas e ontológicas. Na sua projecção literária, o "critério da verdade" para Pessoa é a poesia pura, e o seu contexto é a civilização decadente da Europa actual. A verdade consta de um conjunto de factos determinado: é uma realidade que não pode revelar-se (por assim dizer) a um observador único, nem mesmo àquela perspectiva que se pode designar como "privilegiada." Se o critério da verdade se revelasse completo, unívoco, e unidirecional no passado, era porque a mecânica newtoniana e a filosofia da Ilustração permitiram-no. No início do século XX, no entanto, sabe-se que não há nenhuma realidade cuja descrição ou definição não dependa da posição do observador relativa àquilo que ele observa, e que todos os observadores têm o mesmo valor, *qua* observadores.[3] A ideia mais "completa" de um fenómeno é portanto aquela que reune o maior número de observações pelo maior número possível de observadores numa aproximação plausível a um objectivismo idealmente inalcançável.

A Relatividade e o Relativismo no Pensamento de Pessoa

o conhecimento scientifico é puramente relativo (*Pessoa inédito* 409)

A evidência textual sugere que era lento o processo pelo qual Pessoa converteu a relatividade estrita de Einstein em uma justificação pseudo-científica do perspectivismo poético representado pelos heterónimos. Há de facto uma coincidência inegável e significativa entre o período que vai de 1905, o *annus mirabilis* Einstein, até ao *annus mirabilis* de Pessoa: eram os anos em que Pessoa aprofundava os seus conhecimentos científicos ao mesmo tempo que os heterónimos gestavam na sua imaginação, para saírem ao mundo em 1914.

Diferente do físico alemão-suiço-americano e do seu pensamento já maduro, Pessoa em 1905 tinha apenas 16 anos embora pressentisse que o seu génio exigir-lhe-ia sacrifícios especiais, não sabia muito bem que forma esses sacrifícios tomariam. Neste ano, o poeta dedica-se a elaborar os inquéritos poéticos e filosóficos do primeiro heterónimo que a crítica considera importante, Alexander Search, um Alexandre britânico-africano que, como o seu homónimo grego, busca a fortuna. De 1905 conservam-se poemas de Search como "Beginning," que termina:

> Blow hard, thou wind: look pale, thou awful day!
> Ye cannot in your dread and horror match
> The thing that I bear in me and is me,
> These idle thoughts that stray
> Subordinate to the deep agony
> Of him who hears the gates of reason's latch
> Fall with a sound of termination,
> As of a thing locked past and for e'er done.

Outro da mesma época é "Resolution." As linhas finais são:

> ... I'll to my work then, so God make me strong
> To bring the Demons of mine own self to
> Their knees, and take the Devil by the throat. (*Poesia* 44, 50)

Não é este o lugar para indagar sobre esses Demónios e o Diabo que os rege: basta dizer que dão uma ideia do estado psíquico do jovem Pessoa.

1905 é também o ano do primeiro texto conservado da correspondência de Fernando Pessoa, uma carta de protesto à "ignomínia e insensibilidade humanas" (human ignobleness and unfeeling) do jornal *The Natal Mercury* ao ridicularizar os russos (Bréchon 63). O autor da carta é o segundo heterónimo importante, Charles Robert Anon (nascido por volta de 1905 em Durban, África do Sul). Escreve: "To us, Englishmen, of all men the most egotistic, the thought has never occurred [sic] that misery and grief ennoble, despicable and self-caused though they may be" (Pessoa, *Correspondência* 14). É a voz do idealismo juvenil, em boca de um heterónimo que se transforma mais tarde em céptico de ofício. Essa mostra da pluralidade de perspectivas é um primeiro indício do percurso poético de Pessoa durante a década de 10 e 20, que coincide com o seu interesse crescente nas ciências, entre elas a física einsteiniana.

Os estudos da teoria da relatividade que figuram no inventário da biblioteca Fernando Pessoa—de uma leitura muito mais acessível—são:

1. Anónimo, *Einstein: ABC das suas teorias, explicadas por 26 gravuras e fácil texto* (Lisboa: Sá da Costa, s.d.). 39 páginas em francês, inglês, português e espanhol.
2. Henry L. Brose, *The Theory of Relativity* (Oxford:B.H. Blackwell, 1920 [1919]). 32 páginas.
3. Gaston Moch, *Initiation aux Théories d'Einstein* (Paris: Bibliothèque Larousse, s.d. [1922]. 160 páginas.
4. James Rice, *Relativity: An Exposition without Mathematics* (Londres: Ernest Benn Ltd., 1928 [1927]). 79 páginas.

O folheto *Einstein: ABC das suas teorias* fica fora da conta, também o livro ainda mais breve do Professor Rice, da Universidade de Liverpool: nos dois casos a apresentação é pouco substancial. Pessoa marcou somente quatro passagens do livro de Brose, uma das quais se cita a continuação. O trabalho de Gaston Moch, por outra parte, além do seu interesse intrínseco está amplamente anotado pelo poeta.[4]

Initiation aux Théories d'Einstein

Pessoa destaca o parágrafo em que Moch identifica três ideias que na física clássica têm um valor absoluto: o espaço, o tempo e a massa. O físico lembra ao leitor que, segundo a teoria da relatividade, nenhuma dessas três tem um valor absoluto, muito pelo contrário: o seu valor depende sempre e exclusivamente "de l'etat de mouvement de l'opérateur par rapport à l'objet de la mesure" (13), como no "thought experiment" dos quatro relógios.

No entanto as consequências da teoria vão muito além das medidas de longura, largura e altura, pondo em questão a natureza da própria causalidade. Em outra passagem marcada por Pessoa, Moch explica que todos os fenómenos naturais estão sujeitos à "correição" relativista:

Théoriquement, une loi physique rattache un phénomène à une cause. Mais comme il n'existe pas de phénomène qui ne soit influencé par une multitude de causes, il se trouve qu'à l'application, chaque loi est contrariée par d'autres, suivant une proportion qui peut être insensible ou considérable. (20)

Sem dúvida foi o matiz epistemológico desta formulação o que lhe chamou a atenção ao Pessoa que para 1922 (o ano da publicação de *Initiation...*) explorara a projecção literária do relativismo einsteiniano através da criação dos heterónimos, realizando um trabalho de síntese intelectual-poética parecido àquele realizado por outros escritores "experimentais" da época como Unamuno em *Niebla* (1914, escrita em 1907), Pirandello em *Sei personaggi in cerca d'autore* (1921) e James Joyce em *Ulysses* (1922), cujo *stream of consciousness* e pluralismo estilístico parecem-se com a multiplicidade expressiva dos heterónimos.[5] Moch afirma, em palavras assinaladas por Pessoa, que, graças aos achados de Einstein, o indivíduo nunca mais poderá pressupor que a sua visão do mundo tenha qualquer coisa que ver com a maneira em que os outros percebem o mundo, a não ser que se comuniquem na linguagem impessoal da matemática:

> ... la configuration des étoiles, telle que nous la voyons, n'est qu'une apparence fallacieuse, provenant de la rencontre, sur notre rétine, d'impressions impossibles à classer dans le temps et dans l'espace. Le spectable du ciel étoilé, que poètes et théologiens vantent comme l'exemple de l'harmonie parfaite, est celui de l'incohérence la plus désordinnée. (53)

Na mesma maneira em que o relativismo condena o homem a não poder resolver os grandes enigmas cosmológicos, o perspectivismo epistemológico análogo condena o indivíduo a nunca perceber o significado dos fenómenos, nem sequer ao nível particular.

Não se deve desdenhar o impacto que palavras semelhantes tiveram em Pessoa, mesmo oito anos depois do nascimento de Alberto Caeiro. Sempre absolutista no seu afã de alcançar os primeiros princípios e as últimas verdades, Pessoa teria percebido a conclusão de Moch como uma prova da impossibilidade de abranger qualquer verdade absoluta, de realizar uma obra de arte perfeita ou completa. Pior: embora o poeta conseguisse milagrosamente escrever um poema perfeito, este seria recebido e percebido de acordo com a perspectiva limitada do leitor individual, possivelmente de uma maneira que sem dúvida evade a intenção do autor. Que fazer? Cortado o caminho da perfeição à voz única do poeta solitário, resta o caminho da multiplicação de vozes. A declaração de Moch: "la question de savoir de l'Univers est infini ou sphérique est à jamais invérifiable" (138-139), traduz-se na vivência particular de Pessoa em um processo de interiorização que desemboca na "externalização" psicológica e poética da pluralidade mais variada de perspectivas sobre a realidade. Se nenhum ponto de vista pode ser compreensivo, então o maior número possível de perspectivas dará a visão mais completa do fenómeno observado.

É neste ponto que a física einsteiniana coincide com a teoria da evolução, *sensu lato*. Pessoa aceita uma das teses evolucionistas menos controvertidas, isto é, que a vida orgânica adapta-se às mudanças do ambiente através do desenvolvimento de órgãos especializados. Partindo de uma forma relativamente menos complexa, os organismos desenvolvem-se no sentido de maior complexidade para melhor garantir o domínio sobre o ambiente e portanto a sobrevivência da espécie. Como escreveu Herbert Spencer, autor lido e comentado por Pessoa: "[Matter] passes from an indefinite incoherent homogeneity to a definite coherent heterogeneity" (73).[6] Pessoa descreve o processo no artigo "Organizar," publicado n' *A Revista de Comércio e Contabilidade* a 25 de abril de 1926: "Um organismo complexo formou-se, no decurso do que se chama 'evolução,' por o que os biologistas denominam 'diferenciação,' isto é, a formação—lenta e confusa no tempo, definida nos seus resultados últimos—de órgãos especiais, cada um para uma função especial, e concorrendo todos, cada um adentro da sua função, para a mutenção da vida do organismo em seu conjunto" (*Crítica* 306-307). Os três princípios fundamentais dessa organização são:

> (1) o conjunto deve ser dividido no número de elementos, ou órgãos, que é preciso, e nem em mais, nem em menos, que esses; (2) cada elemento, ou órgão, do conjunto tem que ter uma função absolutamente distinta da de qualquer outro elemento, e relacionada com a função desse outro apenas pela circunstância do comum concurso para o funcionamento do conjunto; (3) adentro de cada elemento ou órgão do conjunto se observará a mesma distinção de funções que se estabeleceu para o próprio conjunto, visto que cada elemento ou órgão, por distinto e diferenciado, é um conjunto em si mesmo. (307-308)

Para o pensamento evolucionista, é um processo análogo que cria a complexidade das civilizações avançadas, em que o funcionamento de cada indivíduo atinge o máximo grau de perfeição, definida como a realização do seu papel para dentro da comunidade, e para o máximo bem dela. É por isso que Spencer diz que o homem difere dos outros animais porque só ele desenvolve "a formula for complete life which specially recognizes the relations of each individual to others, in presence to whom, and in co-operation with whom, he has to live" (153). A consequência deste utilitarismo evolucionário para a ética é evidente: "Ethics becomes nothing else than a definite account of the forms of conduct that are fitted to the associated state, in such wise that the lives of each and all may be the greatest possible, alike in length and in depth" (153). A nível artístico, os órgãos especializados são os heterónimos, que em tudo parecem-se aos órgãos do corpo, pois "quanto mais diferenciados esses orgãos, menos capaz é cada um deles de exercer a função que compete ao outro" (*Crítica* 307), o que Luís de Oliveira e Silva caracterizou como a "experiência paradigmática" de cada um dos heterónimos (224). Alberto Caiero não pode ser Ricardo Reis que também não pode ser Álvaro de Campos, e este não pode ser Pessoa, embora houvesse certa confusão na mente (e no comportamento) do seu criador a respeito dessa identificação. Pode-se perceber os heterónimos anteriores, desde le Chevalier de Pas até a Raphael Baldaia, como vestígios de etapas anteriores na evolução do organismo "total" que é a constelação dos quatro grandes poetas que, segundo o próprio Pessoa, existe principalmente para fomentar a actividade de Alberto Caeiro como o Super-Camões e salvador do espírito europeu. Também se poderia identificar o organismo total com a civilização europeia do início do século XX, aquele organismo que Pessoa encontrou em vias da auto-extinção por não saber adaptar-se ao novo ambiente racionalista e científico.

Finalmente, repare-se que dentro do esquema organizacional esboçado por Pessoa, há sempre um chefe de organização que dirige as actividades dos chefes de elemento. O chefe de organização "estabelece um plano geral, em linhas gerais," logo reparte "a cada chefe de elemento a divisão dos serviços adentro do elemento que lhe compete." Para garantir a unidade ou uniformidade da organização, Pessoa especifica que "cada chefe de elemento tem de ser, adentro do elemento de que é chefe, uma reprodução ou imagem do chefe de organização"—razão pela qual os "sobreviventes" da evolução poética pessoana são todos poetas (lembre-se que segundo o próprio Pessoa, Bernardo Soares não é um heterónimo mas um alter-ego). O chefe de organização, portanto, ao delegar determinada função ao chefe de elemento, torna-se, "por assim dizer, voluntariamente, incompetente para o seu exercício." Pessoa conclui: "E é este o segredo de toda a organização eficaz: *há hierarquia de cargos, não há hierarquia de funções.*" Substituir Fernando Pessoa como chefe de organização e os heterónimos como chefes de elemento, e a descrição evolucionista vale tanto para a poética dos heterónimos—dir-se-ia, para toda a poética modernista europeia—como para o comércio.

A Aplicação Epistemológica

> A luta pela compreensão, que é o *esfôrço para a consciência*, é, no homem, a forma essencial e profunda do seu ser psíquico (Coimbra 237).
> Frase sublinhada por Pessoa no seu exemplar do livro (1923).
> As "dimensões" dos objectos não estão nelles, mas sim em nós. (*Pessoa inédito* 269)

O Pessoa de 1912, ano da fundação do movimento da Renascença Portuguesa no Porto, é bem diferente do jovem do ano da divulgação da teoria restrita da relatividade. É neste ano que Teixeira de Pascoes e Leonardo Coimbra (que estudara com Sampaio Bruno, o outro filósofo "profissional" do movimento) lançam o seu projecto de renovação cultural com o programa filosófico duplo do Saudosismo e do Criacionismo, "sistemas ou ideações aliás convergentes" (escreve António Quadros) "que se irmanam na crítica tanto ao velho regime, ao absolutismo e à ideologista positivista triunfante, como às formas de socialismo e de materialismo, que despontam e crescem" (29). Para essas datas Pessoa já tinha experimentado com a poesia e a prosa, até 1909 principalmente em inglês, depois em português. Através de sua revista, *A Águia*, a Renascença Portuguesa deu-lhe um fórum e uma entrada no "grande" mundo das idéias. Os três ensaios que Pessoa forneceu à revista no seu primeiro ano—"A nova poesia portuguesa sociologicamente considerada," "Reincidindo," e "A nova poesia portuguesa no seu aspecto psicológico"—representam, segundo Quadros, "o primeiro acto de presença de Fernando Pessoa na vida cultural" do seu país e portanto da Europa (30). Embora a temática dos artigos pouco tenha a ver com o tema deste estudo, são uma amostra retrospectiva da atividade intelectual que o poeta desenvolvera desde o seu regresso definitivo a Portugal.

Outro indício da maturidade filosófica de Pessoa, por assim dizer, encontra-se na carta que escreveu a Leonardo Coimbra para agradecer-lhe o envio do seu livro *A morte*, publicado em 1913. Em plena época de seu compromisso com a Renascença Portuguesa. Pessoa reconhece o valor da obra do seu "querido camarada," título que o poeta reservava para os amigos mais íntimos. Escreve:

> Eu conhecia já, da sua obra-base [i.e. *O criacionismo*], as grandes qualidades e os (a meu ver) alguns defeitos do seu espírito, alto porventura, porque plenamente

> lúcido e intelectual, que a nossa Raça hoje reveladamente possui... Logo do princípio notei, através da aparente e ilusória analogia com os de alguns filósofos recentes, a sua íntima e real originalidade. E nunca haverá em mim entusiasmo que eu sinta que me basta perante o panorama de alma que é a sua obra [etc.]. (*Correspondência* 101)

A crítica pessoana aos "defeitos do seu espírito" de Leonardo Coimbra é tópico para outro estudo; é mais fácil afirmar que a referência aos "filósofos" recentes e à "ilusória analogia" com o pensamento do Coimbra provavelmente oculta uma alusão ao neo-kantiano francês Charles Renouvier e, mais importante, a Henri Bergson, um dos filósofos de mais prestígio na Europa a começos do s. XX. O pensamento de Bergson, que sentiu a influência de Herbert Spenceriano na sua juventude, abraçava a ideia da evolução mas rejeitava os mecanismos materialistas propostos por Darwin, Huxley, Haeckel, e outros. Em vez da selecção natural, Bergson mantém no seu livro mais importante, *L'Évolution Créatrice* (1907), que há um *élan vital* (impulso ou força vital), inacessível aos sentidos humanos, que anima e rege a evolução da vida. A sua filosofia é a primeira que explora substancialmente o papel do tempo na epistemologia, portanto assemelha-se em certos aspectos à relatividade einsteiniana. O seu estudo *Durée et simultanéité de la théorie de Einstein* (1922) testemunha a sua vontade de reconciliar a filosofia e a física (embora o próprio Einstein achou o livro deficiente).

Em Portugal, a análise mais importante desse projecto é *A filosofia de Henri Bergson* de Leonardo Coimbra, publicado em 1934, um ano antes da morte de Fernando Pessoa. Nela o filósofo português comenta o que ele chama "a questão Bergson-Einstein," nomeadamente a interpretação que Bergson faz à epistemologia implícita à teoria restrita da relatividade. Coimbra vê uma contradição na posição de Bergson, para que a teoria da relatividade restrita "marca... uma maior exigência de um universal do que a própria mecânica clássica [q.d. de Newton], visto que para esta ainda existiam observadores privilegiados, que desaparecem inteiramente naquela" (Coimbra, *A Filosofia* 200).[7] Para provar o seu ponto de vista, escreve Coimbra,

> Bergson supõe os dois sistemas S e S¢ em movimento de translação uniforme um em relação ao outro—num mora um físico Paulo e no outro um físico Pedro. Cada um destes faz as suas medidas e encontra os comprimentos e os tempos da

mecânica clássica. A física efectiva de cada um deles é, pois, fundamentalmente clássica. Só cada um deles para imaginar a física do outro é que tem de supor as contracções e dilatações correlativas do espaço e do tempo.

— mais uma lembrança dos quatro relógios de Schlick.

Mas esta física é uma simples explicação que cada um dá a si mesmo do facto da identidade das suas visões científicas: qualquer coisa como a necessária explicação de perspectivas diferentes darem o mesmo aspecto de um objecto. Se o objecto é suposto irregular, o fato de perspectivas de pontos de vista diferentes poderia explicar-se por uma deformação de uma imagem por convenientes e apropriadas refracções, por exemplo.

Se, no entanto, nada na natureza, seja, na experiência, me revela a existência desses meios refringentes, não deverei antes concluir que a identidade resulta de secções feitas num objecto regular e que de facto são idênticas?

Bergson argumenta com a *reciprocidade*, isto é, com o facto de Paulo dizer de Pedro o que Pedro tem de dizer de Paulo; mas é isso mesmo que está inscrito no grupo de Lorenz e que só pode dar-se porque o tempo e o espaço são relativos. (Coimbra, *A Filosofia* 201).

É de presumir que o universal torna-se mais necessário no mundo einsteiniano porque sem ele seria impossível afirmar qualquer verdade sobre o mundo: haveria só um caos de percepções sem conexão uns com os outros, e a comunicação humana—a própria linguagem e todas as disciplinas e artes que dela dependem—não seria mais que a ilusão absurda de solipsistas desesperados e auto-enganados. Não foi Bertrand Russell que comentou: "If everything is relative, nothing is relative"? Por outras palavras, a objecção de Bergson não é válida, segundo Coimbra, porque não nega o essencial da teoria de Einstein, disfarça-o em termos diferentes que no fundo dizem a mesma coisa.

Pessoa, por outro lado, prefere o perspectivismo radical que a teoria da relatividade, na sua interpretação, lhe oferece. Ele tira da análise de Coimbra o que lhe convém e deixa o resto: neste caso, reconhece a validez do exemplo atribuído a Bergson sem aceitar a interpretação do seu amigo português. Por outras palavras, acercando-se à mesma problemática a partir do mesmo contexto cultural e intelectual, os dois amigos chegam a conclusões mutuamente contraditórias. Para Coimbra, embora Bergson tivesse razão em rejeitar o relativismo de perspectiva epistemológica, erra, como a imensa maioria dos cientistas e dos pensadores não-teológicos da sua época, em reduzir o conhecimento da realidade à reciprocidade de percepções que só tem em comum o facto de procederem de sujeitos biologicamente parecidos. O seu ponto de vista é essencialmente tomista. Como escreve, no seu estilo altamente metafórico:

> Sim, a intuição directa, o contacto, a experiência osculadora é um ideal de presença e conhecimento; mas nem só o intuído existe, também existe para nós o representado que a realidade exige como real, quando fazemos não a intuição directa desse real, no caso impossível, mas a intuição das operações efectivas do pensamento que o concluiu.
> E é este o caso. O que pretende o físico é achar as *leis*, seja a estrutura da realidade e tais são esses leis, ele exigirá que sejam elas o absoluto (no seu planto ontológico) e não os elementos que elas envolvem na sua expressão. (Coimbra 202)

Ou como escreve no seu *A razão experimental* (1923), num esforço por admitir a relatividade divorciada do relativismo (são palavras destacadas por Pessoa no seu exemplar do livro): "a cada Universo einsteiniano ou super-einsteiniano corresponderá sempre um Universo galíleo-newtoniano tangente, como a cada espaço *não-euclidiano* há sempre um espaço euclidiano tangente ou limite" (Coimbra, *Razão* 258). É possível que Pessoa pensasse no conflito entre o Coimbra-progressista e o Coimbra-tomista quando escreveu, num fragmento inédito, que o seu amigo era "um archanjo cahido com pesadellos do Céo" (*Espólio*15-76): "arcanjo" porque aferrava-se a crenças que o Pessoa achava inteiramente anacrónicas, sobretudo a partir da sua conversão ao Catolicismo; "com pesadelos" porque desejava realizar a conciliação entre o seu idealismo cristão e a filosofia evolucionista, o que para Pessoa era o equivalente a ver-se perseguido por demónios de duas raças.

Conclusão

Fernando Pessoa viveu a luta entre a ambição impossível de realizar a unidade absoluta na forma de uma poética perfeitamente reconciliada com a sua personalidade básica ou nuclear, e a necessidade de aproximar-se àquela expressão ideal (e idealizada) através da multiplicação de vozes e de vivências. Como Luís de Oliveira e Silva comenta: "Através da obra de Fernando Pessoa corre um motivo que ele repete *ad nauseam*: a incapacidade para captar o seu eu interior unitário" (169). A melhor solução, o ponto intermédio entre os extremos do fim desejado mais inalcançável, por um lado, e a necessidade de salvar-se da sua própria estagnação "ortonímica," por outro é a evolução da pluralidade de vozes. Pessoa opta pela auto-libertação: "Em vez de se fechar num auto-escrutínio solitário, resolve livrar-se através da acção imaginativa" (Oliveira e Silva 187), acção que implica a divisão paradoxal entre o sujeito pensante e observante que é o Pessoa-pessoa, e aqueles outros sujeitos denominados heterónimos. José Gil escreve: "Agora, no plano de consistência da heteronímia, é possível ser-se ao mesmo tempo dois universos e dois espaços diferentes; é-se mesmo obrigado a sê-lo, já que a heteronímia permite obter a expressão mais variada, mais intensa e mais inesgotável" (226). Acrescenta-se que para Fernando Pessoa a obrigação deriva em parte do perspectivismo relativista inelutável do século XX, e em parte das exigências da civilização ocidental no seu passo evolutivo para uma cultura—e uma verdade—nova. Como George Rudolf Lind observou no seu estudo pioneiro: "Escrever poesia não tem modernamente a ver com inspiração; põe-se aos artistas como um processo de trabalho" (312).

O dilema moderno da subjectividade desterrada cientificamente e filosoficamente do objecto da sua percepção, dilema fomentado indirectamente pela teoria da relatividade, encontra na heteronímia a sua expressão poética mais original e mais completa. A génese dessa poesia é tão inseparável da génese intelectual de Fernando Pessoa quanto a sua sensibilidade filosófica é inseparável da sua sensibilidade literária. Ao considerarmos ambas como faces da mesma moeda, apreciamos mais intensamente—mais perfeitamente—o génio de um grande homem atormentado.

Notas

[1] Trata-se de "Zur Elektrodynamik bewegte Körper" (Sobre a electrodinâmica dos corpos em movimento). *Annalen der Physik* (1905).

[2] Paráfrase do artigo sobre Einstein na *Encyclopedia Britannica,* 15ª edição (1980), vol. 6.

[3] Entenda-se a observação no sentido einsteiniano, embora também lembra a famoso príncipio da indeterminabilidade, que faz parte da física quántica de Heisenberg.

[4] É curioso que o livro do próprio Einstein sobre o assunto, que Pessoa poderia ter lido em tradução inglesa, não figura no inventário da sua biblioteca: *Relativity* (Londres, 1920; traduzido da terceira edição alemã por Robert Lawson). É possível que Pessoa o vendera, o que era um destino bastante normal para os seus livros; é também possível que a prosa do grande físico, melhor matemático do que escritor, o desencorajasse.

[5] Há um exemplar do romance na biblioteca de Pessoa, na edição de The Odyssey Press (Hamburg, 1932). Pessoa não escreveu nada nas suas páginas.

6 Hoje em dia a biblioteca de Pessoa conta com só três obras de Spencer. O exemplar de *Spencer's Essays* (Londres: Watts & Co., 1907 [ensaios escritos entre 1850 e 1860]) dá pouca evidência de leitura de parte do poeta, que por outro achou várias passagens de interesse em *Social Statics* (Watts & Co., 1910 [1850]) e *The Man versus the State* (Watts & Co., 1914 [1884?]), passagens que versam maiormente sobre a relação entre o indivíduo e o estado. Que Pessoa tivera um conhecimento mais amplo das ideias do Spencer é evidente nos seus escritos geralmente.

7 Este livro de Coimbra não figura no inventário da biblioteca de Pessoa. Além da obra citada (*A razão experimental*), Pessoa possuía duas outras do seu amigo: *O criacionismo* (Porto: Renascença Portuguesa, 1912) e *A morte* (Porto: Renascença Portuguesa, 1913). Este foi-lhe dado de presente polo autor, que na dedicatória se afirma "o amigo e o admiradôr leal"; não aparenta nenhuma marca, mas o próprio Pessoa reconhece havê-lo lido na carta de agradecimento citada acima. O exemplar de *O criacionismo* sim está marcada, mas somente nas últimas 100 páginas. Pessoa anota quase exclusivamente passagens referentes à religião, o que não vem ao caso do estudo presente.

Obras Citadas

Anónimo. *Einstein: ABC das suas teorias, explicadas por 26 gravuras e fácil texto.* Lisboa: Sá da Costa, s.d..

Bergson, Henri. *A evolução criadora.* Trans. Pedro Elói Duarte. Lisboa: Edições 70, 2001.

Bréchon, Robert. *Estranho estrangeiro.* Trans. Maria Abreu e Pedro Tamen. Lisboa: Quetzal Editores, 1996.

Brose, Henry L. Brose. *The Theory of Relativity.* Oxford: B.H. Blackwell, 1920 [1919].

Coimbra, Leonardo Coimbra. *A filosofia de Henri Bergson.* Lisboa: Imprensa Nacional-Casa da Moeda, 1994 [1934].

———. *A razão experimental: lógica e metafísica.* Porto: Renascença Portuguesa, 1923.

Einstein, Albert. *Relativity.* Trans. da terceira edição alemã (1918) de Robert Lawson. Londres, 1920.

"Einstein." *Encyclopedia Britannica.* 15ª ed. 1980.

Gil, José. *Fernando Pessoa ou a metafísica das sensações.* Trans. Miguel Serras Pereira e Ana Luisa Faria. Lisboa: Relógio d'Àgua, s.d.

Lind, Georg Rudolf. *Teoria poética de Fernando Pessoa.* Trans. Margarida Losa. Porto: Editorial Nova, 1970.

Lopes, Teresa Rita. *Pessoa Inédito.* Lisboa: Livros Horizonte, 1993.

Moch, Gaston Moch. *Initiation aux Théories d'Einstein.* Paris: Bibliothèque Larousse, s.d. [1922].

Pessoa, Fernando. *Correspondência (1905-1912).* Edição de Manuela Parreira Silva. Lisboa: Assírio e Alvim, 1998.

———. *Crítica.* Edição de Fernando Cabral Martins. Lisboa: Assírio e Alvim, 1999.

———. *Espólio.* Lisboa: Bibiloteca Nacional.

Oliveira e Silva, Luís de. *O materialismo idealista de Fernando Pessoa.* Lisboa: Clássica Editora, 1985.

Pina Coelho, António de. *Os fundamentos filosóficos da obra de Fernando Pessoa.* Vol. 2. Lisboa: Editorial Verbo, 1971.

Quadros, António. *Fernando Pessoa: vida, personalidade e génio.* Lisboa: Publicações Dom Quixote, 1984.

Rice, James. *Relativity: An Exposition Without Mathematics.* Londres: Ernest Benn Ltd., 1928 [1927].

Schlick, Moritz. *Space and Time in Contemporary Physics.* Oxford: Clarendon, 1920.

Search, Alexander. *Poesia.* Ed. and Trans. de Luísa Freire. Lisboa: Assírio e Alvim, 1999.

Spencer, Herbert. *First Principles of Sociology.* 1862.

————. *Social Statics.* Londres: Watts & Co., 1910.

————. *Spencer's Essays.* Londres: Watts & Co., 1907.

————. *The Man Versus the State.* Londres: Watts & Co., 1914.

Kenneth Krabbenhoft is Professor of Spanish and Portuguese at New York University. He has written on Luso-Brazilian literature, early-modern Spanish literature, mysticism, and science-fiction. His translations include essays by Eduardo Lourenço and Sofia de Mello Breyner and books by Saint John of the Cross, Pablo Neruda, and Eugenio Trías. Some recent publications are *Abraham Cohen de Herrera: Gate of Heaven* (Leiden: Brill, 2002), *Neoestoicismo e género popular* (Salamanca: Universidad de Salamanca, 2001), and "José Saramago, Cognitive Estrangement, and Original Sin?" *Portuguese Literary & Cultural Studies* 6 (Spring 2001). He is currently working on *Darwin e Pessoa*, a study of evolutionary theory and its impact on Fernando Pessoa's poetics of heteronimity. E-mail: kk1@nyu.edu

Joyce and Pessoa: Authors of Polyphony

David Butler

Introduction

At first sight, William Butler Yeats (1865-1939) is the obvious candidate to place in fruitful comparison to his great Portuguese contemporary, Fernando Pessoa (1888-1935). This is not merely a question of the theatre of masks through which each voiced their intrinsically plural poetries. Both figures were deeply interested in their respective nation's historical identity and both inclined to a heroic view of myth, conceiving of history in terms of great, messianic cycles. Both authors were deeply immersed in the occult, and both inclined in later years towards an elitism that was tolerant of the rise of the far right. Or consider the following distinction, from Pessoa's *O livro de desassossego* (fragment 260):

A arte mente porque é social. E há só duas grandes formas de arte—uma que se dirige à nossa alma profunda, a outra que se dirige à nossa alma atenta. A primeira é a poesia, o romance a segunda. A primeira começa a mentir na própria estrutura; a segunda começa a mentir na própria intenção.

[Art lies because it is social. And there are only two great forms of art—one which is directed towards our profound soul, the other directed towards our attentive soul. The first is poetry, the novel is the second. The first begins to lie in its intrinsic structure; the second begins to lie in its intrinsic intention.]

Portuguese Literary & Cultural Studies 7 (2008): 283-95.
© University of Massachusetts Dartmouth.

At first sight, the understanding of the intensely personal poetic audience in such an observation suggests Yeats' much quoted assertion that "we make out of the quarrel with others, rhetoric, but of the quarrel with ourselves, poetry."

I have said at first sight, however, for once we begin to examine the men in more detail, and in particular the nature of the great theatre of the self that plays itself out in their respective poetries, we find that Pessoa has less in common with Yeats and much more with those expatriated precursors of post-modernism, James Joyce (1882-1941) and Samuel Beckett (1906-1989). When Beckett coins the term "vice-existers" in relation to his series of narrators, Molloy, Moran, Malone, Mahood etc., he comes far closer to Pessoa's conception of the "heteronym" than do any of Yeats' rhetorical masks. What is more, a comparable compulsion to write which is entirely vitiated by doubt is expressed by the two authors. Thus when Pessoa has the semi-heteronym Bernardo Soares declare: "Tenho de escrever como cumprindo um castigo. E o maior castigo é o de saber que o que escrevo resulta inteiramente fútil, falhado e incerto" ["I am compelled to write as though fulfilling a punishment. And the greatest punishment is the knowledge that what I write ends in futility, failure and incertitude" (fragment 231)], it takes no great leap of the imagination to hear Beckett's dry complaint concerning his aesthetic dilemma of having "nothing to express, nothing with which to express, nothing from which to express […] together with the obligation to express" (from *Three Dialogues with Georges Duthuit*). Pessoa also occasionally approaches Beckett in tone, as when he talks of the soul as "um poço sinistro cheio de ecos vagos, habitado por vidas ignóbeis, viscosidades sem vida, lesmas sem ser, ranho da subjectividade" ["a sinister well full of vague echoes, inhabited by ignoble lives, lifeless slime, slugs without being, the snot of subjectivity" (fragment 242)] Try to imagine Yeats saying that! However, it is with points of comparison between Fernando Pessoa and Beckett's first mentor, James Joyce, that the present paper is principally concerned.

Although Joyce and Pessoa were immensely eclectic authors who were widely read in everything from classical epic through Shakespeare, Whitman and Mallarmé to Italian Futurism, there can be little question of either author having a direct influence on his contemporary. There is no evidence that James Joyce was ever aware of the existence of Fernando Pessoa, an ignorance that has unfortunately tended to persist among Anglophone authors, and although Pessoa took an interest in the writing of Joyce, he tended to be somewhat dismissive of what he saw as its excessive formality. He wrote of *Ulysses* that "it is a hallucinatory delirium—the kind treated by psychiatrists—presented as an end in itself," and felt that Joyce's writing was "an art preoccupied with method, with how it's made," thereby placing the Irishman's aesthetic squarely in the tradition of the *fin de siècle* French Symbolists.

There are on the other hand a number of similarities and symmetries between the authors that are immediately apparent. The two bespectacled men, who bore an uncanny resemblance to one another, accumulated an inordinate number of addresses in the course of their lives, an uncertainty of abode that was established from early childhood and whose trauma informs much of their subsequent writing. Partly as a corollary of their migratory lifestyles, both felt at home in a number of European languages, and each took a keen interest in the problem of translation. If Joyce is the self-exiled writer whose art is eternally obsessed with the city from which he is absent, Pessoa is the internal exile who becomes an absence at the heart of the city to which he has returned. Curiously, the name of this city, Lisbon, is said to derive from the Latinized form of that archetypal wanderer, Ulysses.

The purpose of comparative literature must be to draw out such similarities and contrasts so as to throw new light on the concerns of authors rather than to dwell on coincidental trivia, no matter how Joycean they may appear. With a view to this, the remainder of the present paper will examine the art of Joyce and Pessoa under four categories, none of which can rightly be understood in isolation: (i) the Recourse to Myth; (ii) the City as a Labyrinth; (iii) Language as a Labyrinth and, to borrow from the Russian critic Mikhail Bakhtin, (iv) the Dialogic Imagination. The central contention to be tested is that Pessoa's extraordinary poetic project and Joyce's masterpiece, *Ulysses*, are informed by a comparable aesthetic of authorial absence. This is perhaps best summarized in the following position, advanced by Stephen Dedalus in *A Portrait of the Artist as a Young Man*:

> The personality of the artist, at first a cry or a cadence or a mood and then a fluid and lambent narrative, finally refines itself out of existence, impersonalises itself, so to speak. [...] The artist, like the God of the creation, remains within or beyond or above his handiwork, invisible, refined out of existence, indifferent, paring his fingernails.

The quote could almost be taken as a commentary on Fernando Pessoa, the salient features of whose life the Mexican Nobel Laureate Octavio Paz famously described as "the footprints of a shadow" ("*El desconocido de sí mismo*"). For a figure such as Pessoa, Paz suggests that "his history could be reduced to the passage between the unreality of his daily life and the reality of his fictions."

(i) The Recourse to Myth

"Ah, curse you! That's Saint Augustine."

In his well-known but somewhat misguided essay of 1923, "Ulysses, Order and Myth," T. S. Eliot accredits Joyce's reworking of Homer's *Odyssey* as having "the importance of a scientific discovery," and goes on to suggest that "in using the myth, in manipulating a continuous parallel between contemporaneity and antiquity, Mr. Joyce is pursuing a method which others must pursue after him." It has become something of a commonplace that Eliot's view was colored, to say the least, by the publication of "The Wasteland," which appeared in the same year as *Ulysses,* and which is perhaps the definitive exemplar of what Eliot terms the "mythic method." What is of interest to the present paper is not so much the extent to which Joyce manipulated the Homeric myth as the fact that he should have recourse to myth in the first place.

Although *Ulysses* is justifiably considered to be a flagship of modernism, revolutionary, irreverent and iconoclastic, there is a deep paradox running through the mind of its author. In his 1962 study entitled "The Aesthetics of Chaosmos," the Italian medievalist Umberto Eco has perceptively characterized Joyce as "the node where the Middle Ages and the avant-garde meet." I would argue that the same is essentially true of Pessoa, although the form of the encounter between the scholastic and the modernist in each author is distinct. Joyce's medievalism extends beyond the aesthetics of the scholastically minded Stephen Dedalus and rubs shoulders continually with a fragmented modernism. As Eco comments in regard to the deep structure of the 1922 text, "the characteristics of an organism arranged according to the most rigorous criteria of a traditional formalism are found in that reverse *Summa* which is *Ulysses.*" What Eco terms a "medieval *forma mentis*" orchestrates the continual clash of contemporary voices throughout Joyce. By contrast, the generation of a number of heteronyms allows Pessoa to distinguish between his variety of affective and seemingly incompatible sensibilities, and to give each a distinct voice. The explicit nominalism of Alberto Caeiro, the pagan classicism of Ricardo Reis, and the millennial "Sebastianismo" of the Fernando Pessoa who authored

Mensagem are all manifestations of a "medieval *forma mentis.*" Indeed, the cast of mind of the last mentioned bears certain formal similarities to the cyclical view of history, derived in part from Vico's *La Scienza Nuova,* that informs the later Joyce. It is also of interest, though beyond the scope of the present essay, that it should be precisely a maritime myth that shapes both *Ulysses* and *Mensagem.* But what of their authors' respective modernisms?

In 1912, precisely two years before Joyce began to commit to paper the evolving text that he was already calling *Ulysses* and Fernando Pessoa conceived of his project of the heteronyms, Guillaume Apollinaire published his extraordinary collection *Alcools,* in which the poem "Zone" makes the claim:

> Tu lis les prospectus les catalogues les affiches qui chantent tout haut
> Voilà la poésie ce matin et pour la prose il y a les journaux

It is a celebration of mass media and the transient, in which posters and catalogues are to be the new poetry, while for prose, there are newspapers. Within the decade, James Joyce's great flagship of modernism, *Ulysses,* would elevate an advertising canvasser to the role of latter-day Odysseus, condemned to wander the semantic urban labyrinth of newspaper headline, music-hall refrain, evangelical flier, nationalist catch-phrase and advertising jingle. But as much as a newspaper, *Ulysses* is a compendium of noises. There are trams, whistles, farts, gas-jets, hooves, printing-presses, squabbling gulls, marching boots, jingling harnesses, all the noise of the modern metropolis. Much the same can be said, and indeed has been said, of "Ode Triunfal" (1914), the text written "in one fell swoop, without hesitation or correction," with which Pessoa launched the career of Álvaro de Campos. It has been called the noisiest poem ever written, and ends in an onomatopoeic flourish not unlike that of the "Sirens" chapter of *Ulysses:*

> Eia! e os rails e as casas de máquinas e a Europa!
> Eia e hurrah por mim-tudo e tudo, máquinas a trabalhar, eia!
> Galgar com tudo por cima de tudo! Hup-lá!
> Hup-lá, hup-lá, hup-lá-hô, hup-lá!
> Hé-la! He-hô! H-o-o-o-o!
> Z-z-z-z-z-z-z-z-z-z-z-z!
> Ah não ser eu toda a gente e toda a parte!
> Prrprr.

Must be the bur.

Fff! Oo. Rrpr.

Nations of the earth. No-one behind. She's passed. *Then and not till then.* Tram kran kran kran. Good oppor. Coming. Krandlkrankran. I'm sure it's the burgund. Yes. One, two. *Let my epitaph be.* Kraaaaaa. *Written.*

I have.

Pprrpffrrppffff.

Done.

I will be arguing in Part IV below that the relentless collage of noises and voices is part of a dialogic impulse that takes the art of Joyce and Pessoa far beyond similar orchestrations of sound in Whitman, Mayakovsky or Marinetti. At one level, however, they are manifestations of the increasing mechanization of urban life, and the art of both Joyce and Pessoa is entirely inseparable from the cityscapes which they evoke.

(ii) The City as Labyrinth

> Cidade da minha infância pavorosamente perdida...
> Cidade triste e alegre, outra vez sonho aqui...

The wanderings of Odysseus are by no means the only, nor indeed the first classical myth to give shape to a Joycean text. As early as 1904, when the first three stories of *Dubliners* were published in the *Irish Homestead,* Joyce chose Stephen Dedalus as what one suspects was to have been a quite literal *nom de plume.* The flight of Daedalus and Icarus from Minoan Crete would later form a framing narrative for *A Portrait of the Artist as a Young Man,* the Icarus aspect of which is wryly alluded to by Stephen Dedalus in the later *Ulysses.* But the Daedalus aspect was equally important to Joyce, for Daedalus was the builder of the great labyrinth at Crete that was to house the Minotaur, and it is this oppressive labyrinth that he later flees. When, towards the end of the second chapter of *A Portrait of the Artist as a Young Man,* the young Dedalus has taken to playing truant from Belvedere College and wandering the tenements of the north inner city in search of sin, the bestial and labyrinthine are evoked in equal part:

His blood was in revolt. He wandered up and down the dark slimy streets peering into the gloom of lanes and doorways, listening eagerly for any sound. He moaned to himself like some baffled prowling beast. He wanted to sin with another of his kind, to force another being to sin with him and to exult with her in sin. […] He had wandered into a maze of narrow and dirty streets.

It will not be the mythical Daedalus, "old father, old artificer," who allows the young artist egress out of the notorious "Nighttown" area into which he has wandered. Rather, it will be the humanitarian impulse of Leopold Bloom, that latter-day Odysseus, in the climactic "Circe" episode of the novel to follow.

From the outset, Joyce's Dublin is very much the inner city of working-class tenements in which he had grown up, a landscape of crumbling Georgian façades still haunted by their ascendancy past:

A horde of grimy children populated the street. They stood or ran in the roadway or crawled up the steps before the gaping doors or squatted like mice upon the thresholds. Little Chandler gave them no thought. He picked his way deftly through all that minute vermin-like life and under the shadow of the gaunt spectral mansions in which the old nobility of Dublin had roistered. ("A Little Cloud")

Pessoa's engagement with Lisbon is by no means as meticulous as is Joyce's in his exposition of the human geography of Edwardian Dublin. If the Irishman could say of *Ulysses* to his friend Frank Budgen that he desired "to give a picture of Dublin so complete that if the city one day suddenly disappeared from the earth it could be reconstructed out of my book," Pessoa would never have inclined to such a boast. Indeed, his terrain is very much the generic city, and the garret overlooking the street with the tobacco-shop in "Tabacaria" could be in almost any Mediterranean town.

When history does impinge on the present, it is as often as not the history of the imagined past: "O Tejo tem grandes navios / E navega nele ainda, / Para aqueles que vêem em tudo o que lá não está, / A memória das naus." ["The Tagus has large ships, / And still navigating on it, / For those who see in everything that which isn't there, / The memory of caravels."] It is no coincidence that, as with Joyce, the river should be a central axis of the imagined city. Lisbon becomes a far more tangible presence, not unlike the Paris of Rilke's *Notebooks of Malte Laurids Brigge* (1906), in the prose fragments penned under the name Bernardo Soares, which have been assembled to form *O livro do desassossego.* Soares, the petty clerk who dreams of escape from the drudgery of his office, is in some ways the counterpart of such trapped figures as Little Chandler and Farrington of *Dubliners*, although, unlike these two, he has decidedly no familial commitments:

> Hoje, em um dos devaneios sem propósito nem dignidade que constitutem grande parte da substância espiritual da minha vida, imaginei-me liberto para sempre da Rua dos Douradores, do patrão Vasques, do guardo-livros Moreira, dos empregados todos, do moço, do garoto e do gato. (fragment 7)

> [Today, in one of those reveries with neither purpose nor dignity which constitute a large part of my spiritual life, I imagined myself free forever from the Rua dos Douradores, from my boss Vasques, from Moreira the bookkeeper, from all the employees, from the porter, the office boy, the cat.]

But of course the city is as much a part of Soares as he is a figure in the cityscape: "Não há diferença entre mim e as ruas para o lado da Alfândega, salvo elas serem ruas e eu ser alma" ["there is no difference between myself and the streets by the side of the Custom House, except that they'd be streets and I a soul"] (fragment 3). In this he is not unlike Bloom, who might idly dream of escape to the "orangegroves and immense melonfields north of Jaffa" or the country mansion idyll he names "Flowerville," but who remains ineluctably wedded to the city of his birth and berth.

(iii) Language as Labyrinth

> "A minha pátria é a lingua portuguesa"

The Dublin that Joyce resurrects for us is very much a city of jostling argots, a forum in which slang and swear-word rub shoulder with flier, advertisement, headline and official proclamation. Words are not merely sounds. They are inscribed on the city as text. No sooner does Bloom appear in *Ulysses* than this tangibility is suggested by the detail of the partly erased label "*Plasto's high grade ha.*" Pessoa's Soares writes that "as palavras são para mim corpos tocáveis, sereias visíveis, sensualidades incorporadas" ["Words for me are touchable bodies, visible sirens, embodied sensualities"] (*O livro do desassossego*, fragment 260). Words are touchable, visible, embodied. This is precisely the experience of the young Stephen Dedalus at Clongowes Wood College: "Suck was a queer word […] the sound was ugly. Once he had washed his hands in the lavatory of the Wicklow Hotel and his father pulled the stopper up by the chain after and the dirty water went down through the hole in the basin. And when it had all gone down slowly the hole in the basin had made a sound like that: suck. Only louder" (*Portrait* 8-9).

Words are also slippery affairs, and both authors make much of the homophone, the neologism and the pun. One thinks of coinages such as "infinitupla" [*O livro do desassossego*, fragment 269, dated Dec. 1931] which seems to combine "infinita" and "dupla" in much the way César Vallejo's "Trilce" of 1922 conflates "triste and "dulce." Pessoa's most translated poem is the brief "Autopsicografia" ["Autopsychography"], the title of which nods to the term autobiography. It begins:

> O poeta é um fingidor.
> Finge tão completamente
> Que chega a fingir que é dor
> A dor que deveras sente.
>
> The poet's a man who feigns.
> He feigns so completely
> That he comes to pretend pain
> For pain that he actually feels.

The point of the poem is contained in the epigrammatic first line, and centers on the word "fingidor," the final syllable of which is itself the term "dor," or "pain." As the third line seems to suggest, the pun could be written "O poeta é um '*finge-dor*'"; perhaps a Joycean translation might read "the poet is a man who *f-aches*."

The facility with which Joyce and Pessoa move between not only language-registers—what post-structuralists like to term discourses—but equally between a number of European languages is, perhaps, the most obvious point of comparison. Indeed it was a source of immediate income, Joyce as a teacher of English and Pessoa as a translator of business correspondence. Pessoa, who was adept in French and English in addition to Portuguese, produced bodies of poetry in both these languages, but his fascination with languages pales a little in comparison to that of Joyce.

That Joyce wrote letters in Italian, French and German is well known. While still a teenager, he privately studied German and Dano-Norwegian specifically with a view to translating the plays of Gerhard Hauptmann and Henrik Ibsen into English. During his sojourn in Trieste, he chose the opposite course, and in 1909 translated J. M. Synge's play *Riders to the Sea* into Italian. Then, in 1921 Paris, he actively collaborated with Jacques Benoîst-Méchin in the task of translating the "Penelope" episode of *Ulysses* into French. Indeed, a true Europhile *avant la lettre*, Joyce was also active in helping Georg Goyert revise an unsatisfactory 1927 translation of *Ulysses* into German, and in 1936 he traveled to Copenhagen to aid Tom Kristensen with a Danish version. This openness to linguistic pluralism would culminate in the colossally difficult Babel of his final work, *Finnegans Wake*.

It can hardly be doubted that this intense exposure to a plurality of tongues led directly to an interest not only in the possibilities and restraints within a single language but also in the problems of voicing within that language. No monolithic discourse can possibly be adequate to the multiplicity of experience within the modern metropolis. Bernardo Soares puts this difficulty very succinctly when he asks: "mas que linguagem estilhaçada e babélica falaria eu quando descrevesse o Elevador de Santa Justa, a Catedral de Reims, os calções dos zuavos, a maneira como o português se pronuncia em Trás-os-Montes"—"But what splintered Babel-like language would I speak when I would describe the Elevator of Santa Justa, the Cathedral of Reims, the trousers worn by the Zouaves, the way in which Portuguese is pronounced in Trás-os-Montes?" (fragment 123).

The attempt to solve this problem is not only the basis of the recourse to onomatopoeia and citation in Álvaro de Campos but should also be understood to be fundamental to the entire project of the heteronyms. For Joyce, too, the impulse lies far deeper than the onomatopoeia of, for instance, the "fourworded wavespeech, seesoo, hrss, rsseeiss, ooos" or the "thump, clank, sllt" of the printing presses in the offices of the *Freeman's Journal*. It also lies behind his radical decision "to allow each adventure [...] to condition and even to create its own technique."

(iv) The Dialogic Imagination

"Do I contradict myself? Very well then, I contradict myself."

The epigraph is a quotation from Walt Whitman's "Song of Myself." That the American poet was a major influence on Fernando Pessoa is well known, and opening lines such as Ricardo Reis's "Vivem em nós inúmeros"—"A multitude lives in us" might almost be translations of Whitman. However, the above quotation is taken, not from any of the various poetic manifestations of Pessoa, but from the opening chapter of *Ulysses*. The fact that it is recited by Buck Mulligan should not distract us. Joyce's multifarious opinions have a tendency of appearing in the most unlikely mouths, very often with ironic or self-deprecatory intent, as when the citizen articulates a number of Joyce's own positions on the vexed question of Irish nationalism.

We began this paper by making reference to Stephen Dedalus's aesthetic of the dramatic form:

> The personality of the artist, at first a cry or a cadence or a mood and then a fluid and lambent narrative, finally refines itself out of existence, impersonalises itself, so to speak. [...] The artist, like the God of the creation, remains within or beyond or above his handiwork, invisible, refined out of existence, indifferent, paring his fingernails.

This agenda is most fully realized by Joyce in *Ulysses*, which might be described as a drama in three main voices, with a supporting cast of dozens. It is impossible to locate the author's position or voice within this polyphony, still less to privilege it. Thus, writing from a post-colonial perspective, Irish critic Declan Kiberd has noted "the refusal of *Ulysses* to ground itself in a narrating subject or an identifiable author: instead [Joyce] offered a text without any final authority."

In this regard, the Russian cultural theorist Mikhail Bakhtin made a number of claims for the novels of Fyodor Dostoevsky that might equally be applied to *Ulysses*:

> A plurality of independent and unmerged voices and consciousnesses, a genuine polyphony of fully valid voices is in fact the chief characteristic of Dostoevsky's novels [...] a plurality of consciousnesses, with equal rights and each with its own world, combine but are not merged in the unity of the event. Dostoevsky's major heroes are, by the very nature of his creative design, not only objects of authorial discourse but also subjects of their own directly signifying discourse. ("Dostoevsky's Polyphonic Novel," italics in the original)

Personalities in Joyce are not differentiated merely in terms of their perspectives, their trajectories, their biographies, their opinions and their emotions as might be true, say, of the cast of characters in Tolstoy's *War and Peace*. What differentiates is rather the entire *Lebensweld* or lived-world of their language.

I would like to suggest that, with the project of the heteronyms that constituted his life, Fernando Pessoa achieved precisely this form of polyphony. Let us now turn to a claim that Bakhtin makes in regard to poetry:

> The language of the poetic genre is a unitary and singular Ptolemaic world outside of which nothing else exists and nothing else is needed. The concept of many worlds of language, all equal in their ability to conceptualize and to be expressive, is organically denied to poetic style.
>
> The world of poetry, no matter how many contradictions and insoluble conflicts the poet develops within it, is always illumined by one unitary and indisputable discourse. Contradictions, conflicts and doubts remain in the object, in thoughts, in living experiences—in short, in the subject matter—but they do not enter into the language itself. In poetry, even discourse about doubt must be cast in a discourse that cannot be doubted. ("Discourse in the Novel" 286)

Bakhtin had clearly never encountered Fernando Pessoa! If we accept Bakhtin's claim that "the poetic genre is a unitary and singular Ptolemaic world" as having a validity prior to the appearance of projects such as that of the heteronyms, then Pessoa is cast in the light of a Copernicus, wrenching the unitary self from the gravitational center of the poetic solar system. Put less grandly, one might say that the poetic project that involved Pessoa for his entire life was just as deserving of those Bakhtinian accolades "polyphonic" and "dialogic" as was anything that Dostoevsky, or for that matter Joyce, put pen to.

Octavio Paz says of the heteronyms that they were "los héroes de una novela que nunca escribió Pessoa" ["the heroes of a novel that Pessoa never wrote"]. In a variation, Pessoa (or is it Soares?) writes: "Sou os arredores de uma vila que não há, o comentário prolixo a um livro que se não escreveu" ["I am the outskirts of a town that doesn't exist, the wordy commentary on a book that was never written"]. Perhaps Bakhtin would accept our claim if we couched it in the following terms. Fernando Pessoa was the author of a polyphony of discourses, and these were in constant dialogue, in a forum from which his own finalizing voice was absent. What differentiates Pessoa from Joyce and Dostoevsky is that he dispensed with the framework of a novel within which to frame the encounter between these voices.

David Butler completed his doctoral research at Trinity College, Dublin in 2002. His *Selected Pessoa* was published by Dedalus Press, Dublin (2004), and *James Joyce / Fernando Pessoa: "A Máscara e o Espelho,"* co-authored with Richard Zenith, by Instituto Camões, Lisbon (2004). He is currently Education Officer at the James Joyce Centre, Dublin, and is working on a translation of the poet Alexandre O'Neill.

Tangled Threads: World History through a Portuguese Lens

Liam M. Brockey

Abstract. Using the example of the headquarters of the Society of Jesus in Lisbon during the sixteenth and seventeenth centuries, this article presents a vision of world history as seen from the perspective of the Portuguese empire. It evokes the air of "pious agitation" that once filled the historic church of São Roque, describing the figures who fill the space in paintings, tombs, sculptures, or in memory alone. Through the prism of the Portuguese Jesuits, it shows that notions of globalization and cosmopolitanism had roots that stretched back over at least five hundred years to the heyday of the Iberian Expansion.

Sitting atop a hill overlooking the central plaza of the city of Lisbon, the church of São Roque has an unassuming façade of unadorned pinkish marble and a similarly unremarkable bell tower. Thanks to the same 1755 earthquake that reduced the city to rubble and provoked Candide to ponder the question of evil, only a short set of steps and an imposing door suggest something of the treasures held within. Once inside, however, one is immediately confronted by a spacious open hall lined with high rounded arches whose volume appears larger due to the optical illusion of three openings to the heavens painted on its flat wooden ceiling. Clear windows forming the highest gallery flood the church with light, illuminating its eight lateral chapels and revealing the richness of the materials used in its construction. Two mar-

Portuguese Literary & Cultural Studies 7 (2008): 297-310.
© University of Massachusetts Dartmouth.

ble pulpits face each other across its center, mounted high up to provide gathered listeners with unimpeded lines of sight and sound for preachers. Recessed side altars in the church's chapels contend with the main altar for beauty, each a composition of inlaid marble, painted tile panels, and gilt carved wood, and all striking examples of the Portuguese baroque style. The primary altar, however, towers above these smaller chapels, itself an architectural composition with columns, paintings, and four life-sized statues of saints, all covered with a layer of gold. On either side of this central sanctuary are two further alcoves, each the size of a small chapel, with reliquaries ranked in ascending rows, their painted heads and blessing arms appearing as a stilled choir. Yet for all of its majestic beauty, the church is more compelling for another reason—it is where the course of many of the otherwise parallel strands of world history converge.

The church of São Roque is a space filled with figures: some painted, some sculpted, some partially present in the flesh, some wholly present, and some present only in the long-faded echoes of their words, but whose crossing in this edifice has given it a global significance. In this respect, it mirrors more recognizable sites such as the United Nations Building in New York, the Hall of Mirrors at Versailles, or the imperial audience chambers of the Forbidden City in Beijing. It is far from recognizable to most, however, since it belongs to a world whose institutional trappings and cultural influence have long since decayed or been actively dismantled. Yet in the early modern period, from the middle of the sixteenth until the middle of the eighteenth century, it was one of the busiest spaces in the city of Lisbon, reflecting the glory of the Portuguese capital during its age of greatest prosperity. During that age, the concerns of the denizens of that space were truly global, involving affairs from the remote jungles of the Congo to the even remoter jungles of Brazil. Their involvement in matters temporal and spiritual stretched from the bustling markets of the Swahili coast to the commercial entrepôts of the South China sea, not to mention all of Europe, from the yet unformed Catholics of Lithuania to the rebellious Calvinists of the Dutch Republic and on to the galley slaves of Mediterranean fleets and isolated rustics of the Azorean archipelago. Indeed, few spaces can boast of having had inhabitants with such ambitious worries or such grandiose plans as the church of São Roque, the former headquarters of the Society of Jesus in Portugal.

Upon entering São Roque, the visitor, awed by the church's silence, directs the eye towards the artistic beauty that fills the space. Yet, without the crucial dimension of human action, the historical importance of this space is hard to discern. From our modern vantage point, we may find it hard to envision the church full of movement, abuzz with pious agitation far surpassing the subdued atmosphere of current worship there. In fact, even before the Jesuits commissioned the present church of São Roque in the 1570s, the spot that it stands upon was thronged by pilgrims. They made the climb up to one of the highest points in the city, just outside the farthest northwestern corner of the city walls, to pray for health at a shrine to Saint Roque (also known as Roch or Rocco), the patron saint of plague victims. In what appears to have been a shrewd combination of piety and public health planning, a small chapel was built at the beginning of the sixteenth century to accommodate the cult of this popular devotional figure as well as to encourage the afflicted to leave the densely packed heart of the city below. On the hilltop, however, they could get some of the best medical treatment that contemporary science had discovered: a constant breeze bringing fresh air from the waterfront, the services of clergy devoted to helping the infirm, and the chance for prayers at the shrine of a heavenly intercessor.

For sixteenth-century Europeans, an opportunity to pray for health in times of plague was often the best therapeutic measure available. Given the variety of treatments for illnesses—ranging from bleeding to herbal potions or compresses—the expense of hiring anyone with enough knowledge to be beneficial, as well as the normal estimate that medical interventions most often made matters worse, devotions to figures such as St. Roque promised to be in their own way more efficacious. If nothing else, they comforted the soul and prepared the afflicted for their impending eternal reward. Yet one could hope for more. Through praying to a saint who had devoted himself to helping victims of the bubonic plague, one might be cured by the lingering miraculous effects of his presence or by his personal supplications to the Almighty. According to tradition, St. Roque had gained his powers on leaving his native Languedoc for Italy, where he tirelessly attended others, saving enough of them to earn a reputation as a healer. Intimate contact with contagion eventually left him infected and desirous to return to France. As recounted in the paintings and tile panels on the walls of the Lisbon church, he collapsed on his way home under a tree where he engaged with angels and had his daily bread delivered by a faithful greyhound until he recovered— only to be imprisoned as an impostor or spy in his hometown. Soon after his death and subsequent burial in Venice, reverence for his healing powers spread along with the deadly waves of disease that repeatedly swept across Southern Europe. After an outbreak of plague in 1505, supposedly brought to Lisbon by a Venetian ship, King Manuel I requested a relic of the saint from the Signoria of the Most Serene Republic. "In this way," wrote a later Jesuit author, the city that "caused our illness gave us the medicine"—in the form of a part of a leg bone. Recent excavations under the paving stones in the floor of the Jesuit church confirm St. Roque's popularity in Portugal. The numerous hastily dug graves found there attest to the desperate efforts plague sufferers made to worship in his chapel.

While the dance of death dominated this corner of Lisbon in the early sixteenth century, its rhythms gradually faded under the din of other activities that occurred on this spot after the Society of Jesus moved in. The arrival of the Jesuits in Portugal, the prelude to their spread into the Portuguese overseas empire, occurred within a year after the order itself was officially founded in 1540. In tune with the heightening tenor of spiritual renewal then on the rise in Iberia—the same that produced the mystics Teresa of Avila and John of the Cross—King João III invited Ignatius Loyola to send a pair of his followers to Lisbon for service both there and abroad. The two who came, Simão Rodrigues and Francis Xavier, had been Ignatius's colleagues at the University of Paris and later in Italy, and were counted among his most trusted friends. Shortly after they arrived, Dom João, the man who styled himself "King of Portugal and of the Algarves, and of the Near and Far Seas of Africa, the Lord of Guinea and of the Conquest, Navigation, and Commerce of Ethiopia, Arabia, Persia, and India," requested that Xavier head off to convert the masses of heathens nominally under his control. Rodrigues, the only Portuguese member of Loyola's original band, was asked to stay in Lisbon in order to tend the new order's roots there. The Society grew quickly in Portugal under Rodrigues's stewardship. The new houses founded under his direction in the country's key cities would turn out generations of confessors, scholars, preachers, and missionaries. Similarly, Xavier started missions throughout maritime Asia, following Portuguese traders and adventurers to ever-farther shores. Both founding fathers would find their places amid the figures on the walls of São Roque within two generations— Rodrigues in an ossuary, Xavier in a set of statues and narrative paintings.

Of these two individuals, however, it was Francis Xavier who was directly responsible for creating the global enterprise that would be run from São Roque. To be sure, his actions merely laid the groundwork for what his

Portuguese, Italian, French, Spanish, German, Polish, and Flemish (not to mention Indian, Chinese, and Japanese) successors would develop in Asia. The powerful impulse to follow in the footsteps of Padre Mestre Francisco by embarking at Lisbon or Seville for the overseas missions, cited in the numerous requests for such assignments held in the order's Roman archives, was both encouraged and commemorated by the images of the saint at São Roque. In a lateral chapel, above the high altar, and most dramatically in a series of paintings ringing the massive vestment drawers in the sacristy, the figure of Xavier reminds the visitor of the Society's missionary vocation— always appearing cloaked in the order's simple black robes and with cross and gospel in hand. The priests and brothers who were bound for the East or West Indies, no less than the provincial superiors who lived in the residence adjoining the church, were meant to derive inspiration from the key episodes of the saint's life. As they prepared for mass, they could contemplate his preaching to a crowd of Indian men, women, and children in the colonial Portuguese city of Goa. They could wonder at his ability to communicate with a group of fierce samurai, all bedecked in kimonos and bearing swords, at Yamaguchi on the Japanese island of Honshu. For these Jesuits, however, the most stirring episodes in Xavier's life were, in all likelihood, the miracles shown in these paintings: Francis dangling his cross from the deck of a troubled ship into crashing waves and imploring the Lord to spare the lives of its passengers; or Francis himself being lowered from a ship's deck into the sea along with an empty porcelain jar only to return with fresh water for the parched crew. Many men said their last confessions in Europe at São Roque before sailing out of Lisbon harbor on a one-way voyage to unknown lands, emboldened by the saint's example.

While the triumphant figure of Francis Xavier may have been captivating enough to spark many missionary vocations, the images of martyrs found in the church also contributed to maintaining the tenor of zeal required for a global enterprise. Although it may be difficult to understand nowadays, martyrdom was a very real goal and a very desirable fate for many early modern Christians, and it did not necessarily require sailing to remote corners of the world. Yet since the Society of Jesus depended on its Portuguese and Spanish provinces to provide the bulk of the missionaries for the Iberian empires in Asia, Africa, and the Americas, these Jesuits had to content themselves with the possibility of suffering for the faith at the hands of infidels overseas. At times, such as in the violent destruction of the Japanese mission by the shoguns bent on national unification in the first half of the seventeenth century, foreign rulers were only too happy to oblige. On either side of the main altar at São Roque, three life-sized painted figures bearing the palms of martyrdom peer down, warning viewers of the mortal dangers—and glorious rewards—of missionary work. These three Japanese martyrs, Paulo Miki, Diogo Kisai, and João de Goto, had joined the Society of Jesus as brothers and perished in Nagasaki at the order of Toyotomi Hideyoshi in 1597. While only these men appeared in this space on gilt panels, the builders of São Roque might just as easily have affixed images of João de Brito (slain in Southern India in 1693), Inácio de Azevedo (killed by French Calvinist pirates along with thirty-nine other Jesuits near the Canaries in 1570), or Luiz de Figueira (consumed by Brazilian cannibals in 1643). Any of these could have served the same purpose of providing the fervor necessary to maintain morale in regions where many missionaries found only despair.

One should not think, however, that the church of São Roque merely served as a starting point for overseas adventures. It was one of the first places visited by some of the Asians, Africans, and Americans who returned to Europe in Jesuit care. Although its trace is impossible to discern today due to a lack of artistic representations, São Roque served as the guest quarters for the first Japanese "embassy" to the West. Four youths, specifically chosen by the Jesuits for their relations to the recently converted daimyo (regional lords) of Kyushu, were escorted to Portugal and onward to Spain and Italy by the missionaries in 1584. This grand tour, a dramatic publicity coup for the Society of Jesus, saw the teenagers, bedecked in either their Japanese finery or European costume, paraded through the streets of many cities such as Madrid, Alicante, Florence, Milan, Rome, Naples, and Coimbra, as evidence of the Jesuits' apostolic triumphs overseas. During their travels, their hosts included the King of Spain, the Grand Duke of Tuscany, and the Pope, not to mention the local nobles and clergy (especially Jesuits) in each place they visited. Not only did this permit the "ambassadors" to learn more about Europe with the hope of them telling their compatriots of the glories of Europe, it gave many Europeans their first glance at the people of East Asia. Subsequent visitors from China, India, Kongo, and Brazil would also pass through São Roque to admire its splendor in the company of returning missionaries, aiming to foster European interest (and financial support) for the Society's activities throughout the globe.

The Jesuits of São Roque intended for all those who passed within, including foreign visitors, to be awed by the majesty of their surroundings. But religious awe for the Catholic men and women of four hundred years ago went beyond remarking the lifelike statues of the Jesuit saints Loyola, Xavier, Gonzaga, and Borja mounted above the main altar—their piety required the physical presence of the blessed. This meant relics. Here too, the presences at São Roque originated far beyond the narrow confines of Lisbon or even Portugal itself, from a realm encompassing the better part of Europe. Seated inside the numerous niches within the golden carved wood panels of the chapels of the *Santo Sacramento* and *Nossa Senhora de Piedade*, as well as in the enclosed reliquary stands on either side of the main altar, one finds a considerable collection of holy bones. These range in size from the smallest sliver of a femur to an entire skeleton (and perhaps more). Most of them belong to the trove of relics given by Juan de Borja, son of former Spanish Duke of Gandía and third General of the Society of Jesus St. Francis Borja, to the Lisbon Jesuits in 1587. The younger Borja, acting as the ambassador of Philip II to the king's Austrian Hapsburg cousin Emperor Rudolph II, purchased most of the pieces from German Catholics who had smuggled them out of Protestant territories. Knowing that the Society's new church had recently been completed, he sent them to Portugal where they might be "more decently kept and more venerated, honored, and visited by the faithful with more devotion than in other parts"—especially the heretical North where iconoclasm was the order of the day. Although the late sixteenth century witnessed the active efforts of reforming clergy to remove relics from the hands of lay men and women and collect them in guarded sanctuaries, the traditional Catholic devotion to holy objects retained its luster. On the occasion of this donation, the Jesuits held an elaborate celebration where a figure of St. Roque was mounted on the church's façade, welcoming a procession bearing the Borja legacy through the city streets. Among the new acquisitions were to be found golden heads of some of the 11,000 virgins slaughtered at Cologne along with St. Ursula, arm bones of bishops and cardinals whose painted reliquary cases extended a gesture of blessing, and a skull reportedly from the brilliant fifth-century nun, St. Bridget of Ireland, in a golden coffer.

But besides housing bits of the mortal remains of the blessed in reliquaries, São Roque serves as the final resting place for other individuals who passed through its doors. In the church's central area, today covered by ranks of pews, one finds scores of unmarked (yet numbered) graves covered by polished pine planks. Likely belonging to the Jesuits from the adjacent Professed House (for the highest, or professed, members of the order), these tombs purposely reveal nothing about whose bones they contain—perhaps in deference to the Society's ideals of poverty, humility, and corporate identity. Nevertheless, the church contains the clearly marked resting place of more than one Jesuit. In addition to Simão Rodrigues's ossuary, the visitor also finds that of Francisco Suárez, the famous Spanish theologian and philosopher who contributed to the reinvigoration of Aristotelian philosophy in the sixteenth century. Suárez spent the last twenty years of his life at the University of Coimbra, the Society's main intellectual center in Portugal, after having taught theology at Salamanca and Rome. At that university he joined the set of Jesuit scholars who produced the *Cursus Conimbricensis,* a set of commentaries on the works of Aristotle that became the standard philosophy textbook used in Jesuit schools across Europe and throughout the globe for the following two hundred years. His own famous work, the *Disputationes metaphysicæ,* would have a similar impact on the study of scholastic thought, influencing such intellectuals as Leibniz and Descartes. More importantly for the modern world, however, Suárez is also remembered for the concept of international law that he helped create with Spanish Dominican Francisco de Vitória. Drawing on both Stoic precepts and the Aristotelian definition of Natural Law, he developed a concept of national sovereignty that he employed to philosophically challenge the notion that the Spanish empire had a right to enslave the native populations of the Americas. In Suárez's view, the world consisted of a community of nations whose interactions were governed by certain universal principles—granting none any more legitimacy than another.

A further figure, not a Jesuit, is also conspicuously present in the middle of the Lisbon church. According to the plaque attached to his vertical tomb, he is Francis Tregian, an Englishman who was sent to prison for twenty-eight years by Queen Elizabeth I for standing "in defense of the Catholic religion." Among the many crimes he committed in Britain was the damnable offense of remaining faithful to his wife despite the Virgin Queen's unwanted romantic overtures at court. When finally freed from captivity in 1606, he abandoned his homeland for Lisbon where he joined the ranks of other English and Irish Catholics living in exile, awaiting the return of a monarch willing to take the British Isles back into the Roman church. In Portugal, France, the Lowlands, or neighboring Spain, Tregian and other Britons sent their sons to seminaries such as the

Jesuit-run College of St. Patrick in Lisbon where they might be trained as priests for covert pastoral work back home. They also contributed to the welfare of the poor of their adopted cities, at times gaining a reputation for piety, as Tregian did. Such was his fame that seventeen years after his burial in 1608, his body was exhumed at the behest of the other English expatriates in Lisbon. Finding it uncorrupted—a sure sign of saintliness—they created another tomb for him in a wall under one of São Roque's pulpits, and enclosed him standing, a literal reminder for posterity of his uprightness.

Today, neither Rodrigues, Suarez, nor Tregian make any sounds from beneath their stone covers, and only periodically do musicians come to play the beautifully painted organ hung from the interior balcony. This is a pity since the church has wonderful acoustics, and in fact was specifically designed according to standard Jesuit practice as an open hall to give pride of place to preaching. As such it represented a dramatic improvement over the cavernous Romanesque cathedral across the city in the Alfama quarter, or the gothic expanses of either the Carmelites' or Hieronymites' churches where soaring columns and tent-like vaults diffused the human voice. The pulpits at São Roque were frequently filled with gifted sermonists, men whose fame commanded capacity crowds and whose oratorical style won them multiple invitations to preach each Lent at cities around Portugal. Foremost among the voices heard from above the crowds at the Society's church was António Vieira, the most talented Portuguese-language author of the seventeenth century and a preacher unmatched in his day. In the present silence of the church one can strain to hear the echoes of this Jesuit's voice, filling the space from end to end and commanding attention and reflection. In an age when sermons were considered spectacle, Vieira was a superstar who combined the intellectual subtlety of the most sophisticated contemporary thought with stylistic elegance and dramatic incisiveness. Of all the renowned preachers in seventeenth-century Lisbon, it was he who made "laying a rug in São Roque at dawn" a popular expression for the only sure way to hear the best oratory.

Surprisingly, António Vieira is little known in the Anglophone world despite his colossal importance in its Lusophone counterpart. Born in Lisbon in 1608, he spent most of his early life in Brazil where he joined the Society of Jesus as a novice at the age of fifteen. At the Jesuit college of Salvador da Bahia he was exposed to both the study of the Latin classics and the rigors of missionary work among the Brazilian Indians. It did not take long for his talents as a writer and preacher to be noticed by his superiors, who entrusted him with producing official correspondence and presenting sermons on major feast days. Sent back to Lisbon in 1641 as one of the city of Bahia's representatives to the restored Portuguese monarchy (restored after sixty years of Castilian domination), Vieira quickly gained renown as a talented orator. After impressing the new king, João IV, he was made the royal preacher and sent on diplomatic missions to England, France, and the Netherlands. Still committed to his earlier formation as a missionary, he returned to Brazil in the 1650s where he devoted himself to organizing the Society's efforts in the Amazon basin. Thoroughly disgusted with how the area's colonists treated the local Indians, he left for Lisbon again where he actively denounced the settlers at court. Back in Europe, he returned to writing, producing a number of messianic texts that spoke of the dawning of a new era of world peace under the aegis of the Portuguese crown. Many of the ideas he used in these texts came from the friendly contacts he had made with the Portuguese Jewish communities in Northern Europe—and for this he ran afoul of the Inquisition. Only a direct appeal to the papacy in the 1670s, based in large part on his fame as a preacher, saved him from a life sentence from the Holy Office or worse. After spending almost a decade in Rome, Vieira returned to Brazil where he served as missions inspector and continued to write until his death in 1697.

On several occasions, António Vieira climbed up to the pulpit at São Roque to deliver sermons designed to shake his listeners from their complacency. For example, on the saint's feast day (August 16) in 1642, he combined the exegesis of that day's reading from the gospel of Luke with a retelling of the legend of that day's patron saint. Following this initial part, Vieira shifted his discourse to a current topic, the defeats that signaled the waning of Spanish power in Europe and the danger that even this decaying power still posed to Portugal. For although Spain had recently strained to control revolt in Catalonia, had lost its hold over the Portuguese empire, had suffered surprising reversals at the hands of the Dutch rebels during more than seventy years of war in the Netherlands, had seen official revenues from the American silver mines dry up and bankruptcy recur, and had been eclipsed militarily (and soon culturally) by France, it remained a major force in Europe. From the pulpit, therefore, Vieira chastised his listeners for collective dismissal of this danger. He decried their unwillingness to pay for the war against Castile and their excessive confidence in their military prowess, calling these faults "two very dangerous plagues" and imploring Saint Roque for aid. Vieira warned of too much self-congratulation in the wake of the

1640 rebellion, recalling that Portugal had shared prosperity under Castilian power for the previous sixty years:

> Why, when Castile heads precipitously toward such a heralded ruin, do we see ourselves safe? What misery! Why, when Castile is found in such as state that it can no longer resist its enemies, do we imagine ourselves to have conquered ours? What blindness! […] I ask you, gentlemen, why God is enraged with Castile and punishes her so rigorously? No doubt it is for her sins, for her iniquities, for her injustices, for her vanity, for her incontinence, etc. We are good witnesses since we were complicit for a time of the same crimes. I ask further, is the God of Castile the same as that of Portugal, or some other? This question has no answer, for if the God is the same, and in Castile punishes sins, how can He reward sins in Portugal? If Castile finds her ruin in her vices, how can we find security in ours?

The remedy that Vieira suggested consisted in a return to prudence, liberality, and renewed virtue, qualities the Spanish oppressors clearly had lacked. Before ending his sermon, he issued a last warning, urging those gathered in São Roque to consider the fate of the Israelites during the Exodus and fear that it might become their own: "God liberated them because they were tormented, and then punished them because they were ungrateful." Yet by the time that Vieira had made this call, the God of Portugal and Castile had chosen other stars to rise in the East (and the West) to outshine their deeds.

Sounds from the pulpit at São Roque, such as the final intonation of *Laus Deo* ending a dramatic oration, dissipate quickly. With a last shuffle of leather soles on marble, the figure of António Vieira disappears, leaving the visitor back in the beautiful, yet silent, space filled with inanimate figures. To those who cannot read the inscriptions on the walls, nor understand the significance of the artifacts stacked in the chapels, the church is a place without memory of the individuals who passed through it. Yet to those who stood here in centuries past, São Roque brimmed with global significance. It was here that King Philip II, whose domains stretched from Manila to Madrid and from Peru to Portugal, had passed to observe the construction of the new church during his stay in Lisbon in the 1580s, arranging afterwards for the purchase and shipment of its massive roof beams from the forests of Prussia. It was for this community that António Andrade longed as he became the first European to venture up to the highlands of Tibet in the 1620s. It was to the priests of this residence that Pedro Dias dispatched his *Art of the Angolan Language* for publication in the 1690s. It was in this church that King João V decided to install the extremely ornate chapel of St. John the Baptist, commissioned from the most talented Italian artists in the 1740s and paid for with part of the royal share of Brazilian diamonds and gold. And it was to this building that the Marquis of Pombal sent royal troops in 1759 to enforce the suppression of the Society of Jesus in Portugal and its empire, beginning the series of extinctions of the order in European nations that would culminate in the final disbanding of the "Old Company" by Pope Clement XIV in 1773.

The figures mentioned above constitute a select group whose personal paths took them all over the globe, but who shared the common experience of having been present at São Roque. In this way, they suggest a historical pedigree for the fashionable term "globalization" when defined as the interconnectedness of peoples throughout the world. The movements of the individuals mentioned above created new links between the largely parallel histories of many of the world's peoples. The threads of their own personal histories therefore cut through those of others much in the same way Broadway cuts across the rigid parallels of the Manhattan city grid. Their paths, converging in São Roque, reveal the church as one of the first physical spaces in human history where those passing through could behold an image of a single world. In this way, these men possessed the uniquely modern capacity to think on a global scale. Beyond merely conceiving of a vast world as many of their predecessors had done, they envisioned the earth as a space proportionate to the ambitions of their order. Their universal Christian ideals—similar to our modern concerns of individual liberty, democracy, or free trade—impelled them to move throughout the world. And their common bond of membership in the Society of Jesus, one of the largest Catholic religious orders then as now, provided them with an institutional legacy molded by the worldwide travels of their brethren. As such, they represent an identifiable group of the early modern precursors of those people today whose personal combinations of travel and education permit them to understand the sheer scope of global interconnectedness.

The presences found in the church of São Roque were not, however, the only people to have possessed this scope of vision. While other "worldly" individuals since antiquity have at times left their marks on the historical record, their numbers only begin to expand in the early modern period. Besides the Portuguese Jesuits in the sixteenth and seventeenth centuries, one could sketch the history of Dutch merchants of the United East India

Company, the Catholic prelates of the Roman curia, the South Asian nobles gathered at Akbar's court, or the English adventurers led by Walter Raleigh in a similar fashion. By substituting an Amsterdam council chamber, the Piazza Navona, an audience chamber in Agra, or the Tower of London for São Roque, one can find other tangles in the strands of world history. Still further spaces emerge as useful starting points for such analyses when one scans the early modern globe for points of interaction: the wharves of Cartagena de las Indias on the Spanish *Tierra Firma*, the warehouses on the banks of the Pearl River in Canton, the pilgrims' hostels surrounding the central sanctuary at Mecca. Like the space enclosed by the walls of São Roque, these places were where the paths of diverse groups of people crossed for a variety of reasons—political, religious, or economic—and where the lingering presence of their passage was felt by others.

Although it is not a towering presence on the Lisbon skyline today, the church of São Roque is a potent reminder for us to think in historical terms about our present global awareness. The church's history challenges us to try to understand the breadth of vision of those who passed through it, either as missionaries, ambassadors, martyrs, or preachers. The vision of these individuals, so similar to our own in its scope but so different in its origins, was created through movements, again reminiscent of our global wanderings yet unlike in their purpose, and through the convergence of ideas. In this way, the figures at São Roque foreshadowed today's global citizens whose restless intellects produce the types of intercultural encounters that we prize so highly. This does not mean that those men and women whose lives did not intersect with others around the globe do not constitute equally important subjects for historical inquiry, or that their pasts do not tell us even more about today. Rather, the presences in the Lisbon church remind us that our form of modernity is much older than we think and that our novel thoughts on global interactions also have a history.

Works Cited

Boxer, Charles R. *A Great Luso-Brazilian Figure, Padre Antonio Vieira, S. J., 1608-1697*. London: Hispanic and Luso-Brazilian Councils, 1957.

Alden, Dauril. *The Making of an Enterprise: The Society of Jesus in Portugal, Its Empire, and Beyond: 1540-1750*. Stanford: Stanford UP, 1996.

Campos, Manuel de. *Relaçam do Solenne Recebimento que se fez em Lisboa as Santas Reliquias que se levaram a Igreja de S. Roque da Companhia de Iesu aos 25 de Ianeiro de 1588*. Lisbon:

Antonio Ribeiro, 1588.

Elisonas, J. S. A. "Acts, Legends, and Southern Barbarous Japanese." *Portugal e a China: Conferências nos Encontros de História Luso-Chinesa.* Ed. Jorge M. dos Santos Alves. Lisbon: Fundação Oriente, 2001. 15-60.

Ribeiro, Victor. *Obituários da Igreja e Casa Professa de São Roque da Companhia de Jesus desde 1555 até 1704.* Lisbon: Academia das Ciências, 1916.

Rodrigues, Francisco, S. J. *História da Companhia de Jesus na Assistência de Portugal.* 3 vols. Porto: Apostolado da Imprensa, 1931-1945.

Teles, Baltazar, S. J. *Chronica da Companhia de Jesus na Provincia de Portugal.* 2 vols. Lisbon: Paulo Craesbeeck, 1645-1647.

[Veiga, Manuel da]. *História da Fundaçam e Progresso da Casa de Sam Roque.* Post 1588. Lisbon, Biblioteca Nacional Mss. Codex 4491.

Vieira, António, S. J. *Sermam que Pregou o P. Antonio Vieira da Companhia de Iesus na Caza Professa da mesma Companhia em 16 de Agosto de 1642.* Lisbon: Domingos Lopes Rosa, 1642.

Liam M. Brockey is Assistant Professor of History at Princeton University and a specialist in the history of early modern Europe and the European Expansion. His recent publications have appeared in the *Journal of the Metropolitan Museum of Art,* the *Revista da Cultura* (Macau), and *Archivum Historicum Societatis Iesu.* Brockey is currently working on a study of the Jesuit missionary enterprise in China in the seventeenth century, as well as other projects on the Society of Jesus in Portugal and its empire. E-mail: lbrockey@Princeton.edu

Portuguese-Brazilian (Dis)Connections

Fernando Arenas

Abstract. Focusing on Luso-Brazilian cultural relations through recent history, this essay offers a series of reflections from within the realm of mentalities and the symbolic regarding the current state of the relationship between Portugal and Brazil, with special attention given to the fields of high and popular culture, media, and geopolitics.

Para o discurso cultural português, o Brasil existe superlativamente, mesmo que essa existência seja quase sempre mítica, sobretudo como suporte simbólico dos nossos antigos sonhos imperiais. Para o discurso cultural brasileiro, Portugal existe pouco ou nada, mas, se existe, é apreendido como o pai colonizador que o Brasil teve de matar para existir (Lourenço, "Nós e o Brasil: ressentimento e delírio," *A nau de Icaro* 150)

Within Portuguese cultural discourse, Brazil exists superlatively, even if such existence is almost always mythical, particularly as the symbolic basis for our most ancient imperial dreams. Within Brazilian cultural discourse, Portugal exists very little or not at all, yet, if it does exist, it is seen as the colonizing father that Brazil had to kill in order to exist (Lourenço, "Us and Brazil: Resentment and Delirium," *The Ship of Icarus*)

Portuguese Literary & Cultural Studies 7 (2008): 311-24.
© University of Massachusetts Dartmouth.

The myth of the "land of the future," which has governed the modern Brazilian imaginary, has inevitably entailed the gradual erasure of Portugal as a primary cultural point of reference. This myth is the result of a complex historical and cultural metamorphosis that started with the Christian utopian vision of the "earthly paradise," projected onto Brazil from the moment of the Portuguese arrival in 1500. Both asymmetrical mythical-utopian visions underscore the movement from a colonial to a postcolonial era, as well as the peculiar relationship between a weak (former) colonial power on the edge of Europe and the enormous potential of a (formerly) colonized giant in the New World. Thus, Brazil has historically functioned as an imaginary compensatory mechanism for Portugal due to its smaller dimensions, as well as its economical limitations. Brazil was in fact the "crown jewel" of the Portuguese colonial empire, thus, its "superlative" place, according to Lourenço, within the Portuguese cultural discourse before and after Brazilian independence. Yet, in the earlier colonial period, there was a convergence of interests between the white ruling classes of both the colony (i.e., the Luso-Brazilians) and the metropole, as they administered the territory and managed the trans-Atlantic slave trade. However, as the metropolitan rule increasingly became an obstacle to the political and economic aspirations of the white elites (now more decidedly Brazilian and far less Luso) in their quest for greater autonomy, independence became the only viable option. Conversely, in a subsequent postcolonial moment (which is still evolving), Portugal has become, from a Brazilian perspective, a mixture of a distant historical echo, a suppressed memory, a distant parent, a relatively important piece of a much larger cultural mosaic that is contemporary Brazil, as well as an "impoverished reality" in relationship to the vision of a country that sees itself as "forever modern," at the risk of obliterating its cultural memory.

The year 2000 marked the 500th anniversary of the Portuguese arrival at what would eventually become Brazil. No one in 1500 could possibly imagine what this new geographical space would become or what new human reality would emerge here, but Pêro Vaz de Caminha's "Letter of Discovery" eloquently provides hints. This "birth certificate" of Brazil reveals all the cultural underpinnings and ideological biases of Renaissance Europe, thus preparing the terrain for the colonial enterprise that would ultimately ensue. The utopian vision of paradise initially deployed inevitably gave way to the utilitarian task of catechization and submission of the infantilized natives, the extraction of raw materials, and the setting up of the necessary infrastructure for empire-building. The Portuguese colonization of Brazil initiated in 1500 with all of its contradictions, excesses, and epic feats constitutes the basis for the emergence of a nation that eventually organized itself as the state that we know today.

The festivities and counter-festivities that surrounded the 500 years of Brazil underscored the fact that Brazil and Portugal are living in vastly different historical times in the year 2000, as well as the fact that there is a multiplicity of interpretations in both countries regarding the meaning of the quincentennial. This is clearly reflected in the contrasting approaches taken by the Portuguese and Brazilian presidents during the occasion: the perspective advanced by Sampaio emphasized past Portuguese glories, paid tribute to the cultural richness of Brazil (to which Portugal partly contributed), politely acknowledged present and future socio-economic challenges for Brazil, while offering no apologies for the misdeeds of colonial-era Portugal. Meanwhile, the point of view offered by Cardoso inevitably focused on the present social ills that predictably marred the 500 year celebration. Even though he still evoked the heroic deeds of past Brazilian leaders, Cardoso's speech forcibly accentuated the huge socio-economic gaps that continue to plague Brazil, stating that his country is "one of the world's most unfair societies." [1]

In the early twenty-first century, both Brazil and Portugal are striving to become active players in the global economic, political, and cultural arenas. Portugal is consolidating its (irrevocably peripheral) place within one of the world's major power blocs (i.e., the European Union), at the same time as it endeavors, together with Brazil and Lusophone Africa, to give shape to a community of Portuguese-speaking nations that also encompasses East Timor. At the same time, Brazil has become a de facto regional power in Latin America from an economic and political point of view, at the same time as it struggles to attain socio-economic stability and political democratization. Brazil is also fast becoming a world agricultural superpower, and under president Luiz Inácio Lula da Silva, Brazil is assuming a more proactive diplomatic role in the global South.

The (post)colonial relationship between Brazil and Portugal is exceptional in ways that differ greatly even from the special relationship between the United States and Great Britain. Already before its independence, Brazilian economic output and natural resource base was far greater than that of the metropole, thereby creating a relation of economic dependence of the mother country vis-à-vis the former colony. No other colonial power transferred its capital from the metropole to the colony as Portugal did between 1808-1821 due to the Napoleonic wars. This particular move led to the emergence of Rio de Janeiro as the center of the Portuguese empire. In fact, as Mota and Novais point out, during this era there was an inversion of the colonial pact between Portugal and Brazil whereby the metropole became a de facto appendix of the colony (as also cited in Santos's *Pela mão de Alice,* pages 130-31). This is one of the most blatant examples of a Portuguese condition that Boaventura de Sousa Santos describes as intermediate and semi-peripheral from a geopolitical point of view; simultaneously semi-colonizers and semi-colonized (this, in relationship to Brazil but also to England). Borrowing a major trope from Shakespeare's *The Tempest,* but also from Hispanic American postcolonial re-elaborations of this trope, Santos adds that the Portuguese colonizer was a hybrid who combined aspects of Prospero and Caliban: "If Prospero ever disguised himself as Caliban, it was through the mask of the Portuguese" ("Espírito de Timor Invade o Rio" 2). In his article, "Between Prospero and Caliban: Colonialism, Postcolonialism, and Inter-Identity" (2002), Santos develops the suggestive trope by arguing that the identity of the Portuguese colonizer does not only encompass the identity of the colonized other, but also that the identity of the Portuguese colonizer is in itself colonized: "The Portuguese Prospero is not just a Calibanized Prospero; he is a very Caliban from the viewpoint of European super-Prosperos. The identity of the Portuguese colonizer is thus doubly double" (17). I partially subscribe to Santos's re-codifying of the colonial bipolarity between Prospero and Caliban by introducing the figure of the "hybrid Portuguese colonizer" on account of Portugal's subalternized position in the world system after the late sixteenth century, or because of the fact that the Portuguese have been viewed at various points in history as a "barbaric other" by Northern Europeans or by many Brazilians who after independence harbored deep feelings of anti-colonial resentment towards the Portuguese and/or disdain for the condition of many of them as poor rustic immigrants to Brazil. Nevertheless, I still would like to bring attention to unambiguous Prospero-like figures in the history of Portuguese colonialism, such as Mousinho de Albuquerque, commander of major war campaigns against native populations in southern Mozambique in 1895; Kaúlza de Arriaga, commander in chief of Portuguese armed forces in Mozambique in the war against nationalist forces between 1969-74; or Tomé de Souza, the first governor general of Brazil, who in 1549 was in charge of centralizing the colonial administration as well as of pacifying the native populations through extermination and/or catechism.

In spite of the autonomy gained by Brazil in all spheres of its national life after 1822, the political framework that was established at first was a bi-national monarchy, whereby the same monarchical family ruled both countries (the father, João VI in Portugal, and the son, Pedro I in Brazil). Thus, strong political ties (as well as economic and cultural ones) between both countries continued after independence. However, Emperor Pedro II's rule (1840-88) was characterized by a gradual but definitive disentanglement and distancing from the European colonial matrix. Nevertheless, the Brazilian Empire was firmly anchored in a conservative, plantation-based, slave-holding system that critics (see, for example, Nelson Vieira and Boaventura de Sousa Santos) describe as tantamount to the continuation of colonialism but in the form of an internal colonialism (this is a socio-historical dynamic dramatized by the epic historical novel *Viva o povo brasileiro* (1984) [*Invincible Memory*, 1989] by João Ubaldo Ribeiro). In fact, the key importance of slave labor to the economic survival and development of colonial Brazil meant that the Portuguese as well as the Luso-Brazilian elites had as much at stake in the continuation of the slave trade. Thus, in the struggles against the Dutch occupation of the Brazilian Northeast and Angola during the first half of the seventeenth century, Luso-Brazilians and Portuguese acted as co-colonizers in their quest to recover the Angola-Brazil lifeline that the Dutch had wrested away from them. The continued dependence on slave labor in independent Brazil during the nineteenth century meant that even after independence Brazil was still inextricably linked to the colonial Black Atlantic matrix until the abolition of slavery, lending credence to Luiz Felipe de Alencastro's view of the aterritorial basis for the formation of Brazil.[2] He argues that Brazil emerged from an economically and socially bipolar space located in the south Atlantic, created by Portuguese colonialism and largely based upon slave labor, encompassing an area of slave reproduction centered in Angola and an area of slave production in various enclaves throughout Portuguese America. Hence, this line of reasoning suggests a space-time disjuncture occurring during Brazilian independence, that is, a break from the European colonial matrix that empowered the Luso-Brazilian ruling class who, by the same token, became responsible for extending Brazil's colonial economic dependence on the African slave-trading matrix. Consequently, Brazilian independence entailed the passage from colonial power structures to the power structures of "coloniality" (a term borrowed from Santos) both internally and externally.

Even though Brazil severed formal ties from Portugal in the course of the nineteenth century, the large Portuguese presence in the daily life of Brazil, especially in Rio de Janeiro, continued unabated (this phenomenon is widely documented in nineteenth-century Brazilian literature, from Manuel Antônio de Almeida to Machado de Assis, Adolfo Caminha, and Aluísio Azevedo). Heavy immigration from Portugal to Brazil did not come to a halt in 1822 but in fact continued well into the twentieth century, only subsiding after the Portuguese Revolution of 1974 that toppled the Salazar/Caetano right-wing authoritarian regime. The constant migratory wave from Portugal to Brazil is a manifestation of a peculiar (post)colonial dependence. In fact, emigration throughout the history of Portuguese colonialism in Brazil since the sixteenth century (as well as in Angola and Mozambique, particularly after Salazar's ascent to power in 1933) served as an escape mechanism for millions of rural Portuguese in search for a better life, at the same time as it served as an economic strategy to rid the country of its poor, while avoiding some of the pressing developmental problems that plagued Portugal since the "epic navigators" set sail to India in the fifteenth century. This would constitute one of the tragic aspects of the "discoveries" suggested in the speech proffered by the old man of Restelo in Camões's epic poem *The Lusiads*. Hence, colonialism and emigration went hand in hand in the case of the Portuguese, and its relationship of dependence vis-à-vis Brazil continued on after Brazilian independence.

Today, millions of Brazilians have grandparents or even parents who are Portuguese. On the other hand, Portuguese emigration to its traditional points of destination (Brazil, France, Canada, the United States, South Africa, Venezuela, etc.) has greatly diminished since Portugal entered the European Union in 1986. European integration has been to a large extent the catalyst for Portugal's rapid modernization, renewed economic prosperity, and the guarantor of its political stability. This situation has attracted tens of thousands of immigrants from Brazil during the Brazilian economic and political crisis of the 1980s and early nineties, from Africa, primarily from the drought-prone Cape Verde Islands and war-torn Angola, and increasingly from the former Soviet Union (Russia, Ukraine, Moldova).

In the cultural sphere, it is a well known fact that Brazilian popular music and media exert an enormous influence in contemporary Portugal (as well as in Lusophone Africa). This is reflected in the proliferation of Brazilian soap operas *(novelas)* on a daily basis on Portuguese public and private television channels, together with several Brazilian TV channels via satellite or on cable. The intense exposure to Brazilian culture in Portugal is only surpassed by the exposure to American (and to a lesser extent, British) pop and media culture (this is also applicable to popular music where Anglo-American and Brazilian music have a large share of the Portuguese consumer market). The daily contact with Brazilian culture has produced significant changes in Portugal, particularly from a linguistic point of view, but also within the realm of mentalities (for example, regarding sexual, gender, ecological, race, and class dynamics. This is not only true for Portugal but also for Angola, Mozambique, Cape Verde, Guinea Bissau, and São Tomé & Príncipe).

While British popular and elite cultures are quite present in the daily life of the United States, the same cannot be said of Portuguese culture in Brazil, especially regarding Portuguese popular culture (music, TV), which has a minimal presence in everyday Brazilian life. In the realm of elite culture, some of the greatest writers of Portuguese literature, such as Camões or Eça de Queiroz are indeed familiar to well-educated Brazilians through secondary and/or college education, while celebrated Modernist poet Fernando Pessoa has achieved near cult status among well-read Brazilians. For his part, 1998 Nobel Laureate José Saramago has constantly figured on Brazilian lists of bestsellers. Saramago's literary award was perceived in Brazil as being Brazilian as much as Portuguese. By the same token, the Nobel Prize has boosted the presence and prestige of Portuguese literature in Brazil, as well as throughout the world. However, even before this significant development, Portuguese literature already had been widely disseminated throughout the Brazilian university system where there are MA and PhD programs in the area at all major Brazilian universities. Unfortunately, the same cannot be said about the institutionalization of Brazilian literature in the Portuguese university system, where there are few courses or degree programs in the area. In fact, it can be argued that Brazilian literature today is much less known in Portugal than Portuguese literature is in Brazil. This can be attributed to ethnocentric attitudes that have dominated the educational system in Portugal and hence literary studies' curricula as well. Despite this contemporary literary chasm, Brazilian literature of the 1930s (Graciliano Ramos, Jorge Amado, José Lins do Rego, among others) profoundly influenced Portuguese Neo-realist writers (as well as emerging Cape Verdean writers of the time) and enjoyed wide readership. Meanwhile, the greatest Brazilian twentieth-century literary figures, such as poets Carlos Drummond de Andrade and João Cabral de Melo Neto, as well as prose writers João Guimarães Rosa and Clarice Lispector remain well-known within academic and intellectual circles in Portugal.[3]

In the realm of literature and other "high" cultural expressions, Brazil has a rather limited presence in Portugal. This can be partly explained by the obvious limitations experienced by cultural and artistic productions aimed at highly educated and specialized segments of the population, even in wealthier societies. Nonetheless, the dramatic increase in cultural exchanges between Brazil and Portugal as a result of the 500 years of Brazil has led to a (re-)discovery of Brazilian culture on the part of the Portuguese, particularly of Brazilian "high" cultural expressions such as the visual and performance arts, classical music, and cinema, with major retrospectives that aim at not only educating Portuguese audiences but also changing the perception of Brazil as a producer of exclusively pop cultural expressions such as *novelas* and *MPB*.

Yet, it remains *de rigueur* for Brazilian pop music artists to include various Portuguese cities in their European tours, where they have thousands of loyal fans. The intense exposure to the Portuguese language spoken in Brazil has made the Portuguese population very familiar with its sounds and nuances to the point of decisively influencing the vocabulary and grammar used in Portugal, especially among youth. The opposite is not at all true, where Brazilians, particularly less-educated ones, experience great difficulty in comprehending Lusitanian Portuguese. Linguistically, European Portuguese today sounds exotic to many Brazilians and more often than not somewhat shocking, if not altogether jarring to their ears. In spite of the substantial growth, renewed vitality, and high quality of contemporary Portuguese pop music, Brazilian radio stations and audiences are rather reluctant to include it in their repertoire of sounds. Yet, in the past fifteen years there has been a veritable explosion of new artists and a proliferation of styles ranging from new folk and fado to jazz, rock, hip hop, funk, soul, and electronic music. Fado, in spite of the huge loss of Amália Rodrigues in 1999, has experienced a remarkable boom with numerous outstanding new and not so new voices, such as Mísia, Dulce Pontes, Teresa Salgueiro (from the group Madredeus), Nuno Guerreiro (from the group Ala dos Namorados), Mafalda Arnauth, Cristina Branco, Camané, Paulo Bragança, Ana Sofia Varela, Mariza, Kátia Guerreiro, Ana Moura, Marta Dias, and Ana Maria Bobone, among others.

Portuguese state-sponsored organizations and private enterprises sporadically organize large cultural events throughout Brazil that showcase contemporary visual and performance art, film, or classical, jazz, pop, or fado music produced in Portugal. These events have a limited scope and tend to reach primarily elite Brazilian audiences or Portuguese immigrants in large cities such as São Paulo, Rio de Janeiro, and others. Since Expo '98, which took place in Lisbon, and the 500 years of Brazil there has been an increase in the number of joint events, such as concerts featuring well-known Brazilian artists together with Portuguese in the hopes of providing more visibility to Portuguese popular music in Brazil with, for example, concerts on Ipanema Beach in Rio de Janeiro and at Ibirapuera Park in São Paulo. Beyond these highly specific instances, the presence of contemporary Portuguese high or popular cultures in Brazil is fairly limited.

In terms of literary representations, Portugal and Brazil have been historically present in each other's national literature, especially during colonial times but also throughout the nineteenth century, as well as in the postmodern historiographical metafiction of the late twentieth-century with authors such as Ana Miranda, Haroldo Maranhão, Eduardo Bueno, and João Ubaldo Ribeiro, among others. Within the abundant literature of Portuguese navigations and "discoveries" of the sixteenth century, Brazil is primarily an object of description.[4] Throughout the colonial period, most literature produced in Brazil was inevitably linked to the metropole, as much as it was linked to the colony itself; the most outstanding examples would be the great baroque figures of Luso-Brazilian letters, the Jesuit Father Antonio Vieira and poet Gregório de Matos. Within Brazilian colonial literature we find nascent signs of a distinct nationality that undergoes an evolutionary process, much akin to what is seen in Angolan or Cape Verdean literature between the nineteenth and twentieth centuries, which culminates in the works of the greatest Brazilian (and Latin American) writer of the nineteenth century, Machado de Assis. In Machado's fiction, Brazilian national identity is no longer a primary or explicit concern, while Portugal practically disappears as an obvious cultural or historical point of reference or comparison.[5] A large part of the fiction and poetry produced in Brazil after independence (1822) and until the Modernist movement of 1922 is invested in the construction of a national literature intended to reveal—or propose—the contours of an independent and distinct nation. In this context, it is evident that Portugal will necessarily appear under a negative limning or as a point of contrast, i.e., that which is not Brazil. Here, the figure of the Portuguese immigrant to Brazil plays a major role. Nelson Vieira offers the most exhaustive study of the representations of Portuguese and Brazilians in each other's literature. In his study, Vieira concludes that in spite of the degree of familiarity and affection that has existed between both nations throughout history, the dominant images of each other's peoples have generally been negative. The figure of the Portuguese immigrant to Brazil appears as the loaded signifier through which Brazilian authors (particularly of the nineteenth century) express a lingering and complex colonial resentment, as well as a feeling of revenge vis-à-vis the former mother country, viewed as an impoverished nation of rustic yet ambitious and arrogant immigrants. Vieira also argues that the negative relationship with Portugal underscores the insecurity of nineteenth-century Brazil, which was in the process of defining its identity and place in the world (122).

In nineteenth-century Portuguese literature, on the other hand, "Brazilian" figures are really the Portuguese who emigrated to Brazil but who returned to Portugal. These "Brazilians" are also an object of satire and scorn on the part of Portuguese writers and are represented as unsophisticated and materialistic *nouveaux riches*.[6] This stereotype may indicate a classist, as well as neo-colonialist attitude on the part of Portuguese intellectuals. Interestingly, in neither case do we observe an attempt on the part of Brazilian or Portuguese writers to accurately represent the actual peoples living in the other country. In the literature of both nations, realistic and more accurate representations based on lived experiences in each other's country have been rather rare, and, unfortunately, the negative stereotypes of the immigrant/emigrant still largely prevail.[7]

The dominant notions that Brazil and Portugal have about each other in their collective imaginaries are doubtless manifold. When spending time in either country one confronts the postcolonial paradox of a generalized contemporary indifference toward Portugal in today's Brazil, and, on the other hand, the impossibility of ignoring Brazil in everyday Portuguese life. This paradox is also palpable at an interpersonal level when encountering Portuguese and Brazilians elsewhere in Europe or in the Americas. There is a complex spectrum of feelings and perceptions that Brazilians and Portuguese have for each other (which Vieira amply describes in the realms of literature and oral folklore) that range from a sense of familiarity with each other's culture, the discovery of uncanny similarities between them, a mutual feeling of "home" when Brazilians are in Portugal or vice-versa, and sincere affection for each other, to feelings of culture shock, national chauvinism, active ignorance, paternalism, arrogance, mutual mistrust, or alienation (the latter feeling is dramatized in Walter Salles's film *Foreign Land* [1995]). On the other hand, occasional tensions also have arisen in recent years on the diplomatic front due to the difficulties Portugal has encountered in adapting to the sizable immigration from Brazil and Lusophone Africa since the 1980s and the demand made by the European Union that countries such as Portugal—which have special ties with former colonies—curtail and control the migratory flow of non-EU citizens. These diplomatic tensions have led at times to interpersonal tensions or to inflamed comments in the respective national media.

Brazil and Portugal continue to evoke images of the "exotic other" in their respective imaginaries. The "exoticism" associated with each other may at times reach extremes of caricature or sardonic humor (see Vieira). For instance, Brazil (in the most extreme cases) may evoke in Portugal a whole repertoire of clichés associated with it in other countries as well, such as the images of a lush tropical beach paradise, sensuous mulattas, soccer players, or a country in a state of endless *carnaval.* In addition, Brazil may evoke images of poverty, violence, corruption, and vast socio-economic injustices. In Brazil, Portugal may still appear in the popular imaginary of clichés as an archaic poverty-stricken country, frozen in time, where black-clad rustic peasant women sing an interminable litany of melancholic *fados.* These stereotypes reveal yet another and no less important facet of the highly complex world of Luso-Brazilian relations. These over-simplistic and distorted images of each other's country may in time be superseded by more balanced and accurate notions, based on increased cultural and economic contacts (which are already occurring), as well as through greater direct human contact, which continues to take place via immigration (a trend that is now directed more toward Portugal), or increasingly through tourism (in both directions), among other vectors.

Is it possible, as Eduardo Lourenço asks (141), to overcome the historical-psychic-cultural complex of colonizer/colonized or father/son in the context of Luso-Brazilian relations? Or must current and future relations between both countries be inexorably condemned to a dynamic of resentment, fascination, delirium, mythification, active ignorance, or indifference in relationship to each other, stemming from their colonial past? The answers to both questions are inevitably yes and no. The (post)colonial link will always inform to one degree or another the cultural memory of both countries; yet, such memory will be differently lived by Brazil as well as by Portugal. On the other hand, the evolution of bi-national relations will largely depend on the level and intensity of the economic, financial, political, cultural, interpersonal, academic, and media-based *exchanges* between Portugal and Brazil. Such exchanges will take place within a decidedly postcolonial framework and as part of a much wider global network of relations. In this context, both nations must defend their common interests and, together with the Portuguese-speaking nations of Africa, safeguard the place of the Portuguese language—while respecting cultural differences—in a world that is tending more and more toward linguistic and cultural homogenization. I hope that within the realm of intellectual-academic exchanges, to contribute to an updated and perhaps more nuanced view of national identities in Brazil and Portugal in an era of postmodern globalization, shedding new light on Luso-Brazilian intercultural connections, while at the same time recognizing the fact that both countries are today inhabiting highly differentiated historical and cultural moments in relationship to each other.

Notes

[1] In "FHC pede tolerância com divergências" (*Folha de São Paulo* Online, April 23, 2000).

[2] See, *O trato dos viventes: a formação do Brasil no Atlântico sul* (2000).

[3] Until the rise of Brazilian Modernism in 1922 the Portuguese and Brazilian literary fields were closely intertwined since poets from both countries were known across the Atlantic due to their being featured in anthologies that simultaneously included poetry written in both countries. Brazilian authors were regularly published in Portugal as were Portuguese authors in Brazil, and between the late nineteenth and early twentieth centuries, writers from both countries often jointly contributed in Portuguese literary journals or were regularly featured in Brazilian newspapers, such as Eça de Queiroz (and other nineteenth-century figures such as António Castilho, Pinheiro. Chagas, and Ramalho Ortigão. In fact, as Antonio Candido has argued (*Literatura e sociedade* 132), until 1922 Portuguese literature (alongside French and English) exerted an enormous influence among Brazilian elites. Nevertheless, even if Brazilian Modernism broke culturally and linguistically with Portuguese literary influences, joint collaboration between Portuguese and Brazilian writers or the attempts to foster cultural exchanges between both countries never entirely ceased (for more information on this subject see Arnaldo Saraiva as well as João Almino).

[4] Alfredo Bosi distinguishes between the Portuguese chronicles that center on the "discovery" and description of Brazil and actual histories that reflect the experience of a colonial subject engaged in the construction of a new Luso-Brazilian reality (*História concisa* 24-25). In the first category, the most notable examples are the "Letter of Discovery" or *Carta de achamento* (1500) by Pêro Vaz de Caminha, as well as Pêro de Magalhães Gândavo's *História da Província de Santa Cruz a que vulgarmente chamamos Brasil* (1576), and Gabriel Soares de Sousa's encyclopedic *Tratado descritivo do Brasil em 1587*. In the second category, where a "proto-Brazilian" consciousness can already be detected, we find Frei Vicente do Salvador's *História do Brasil*

(1627), and André João Antonil's *Cultura e opulência do Brasil* (1711).

[5] The most prominent critics of Machado de Assis (Roberto Schwarz and John Gledson) consider him to be the first major Brazilian writer who succeeds in transcending national borders, not only due to his masterfully subtle art, but also through the "universal" resonance of his thematic concerns.

[6] The stereotype of the "Brazilian" (i.e., the Portuguese emigrant who goes to Brazil and eventually returns home rich) is particularly present in the works of one of the greatest nineteenth-century Portuguese novelists, Camilo Castelo Branco (see *Eusébio Macário* [1879] and *A brasileira de Prazins* [1882]).

[7] The most virulent manifestations of lusophobia appear in Brazilian naturalist novels of the late nineteenth century, namely in the works of Aluísio Azevedo (*O mulato,* 1881, or *Mulatto,* and *O cortiço,* 1890, or *The Slum: A Novel*) and Adolfo Caminha *(Bom Crioulo,* 1895, or *Bom-Crioulo: The Blackman and the Cabin Boy*). Raúl Pompéia, another prominent Brazilian naturalist, was notorious for his caustic journalistic attacks against the Portuguese (Vieira 127-29). They all reveal a profound resentment toward the large presence of Portuguese immigrants in Brazil during this period, where they held a virtual monopoly over the small business sector of the economy (i.e., small grocery stores, bakeries, restaurants, etc.). This was seen as a pernicious extension of Portuguese colonialism, even though Brazil had been independent for almost a century. This dynamic also attests to the amount of frustration on the part of Brazilian intellectuals with the lack of progress in Brazil; thus, the Portuguese became a convenient scapegoat, representing a possible cause of Brazil's socioeconomic ills (122).

Works Cited

Alencastro, Luiz Felipe de. *O trato dos viventes: Formação do Brasil no atlântico sul, séculos XVI e XVII.* São Paulo: Cia. das Letras, 2000.

Almino, João. "O diálogo interrompido." *Rumos* 1 (1999): 26-35.

Antonil, André João. *Cultura e opulência do Brasil.* São Paulo: Cia. Editora Nacional, 1967.

Azevedo, Aluísio. *O cortiço.* São Paulo: Ática, 1984.

———. *Mulatto.* Trans. Murray Graeme MacNicholl. Rutherford, NJ: Fairleigh Dickinson UP, 1990.

———. *O mulato.* São Paulo: Ática, 1992.

———. *The Slum: A Novel.* Trans. David H. Rosenthal. New York: Oxford UP, 2000.

Baganha, Maria Ioannis B. "Portuguese Emigration After World War II." *Modern Portugal.* Ed. António Costa Pinto. Palo Alto, CA: Society for the Promotion of Science and Scholarship, 1998.

Bosi, Alfredo. *Dialética da colonização.* São Paulo: Cia. das Letras, 1992.

———. *História concisa da literatura brasileira.* 32nd ed. São Paulo: Cultrix, 1994.

Branco, Camilo Castelo. *A brasileira de Prazins.* Mem-Martins: Europa-América, n. d.

———. *Eusébio Macário.* Mem Martins: Europa-América, n. d.

Caminha, Adolfo. *Bom-crioulo.* São Paulo: Ática, 1983.

———. *Bom-Crioulo: The Black man and the Cabin Boy.* Trans. E. A. Lacey. San Francisco: Gay Sunshine, 1982.

Caminha, Pêro Vaz de. *Carta de Pêro Vaz de Caminha a El-Rei D. Manuel sobre o achamento do Brasil.* Mem Martins: Europa-América, 1987.

Candido, Antonio. *Literatura e sociedade.* São Paulo: Cia. Editora Nacional, 1967.

Cervo, Amado, e José Calvet de Magalhães. *Depois das caravelas: as relações entre Portugal e Brasil, 1808-2000.* Brasília: Universidade de Brasília, 2000.

"FHC pede tolerância com divergências." *Folha Online.* 23 Apr. 2000 <http://www.uol.com.br/fsp/>.

Gândavo, Pêro de Magalhães. *Tratado da terra do Brasil; história da província de Santa Cruz.* Belo Horizonte: Itatiaia, 1980.

Linhares, Maria Yedda, ed. *História geral do Brasil.* Rio de Janeiro: Campus, 1990.

Lourenço, Eduardo. *A nau de Ícaro seguido de Imagem e miragem da lusofonia.* Lisboa: Gradiva, 1999.

Marques, A. H de Oliveira. *Breve história de Portugal.* Lisboa: Presença, 1995.

Mota, Carlos Guilherme and Fernando Novais. *O processo político da independência do Brasil.* São Paulo: Moderna, 1982.

Ribeiro, João Ubaldo. *Viva o povo brasileiro.* Rio de Janeiro: Nova Fronteira, 1984.

Salvador, Frei Vicente do. *História do Brasil.* Belo Horizonte: Itatiaia, 1982.

Santos, Boaventura de Sousa. *Pela mão de Alice.* Porto: Afrontamento, 1994.

————. "O espírito de Timor invade o Rio." *Jornal de letras, artes e ideias* (1999): 2.

————. "Between Prospero and Caliban: Colonialism, Postcolonialism, and Inter-Identity." *Luso-Brazilian Review* 39.2 (Winter 2002): 9-43.

Santos, Gilda, ed. *Brasil e Portugal: 500 anos de enlaces e desenlaces.* 2 vols. Rio de Janeiro: Real Gabinete Português de Leitura, 2001.

Saraiva, Arnaldo. *O modernismo brasileiro e o modernismo português.* Porto: Afrontamento, 1986.

Saraiva, José Hermano. *História de Portugal.* Mem Martins: Europa-América, 1993.

Sousa, Gabriel Soares de. *Tratado descriptivo do Brasil em 1587.* Rio de Janeiro: Cia. Editora Nacional, 1879.

Terra Estrangeira [Foreign Land]. Dir. Walter Salles. VideoFilmes, 1995.

Vieira, Nelson. *Brasil e Portugal: a imagem recíproca.* Lisboa: Instituto de Cultura e Língua Portuguesa, 1991.

Fernando Arenas is Associate Professor of Portuguese, Brazilian, and Lusophone African literary and cultural studies in the Department of Spanish and Portuguese Studies at the University of Minnesota. He is the author of *Utopias of Otherness: Nationhood and Subjectivity in Portugal and Brazil* (University of Minnesota Press, 2003) and co-editor together with Susan C. Quinlan of *Lusosex: Gender and Sexuality in the Portuguese-Speaking World* (University of Minnesota Press, 2002). In 2005-06, he received a Guggenheim Fellowship to finish working on his new book on Lusophone Africa, *After Independence: Globalization, "Neo-colonialism," and the Cultures of Portuguese-Speaking Africa.* He is also developing an on-going project on homoerotic desire in Brazilian and Portuguese cultures and literatures. E-mail: arena002@umn.edu.

Why Do Scholars Write Autobiographies? or: Exile as a "Comfortable" Metaphor[1]

João Cezar de Castro Rocha

Abstract. In the past decade an increasing number of scholars have written autobiographies, notably in the field of literary criticism. Is it possible to identify a pattern to those works? How do contemporary scholars face the dilemma of autobiography as a genre? Such questions aim at discussing autobiography as a fictional genre. Therefore, to read an autobiography one must pay attention to the rhetorical frame chosen by the author.

In the past decade an increasing number of scholars have written autobiographies, notably in the field of literary criticism. Indeed, Henry Louis Gates's *Colored People: A Memoir* (1994) and Frank Lentricchia's *The Edge of Night: A Confession* (1994) seem to have stimulated several colleagues to take up the pen. Is it possible to identify a pattern to these works? How do contemporary scholars face the dilemma of autobiography as a genre? After all, literary critics should be aware of the pitfalls of the genre. Among so many examples, two autobiographies have caught the eye of readers who are not necessarily concerned with literary studies: Edward Said's *Out of Place* (1999) and Terry Eagleton's *The Gatekeeper* (2001).

Edward Said portrays himself as being torn apart between two worlds as well as between two languages. In his words: "I have never known what language I spoke first, Arabic or English, or which was really mine beyond any

Portuguese Literary & Cultural Studies 7 (2008): 325-38.
© University of Massachusetts Dartmouth.

doubt. What I do know, however, is that the two have always been together in my life, one resonating in the other, sometimes ironically, sometimes nostalgically, most often each correcting, and commenting on, the other."[2] Indeed, this nomadic condition runs throughout the narrative and provides the frame for his self-definition: "I occasionally experience myself as a cluster of flowing currents. I prefer this to the idea of a solid self [...]."[3]

Terry Eagleton, one of the stars of (and rebels against) the "Oxbridge" system as well as the author of numerous works of literary criticism, also pictures himself as being torn apart. In his case, he feels divided between classes. Recalling his early years, he writes: "Literacy was not the strongest point of my childhood community. It was a world which would no more have understood how you could make a living by writing books than how you could make one by picking wax from your ears."[4] Both authors frame themselves as being fundamentally marginal, exiled in a potentially hostile environment.

As a matter of fact, the composition of scholars' autobiographies has a long tradition in which two models have become prevalent. On the one hand, the life of an accomplished scholar is commonly portrayed as being as uneventful as his work is regarded important. In this model, the true autobiography is the collection of his writings or the intensity of his readings—as Jorge Luis Borges would have it. David Hume conveyed it in the opening paragraph of *My Own Life*: "It is difficult for a man to speak of himself without vanity; therefore, I shall be short."[5] Dutiful in his observance of this creed, Hume summed up his existence in no more than a few eloquent pages, producing what today would be called a *curriculum vitae*: "It may be thought an instance of vanity that I pretend at all to write my life; but this Narrative shall contain little more than the History of my Writings."[6] This ideal of a life as unperturbed as possible by worldly affairs reveals how close the religious life was taken as a model to the scholar.

On the other hand, the figure of the uprooted has often been used to characterize both scholars and artists. From Ovid's poems in exile to Dante's memories of his own ostracism, the condition of the exile has almost become an existential commonplace to men of letters. Is it not true that in the nineteenth century the Romantic artist was an expert in presenting himself as a tormented soul exiled in his own complexity? Historically closer to our contemporary scholars, it is enough to recall the American writers of the 1920s: they made themselves famous as the "lost generation"—and happily so long as they were lost in the uncomfortable exile of Paris's avant-garde milieu. As

Said has himself acknowledged in a well-known essay: "If true exile is a condition of terminal loss, why has it been transformed so easily into a potent, even enriching, motif of modern culture? We have become accustomed to thinking of the modern period itself as spiritually orphaned and alienated."[7]

Said's and Eagleton's autobiographies are inextricably related to such models. Nonetheless, and in spite of being acclaimed literary critics, their efforts ironically fall short because they seem to believe in the capacity of their texts to live up to those models, especially to the *topos* of the exile. This will be my contention, and in order to unfold it I shall bring to the fore some earlier examples of intellectual autobiographies.

Hume wrote *My Own Life* in 1776. Some decades earlier, Giambattista Vico had already radicalized the convergence between life and work—or rather the absorption of life by work. In his *Life of Giambattista Vico written by Himself,* Vico resurrected Julius Caesar's rhetorical device of referring to oneself in the third person. His autobiography begins: "Giambattista Vico was born in Naples in the year 1670 of upright parents who left a good name after them."[8] This rhetorical device allowed for an unexpected answer to the often overlooked impossibility of the autobiography as a genre. Is it not true that it should always be too early to properly begin its composition? And is it not even truer that it should always be too late to adequately conclude it? After all, how to find a proper conclusion to the narrative while the writer is composing it? How to reconcile the paradox of temporarily suspending the act of "living" in order to recall one's own life through its writing? The endless fascination caused by Laurence Sterne's *Tristram Shandy* seems to be directly related to this inner contradiction. The main character of the novel cannot reconstruct his life in an orderly fashion precisely because he keeps on living it intently in his infinite digressions and chaotic dialogues.

If the beginning of any autobiography is always arbitrary, how to write the scene of one's own death, unless the autobiographer becomes a fictional afterlife narrator of his passing away? Vico started his autobiography in 1723, added a new section in 1728 and "completed" it in 1731. However, he would "only" die in 1744. A curious reader cannot fail to wonder what happened in the remaining years of Vico's life. Hume intuited it keenly while referring to his autobiography as "this funeral oration of myself."[9]

The Brazilian writer Machado de Assis, a creative and productive reader of Sterne's *Tristram Shandy* as well as of Lucian's *Dialogues of the Dead,* imagined an ingenious solution to the dilemma of autobiography by developing Hume's self-irony. In *The Posthumous Memoirs of Brás Cubas*, the main character decides to produce an account of his life at the indisputably proper moment of doing it, namely, after his death. As a "deceased author" he is perfectly equipped not only to remember episodes of his entire life, but as a traditional third person narrator he is able to locate them in a meaningful account, attributing to each episode a specific place. Seemingly, a "deceased author" is the ideal narrator to remember episodes of all phases of his life, including above all his own death. As the character ponders over his narrative choice, he thinks: "I am not exactly a writer who is dead but a dead man who is a writer, for whom the grave was a second cradle."[10] The autobiography, then, should become the writing of "mémoires d'outre tombe." In other words, the autobiography as a genre would not be an impossibility so long as it learns to overcome Daniel Defoe's description of the hardships involved in providing a full account of Moll Flanders's story: "We cannot say indeed, that this History is carried on quite to the End of the Life of this Famous *Moll Flanders*, as she calls her self, for no Body can write it after they are dead [...]."[11] Charles Darwin understood this paradox perfectly, transforming it into the underlying motivation of his autobiography: "I have attempted to write the following account of myself, as if I were a dead man in another world looking back at my own life."[12]

It should also be stressed that the solution adopted by Vico has a practical advantage: once the philosopher employed the third person in his narrative, 74 years after Vico's death, an admirer of his work, the Marquis of Villarosa, could satisfy the curious reader concluding Vico's autobiography with no difficulty. In 1818 he added the section, "Vico's Last Years." The Marquis only needed to provide a brief transition and then to keep the same third person narrator: "Now that Vico had become, as he himself tells us, the father of a large family [...]." This fine transition is a powerful illustration of the overlooked impossibility of the autobiography as a genre unless its fictionality is fully acknowledged. Vico's 1728 and 1731 additions to his original narrative already conveyed the dilemma of finding a plausible manner of "concluding" the account.

Indeed, Defoe had already fictionally offered an answer to Vico's difficulties. In the sequence from which the above-mentioned passage is taken, he informs the reader: "[...] but her Husband's Life being written by a third Hand, gives a full account of them both."[13] Nevertheless, it should be noted that Vico's choice meant much more than simply a stylistic device, once the "third Hand" literally became Vico's use of a third person narrator. That is to say, while choosing this usage to refer to his life, Vico concocted a new genre, in which life molds itself after the work. In this sense, every work is always already autobiographical, since life is (or should be) the embodiment of work.

How does this take place in Vico's text? His conception of history, as developed in his masterpiece, *New Science*, implied the underlying design of Providence guiding the actions of humankind. Ultimately, Vico's autobiography reproduces the same pattern. It is as if every single accident in his life destined him to become the author of *New Science*. Immediately at the beginning of his account, the reader is offered a key to interpret it. Vico describes a tremendous fall from a ladder when he was seven years of age. Doctors thought that he would not recover. In the best scenario, he would survive but with serious consequences: "The surgeon, indeed, observing the broken cranium and considering the long period of unconsciousness, predicted that he would either die of it or grow up an idiot."[14] As the reading of *Life of Giambattista Vico written by Himself* suggests, the diagnosis was mistaken. Moreover, through this incident, Vico establishes the model of his intellectual journey: a self-taught man, independent from institutions; a person always able to recover from unhappy events, the most notorious being his defeat in the election of a Chair at the University of Naples;[15] someone willing to bear any sacrifice and seclusion in order to fully develop his mind. In a nutshell, the young Italian already appears as the predestined creator of a new science. In this way his own life prefigures the philosophy he later developed.

Edward Said resorts to a similar pattern, and at the beginning of his narrative offers a metaphor for its reading: "All families invent their parents and children, give each of them a story, a character, fate, and even a language. [...] Thus it took me about fifty years to become accustomed to, or, more exactly, to feel less uncomfortable with, 'Edward', a foolish English name yoked forcibly to the unmistakably Arabic family name Said."[16] The author seems to project retrospectively his reflections on exile upon his own christening, evidencing the rhetorical construction of individual memory: the apparently odd mixture of an English and an Arabic name would have "contributed" to Said's future personal dilemma. This operation brings to one's mind Sterne's character, Tristram Shandy, whose name was mistakenly attributed at the moment of his registry. Tristram's father had chosen an honorable name for his son: "He shall be christened *Trimegistus*."[17] The reasons could not be more persuasive; after all, "he was the greatest king—the greatest lawgiver—the greatest philosopher."[18] Nonetheless, thanks to an unhappy misunderstanding, the newborn is christened Tristram, an incident that seemingly "determines" most of his personality as well as his awkwardness throughout his life.

Eagleton too utilizes a similar strategy in order to provide an interpretive frame for his account. We have already seen how uncommon literacy was in his childhood community. It will not be surprising then to find that, "Later in life, I was to overcompensate for the uncertain literacy of my early environment. Whereas other academics worry about not being productive enough, my embarrassment has always been the opposite. Instead of finding myself unable to write books, I find myself unable to stop."[19] In other words, both authors cope with the challenge of the autobiographical genre by employing a traditional nineteenth-century narrative device used widely in realist novels, according to which the life of the character, that is, Said's and Eagleton's lives, unfold in accordance to a powerful event or a decisive drive, providing coherence and cohesion to a myriad of events.

On the contrary, while Vico also provided an all-encompassing metaphor that meaningfully organized his experiences, his solution to the dilemma of autobiography is far more complex. It actually implies the discovery of a novel relationship. Instead of primarily recalling one's private life, a scholar's autobiography should become the story of the work accomplished, an account of the development and succession of themes and ideas. In this sense, David Hume followed the Italian's lead. Vico's use of the third person remains an extremely insightful finding. On the one hand, it textualizes the subsumption of life into work. On the other hand, it prompts a level of self-reflexiveness that in itself brings to the fore the model of critically detaching the autobiographer from his own "life" in order to stress the results of the "work."

In other words, given the inner contradiction of autobiography as a genre, it demands a narrative structure within which this contradiction becomes functional. Therefore, in order to write one's autobiography it is necessary to fictionally see one's life as if it is already "finished." Let us recall the beginning of Vico's *Life*, which is a case in point: "Giambattista Vico was born in Naples in the year 1670 [...]."[20] Vico was born in 1688. Why Vico "forgot" the exact date of his own birth is due simply to his desire to picture himself as a prodigy. Thus, the detachment propitiated by the usage of the third person does not necessarily keep one from the vanity associated by David Hume with the writing of autobiographies.

Therefore, because the autobiography should rely on an immediate level of referentiality—the life of the writer who writes of his own life (and the tautology is insurmountable) can only become possible through the acknowledgement of its own fictionality. Silviano Santiago, one of the most important Brazilian contemporary writers as well as a noted literary critic, in his latest novels and short stories has put forward the thought-provoking model of "faked memories" or "true lies." His latest collection of short stories, *Histórias mal contadas*, represents an insightful re-reading of the genre, and it is worth mentioning his achievement in the context of acknowledging the fictional drive implied in the autobiographical gesture. After all, is it not true that the gesture implied in the autobiographical narrative necessarily involves the most fictional act of temporarily suspending the act of "living?" Thus, if, according to Wolfgang Iser, fictionality, in its specific literary form,[21] is an anthropological device through which we can approach what otherwise could not be conceived, and if, "inaccessible to us are the cardinal points of our existence—the beginning and the end," then the autobiography as a genre reveals itself as a powerful fictional gesture that, given "the impossibility of being present to ourselves becomes our possibility to play ourselves out to the fullness that knows no bounds."[22] Is it not also true that autobiography allows the temporary overcoming of the most rigid bound of all? Death itself seems to be indefinitely postponed by the adversary register of one's life.

For this reason, Philipe Lejeune's *Le Pacte autobiographique* must be called into question. According to Lejeune, the autobiographical pact implies a direct link between the author, the narrator and the character depicted in the narrative: "Pour qu'il y ait autobiographie (et plus généralement littérature intime) il faut qu'il y ait identité de l'*auteur*, du *narrateur* et du *personage*."[23] This pact implies that the author uses the first person narrator since he is truthfully writing about a character that happens to be himself. Of course, an immediate relationship between the author and the object of the text cannot be denied, since it is the minimum prerequisite of the autobiography as a genre. However, and contrary to what Lejeune seems to believe, this relationship does not preclude the fictionality of the text; rather, it requires the constitutive presence of a fictional drive in the autobiographical account. Again, in order to write one's autobiography it is necessary to see one's life as if it is already "finished." As Hayden White proposes in *Metahistory*, the historian can only cope with the past when he organizes it through the ordering of the events into the mold of a specific narrative structure.[24] I am suggesting that similarly the author of an autobiographical text can only see himself and his own unfinished "past" through the lens of a literary model. Hence, to read an autobiography one must pay attention to the rhetorical frame chosen by the author to publicly present his life, although very often the rhetoric of the genre proclaims itself indifferent to the nature of its composition. Charles Darwin's statement is a common place: "I have taken no pains about my style of writing."[25] Edward Gibbon was equally straightforward: "the style shall be simple and familiar."[26] Simplicity and verisimilitude are supposed to strengthen each other, as we have learned since the classical codification of genres.

This rhetorical framing brings us back to Edward Said and Terry Eagleton. Contrary to the model of the uneventful existence of a scholar, they willingly share intimate details of their lives, not bothering to relate them to their intellectual achievements. For instance, Eagleton introduces the reader to his family without reservations. We meet his father, whose "life had the unattractiveness of the victim. Like many a parent, he sacrificed himself for his children, but that made him precisely not a model to emulate."[27] We also become acquainted with his grandmother, who "combined working-class poverty with petty-bourgeois values, and so was afflicted with the worst of both worlds."[28] This caricature of intimacy was already present in Frank Lentricchia's *The Edge of Night*: "About a year ago, in New York, an editor of a major publishing house said to me that I ought, up front, tell my readers who I am. Otherwise readers would have to crawl inside my head."[29] It seems that not only Lentricchia but also Said and Eagleton believe the editor's unexpected assumption. They have produced autobiographies that are full of intimate episodes and only incidentally concerned with their readings and writings. Maybe this is the reason why Lentricchia entertains the reader with such important information as this, conveyed with remarkable precision: "I leave on the USAir Ticket counter the sunglasses I wear 300 to 325 days per year."[30] Sometimes, literary critics can also indulge in unabashed narcissism, or vanity, to recall Hume's vocabulary: "I'll tell you what I like about writing. When I'm doing it, there's only the doing, the movement of my pen across the paper, the shape of the rhythms as I go, myself the rhythm."[31] A couple of years later, allowing the reader to enter his mind without having to make too much effort, Lentricchia provides another confession, this time a little more surprising, if not embarrassing. He reveals the name of his mistress: "My silent encounters with literature are ravishingly pleasurable like erotic transport. In private I was tranquility personified; in public, an actor in the endless strife and divisiveness of argument […]."[32] Of course, it is an important symptom that a noted literary theorist has to entertain a secret life in which he mainly reads… literary works.

It is indeed not a novelty that an editor's invitation prompts the composition of an autobiography. Vico's *Life* was written under the patronage of the Count Porcía, who sponsored "autobiographies for the edification of young students and with a view to the reform of school and curricula."[33] Darwin similarly justified his incursion into the genre: "A German editor having written to me to ask for an account of the development of my mind and character with some sketch of my autobiography."[34] Vico and Darwin were engaged in the classical tradition of transmitting one's experiences and knowledge to posterity, which implied circumspection and an emphasis on the work accomplished. Gibbon's opening lines of his autobiography are paradigmatic: "In the fifty-second year of my age, after the completion of a toilsome and successful work, I now propose to employ some moments of my leisure in reviewing the simple transactions of a private and literary life."[35] Said's, Eagleton's, and above all Lentricchia's memoirs are symptomatic of the contemporary state of affairs in the academic world, which has been poignantly unveiled by David Shumway in his critique of "the star system in literary studies," whose most visible sign is directly related to the unheard-of exposition of the intimacy of scholars: "The importance of gossip and of other types of public discussion of the private lives of the stars is manifested in the current rash of autobiographies written by literary academics."[36]

This difference prompts another one regarding the *topos* of the exile. While employing this classical *topos*, Said and Eagleton refer to a literary tradition that ultimately prevents them from seriously "believing" in the uniqueness or in the "truth" of their narratives. The rhetorical codes are well-known: the exiled feels torn between his homeland and his present location, and often this feeling is conveyed through the difficulties with an unknown or a poorly controlled language; this feeling favors a melancholic mood, which aims at winning the audience's sympathies for the author's condition. In other words, the *topos* of exile fosters an amicable reception that should in itself provide shelter to the exiled writer. Perhaps this is why the exile has "been transformed so easily into a potent, even enriching, motif of modern culture," recalling Said's question mentioned above. The exile offers a compelling metaphor as well as, at least in some cases, a complex manner of finding an especially detached vantage point that potentially fosters an acute critical perspective. According to Said, "James Joyce *chose* to be in exile: to give force to his artistic vocation. […]

And although it is rare to pick banishment as a way of life, Joyce perfectly understood its trials."[37] Vilém Flusser—a Czech philosopher who had to flee his homeland in order to escape the Nazis and who lived in Brazil for several decades until he returned to Europe and became widely acclaimed as an innovative media theorist—has developed a challenging "philosophy of emigration."[38] In this philosophy, Flusser proposes that "taking up residence in homelessness,"[39] although initially a painful experience, makes it possible "to interpret the exile situation as a challenge to creativity."[40] Of course, Flusser is not romanticizing the condition of being expelled from one's own country. Nonetheless, he is proposing a crucial critical distinction between intellectuals and those who usually do not have the opportunity to voice their indignation and protest while exiled. This distinction is obviously at stake in my reading of the recent autobiographies written by literary critics.

The problem with Said's *Out of Place* and Eagleton's *The Gatekeeper* is that they seem to believe that the *topos* of exile properly fits the social role of stars in the academic world. They apparently do not realize that they have created a paradoxical instance: the institutional and officially supported exile. Usually scholars who portray themselves as exiled or marginalized in autobiographies are successful enough to have caught the eye of publishers eager not to engage the reader in their intellectual achievements but to expose their lives as if they had suddenly become celebrities. These "exiled" scholars are indeed acclaimed authors, and worldwide respected academics. Ovid's exile, for instance, was much more than a *topos*. While exiled, he composed *Tristia* (A.D. 9), hoping to bridge a return to Rome with his poetry: "*Parve, nec invideo, sine me, Liber, ibis in Urbem, / Hei mihi! quo domino non licet ire tuo*" ["Go alone, Book that I envy, to the Urbis, / Where, poor me!, your master is not allowed to go"]. In spite of lines such as these, neither Augustus nor Tiberius forgave the poet. Exiled from Rome to the peripheral village of Tomos in A.D. 8, Ovid died there ten years later.

By contrast, for successful scholars exile has become a literary model through which they try to anticipate a criticism that, precisely because they are successful, is not often voiced. While mainly writing on behalf of marginalized cultures or classes, they have manufactured their careers at the very center they strongly criticize. The irony is self-evident. Perhaps through the *topos* of exile they attempt to see themselves as not having reached the top—where indeed they have been throughout their professional lives, due to their own intellectual merits, it must be noted. The problem is that to do so they have to write denying the critical gaze with which they taught their students to read. In other words, they become not exactly "naïve readers," that ideal figure dreamed of by some schools of close reading, but "naïve authors," the ideological figure denounced by critics such as Lentricchia, Said and Eagleton.

Let me then conclude by bringing to this discussion Joseph Brodsky's uncompromising reflection on exile, which echoes Vilém Flusser's distinction mentioned above. We have not yet fully developed an approach that might be able to carry forward the toughness of a writer who resists any self-indulgence regarding the understanding of his troubled and complex personal circumstance:

> As we gather here, in this attractive and well-lit room, on this cold December evening, to discuss the plight of the writer in exile, let us pause for a minute and think of some of those who, quite naturally, didn't make it to this room. [...] Whatever the proper name for this phenomenon is, whatever the motives, origins, and destinations of these people are, whatever their impact on the societies which they abandon and to which they come, one thing is absolutely clear: they make it very difficult to talk with a straight face about the plight of the writer in exile.[41]

Notes

[1] A much shorter version of this essay was originally published in the *Geisteswissenschaften* section of the *Frankfurter Allgemeine Zeitung*, on 4 September 2002, as "Exil as Metapher des Behagens." I would like to thank the encouragement given to me by Henning Ritter and Hans Ulrich Gumbrecht, as well as their friendly and yet rigorous criticism.

[2] Said, *Out of Place* 4.

[3] *Idem* 295.

[4] Eagleton 51.

[5] Hume xxxi.

[6] *Idem, ibidem.*

[7] Said, "Reflections" 173.

[8] Vico 111.

[9] Hume xli. The full passage reads: "I cannot say that there is no vanity in making this funeral oration of myself, but I hope it is not a misplaced one; and this is a matter of fact which is easily cleared and ascertained."

[10] Assis 7.

[11] Defoe 5.

[12] Darwin 21.

[13] Defoe 5.

[14] Vico 111.

[15] "The decisive event in Vico's life was his failure in the academic 'concourse' or competition of 1723. He was then fifty-five years of age, and had lingered for nearly a quarter of a century in the propaedeutic chair of rhetoric, whose main function was to prepare students for admission to the law course. It paid a miserable hundred ducats a year" (Fisch 8).

[16] Said, "Reflections" 3.

[17] Sterne 202.

[18] *Idem* 205.

[19] Eagleton 54-55.

[20] *Idem, ibidem.*

[21] It is important to realize that, "since both the fictive and the imaginary feature anthropological dispositions, they are not confined to literature but also play a role in our everyday lives" (Iser xiii).

[22] *Idem* 297.

[23] Lejeune 15. Regarding the referentiality, see the following passage: "L' autobiographie étant un genre referential, elle est naturellement soumise en même temps à l'impératif de resemblance au niveau du modèle, mais ce n'est qu'un aspect secondaire" (40).

[24] "I treat the historical work as what it most manifestly is: a verbal structure in the form of a narrative prose discourse. Histories (and philosophies of history as well) combine certain amount of 'data', theoretical concepts for 'explaining' these data, and a narrative structure for their presentation as an icon of sets of events presumed to have occurred in times past" (White ix).

[25] Darwin 21.

[26] Gibbon 39.

[27] Eagleton 115.

[28] *Idem* 117

[29] Lentricchia 5-6.

[30] *Idem* 62.

[31] *Idem* 7.

[32] Lentricchia 25.

[33] Fisch 2.

[34] Darwin 21.

[35] Gibbon 39.

[36] Shumway 96.

[37] Said. "Reflections" 182, author's emphasis.

[38] Flusser, *Freedom of the Migrant* 21-24.

[39] Flusser, *Writings* 91-103.

[40] Flusser *Writings* 104.

[41] Brodsky 22-23. I owe Henning Ritter for this reference.

Works Cited

Assis, Machado de. *The Posthumous Memoirs of Brás Cubas.* Trans. Gregory Rabassa. Oxford: Oxford UP, 1997.

Brodsky, Joseph. "The Condition we call Exile or Acorns Aweigh." *On Grief and Reason: Essays.* New York: FSG, 1994.

Darwin, Charles. *The Autobiography of Charles Darwin.* Ed. Nora Barlow. New York: Norton, 1993.

Defoe, Daniel. *Moll Flanders.* Oxford: Oxford UP, 1971.

Eagleton, Terry. *The Gatekeeper. A Memoir.* London: Penguin, 2001.

Fisch, Max Harold. Introduction. *The Autobiography of Giambattista Vico.* Trans. Max Harold Fisch & Thomas Goddard Bergin. Ithaca: Cornell UP, 1995.

Flusser, Vilém. *Writings.* Ed. Andreas Ströhl. Trans. Erik Eisel. Minneapolis: U of Minnesota P, 2002.

———.*The Freedom of the Migrant. Objections to Nationalism.* Ed. Anke K. Finger. Trans. Kenneth Kronenberg. Urbana: U of Illinois P, 2003.

Gates, Henry Louis, Jr. *Colored People: A Memoir.* New York: Vintage, 1994.

Gibbon, Edward. *Memoirs of my Life.* London: Penguin, 1984.

Hume, David. "My own Life." *Essays. Moral, Political and Literary.* Indianapolis: Liberty Fund, 1985.

Iser, Wolfgang. *The Fictive and the Imaginary. Charting Literary Anthropology.* Baltimore: Johns Hopkins UP, 1993.

Lejeune, Philippe. *Le Pacte autobiographique.* Nouvelle edition augmentée. Paris: Éditions du Seuil, 1996.

Lentricchia, Frank. *The Edge of Night. A Confession.* New York: Random House, 1994.

———. "Last Will and Testament of an ex-Literary Critic." *Quick Studies. The Best of* Lingua Franca. Ed. Alexander Star. New York: FSG, 2002.

Lucian. *Dialogues of the Dead, Dialogues of the Sea-Gods; Dialogues of the Gods, Dialogues of the Courtesans.* Trans. M.D. Macleod. Cambridge, MA: Harvard UP, 1961.

Rocha, João Cezar de Castro. "Exil as Metapher des Behagens." *Frankfurter Allgemeine Zeitung* 4 Sept. 2002.

Said, Edward. *Out of Place. A Memoir.* London: Granta, 1999.

———. "Reflections on Exile." *Reflections on Exile and Other Literary and Cultural Essays.* London: Granta, 2001.

Shumway, David R. "The Star System in Literary Studies." *PMLA* 112.1 (Jan. 1997): 85-100.

Sterne, Laurence. *The Life and Opinions of Tristram Shandy. A Gentleman.* New York: Norton, 1980.

Vico, Giambattista. *The Autobiography of Giambattista Vico.* Trans. Max Harold Fisch & Thomas Goddard Bergin. Ithaca: Cornell UP, 1995.

White, Hayden. *Metahistory. The Historical Imagination in Nineteenth-Century Europe.* Baltimore: Johns Hopkins UP, 1973.

João Cezar de Castro Rocha is Professor of Comparative Transatlantic Studies at the University of Manchester, where he is Program Director of the MA in Latin American Cultural Studies. Author of *Literatura e cordialidade—o público e o privado na cultura brasileira* (1998, "Mário de Andrade Award," Biblioteca Nacional) and *O exílio do homem cordial—ensaios e revisões.* E-mail: Joao.De-castro-rocha@manchester.ac.uk

The God Factor

José Saramago
Translated by
George Monteiro

Somewhere in India. A row of artillery pieces in place. Attached to the mouth of each one of them there is a man. In the first frame of the photograph a British officer raises his sword and is about to give the order to fire. We are not exposed to images showing the effects of those discharges, but even the most obtuse imagination can "see" heads and torsos scattered over the killing field, bloody remains, viscera, amputated members. The men were rebels. Somewhere in Angola. Two Portuguese soldiers lift up by his arms a negro who quite possibly is not dead; another soldier grasps a machete and gets ready to separate his head from his body. That's the first photograph. In the second one—this time there is a second photograph—the head has already been cut off and spiked on a stick; the soldiers are laughing. The negro was a guerrilla. Somewhere in Israel. While some Israeli soldiers immobilize a Palestinian, another soldier hammers into the bones in his right hand. The Palestinian had thrown stones. The United States of North-America, New York City. Two North-American commercial planes, hijacked by terrorists connected to Islamic righteousness, smash into the towers of the World Trade Center and bring them down. Following the same procedure a third plane causes enormous damage to the Pentagon, the seat of United States war power. The dead—buried in the rubble, reduced to crumbs, vaporized—are counted by the thousands.

The photographs of India, Angola and Israel hurl their horror in our

Portuguese Literary & Cultural Studies 7 (2008): 339-42.
© University of Massachusetts Dartmouth.

faces; victims are shown to us at the very moment of their torturing, of their agonizing expectation, of their ignoble death. In New York everything seemed unreal at first, an episode, repeated without novelty, of still another cinematic catastrophe, really striking in the degree of illusion achieved by special-effects engineering, but devoid of death rattles, blood-bursts, crushed flesh, shattered bones, or feces. Horror, crouching like an obscene animal, waited until we got over our stupefaction to leap at our throats. Horror said "here I am" for the first time when those persons leapt into space as if they had just selected a form of death of their choosing. Now horror will appear whenever a stone is removed, part of a wall, a sheet of twisted aluminum, to reveal an unrecognizable head, an arm, a leg, an unraveled abdomen, a flattened thorax. But even this will be repetitive and monotonous, already familiar, in a certain sense, from those images that came to us from that Rwanda-of-a-million-dead, that Vietnam scorched by napalm, those executions in crowded stadiums, those lynchings and beatings of Iraqi soldiers buried alive under tons of sand, those atomic bombs that leveled and pulverized Hiroshima and Nagasaki, the Nazi crematorium vomiting ash, those trucks dumping cadavers as if they were trash. We all must die of something or other, but we have lost count of the human beings dead in the worst ways possible that humankind has been able to invent. One of those, the most criminal, the most absurd, the one that most offends simple reason, is that one that, since the beginnings of time and of civilizations, has called for the dealing of death in God's name. It has been said that all religions, without exception, have never served to reconcile or to bring human beings together; that, on the contrary, they have been and continue to be the cause of indescribable sufferings and massacres, of the monstrous physical and spiritual violence that constitutes one of the darkest chapters in mankind's miserable history. As a sign of our respect for life, at least, we should have the courage to proclaim under all circumstances this evident and demonstrable truth, but the majority of the faithful of all religions not only pretend not to know it, but rise up, enraged and intolerant, against those for whom God is nothing more but a name, nothing more than the name that, fearing death, we gave him one day and that would come to block our steps to a real humanization. In exchange they promised us paradises and threatened us with infernos, one as much a fake as the other—shameless insults to the intelligence and common sense that cost us so much effort to bring about. Nietzsche said that all was permissible if God did not exist, and I reply that it is precisely because of God and in God's name that everything has been permitted and justified, principally the worst of things, principally the most cruel and horrendous. For centuries the Inquisition— it, too, a terrorist organization, like today's Taliban, one dedicated to a perverse interpretation of sacred texts that should merit the respect of those who say they believe in them—was a monstrous union between Religion and State against liberty of conscience and against the most human of rights: the right to say no, the right to heresy, the right to chose something else, which is what the word heresy signifies.

And yet, God is innocent. Innocent as something that does not exist, that has never existed or will ever exist. Innocent of having created an entire universe to house beings capable of committing the grossest crimes only to justify themselves by saying that they are celebrations of his power and of his glory, even as the dead mount up, these of the twin towers in New York, and all the others who, in the name of a God turned assassin through the will and actions of men, have covered and insist on covering the pages of History with blood and terror. Gods, I find, exist only in the human brain, prosper or languish in the same universe that invented them, but the "God factor"—that is present in life as if it were effectively life's lord and master. It is not a god, but the "God factor" that is exhibited on the dollar bill and that expresses itself on billboards that ask for a divine blessing for America (the America of the United States, not the other one). And it was the "God factor" the god of Islam transformed itself into that was hurled against the World Trade Center towers in planes revolting against contempt and in vengeance for humiliation. It might be said that one god went around sowing winds and that another god now responds with storms. It is possible; it's even right. But it was not they, those poor, blameless gods, but it was the "God factor," which is terrifyingly equal in all human beings no matter where they come from or whatever religion they profess, which has intoxicated thought and opened the doors to the most sordid forms of intolerance, which respects only it own beliefs, and which having supposedly made the beast into man ended by turning man into a beast.

Of the reader who is a believer (of whatever belief) who has managed to take the repugnance that these words have probably aroused in him, I do not ask that he go over to the atheism of the one who has written them. I simply ask that he understand, through feeling if not reason, that if God exists, there exists only one God, and that, in his relations with him, what matters least is the name by which he has been taught to call him. And that he watch out for the "God factor." The human spirit does not lack for enemies, but "God factor" is among the most obstinate and corrosive of them—as has been demonstrated and shall continue to be so disgracefully demonstrated.

José Saramago is the 1998 Nobel Prize for Literature.

George Monteiro's most recent books are *The Presence of Camões* (1996), *The Presence of Pessoa* (1998), *Stephen Crane's Blue Badge of Courage* (2000), and *Fernando Pessoa and Nineteenth-Century Anglo-American Literature* (2000). Forthcoming are bilingual editions of Miguel Torga's *Poemas Ibéricos*, Pedro da Silveira's *Poemas Ausentes*, and *Selected Poems* by Jorge de Sena. He is currently at work on two other books, *The English Face of Fernando Pessoa* and *Elizabeth Bishop's Brazilian Beat*. "The Bureaucratic Tale of the Harbor-Master and the Collector of Customs," his translation of a story by José Saramago, appeared in *PLCS 6*. Email: georgemonteiro@prodigy.net

The God Maker: A Reply to Saramago

Pedro Schachtt Pereira

> Comment "parler religion?" de la religion? Singulièrement de la religion, aujourd' hui? Comment oser en parler au singulier sans crainte et tremblement à ce jour? Et si peu et si vite? Qui aurait l'impudence de prétendre qu'il s'agit là d'un sujet à la fois identifiable et nouveau?
>
> Jacques Derrida, *Foi et Savoir. Les deux sources de la "religion" aus limites de la simple raison.*

In a long-forgotten text published in 1969,[1] Maurice Blanchot offers a meditation on the elusiveness of atheism, mostly by showing how humanism, understood as the discourse of the death of God, is still a "theological myth" (248). Writing in the aftermath of the publication of *The Order of Things: An Archeology of the Human Sciences,* the French writer-philosopher had as his intended targets those who, primarily in France (but soon after everywhere else), had not been able to read Foucault's (in)famous proclamation about the disappearance of man—"it is reassuring and profoundly calming to think that man is no more than a recent invention, a simple fold in our knowledge, and that he will disappear as soon as he has found a new form" (247)— beyond its superficial facetiousness, and surrendered to a facile and shallow controversy over the scandal of the "end of humanism."

In his serene and piercingly rigorous prose, Blanchot lets us see how the threat to humanism lurks instead within its very formulation. Rather than

Portuguese Literary & Cultural Studies 7 (2008): 343-46.
© University of Massachusetts Dartmouth.

being the victim of a late-coming nihilism, humanism is always already undermined by the Sovereignty that it inherited from the theological era: when God dies, man is endowed with the Promethean powers that allow him to found and create, to found and create *himself,* thus being configured in a relation with finitude as much as with the absolute. Whether God's rival or his replacement, man is still thought with the same categories used to think the divine logos, Blanchot reminds us. This is, after all, the allure and the trap of Feuerbach. We can postulate that man is God's true creator who alienates himself whenever he renders cult to his creation; however, whenever we think man as the bearer of meaning, and we think meaning as light, and language as the expression of a meaning that precedes it, we are insisting on the traits that, within atheism, "perpetuate what is essential to the divine logos." Atheism remains, alas, a pure pretension, and it never speaks in the first person, since the "I," the ego, in its self-founded autonomy, "constitutes itself by way of the unmitigated theological project."

There was a time when statements like these were the bread and butter of public debates. Even in Portugal this text deserved, many years ago, the attention of a young Eduardo Prado Coelho[2] who, trying to stir a debate with the musty Catholicism and social realism that stifled the literary and political milieu of the sixties, managed at least to maintain a sophisticated soliloquy. But *these* are hard times, when, after the recent death of one of the great philosophers of the century, a major newspaper in the United States happily celebrates "the end of theory." When punditry replaces critical inquiry, "theory" becomes anachronistic; we are from now on devoted to the untimely.

These untimely remarks and this delayed homage to Blanchot arrive by way of a brief commentary on a very timely text by José Saramago, previously published in Spanish and Portuguese newspapers and now included in this issue of *PLCS*. In it we are reminded of many of the violent scenarios that tarnished with nameless horror the last and the present centuries; violence perpetrated by man against defenseless man, often in the name of God. Scenarios of what Hannah Arendt once called "the banality of evil." We are also urged to watch out for, not God—who, after all, and in a Feuerbachian fashion, exists "only in the human brain,"—but mainly the "God Factor," a term that Saramago coins in order to convey a religious representation that "is present in life as if it were effectively life's lord and master." Aside from being "the most obstinate and corrosive" of enemies of "the human spirit," he sustains, it is also "terrifyingly equal in all human beings no matter where they come from or whatever religion they profess." Furthermore, this religious representation, "having supposedly made the beast into man ended by turning man into a beast."

These are very momentous statements that, in these times of "the return of the religious," we should all take very seriously. In this limited space, though, and in all seriousness, we have to restrict ourselves to raising some questions and sharing some perplexities.

The first one deals with equality: if the "God factor" is equal in all human beings, shouldn't we include in that number those who do not profess any religion except for that of atheism? Because if, as Saramago sustains (in a very monotheistic language, let us add in passing), God himself is innocent of the violence perpetrated in his name, then we are led to conclude that those who kill in the name of God are the true non-believers, the only consistent atheists. And this leads us to a further, more disquieting perplexity: if the "God factor" is a human product, equally present in all humans, how can we keep thinking of it as the enemy among all enemies of "the human spirit," and how will we keep believing that it is responsible for blocking "our steps to a real humanization"? Instead, isn't it time that we see the "God factor" as the hallmark and the flesh and blood of the "human spirit," one of the least elusive vestiges of what something like a "real humanization" can be? The "God factor" may well have turned man into a beast, but isn't man the only known beast capable of gratuitous violence? If we had the time to investigate, we would find that the bestiary, the *homo hominis lupus,* belongs, after all, to the very language and tradition that Saramago wants us to suspect as a religious one: the tradition that has been called humanism. Wouldn't we be wise to think, taking Blanchot's propositions seriously, that the "God factor" is first of all a certain relationship with language? And that, therefore, "those for whom God is nothing more than a name," to quote Saramago once more, that group to which he wants to belong, are still forgetting how weighty words can be, particularly those words that are capable of making gods? Aren't they still forgetting how elusive atheism can be, especially when it is still and again an affirmation, that of the absence of God?

Because the language of exhortation, injunction, and appellation is used with some degree of comfort—and to comfortably conflate man and beast, atheism and humanism, and, most notoriously, vigilance and the "human spirit"—one is led to presuppose that there is, behind such conflations and comforts, a knowledge of what these words mean and what their use implies.

This knowledge must be what confers authority over he who possesses it (and we find a consistency, perhaps involuntary, in the use of the personal pronoun "he"); yet, interestingly enough, this is an authority that allows the knowledgeable columnist to excuse himself from interrogating the presuppositions of both his knowledge and his authority. However, isn't it precisely by interrogating the theoretical and ideological foundations of one's discourse that we will be able to take strides in preventing, ever so precariously, the threat of the "God factor"?

Thinking interrogatively is now a luxury that very few can afford, and perhaps we should not be too demanding in the face of real adversity. But, in these hard times, when "the human spirit" and "human dignity" are but the commonplaces of the late-coming empire-builders, I would like to give that thinking a chance, by letting Blanchot speak once more, perhaps risking untimeliness: "Let us then not drag the thought of 'humanism' into a debate where this word's use would suffice for its understanding."

Notes

[1] "L'Athéisme et L'Écriture. L'Humanisme et le Cri." *L'Entretien Infini*. Paris: Gallimard, 1965. I am using the English version by Susan Hanson, "Atheism and Writing. Humanism and the Cry." *The Infinite Conversation*. Minneapolis and London: U of Minnesota P, 1993.

[2] See "Notas (polémicas) para um anti-humanismo," in *O Reino Flutuante. Exercícios sobre a razão e o discurso*. Lisboa: edições 70, 1972.

Works Cited

Blanchot, Maurice. "L'Athéisme et L'Écriture. L'Humanism et le Cri." *L'entretien Infini*. Paris: Gallimard, 1965.

Coelho, Eduardo Prado. "Notas (polémicas) para um anti-humanismo." *O Reino Flutuante. Exercícios sobre a razão e o discurso*. Lisboa: Edicões 70, 1972.

Hanson, Susan. "Atheism and Writing. Humanism and the Cry." *The Infinite Conversation*. Minneapolis and London: U of Minnesota P, 1993.

Pedro Schachtt Pereira is an Andrew Mellon Postdoctoral Fellow and Visiting Instructor in the Department of Romance Languages and Literatures at the University of Chicago. His PhD dissertation is entitled *Filósofos de trazer-por-casa. A desconfiança da filosofia como motivo literário na ficção de Eça de Queirós, Machado de Assis e Raul Brandão* (Brown University). He has published articles on Jorge de Sena, Eça de Queirós, Carlos de Oliveira and others. E-mail: pedrop@uchicago.edu

In Nomine Dei? Saramago, Religion, and "The God Factor"

Keith Anthis

The newcomer to José Saramago may be perplexed by the fact that the theme of religion plays such an important role in a number of the Portuguese Nobel laureate's works (most prominently in *O Evangelho segundo Jesus Cristo*) since Saramago has long maintained that he is an atheist. It is important to keep in mind that Saramago is a man of ideas and that his preoccupations concerning religion focus more specifically on how its most fundamental tenets are often considerably altered in the transition between the written word and its realization. It is through his literature that Saramago seeks to communicate his ideas and, when it comes to religion, Saramago attacks the sometimes gross misinterpretations of the writings of the various religions practiced all over the world, as well as the blatant exploitation of religion by people who merely want to take advantage of other people's insecurities, but who in doing so claim that they are doing "God's work." One of his more outstanding critiques is his highly controversial essay, "The God Factor," originally published in Portuguese and Spanish periodicals just one week after the terrorist attacks of September 11 and presently appearing in English translation. Of course, Saramago has never been one to avoid polemics and has proven time and time again that his goal in criticizing various institutions—religious, governmental, educational, among others—is to provoke people to make changes that Saramago believes will improve society.

Portuguese Literary & Cultural Studies 7 (2008): 347-50.
© University of Massachusetts Dartmouth.

Saramago discusses various atrocities committed during the later twenti-eth century in places like India, Angola and Israel, with short descriptions of scenes that seem better suited to a horror movie than to real life, before finally settling on his main discussion involving the September 11 attacks. He makes more references to some of the most horrible moments of the past half cen-tury, citing Rwanda, Vietnam, Hiroshima and Nagasaki, and, finally, the concentration camps of Nazi Germany, explaining that one of the things that ties them all together is what he refers to as the "God factor," stating that "it is precisely because of God and in God's name that everything has been per-mitted and justified, principally the worst things, principally the most cruel and horrendous." At times it seems difficult to identify exactly how the "God factor" figures into some of the examples given by Saramago—because some of the scenarios he chooses to include were definitely more racially motivated than religiously—but the final one, the Inquisition, works perfectly. Especially noteworthy is the manner in which Saramago refers to the Inquisition: a "ter-rorist organization," similar in form and function to the Taliban, and "dedi-cated to a perverse interpretation of sacred texts that should merit the respect of those who say they believe in them."

Another scenario that would work perfectly within the framework of "The God Factor" might be the response made by the United States to the September 11 attacks, and I think it would be interesting to hear what Saramago has to say about this. Saramago once said: "We invent a sort of real-ity for our own sake. We think that this so-called reality we invent is not only the only reality that exists, but the only reality that we *want*. And we react in a very negative way when someone tells us that the reality of the world is not exactly the way that we think it is."[1] This statement could certainly be applied to the religious right in the United States: this group has become increasingly powerful in recent years, to the point that it exerts an alarming amount of influence on the President, as can be evidenced in his decisions on such controversial subjects as cloning, stem cell research, gay marriage, etc. The problem is that the religious right, and the President as well, actually seem to believe that what they are doing is morally correct according to the tenets of their faith; yet in doing so, they exclude all other possibilities by assuming that their way is the only "right" way—and therefore do not seem to understand why others should want to question their methods of reason-ing or the logic behind the choices they make. The actions taken by the President of the United States following September 11 could make for an interesting extension to "The God Factor," as it seems that their mentality is not too different than those of the people Saramago discusses in this essay. The commonality between terrorists and counterterrorists—which is, at the same time, the main theme of Saramago's essay—is the claim these groups make that their acts of aggression/violence are justified and, more specifically, that such actions, no matter how terrible they might seem under otherwise normal circumstances, are tolerated and even supported by those groups' religions. As Saramago indicates in the essay, these people believe that such acts should be admissible because the ends justify the means. However, Saramago wants to deconstruct their argument by means of a rational analysis of the situation, which he bases on his humanistic point of view, underlining the importance of all human life and the fact that it is not up to a minority of people to decide what is good for the majority, whether it be for religious reasons or otherwise.

It is precisely this God factor of which Saramago speaks that compelled George Bush to proclaim the War on Terror, whose primary goal was to locate Osama bin Laden but which soon extended itself to the invasion of Iraq and search for weapons of mass destruction. Again, the similarities between these actions and the terrorist actions that inspired them is this: the people who made the decision to take action believed that what they were doing was necessary for the preservation of their society's way of life. There was technically no reason for the United States to enter Iraq at they time they did since there were no weapons of mass destruction to be found, and, although Saddam Hussein has been removed from power, little progress seems to have been made towards establishing a more democratic society there. As a matter of fact, some might say that the only progress being made is the ever-increasing number of soldiers—and civilians—killed by people who are simply tired of these people who have invaded their country and who continue to force a foreign ideology onto them. None of the activities in Iraq have anything to do, really, with the terrorist attacks of September 11, nor have they yielded any results in bringing Osama bin Laden and other key figures responsible for the aforementioned attacks to justice. This brings us to yet another important question: if bin Laden were to be found, of what, exactly, would "bringing him to justice" consist?

Saramago's response to the September 11 attacks was fitting of the way in which he responds to such acts of terrorism or violence: he uses humanism to denounce the rationale of those who committed what he can only consider to be atrocities. Saramago has always used his writing as a means to criticize what he considers to be wrong with society, and "The God Factor" is no exception. The Portuguese Nobel wants to bring to our attention the fact that there are people who will take up religion as their shield to wage wars and to wreak havoc on the lives of innocent people in the name of someone Saramago says does not exist. Now that he has told us what is wrong with society, all he has to do is give us a possible solution for the problems he has so deftly signaled. The author, however, would probably respond that it is not his place to make such far-reaching decisions for the whole of society but rather only to point out its defects so that the greater majority can decide how to remedy the situation. He does, of course, remind us to avoid becoming victims of the God factor by suggesting that we rely instead on the same human spirit that has the power to make the *Passarola* fly in *Memorial do Convento*. Most importantly, Saramago would rather try to examine the situation with the intent of discovering the best way to ameliorate it: his only war-waging has occurred with the publication of his literature, including "The God Factor." Now if only the right people would stop making war and pay more attention to this literature.

Note

[1] This interview, given on the occasion of the publication of the English translation of *A Caverna*, was originally published under the title "Prophet of Doom" in the November/December 2002 issue of *Book* magazine.

Keith Anthis holds BA and MA degrees from Texas A&M University and is currently pursuing the PhD at Texas Tech University. His dissertation involves a comparative analysis of themes of historiography and (mis)representations of history in the works of José Saramago and the Galician author Gonzalo Torrente Ballester. E-mail: keith.anthis@ttu.edu

Do imemorial ou a dança do tempo

Eduardo Lourenço

Durante três séculos, sem desfalecimento, o homem ocidental tomou de assalto o barco em que até então tinha seguido pilotado pela Providência. Fê-lo em nome da Humanidade, como o D. João de Molière. De uma Humanidade capaz de ser dirigir sozinha, não para o paraíso de onde se supusera expulsa, mas para um futuro cada vez mais liberto dos medos, das opressões, dos males que desde a chamada noite dos tempos se infligiu a si mesma.

Nunca houve outro autor do seu destino que ela própria, mas as máscaras que inventou para endossar a Outrem a sua responsabilidade, não só fazem parte desse destino, como são a única leitura dele que ilumina. O que fomos com essas máscaras, deuses, demónios, anjos, Deus, quando esse destino tinha um sentido que se confundia com o próprio existir, está tão vivo hoje, que as perdemos ou rejeitamos, como sempre esteve.

O tempo do "Humanidade" que não foi tão humano como o sonháramos, já estava esgotado quando o século XX acabou. Tempo da razão, tempo do progresso, tempo da história a si mesma transparente, tempo da utopia com tempo plausível, não recebia só de si mesmo a sua faustica energia, mas daquele tempo que com tanta determinação recusava. Quando o dispensou e parecia que íamos entrar, de olhos bem abertos, naquele espaço que desde Platão designamos como o da plena claridade, por oposição às aparências, descobrimos que o novo tempo, este nosso, é precisamente o da caverna. De uma caverna perpetuamente iluminada, mais fascinante que todos os céus

Portuguese Literary & Cultural Studies 7 (2008): 351-56.
© University of Massachusetts Dartmouth.

supostos, o dos deuses ou o da razão. O antigo tempo do Ser transcendente, natural ou simbólico, converteu-se em tempo da aparência e nela está encerrado. Neste novo tempo sem raiz alguma no Imemorial onde todos, os antigos tempos repousavam, podemos reciclar, como meros tempos virtuais, todos os passados que sem memória não são tempo de ninguém. E nós, de quem somos o tempo, neste começo de um terceiro milénio ainda de evocação cristã, pelo menos no Ocidente? Anjos definitivamente caídos e quase contentes de nos ter libertado da tutela de um deus que nunca prometeu vir, nem mesmo existir, para nos tirar, dos ombros o peso de uma liberdade imaginária, e do coração um sonho de felicidade não menos imaginária? Ou meros animais, como os evocado, num texto célebre de Ernst Jünger, que desde há milhares de anos estão inventando Deus por ser mais fácil que suportar a ideia de que nunca serão mais do que simples homens que se crêem deuses?

De uma maneira, até hoje inédita, pelo seu excesso, não sabemos quem somos, nem onde estamos. Ao menos nós, ocidentais que tínhamos a pretensão de o saber e para isso inventámos todos os romances sobre as origens e outros mais brumosos sobre um impensável fim. Sem dúvida que sabemos mais que todas as gerações passadas sobre essa origem e que o futuro é tão imaginável como o foi sempre. Talvez por isso estejamos parados no meio de um cosmos de que desvendámos quase todos os mistérios, salvo os nossos de passageiros em trânsito para lado algum realmente pensável, salvo como apocalipse domesticado, como em "Independence Day." Mesmo a Morte perdeu a sua função de espelho onde de uma vez para sempre tínhamos aprendido que éramos mortais sem nos resignar a sê-lo. Nada é mais novo neste começo de milénio, que este sentimento de já não termos uma morte credível—colectiva ou individual—depois de a ter tido tanto e em função dela termos inventado os deuses. E, depois da sua glosada fuga, a Arte com que douramos a sua ausência. A sua definitiva ausência. Não é por acaso que nos ecrãs onde vivemos a nossa vida simbolicamente imortal, há tanta morte. Ou antes, tanto morto sem morte. Um morto com morte, à maneira antiga, uma morte onde se morria ou no silêncio oco do coração, ou na praça pública, como se um deus acabasse de desaparecer, é um luxo reservado a poucos. Digamos, aos Kennedys, ou Marylins, figuras recorrentes do poder e da graça.

Somos anonimamente imortais, mas sem aquela inocência que parece ter sido a nossa quando éramos historicamente e naturalmente pagãos, como os gregos e os romanos de outrora. Foi neste tempo sem morte própria que nós entrámos sem sequer nos darmos conta disso. É esta uma das leituras do tão falado "fim da história," em todo o caso da que foi a nossa, até que os relógios onde líamos um destino com rosto ainda humano, pararam ao mesmo tempo, numa aldeia da Polónia e numa cidade do Japão. Este acontecimento não foi como a batalha de Waterloo ou a invenção da máquina a vapor, mas um momento de história e da História, mas uma outra espécie de tempo, uma eternidade vazia, modelo de todo o tempo futuro vivido de olhos inutilmente abertos. O horror puro é invisível.

Por fora, vivemos e consumimos um tempo realmente planetário, como se fôssemos todos, e não apenas os ocidentais que estenderam a leitura do seu tempo próprio ao mundo inteiro, o primeiro actor da história digno desse nome. Por dentro, vivemos simultaneamente uma temporalidade virtual e real sem relação alguma com o que foi, nos tempos arcaicos, tempo circular, e nos tempos cristãos, uma temporalidade ressentida como desejo ou nostalgia activa do tempo de Deus. Podemos organizar todas as festas para nos lembrar que tivemos um nascimento e uma vida memoráveis, podemos mesmo não acreditando um segundo em tão exaltante invenção, que um Jubileu nos devolva ainda viva a memória de um destino análoga ao nosso quando pensávamos ser "filhos de Deus." Nenhuma magia virtual nos restituirá esse mundo que já nem como História somos capazes, ou temos interesse, em revisitar. Estamos numa outra história onde a urgência do presente a si mesma se basta. Tempo indiscernível da sua própria interpretação, sufocados e prisioneiros dela, como a abelha no seu mel ou Creso no seu ouro.

Para quem não é europeu, herdeiro de um passado sem cessar aspirado pelo futuro, de ordem transcendente ou apenas utópica, esta imobilidade na plenitude, não só não lhe causará estranheza como talvez um justificado contentamento. Com riqueza a mais, nós chegámos, penosamente, onde eles nos esperaram sempre, a um mundo, filho do Céu e da Terra, sem metáfora alguma, cheio das tragédias banais da humanidade, mas sem trágico interior por não haver razão alguma para o ser. O que tanto custou a imaginar e a viver a Nietzsche é, no Oriente, um dado natural. E é de supor que também será daqui em diante para nós, tão grande a sedução da quietude budista no mundo ocidental. Aceitamos agora não ter vindo de nenhum paraíso de onde tivéssemos sido expulsos, nem ir para nenhum "além mundo" que magicamente no-lo devolva. Devemos viver a legenda como a verdade e a verdade como um sonho para sempre adiado. Só assim entraremos no tempo onde já estamos, um tempo onde o ídolo História, que durante dois séculos tomámos por Deus ou o seu anjo ambíguo, deixou de emitir sinais.

A inocente fórmula anarquista, "nem deus nem senhor," não escandaliza nem surpreende ninguém, é uma carta de visita que recebemos no berço antes de abrir os olhos na caverna celeste da televisão onde noite e dia reciclamos êxtases e terrores virtuais que nos tocam menos que os da antiga vida inscrita no círculo da "morte," "inferno" e "paraíso." Estamos obrigados a inventar uma imagem de nós mesmos como se nunca a tivéssemos tido, ou a tivéssemos para saber, sem ilusão alguma, que não é aquela que já somos sem ter nome para ela. Nem bárbaros, nem gregos, nem pagãos, nem cristãos, nem filhos da razão, nem íntimos das trevas, nem vencedores nem vencidos de combates de séculos, subitamente tornámo-nos personagens de jogos vídeo, nem mais nem menos reais que os das aventuras intergalácticas. Aquilo que somos e o navio sem piloto onde singramos deixou o cais de um tempo que imaginávamos conhecer como conhecemos o espaço e aborda agora como se fôssemos todos colombos de nós mesmos, o único continente onde sempre estivemos pensando navegar no oceano de Deus: o do Imemorial.

Nos romances de cavalaria o herói à procura de si mesmo deparava no seu caminho com moradas simbólicas sobre a invocação de virtudes que o confortavam no seu sentimento de não estar de todo perdido. No nosso ex-destino de peregrinos de uma História concebida como uma sucessão de carruagens cada vez mais perfeitas—tempos bárbaros, tempos imperiais, idades médias, renascenças, barroquismos, luzes, progressos sem fim, democracia perpétua, paraíso igualitário—cada etapa nos aproximava daquele tempo dos tempos, o nosso, filho de todos os outros e revelação do seu sonho de esperança sem cessar diferidos. Desde o século XVIII vivemos na convicção de sermos, finalmente, os hóspedes de um mundo que sabia o que queria e para onde ia, pois ninguém nos impunha fins que não fossem da nossa invenção e responsabilidade. Mas chegámos a este tempo onde os tempos esperavam por nós para saberem quem foram, e nada nos mostra que tenhamos nele uma imagem, uma identidade, uma existência mais humana para nós mesmos que o dessa série de tempos dedicados cada um a um altar diferente e a uma só adoração, a nossa de simulacros de Deus.

Sem mais Deus que a sua ausência vivida como uma festa, nem por isso deixamos de ser simulacros, agora de nós mesmos. Simulacros virtualmente eternos, clones do deus que não somos, multiplicando sem fim o nosso esplendor de mortais porque tanto almejámos. Sem a ironia bíblica, temos de nos habituar a ser como "deuses," não por receber existência e sentido de um Outro, nosso semelhante inacessível, mas por poder reproduzir, como Andy Warhol sarcásticos, a nossa vida reduzida à imagem de si mesma. De certo, não resolvemos ainda males tão universais e tragédias como as que todos os dias nos dão o sentimento de ser como outrora, "bichos da terra vis e tão pequenos," mas vivemo-los como se nos interessassem menos que todos os jogos e concursos inventados para nos distraírem deles e nos confirmar na nossa nova existência de deuses virtuais. As próprias vítimas sonham com este Las Vegas planetário que as deixa menos sós nos seus infernos, sem outros Dante que os fotógrafos que no-los metem pelos olhos dentro sem que nos comovam.

Com o fim de um tempo como História, e memória dentro, é o sujeito cultural dele que desaparece. Quer dizer, a Europa. Neste fim do milénio e começo de outro, o "espírito do mundo" chama-se América que só tem três séculos de vivida memória ritualizada. Para ela tudo o mais lhe é fábula, como o foram para nós a Grécia ou Roma, antes de as assumirmos como nossas por voluntária viagem nos seus livros ressuscitados. Nada indica que a América possa fazer connosco o que fizemos com a Grécia e depois com todos os Egiptos e Babilónias perdidos. Não o precisa, mas também não tem interesse em recuperar e universalizar um passado onde mal existiu. É no seu tempo e em função dele, como nós fazíamos para reforçar a nossa imagem de gregos e cristãos, que a América vive e é ele que tentará impor, sem pena, como paradigma universal.

Tudo receberá leitura do lugar e tempo onde o "sentido" da aventura humana se produz e concentra: o dessa mesma América. É o que há de verdade no diagnóstico de Fukuyama: o seu "fim da história" é o fim do paradigma europeu e o início de um outro "indiferente à história" como intencionalmente universal e concretamente europeia. Isto não nos deve escandalizar mais do que a antiga convicção de que a Europa e o Mundo eram sinónimos. Devemos aprender a viver neste novo tempo onde a vontade de poderio europeia, em todas as ordens, não regula todos os relógios do mundo, se alguma vez os regulou. Mas não devemos esquecer que, enquanto tal, o "tempo americano" é um tempo de tipo novo que desconhece o travo de inquietude que Santo Agostinho comunicou à temporalidade cristã e a esse título, um "anti-tempo" europeu. Desde que nasceu, a América é um mundo salvo das águas europeias. Não há nenhum mito que lhe seja mais congenital que o de Moisés. O nosso foi e é ainda o de Ulisses, mas na realidade é vestido do americano que Ulisses continua viajando nos espaços que se nos tornaram inacessíveis. Como se a América viajasse neles para se encontrar, temendo não ser ninguém como herói de Homero, enquanto nós, como o mesmo Ulisses, num tempo gloriosamente parado, não temos mais vida que a da nostalgia de uma História que tinha o nosso rosto e já não o tem.

Eduardo Lourenço ensinou na Universidade de Coimbra, onde estudou História e Filosofia. Partiu de Portugal em 1953 para viver na Alemanha e no Brasil. Veio a instalar-se em França, onde foi professor na Universidade de Nice entre 1960 e 1989. Foi Prémio Europeu de Ensaio Charles Veillon em 1988. É um dos maiores especialistas na obra de Fernando Pessoa. Entre a sua vasta e influente bibliografia, contam-se obras como *Heterodoxia I*, 1949, *Pessoa Revisitado*, 1973, e *Nós e a Europa ou as Duas Razões*, 1988.

Portuguese Poetry in Translation

'Once you Experience Love ...'

Camões
Translated by
Landeg White

1

When fortune was disposed to give some
hope of future satisfaction,
the agreeable pleasures of invention
made me write of the likely outcome.

Love, however, fearing what I wrote
would be artless in its candour,
made of my talents a nightmare
to keep its shams inviolate.

You, then, whom love compels to be subject
to various yearnings! When you read
in a brief book such varied cases,

that are plain truths, without defect ....
once you experience love, I'm persuaded
you'll know what I'm on about in my verses.

2

I'll sing of love in a manner so svelte,
with theme and style perfectly matched,

Portuguese Literary & Cultural Studies 7 (2008): 359-73.
© University of Massachusetts Dartmouth.

two thousand amorous parts of speech
will make hearts feel what they never felt.
I'll do it so love confers life,
painting its thousand delicate mysteries,
its blank rages, its heart-felt sighs,
it foolhardy courage, its remote grief.

But in writing of the highborn disdain
of your tender and fastidious eyes,
I'm content to play the lesser part.

For to sing of your face, a composition
in itself sublime and marvellous,
I lack knowledge, Lady, and wit and art.

4
So much of my life is equivocal,
I shiver with cold in the hot season;
I weep and together laugh without reason,
I embrace the world and clasp a bubble.

My impulses mutually contradict,
from my soul comes fire, from my eyes a fountain;
at times I hope, at times am uncertain,
at times I vary, at times I perfect.

Being earthbound, I soar to heaven,
an hour is a thousand years, and my genius
in a thousand years is to miss my hour.

If someone asks why I am so driven,
I reply I don't know. But I surmise
it's because, my lady, I am in your power.

37
Resolute and strong, buoyed by these breakers
I went wherever my luck ordained,

since, buoyed by the tears that rained
for me from those bright eyes, I could embark.
I had reached the end of my setting
out, with every obstacle foreclosed,
when rivers of love interposed
to obstruct the finality of my parting.

I proceeded in that desperate state
in which death, inevitable and glorious,
makes the defeated already obdurate.

In what shape or unfamiliar guise
could furious death then intimidate
one delivered to him, bound and helpless?

43
As when an adroit, exhausted mariner
swimming from some dreadful shipwreck
in mountainous seas, has saved his neck
though only to speak of it makes him shudder;

and he swears even if he sees the ocean
no longer heaving but placid and secure
he will venture out on it no more
unless profiting hugely for his pains;

in the same state, Lady, am I who withdrew
to free myself from your face's torment,
vowing never again to be lost;

but my heart, where you were never absent,
for the simple dividend of seeing you,
steers me back to that dangerous coast.

53
If I have merited such an ordeal
as my wage for bearing such adversity,

practise on me your cruelty, Lady,
having this heart at your disposal.
Experiment on it, if such is your fancy,
the whole gamut of your disfavour,
so I sustain in this life's warfare
even greater anguish and constancy.

But against your eyes, what could avail?
All that surrenders is by force,
but I shielded myself with my heart,

for in such a hard and bitter struggle
it is good that, being defenceless,
my defence is to fling myself on the dart.

63
Perceiving she was taken, the lovely Procris,
wife of Cephalus, consented to the rape;
she fled from her husband to the mountain top
but I don't know whether from design or disgrace.

Because he, as it happened, being horn mad
out of blind love and violent lust,
followed in her footsteps like one lost,
having already pardoned the guilty jade.

Oppressed by such studied deception,
he flung himself at the cruel nymph's
feet, begging forgiveness, begging for life.

Oh the power of misplaced passion!
that for the crime of which he was victim
he asked pardon from her who had tricked him.

64
My heart had always set such store
on its independence, it was unprepared

for a love so unlawful, so daring,
a torment I never felt before.
But the eyes manifested in such fashion
as others I had seen in dreams,
while reason, scared of what seemed,
fled, leaving the field to passion.

'Oh chaste Hippolytus, loved illegally
By Phaedra, your own stepmother,
who had no acquaintance with honour.

Love has avenged your virtue through me;
but so fully avenged is this other
crime, it now repents of what was done.'

65
Wounded, and with no apparent remedy,
by Achilles who had been dipped in water
so nothing iron could inflict a cut,
the strong and brave Telephus trembled.

He sought prescription, to be cured,
from Apollo's oracle at Delphi.
"Be wounded again," came the reply,
"by the same Achilles," and so was restored.

Obviously, lady, my fate's diagnosis
is that, pierced by your loveliness, the pill's
to see you and adore you as at first.

But such is your beauty, my prognosis
is that of a patient swollen with dropsy:
the more I drink in, the greater my thirst.

69
Daliana took bitter revenge against
the scorn of the shepherd she so much loved

by marrying cowman Gil, to reprove
such crass error and faithless disdain.
Her dependable trust, her self-possession,
her fresh face modelled on roses,
withered as her unhappiness
wrought its cruel alteration.

It was hybrid flower in barren soil,
sweet fruit plucked by a coarse hand,
while her memories of the one disloyal,

turned green meadow to arid highland,
as love feigned and vows broken
left planet-struck the loveliest woman.

71
— "How come you, Portia, to be so wounded?
Was it willingly? Or through innocence?"
— "It was love, making the experiment
if it could bear to spill my blood."

— "And is your blood not determined
to resist your own destruction?"
— "It accustoms me to resignation
since death's terrors are no constraint."

— "So why do you now eat hot coals
if you are accustomed to iron?" "To suffer
belongs with death. So love ordains."

— "And the pain of iron is impalpable?
— "Yes. The pain you live with is a cipher,
and I don't want any death without pain."

79
Apollo, Laetona's enlightened son,
who gladdens human hearts each daybreak,

killed the python, the dreadful snake
that so terrified Tessalia's population.
He shot with his bow, and was wounded in turn
By the arrow tipped with glistening gold;
So, on the beaches of Tessalia, spell-bound
By the nymph Peneia, he was overcome.

Nothing availed him, for all his misery,
neither knowledge, persistence, nor respect
for the fact of his being exalted and sovereign.

If such a one, even through treachery
could not win her love, what should I expect
from her who is herself more than human?

85
In vile prisons I was once fettered
as shameful punishment for my sins;
even now I drag along the irons
that death, to my chagrin, has since shattered.

I sacrificed my life as my warning
that love demands more than lambs or heifers;
I saw wretchedness, I saw exile and grief.
It strikes me now all this was ordained.

I satisfied myself with little, keeping
before me the ambiguous happiness
of seeing what a thing it was to be happy.

But by my star, as I only now realise,
unreasoning death and dubious hazard
made enjoyment for me a risk to avoid.

90
A shift of the eyes, gentle and piteous
without seeing; a gentle, honest smile,

as if forced; a sweet gesture, but bashful,
doubting any personal happiness;
an outcaste, shy and barely audible,
a grave and demure serenity,
whose pure goodwill was the fitting
and gracious evidence of her soul;

a timorous daring; a gentleness;
a blameless fear; a tranquil manner:
a prolonged, unquestioning agony:

this was the unearthly loveliness
of my Circe, and the magic poison
that could metamorphose my fancy.

91
Beautiful eyes that for our present epoch
are the surest sign of paradise,
if you wish to see what power you possess
look at me who are your handiwork.

You will see how existing robs me
of that very laughter you brought to life;
you will see I want no more of love
for as time advances, so do my troubles.

And if you care to look inside this heart,
there you will see, as in a clear glass,
your own self, too, angelic and serene.

But I warn you, Lady, my image apart,
you won't like seeing your own likeness
taking such pleasure in all my pain.

100
When prolonged reflection on my grief
dulls my eyes in sleep, I discern

in vivid dreams that dear person
who was for so long the dream of my life.
There in the empty landscape, straining
my pupils at the shimmering vistas,
I pursue her. And she then appears
remoter than ever, and more driven.

"Don't avoid me, gentle shade," I cry out
while, my eyes brimming with tender shame
like one who speaks what cannot be,

she turns aside. "Dina-", I shout,
and before I have added "-mene," I falter
as even that brief illusion's denied me.

124

While Phoebus was lighting up the mountains
of Heaven with his radiant clarity,
to relieve the boredom of her chastity
Diana was killing time in hunting.

Then Venus who was descending secretly
to fetter the desire of Anchises,
seeing Diana so undisguised
addressed her half-jokingly:

'You come with your nets to the thick wood
to ensnare the fast-running deer,
but my own nets capture the mind.'

'Better,' the chaste goddess replied,
to take the nimble deer in my snare
than be caught in one by your husband.'

127

I no longer feel disillusioned, lady,
over how you always treated my love,

nor at seeing the satisfaction I deserved
withheld after so many years' fidelity.
I lament only the anguish, only the distress
at seeing, lady, for whom you exchanged me;
but such as he is, you have merely avenged me
for your ingratitude, your artifice.

Revenge achieves redoubled glory
in according guilt to the culpable
when the vindicated has a just suit.

But reviewing my all too easy victory
over your ill-treatment and denial,
I wish it were not so much to your hurt.

131
That black, terminal day I was born,
let it be expunged from the almanac;
may it never return or, if venturing back,
let it suffer the same eclipse as the sun.

Let the sky darken, and the sun run wild,
let signs herald the world's end,
let the air rain blood, monsters portend,
the mother be stranger to her own child.

Let astonished people, their hearts aghast
in their ignorance, their faces dazed,
reckon the world already lost.

O timid creatures, don't be amazed
this day brought forth the most accursed
wretch on whom mankind ever gazed!

158
Death, what are you taking?—Daylight.
What hour did you take it?—At dawn.

Do you know what you're taking?—I'm unconcerned.
Then who made you do it?—The Creator.
Who's enjoying the body?—The cold earth.
What became of its Light?—Benighted.
What does Portugal say?—Stop, it's not right,
Dona Maria was beyond my desert.

Did you kill whom you saw?—She was dead.
What does bare Love proclaim?—She dares not.
Who made her stay silent?—My caprice.

What's left at the court?—Hopeless regret.
What's there left to remark?—A void.
It remains only to bewail her grace.

Song IX
Under a parched and barren mountain,
treeless, unfarmed, utterly bare,
the most tedious place in all nature
where no birds drift, nor animals make their lair,
without one flowing river or simple fountain,
nor a palm frond's sweet whispering,
and named in the current vernacular
Arabia Felix, or by inversion, unhappy,
somewhere nature
has located in a gulf
where an arm of the sea shoals off
Abbasiya from Arabia the Bitter,
where Berenice was founded by Ptolemy,
and a place the sun blazes
on so ferociously it vanishes;

here looms the cape, where Africa's
coastline continuing from the south
stops. It is named Aromata, though
under the turning heavens of the world's youth,
Aromata was named in the lingua franca

of the inhabitants Cape Guardafu.
Here, where the sea loves to break through
tumultuously the channel to this gulf,
I took myself and there met
my fortune in the wild,
and here in this corner of the world
so hostile and unbearably remote,
I asked brief life for a brief
respite, since the token
of remaining would be a life broken.

Here I whiled away wretched days,
wretched, unwilling, utterly solitary,
toilsome, full of grief and resentment,
and suffering as my adversaries
not only a life of hot suns and cold seas,
with burning winds, harsh and pestilent,
but my fancies, the apt instrument
to seduce me from my true nature,
and I saw, too, reviving
to my chagrin, the memory
of the brief and superseded glory
I knew among mankind when I was alive,
reminding me of my untold
hours of happiness in the world.
Here was I, wasting away time and life,
and raised on the wings of such fancies
to so great a height I plunged down
(and think how light a descent that was!)
from daydreams and illusory relief
to despair of one day being reborn.
Here my imagination was suborned
by fits of sudden weeping, and sighs
that outdid the winds.
Here, my afflicted soul
was again imprisoned in corporeal
form, ambushed by pain, chagrined,

and rudderless, exposed to the arrows
of imperious fortune,
proud, implacable, and importuning.

I had no place to lay myself down,
nor any remaining hope where my head
might lean a little by way of repose.
All was pain to me, a thing to be endured,
not just that it seemed so, but was ordained
in destiny's never gentle decrees.
Oh that I could tame these thundering seas!
These winds, with their truculent voice
that seem a law unto themselves!
But severe heaven and the stars,
along with endlessly ferocious fate, amuse
themselves with my perpetual fevers,
exercising their malignant noise
against this flesh and bone,
this vile earthworm, and so puny.

If only I could banish by such labours
the certain knowledge that sooner or later
I'd recall those eyes I once had sight of;
and if this sad voice, bursting out,
should reach to those angelic ears
of her for whose smile I once lived;
and now, as the memory revives,
turning over in my feverish brain
times now extinct
of me sweet trespasses,
of the gentle pain and madness
endured and longed for on her account
who (long afterwards) had shown
some touch of pity
for all her former asperity.

If I could know this, it would lend
comfort to the time I am still allowed;
to know this would allay my suffering.
Oh lady, lady, you are so endowed
that even here, on this remote strand,
you sustain me, in my sweet feigning.
With you, simply by imagining,
I soar above the toil and pain
and as thoughts of you revive
I can summon up courage
in the face of death's grim visage,
and my conjoined hopes are kept alive,
making my countenance more serene
as the torments metamorphose
to sweet and happy memories.

So secured, I remain here questioning
the amorous winds that sigh for you
from that region where you are, Lady,
ad the migrating birds, if they had sight of you,
what your habits are, what you are doing,
where, when, with whom, what time of day?
Here, my wearisome days make way
for a new spirit, ready to conquer
fortune and toil,
if only to observe you,
if only to find and serve you
as time promises me all will be whole;
Yet ardent desire, that never suffers
delay, against good sense
opens the wounds of fresh disturbance.

So I live; and if someone should ask you,
Song, how I exist,
you can reply it is because I exist.

Landeg White's translation of *The Lusiads* (Oxford World's Classics, 1997) won the Teixeira Gomes prize. He has been commissioned by the Calouste Gulbenkian Foundation to undertake a complete translation of Camões' lyrical poems. E-mail: landeg@oninet.pt

Three Poems

Ruy Belo

Translated by

Richard Zenith

The Game of Quoits

In this square my childhood resurrects
here my life suddenly has a new wellspring
and surges with the force it had when it started
The time hasn't passed only my consciousness
which I feel temporarily transported back a few years
only my familiar sensation of reflecting on that time
of being a spectator of the succession of succeeding days
of not just living of not living without even knowing I live
in a delimited space where things and people
evidently were because they simply were
only that consciousness and sensation make me suspect
that the time that never passed has passed
The churchyard in late afternoon the game of quoits
the clatter of the quoits the iron stakes
the sun setting on itself and round like a simple
quoit tossed by someone through the space of the day
and ready to fall into the sea as onto a stake
the extravagant and thoughtless act of tossing
the quoit as if in that act life itself were at stake
the stock-still profiles of those who look on

Portuguese Literary & Cultural Studies 7 (2008): 375-378.
© University of Massachusetts Dartmouth.

with caps on their heads and hands in their pockets
it all happened it happens here thirty-five years ago
as if here no one had gotten old
or suffered or died or endured
the enormous hunger needed to produce one rich man
as if no one here had gone in search of his country
in countries far far away from here
It's the very same churchyard same afternoon same quoits
Even this café where I sit watching and watch with my thinking
is the same café where I split my first beer
with my father a beer that resisted
the heat of the summer day
in that wicker basket submerged in that well
It's the same taste I've had in my mouth
for many years now chewing wine and bread and life
the taste of women the taste of girls
forever inaccessible like any absolute
forever impossible yet pursued as if possible
the taste of defeat or the taste of palpable
earth day by day running through my fingers
and one day bound to fill my mouth forever
I've aged I know and all I've gained
is what I lost. I'm a grown-up now.
Meanwhile night has engulfed everything the game is over
and across the sky of time there was a man who passed
or a certain quoit that by chance was hurled into life
and that lives in the precarious trajectory before the fall

Hand to the Plow

Happy the man who manages sadness wisely
and learns to divide it among the days
Though months and years pass it will never leave him

How sad it is to grow old on the doorstep
while weaving in our hands a belated heart
How sad to risk against human returns

the blue equilibrium of summer's sheer mornings
by the ocean that overflows with us
in the long farewell of our condition
It is sad to see in the garden the sun's solitude
reaching from the city's houses and din
to a distant hint of river
and the meager life meted out to us
It is sadder to have to be born and to die
and to have trees at the end of the street

It is sad to go through life as if
returning and to enter humbly into death by mistake
It is sad in autumn to conclude that summer
was the only season
The wind passed by in solidarity and we didn't see it
and we didn't know to go to the green depths
like rivers that know where to find the sea
and know which bridges which streets which people which hills to talk with
through the words of a forever uttered water
But what's saddest is to remember tomorrow's acts

It is sad to buy chestnuts after the bullfight
between sunday and the smoke on a november afternoon
and to have asphalt and many people for your future
and behind you a life with no childhood
looking back at all of this some time later
Day by day the afternoon dies
It is very sad to walk among God and be absent

But manage, poet, your sadness wisely

Flower of Solitude
We lived we conversed we resisted
we crossed paths on the street under the trees
we perhaps made a little stir
we traced timid gestures in the air

but what words can explain
that ours was a solitary and silent
profoundly silent heart
and in the end our eyes watched
like eyes that watch in forests
In the midst of the tumultuous city
in the visible angle of its countless edges
the flower of solitude grew lusher each day
We had a name for this
but the ruthless time of men
killed in us the one who was dying
And in this ambitious heart
alone like a man christ dies
What shall we call the void that flows
relentless as a river?
It is born it swells it will empty
and in all of this it's finally a sea
We lived we conversed we resisted
without realizing that in everything we die a little

Richard Zenith lives in Lisbon, where he works as a free-lance writer, translator, and researcher in the Pessoa archives. His *Fernando Pessoa & Co.—Selected Poems* won the 1999 PEN Award for Poetry in Translation, and his new version of Pessoa's *The Book of Disquiet* (Penguin) was awarded the 2002 Calouste Gulbenkian Translation Prize. His many other translations include *Log Book: Selected Poems of Sophia de Mello Breyner* and António Lobo Antunes's *The Inquisitors' Manual*. His own poetry appears in literary reviews. E-mail: rzenith@gmail.com

From *Flash*

Herberto Helder
Translated by
Alexis Levitin

IV

Mouth.
Brûlure, blessure. Where
the many channels disembogue, as the word has it.
Pure consumption, or in a murmur,
amidst venous blood, or
a trace of flame. Gangrene,
music,
a bubble.
The awful art of passion.
A monstrous pore that breathes the world.
In it the dark, the breath,
burnt air are crowned.
Gold, gold.
Sonorous tube through which the body filters.
All of it, flowing away.

IX

I wouldn't want you broken by the four elements.
Or caught by touch alone;
or smell,

Portuguese Literary & Cultural Studies 7 (2008): 379-83.
© University of Massachusetts Dartmouth.

or flesh heard beneath the working of the moons
in the water's deepest mesh.
Or to watch the operation of a star between your arms.
Or that falconry alone darken me like a blow,
the quivering nourishment among linens piled
high
upon the beds.
Magnificence.
It raised you up
in music, a naked wound
—terrified by richness—
that black jubilation. It raised you up in me, a crown.
It made the world tremble.
And you burned my mouth, pure
spoon of gold, swallowed
alive. Our tongue glittered.
I glittered.
Or else that, nailed together into a single, on-going nexus,
a marble stalk of cane
be born from a unity of flesh.
And someone passing cut the breath
of braided death. Anonymous lips, in the gasping
of arduous male and female
intertwining, creating a new organ within order.
That they might modulate.
With flickering tips of flames, faces throbbed, bursting into plumage.
Animals drank, filling themselves with the rushing of water.
The planets closed themselves in that
forest of sound and unanimous
stone. And it was us, this violent splendor, transformer
of the earth.

Name of the world, diadem.

Untitled
I swallowed
water. Deeply—water dammed within the air.

A maternal star.
And I am here devoured by a sobbing,
weightless from my face.
The glass made of star. The water so powerful
in the glass. My nails are black.
I grab hold of that glass, drink from that star.
I am innocent, uncertain, quivering, potent,
tumescent.
The illumination that the stationary water draws from me
from my hands to my mouth.
I enter spacious places.
— The power of an unknown food to shine
in me; my face,
when a dark hand grazes it, above
the shirt sodden with blood,
below hair dried by moonlight. I swallowed
water. The mother and the demonic child
were seated on the red rock.
I swallowed deep
deep water.

Untitled
I cannot listen to such icy singing. They are singing
about my life.
They have brought forth the taciturn purity of the world's
vast nights.
From the ancient element of silence that devastating
song arose. Oh, ferocious world of purity,
oh, incomparable life. They are singing and singing.
I open my eyes beneath silent waters,
and I see that my memory is the furthest thing
of all. They are singing icily.
I cannot listen to their song.

And if they were to say: your life is a rosebush. See
how it drinks in the anonymity of the season.
Blood drips from you when it's the time for roses.

Listen: aren't you lost in wonder
at the subtlety of the thorns and the tiny leaves?
— If they were to say something, I would be graced
with a boundless name.
Do not sing, do not blossom.
I cannot feel life filling up this way
like an icy song and a rosebush
so spread out in me.

It could be this season of the year remained untouched,
and my existence suddenly was flooded
by all that fervor.
I see my ardent sharpness drain until it merges with maturity
in a confluent
summer's minute.—Would I now be
complete for death?
No, do not sing that memory of everything.
Neither the rosebush on blood-streaked fragile
flesh, nor summer with its
symbols of ferocious plenitude.

I would like to think my fingers, one by one,
a zither dropped into my work.
All of sadness like an admirable life
filling up eternity.
Songs like ice leave me a desert, and the rosebush
sows discord among recoiling
roses. Listen: in the sadness of enormous summer
the oneness of my blood collapses.
I myself cold sing a masculine name,
my entire life
so strong and sullied, so filled with the heated silence
of what we do not know.

It isn't sung, it doesn't blossom. No one
ripens in the middle of their life.
Slowly one touches a suspended part of one's body

and a high sadness purifies one's fingers.
For a man is not a song of ice or
a rosebush. He is not
a fruit as if among inspiring leaves.
A man lives a deep eternity that closes
over him, but there his body
burns beyond all symbols, without a soul and pure
as an ancient sacrifice.

Upon icy songs and terrifying rosebushes,
my connected flesh nourishes the miraculous silence
of a vast life.

It could be that all is well in the pluralness
of an intense world. But
love is a different power, flesh
lives from its absorbed permanence. The life
of which I speak
does not drain away or feed our daily
superlatives. Unique,
eternal, it hovers above the hidden fluidity
of all motion.

— A rosebush, even though
incomparable, covers everything with its crimson distraction.
Behind the night of drooping
roses, the flesh is sad and perfect
like a book.

Alexis Levitin's publications include contributions to *APR, Chelsea, Grand Street, Partisan Review, Prairie Schooner, New England Review,* and *Kenyon Review.* He has published twenty-three books, including *Forbidden Words: Selected Poetry of Eugénio de Andrade* (New Directions, 2003), and *Guernica and Other Poems* by Carlos de Oliveira (Guernica Editions, 2004). Levitin also translated poetry by Herberto Helder and Sophia de Mello Breyner Andresen, a project begun under a 2003-2004 NEA Translation Fellowship. E-mail: levitia@plattsburgh.edu

Reviews and Review-Essays

The Disquiet of Influence

George Monteiro. *Fernando Pessoa and Nineteenth-Century Anglo-American Literature*. Lexington: The University Press of Kentucky, 2000.

Anna Klobucka

George Monteiro's most recent book on Fernando Pessoa is also the latest installment in the fertile line of inquiry initiated by Charles David Ley, who dedicated a chapter to the Portuguese poet in his *A Inglaterra e os Escritores Portugueses* (Lisboa: Seara Nova, 1939), and taken up seventeen years later by the present author's homonymous predecessor, Maria da Encarnação Monteiro, in her *Incidências Inglesas na Poesia de Fernando Pessoa* (Coimbra: Coimbra Editora, 1956). In the following years, Pessoa's literary Englishness came to be explored most fruitfully by Jorge de Sena, in several of the essays gathered in his posthumously published *Fernando Pessoa & C^a Heterónima*, and Monteiro's own important—indeed, in some respects groundbreaking—contribution signals on frequent occasions its indebtedness to Sena's investigations and insights in its author's continuing exploration of Pessoa's "genuine biculturalism" (9). Monteiro enters also into a dialogue with other (all too few) critics who over the years have given serious, sustained attention to Pessoa's Anglo-American connections; their views are presented, sometimes endorsed, occasionally contrasted with Monteiro's own, and often symbiotically integrated within his argument. Anyone wishing for a synthetic yet reasoned overview of the English Pessoa's critical fortune need look no further than Monteiro's copious bibliographic endnotes, which, as an added bonus, occasionally hint at rich interpretive opportunities his chapters stop short of exploring. This is, therefore, not merely an accomplished study, but also an inspiring one: one of its substantial merits is that it openly *raises* the questions it chooses not to consider in depth (thus pointing the way to future approaches, as well as preempting the almost inevitable charges of incompleteness that virtually any approach to Pessoa's labyrinthine oeuvre is likely to provoke).

The book's goals are stated simply, so simply as to almost deceive an unsuspecting reader into believing that the task at hand is in fact straightforward:

Portuguese Literary & Cultural Studies 7 (2008): 387-93.
© University of Massachusetts Dartmouth.

"*Fernando Pessoa and Nineteenth-Century Anglo-American Literature* examines the consequences for his work of Pessoa's knowledge of English and American literature in the nineteenth century" (11). However, although Monteiro himself names the vast areas of potential inquiry that he leaves out from his study—most notably, Pessoa's reading of pre-nineteenth-century English writers, including Shakespeare, and the poetry he wrote in English, both published and unpublished in his lifetime—what remains is by no means limited in scope, much less uncomplicated. Although the author steers clear of any founding theoretical engagement with the concept of literary influence, letting himself be guided instead by what he describes as Pessoa's own recognition of the "simple principle [...] that writers influence other writers and that, by implication, the specific consequences of such influence are worth study" (1), his subtle and intricate discussions of this mechanism at work in the Portuguese poet's *oeuvre* reveal that while the principle itself may be simple, its consequences are far more likely to emerge as exceedingly complex. No critical constructs comparable to the elaborate edifice of the Bloomian "anxiety of influence" may be found to sustain Monteiro's arguments, yet his study plunges deeply into the overflowing reservoir of Pessoa's own homegrown *desassossego* over questions of literary influence, creativity, and genius that are a pervasive presence in his writing. As the author notes, the entire "*companhia heterónima*" may be viewed as an exercise in the fertile dynamics of literary discipleship, with its own historical trajectory along which the principal heteronyms played out their multilayered reciprocal relations, informed by varying degrees of loyalty and resistance (116).

Following a useful chronology of Pessoa's life and work and an introductory overview of his largely unsuccessful attempts to establish himself as an acclaimed English poet, the book's ten chapters examine the reverberations in Pessoa's work of writings by nine British men and women (Wordsworth, Gray, Keats, Byron, Elizabeth Barrett Browning, Robert Browning, Ruskin, Alice Meynell, and Caroline Norton) and three Americans (Poe, Hawthorne, and Whitman). The chapters vary considerably in length and scope, ranging from the compact eleven pages on the young Pessoa's poetic apprenticeship, viewed through his engagement with Grey and Keats, to the generously footnoted twenty-eight pages dedicated to discussing the echoes of Wordsworthian inspiration in Pessoa "himself" (notably in his famous "ceifeira" poem), Alberto Caeiro, and Álvaro de Campos. The latter study, which refers the reader to a number of earlier discussions of the Pessoa-

Wordsworth connection, would benefit from being read in concert with another recent contribution to this growing body of criticism, António M. Feijó's article "Pessoa e a correcção de Wordsworth." Feijó's central thesis is that Pessoa "corrects" Wordsworth, first through a rewriting of the English poet's lyric "Solitary Reaper" (in which the subject's "apocalyptic self-consciousness," hinted at but ultimately appeased in Wordsworth's text, is spectacularly revealed and exacerbated in Pessoa's), but especially through the invention of Alberto Caeiro as an "anti-Wordsworth" (360-61). While Monteiro's and Feijó's readings of the Pessoa-Wordsworth textual cross-fertilization are both parallel and remote from each other—given the respective parameters of their distinct critical idioms—perhaps the most inspiring portion of Monteiro's chapter is the final one, in which the author veers off the relatively predictable course of his discussion in order to engage with Campos's sonnet sequence "Barrow-on-Furness." That group of five sonnets offers another instance of Pessoa's "correction of Wordsworth," the process whose symptomatic index is displayed, however, in the (deliberate or accidental) *error* of its title: although "Barrow-on-Furness" situates itself firmly in the Romantic tradition of local-meditative poetry, with Wordsworth's *The River Duddon: A Series of Sonnets* (1820) as one of its most prominent examples, it also betrays that tradition in a number of ways. Staging his sequence in a commercial and industrial setting (as opposed to Wordsworth's pastoral landscape) and addressing the river from the vantage point of a man-made quay (seated on a barrel and not, like Wordsworth, on the river's grassy banks), Campos formulates his meditation so as to "out-romanticize the great Wordsworth himself":

> While Wordsworth thinks of the high purpose of the river flow, a river that seems
> to laughingly dare the poet (the "Adventurer") who has climbed so high to fulfil
> a "rival purpose"—that is to say, a purpose as worthy as the river's—Campos's
> river serves not to challenge the poet to strive to achieve higher purposes or even
> to think higher thoughts but only to put the ironies of the poet's life in relief. (38)

The leading irony of Pessoa-as-Campos's sequence of sonnets is of course the fact that the river Furness does not exist: Barrow-on-Furness is, in the (geographical) reality of the English Lancashire, the seaport of Barrow-*in*-Furness, Furness being the name of a district, not of a river. It is tantalizing to realize that a somewhat different version of this vocalic equivocation (in vs. on) reemerges, with reference to the same group of poems, in Campos's commentary on the circumstances of their composition, casting ambiguous light on a very particular "irony" of the heteronym's life. In the closing section of his discussion, Monteiro refers to a statement submitted by Pessoa in Campos's name in response to a literary survey. Published in 1926 in the newspaper *A Informação*, Campos's comments contained an account of an "amorous adventure" begun while he was sitting on an empty quay in Barrow-in-Furness (he gets the name right in this context), composing a sonnet:

> Aproximou-se de mim uma rapariga, por assim dizer,—aluno, segundo depois soube, do liceu (*High School*) local—, e entrou em conversa comigo. Viu que eu estava a escrever versos, e perguntou-me, como nestas ocasiões se costuma perguntar, se eu escrevia versos. Respondi, como nestes casos se responde, que não. A tarde, segundo a sua obrigação tradicional, caía lenta e suave. Deixei-a cair. (*Fotobibliografia* 143)

The identity of the adolescent "girl, so to speak," who seductively distracts Campos from the poetic labor at hand, has tended to vacillate among various published versions of the testimonial. In his volume of Pessoa's *Páginas de doutrina estética*, Jorge de Sena maintained the version reproduced above (transcribed here from the photo facsimile of *A Informação*), and commented on the titillating disparity between the grammatical genders of "rapariga" and "aluno," stating that "[conforme] testemunho de Carlos Queirós, o próprio Pessoa lhe chamou a atenção para estes dois elementos, apontando a gralha como voluntária" (240). However, the latest version of the passage—to give but one of several examples—included in the second volume of Pessoa's correspondence, published in 1999 by Assírio & Alvim, changes "aluno" to "aluna" without an explanation, thus normalizing Campos's sexuality (and rendering meaningless, in the process, Pessoa's coyly precise qualifier "por assim dizer"). Curiously enough, given his unprecedented attentiveness to the homoerotic import of the Pessoa-Whitman connection (on which more later), Monteiro gives the gender of the young interloper as unequivocally female in his translation of the passage (reinforcing it, in fact, through a repeated insertion of the subject pronoun ["she"], which Pessoa, writing in Portuguese, was able to avoid altogether). He thus misses the opportunity to pose the following question: Is "aluno" to "aluna" as "Barrow-on-Furness" is to "Barrow-in-Furness," a deliberate dislocation of established parameters of geographic and amorous reference? Is the Modernist Campos engaging in a sexual as well as a literary parody of the Romantic canon? While the equivocal spelling of the preposition linking "Barrow" to "Furness" may, after all, be attributed to a simple typographic lapse in the poems' first edition by Ática (an unverifiable proposition, given that Pessoa's manuscript of "Barrow-on-Furness" has been lost), the "aluno/rapariga" ambiguity stands out in plain view, endorsed and emphasized by its author, but all too often disregarded by his editors and critics.

Among the most satisfying "case studies" in *Fernando Pessoa and Nineteenth-Century Anglo-American Literature* are those that proceed from accounts of spirited archival sleuthing (to which Pessoa's sprawling and convoluted legacy lends itself wonderfully) to stimulating openings of promising lines of inquiry. The chapter on Pessoa's translation of Hawthorne's *The Scarlet Letter* is a good example, as it moves from considerations of documentary evidence to "the question of why and to what end Pessoa translated *The Scarlet Letter* in the first place" (105). Monteiro's answer is that it may have had to do with the central problem faced by the character of the minister Arthur Dimmesdale, who attempts to confess his guilty secret to his congregation, only to find that his expressions of self-abasement are taken instead as unmistakable signs of his moral purity and holiness. Monteiro finds echoes of Hawthorne's Dimmesdale in Pessoa's laconic dissection of the artifice of truth-telling in "Autopsicografia" and, most strikingly, in Campos's "Poema em linha recta," whose heteronymous author is said to avail himself of "Dimmesdale's authentically inauthentic voice" in order to forge a bombastic parody of Fernando Pessoa himself. However, perhaps the most valuable aspect of Monteiro's discussion—beyond his important and convincing identification of the Hawthorne connection—is that it draws attention to the centrality of confessional discourse in Pessoa's writing, much of which is concerned, often indirectly but nonetheless pervasively, with resistance and attraction to the revelation of private truth, with courting and escaping recognition, with the embarrassment of disclosure and the temptations of absolute sincerity.

Another generous stimulus of future investigations may be found in Monteiro's groundbreaking revisitation of the question of Walt Whitman's influence on Pessoa. I am aware of no other published study that points in such unambiguous terms to the fact that the Walt Whitman celebrated by Álvaro de Campos was a very different Whitman from that honored, for instance, by Rubén Darío twenty-five years earlier (a contrastive example that

Monteiro considers at some length). According to Monteiro, "The key to the Portuguese poet's Whitman lies in seeing that for Campos the truest and most meaningful Whitman is the poet as 'great pederast,' the poet for whom a man's love for another man realizes, perhaps in its highest form, the love he sees metaphorically as the kelson of creation" (92). The chapter's title, "Walt's Anomaly," refers to *Walt Whitman's Anomaly*, a small book by one W. C. Rivers published in London in 1913 that was entirely devoted to a hostile denunciation of the American poet's homosexuality. While Monteiro seems unaware that Pessoa's own copy of *Walt Whitman's Anomaly*, densely marked and underlined, survives in his library (now housed in the Casa Fernando Pessoa in Lisbon), his analysis is right on target in linking Pessoa to those English readers of Whitman (most notably John Addington Symonds) for whom the homoerotic charge of the American's poetry was its most irresistible aspect. Pessoa's reaction to Whitman was not far different from what Eve Kosofsky Sedgwick has described as "Whitman's electric effect on his English readers"; however, while in the English context *Leaves of Grass* may have "operated most characteristically as a conduit from one man to another of feelings that had, in many cases, been private or inchoate" (113), no such unmediated communion seemed possible in Portugal, where Pessoa was just about the only reader of Whitman. Enter Álvaro de Campos and his unabashedly homoerotic "Saudação a Walt Whitman," a centerpiece of what was to be, as Monteiro notes, an issue of *Orpheu* virtually devoted to Whitman-style *paiderastia* ("One would not be far from the mark in identifying the theme of the projected third issue of *Orpheu* as *pederastia*" [164]).

It is one strong measure of a book's interest when its reviewer finds it difficult to confine his or her remarks to the word limit prescribed by the journal's editors. Several more of Monteiro's chapters invite detailed commentary, not to mention a comprehensive rereading of significant portions of Pessoa's oeuvre. It is to be hoped that this book, the author's second study dedicated to the Portuguese poet's English-language contexts, connections, and consequences (following *The Presence of Pessoa,* published in 1998 also by the University Press of Kentucky), is merely another link in a continuing chain of inspired and inspiring inquiry that readers of George Monteiro have learned to expect and welcome.

Works Cited

Feijó, António M. "Pessoa e a correcção de Wordsworth." *Os sentidos e o sentido. Homenageando Jacinto do Prado Coelho*. Ed. Ana Hatherly and Silvina Rodrigues Lopes. Lisboa: Cosmos, 1997. 357-370.

——. *Fotobibliografia de Fernando Pessoa*. Ed. João Rui de Sousa. Lisboa: Imprensa Nacional-Casa da Moeda, 1988.

Pessoa, Fernando. *Correspondência 1923-1935*. Ed. Manuela Parreira da Silva. Lisboa: Assírio & Alvim, 1999.

——. *Páginas de doutrina estética*. Ed. Jorge de Sena. 2nd ed. Lisboa: Inquérito, n.d.

Sedgwick, Eve Kosofsky. "Whitman's Transatlantic Context: Class, Gender, and Male Homosexual Style." *Delta* 16 (May 1983): 111-24.

Anna M. Klobucka is Professor in the Department of Portuguese at the University of Massachusetts Dartmouth. She is the co-editor of *After the Revolution: Twenty Years of Portuguese Literature 1974-1994* (Bucknell University Press, 1997) and the author of *The Portuguese Nun: Formation of a National Myth* (Bucknell, 2000; Portuguese translation from Imprensa Nacional–Casa da Moeda). She has recently co-edited (with Mark Sabine) a collection of essays on Fernando Pessoa, *Embodying Pessoa: Corporeality, Gender, Sexuality* (Toronto University Press). Her articles have appeared in *Colóquio/Letras, Luso-Brazilian Review, Portuguese Studies, Slavic and East European Journal,* and *SubStance,* among other journals. E-mail: aklobucka @umassd.edu

Worlds of Difference, Words of Equivalence: Pessoa's Prose Writings and the English-language Reader

Pessoa, Fernando. *The Selected Prose of Fernando Pessoa*. Ed. and trans. Richard Zenith. New York: Grove, 2001.

Mark Sabine

For many who still talk of greatness in literature, Fernando Pessoa is at least four great poets. But will he ever be considered more than one great prosodist? Due in part to the comparative ease of translating and marketing prose fiction, Pessoa's recent canonization as a giant of world literature derives in large measure from the international impact of *O Livro do Desassossego de Bernardo Soares*, which an international writers' panel recently declared one of the "100 greatest books of all time."[1] Even Pessoa's greatest admirers might wonder, however, what readers outside his native land and language would make of the vast remainder of his prose, much of it still little read in Portugal. They will be delighted, perhaps even surprised, to discover what an elegant, well-proportioned and richly entertaining anthology Richard Zenith has fashioned from the supposed "also-rans" of the Pessoan catalogue. For many years one of Pessoa's most able ambassadors to the Anglophone world, Zenith has edited, translated and introduced a selection that, for three reasons, represents a watershed in the publication of Pessoa in English. First, the comprehensive range of Zenith's selections grants Anglophone readers unprecedented insight into the full complexity of Fernando Pessoa's universe. Second, in addition to succinctly enlightening the reader who is unfamiliar with the Portuguese cultural context of Pessoa's work, the anthology also directs a spotlight at that work's interaction with, and continuing relevance to, English-language cultures. Finally, the volume, and Zenith's sensitive and imaginative English renderings, vindicate Pessoa in his many incarnations besides that of Bernardo Soares, as a prosodist of subtlety, power and versatility.

Zenith's success in extracting so many memorable and nuanced passages from the generality of Pessoa's prose, and his emphasis on those texts' relationships with English letters, will make this anthology a delight and enhance

Portuguese Literary & Cultural Studies 7 (2008): 395-402.
© University of Massachusetts Dartmouth.

Pessoa's international popularity. The importance of this book, however, is its adept packaging of a much broader sample of prose than any that has yet reached the English-language market, for example, the judicious yet slim selection in Lisboa and Taylor's *Centenary Pessoa* (1995). The refusal of Zenith's volume to treat its raw material as a mere appendage to the "major" poems demonstrates how attention to Pessoa's prose makes him appear, all over again, as a still larger writer than previously imagined: his output more multifaceted yet also better integrated, and more engaged in dialogue with its social and historical contexts.

This is not simply because the collection introduces more than fifteen of Pessoa's lesser-known voices alongside the familiar quintet, though here one must applaud Zenith's pioneering work in transcribing much unpublished material from Pessoa's famous trunk. More significantly, the output of "neo-pagan" theorist António Mora, astrologer Rafael Baldaya and lovestruck, hunchbacked Maria José et al. is not unloaded before the reader in all its bewildering diversity. Rather, Zenith insists—persuasively—on presenting the contradictory, often fragmentary products of the heteronymic enterprise as a system, and that "system in its totality" as "Pessoa's one perfect work."2 Álvaro de Campos's rambunctious rebuttal of Nietzsche in his *Ultimatum* asserts that the "superman" of the modern age will not be the "strongest [...] toughest [...] freest man," but the "most complete [...] most complex [and] most harmonious" (86-7). While Campos's prediction of the riven subject's supremacy is best not taken too seriously, it helps us define the first of three key observations that Zenith's anthology stresses regarding Pessoa's transgression of the constraints of a unitary, singular identity. Heteronymity, on one level, facilitates the articulation of comprehensive debate of questions metaphysical, political and aesthetic, in which both thesis and counterthesis are presented from diverse perspectives, rational and emotional. The vast and systematic nature of this project makes it insufficient for Alberto Caeiro's "neo-pagan" disciples to critique earnestly each other's poetic styles and aesthetic principles. It requires Pessoa, for example, to create the supercilious critic who attributes the "dullness" of *Paradise Lost* to Milton's preference for a "desert of blank verses" over prose (216), and then to counterpose to him the nutty Professor Jones whose "recipe" for blank verse advises poets to chop their "prose effusion" into "bits about four inches or ten centimeters long" (227).

At the same time, however, Zenith enhances our understanding of the foundations of this immensely rich, yet inconclusive, debate. His selection is calculated to stress how Pessoa interposes the question of subjectivity as a central issue in myriad discussions. The collection indicates just how many unsettling propositions Pessoa extrapolates from his favorite Protagorean dictum that "man is the measure of all things" (234; 304). Heteronymity, as a system, constitutes a tool used for opening up philosophical debate and challenging what Álvaro de Campos called a hegemonic "dogma of personal objectivity" wherein objectivity is but "a rough average of partial subjectivities" (84). However, Pessoa's heteronymic voices also articulate uncertainty about whether—assuming the non-existence of a unitary self—one can control this challenge, and—if one can—what epistemological gain follows. Without overloading the reader, Zenith adeptly exposes how these anxieties color Pessoa's disquisitions on every subject. Thus, his hopes of an exalted destiny for the Portuguese are pinned both on what "sub-heteronym" Thomas Crosse calls their cosmopolitanism and talent for depersonalization (63), and, conversely, on their assumption of a singular and specifically national identity predicated on Sebastianist mythology (163). Thus, also, Pessoa offers a reconciliation of these conflicting analyses, in a third text asking "who, if they're Portuguese, can live within the bounds of just one personality?" (162).

An emphasis on the concept of *living* as a subjective plurality is the third feature of Zenith's collection that so enlarges and animates Pessoa for the English-language reader. Zenith suggests that, in addition to their other functions, the heteronyms were "all born to save Pessoa from the life that bored him, or that he didn't care for, or that he had little aptitude for" (301). This view does not, however, contradict Fernando Cabral Martins's recent insistence that Pessoa, while enigmatic, was also "vivo, desconcertante, interventivo e presente no seu tempo" (Cabral Martins 134). The *drama em gente* was never a purely intellectual abstraction, or a retreat into a private literary never-land, but rather an ever-reconfigured interaction of the imagination with the "exterior" social world. Zenith's collection equips the reader to assess the multifarious social manifestations of what Pessoa termed his "relentless, organic tendency to depersonalisation and simulation" (254): the tendency that spurred him to write and publish articles in the names of the major heteronyms (and even in those of their "subheteronyms," such as Thomas Crosse and Federico Reis) as well as to pluralize his identity and aspects of his life history in his letters and personalia. Zenith is the first to have translated many of the most fascinating of these texts; some of them, such as Pessoa's mediumal "automatic" writings, are here edited and published for the first time. Together, they illustrate that the identities introduced into Pessoa's private and public lives represented more than an escapist dressing up in "other" personalities. Increasingly talked of today as an exponent of literary drag, Pessoa was an artist who, in any of his guises, could say "I am what I am" with genuine, though provisional, sincerity.

Zenith notes of Pessoa's prose that while "the untrammelled word did not necessarily probe more deeply than poetry, […] it drew a closer, more naked picture of its subject" (xv). Certainly it is more apparent from this anthology than from the more familiar poems how immediate and spontaneous was the intermingling of what can only problematically be labeled Pessoa's life and his art. Most remarkably, Zenith guides his reader to a clearer view of this without falling victim to the twin perils of reading Pessoa: on the one hand, the temptation to a reductively (and often spuriously) biographical reading of the heteronymic writings and the designated "fictional" works, and, on the other, the temptation to read Pessoa's correspondence, and his pages of psychoanalytical and occultist self-analysis, as a fantastical fiction, rather than as traces of a life lived partly outside the boundaries of a consistent, individual subjectivity. Zenith provides a thorough social and historical contextualization in a series of evocative introductions and meticulously researched footnotes. He also ingeniously organizes the volume into a chapter sequence that constitutes both a thematic and an (approximately) chronological progression, thus aiding evaluation of Pessoa's political and philosophical discussions in relation to the fundamental concern with subjectivity, but also helping the reader assess how the emergence and—in certain cases—the demise of the heteronyms ties in with his milieu and personal history.

Yet, although Zenith offers his own hypotheses, he mostly leaves the storytelling to Pessoa's texts themselves. He lets Pessoa be his own biographer, and define his troubled relationship to relationships—"I've always wanted to be loved but never to love" (201)—his disdain for nostalgia—"I'm unable to be pessimistic" (245)—and his sexuality—"a latent sexual inversion [that] stops in my spirit" (201). Zenith also addresses the tendency in some Pessoan criticism to a simplistic pathologization of the phenomenon of heteronymity. While Zenith suggests Pessoa may have suffered a couple of bouts of mental disturbance (7; 139), he generally leaves Pessoa equally free to be his own doctor, diagnosing his condition as that of a "hysterical neurasthenic" (125) or a masturbator (237), yet elsewhere treating such pathologization with hyperbolic irony, by claiming that "my craziness is no different from Shakespeare's, whatever may be the comparative value of the products that issue from the saner side of our crazed minds" (262).

Zenith's inclusion of such diverse, often neglected, writings, and his limited interpretative intervention, produce an anthology that maintains an evaluative focus on its contents as texts but simultaneously reveals a psychological fascination and emotional intensity to match the philosophical weight and formal elegance more commonly attributed to Pessoa. The revelation of these qualities obviously affects attempts to assess Pessoa's writings as a unity or *oeuvre*, but it impacts equally upon the reading of the most familiar individual texts. The reader of almost any part of Bernardo Soares's *Livro* enjoys greatly increased interpretative options after sampling the work of the Barão de Teive, a fellow "semi-heteronymous" "mutilation" of Pessoa's "own" personality (301-10; 300; 259). This increase becomes exponential, of course, after comparing the Barão's fatally destructive anxiety about his literary legacy, or his regret for his sexual inactivity, respectively, with Pessoa *ele-mesmo*'s *Erostratus: The search for immortality* (205-12) or the "automatically" transcribed dialogues in which 17th-century Rosicrucian Henry More counsels Pessoa on attempting to lose his virginity (103-6).

Likewise every aspect of the *drama em gente* is rendered more literally dramatic when contemplated in relation to Pessoa's love letters to Ophelia de Queiroz. Here, under the veneer of mawkish endearments and clownish humor, a sense of riven identity is painfully apparent in Pessoa's inability either to reconcile or to sustain his two roles as lover and joker. He turns a surreal joke about his unwittingly providing a spectacle for a group of empty chairs into an accusation that Ophelia is forcing the role of clown upon him (136), and allows Álvaro de Campos to intervene and sabotage the relationship, by impersonating him and rowing with Ophelia, or sending her insulting letters (137; 141-2). Pessoa's contrary attitude, forcing Ophelia to accept his subjective plurality and incapacity for consistent, or unqualified, sincerity, while demanding singularity and sincerity from her, can be viewed as a hyperbolic expression of the craving widely experienced in intimate self-other relationships for the self to be "understood" and accepted in all its complexity, and for the other to be reassuringly "understandable." Zenith includes an impassioned and gloomy letter to Mário de Sá Carneiro, in which this craving resurfaces and appears for once half-satisfied when Pessoa claims that "if I weren't writing to you, I would have to swear that this letter is sincere. [...] But you know all too well that this unstageable tragedy is as real as a cup or a coathanger" (90). Whatever the truth was about Sá Carneiro's capacity for understanding, ultimately Pessoa was to channel the angst of the great existential dilemmas into literary creation, rather than dissipating them in love.

It is important to note that Sá Carneiro features in this anthology in regard not just to his apparent emotional impact on Pessoa, but also to his pivotal role in the intellectual ferment surrounding Pessoa in early twentieth-century Lisbon (58-61). It is remarkable how thoughtfully Zenith elucidates unfamiliar aspects of the Portuguese cultural context for his reader, employing his chapter introductions to present the key cultural figures and institutions around Pessoa, to fill in the necessary reference points from Portuguese history, and to relate Pessoa's *Paulismo*, Sensationism and Intersectionism to more familiar Modernist aesthetics. A particularly effective ploy is the inclusion of several of the prefaces written by Thomas Crosse to introduce an Anglophone readership to Portuguese Modernism and, more specifically, the major heteronyms; thus, the editor's interpretations of the original texts are, to a degree, offset by Pessoa's own reappropriations. One might regret the limited space provided in the collection for Pessoa's comments on the Portuguese literary figures and movements that preceded him. However, the root cause for this regret is arguably not the editor's judgment, but the seemingly increasing insularity of the English-speaking markets where he must hope to sell most copies of his book.

Whatever the need for calculated marketing, Zenith's foregrounding of Pessoa the Anglophone and (literary) Anglophile is both appropriate and effective. He highlights stylistic affinities not only with Beckett and Whitman but also with Swift and Carlyle, and brings together the cream of Pessoa's criticism, by turns reverential, iconoclastic, and affectionate, of Shakespeare, Dickens and Milton. This thorough contextualization of Pessoa within the English literary tradition will doubtless benefit the reception of this and future English editions of his work. More importantly, Zenith's generous selection from the English prose permits exemplification of Pessoa's gamut of styles and genres at its fullest. We also discover his extraordinary capacity, as a non-native speaker, to put a hackneyed English idiom to a fresh, often idiosyncratic, use, as when claiming that "[the artist] must be on fire somewhere. Otherwise he will not cook the goose of his human inferiority" (207). Moreover, in Pessoa's English-language juvenilia there are fascinating hints at the literary lights that guided Pessoa towards expressing an experience of subjective plurality, as when teenage alter-ego Charles Robert Anon draws on Rimbaud at his most alienated in a histrionic catalogue of the "greater hell" of "the vast dung-heap of the world": "I feel as lonely as a wreck at sea. And a wreck I am indeed" (11).

For all these riches, however, any collection of Pessoa's prose must center on the texts that appeared when this exiled *bateau ivre* found an uneasy mooring in the harbour of the Portuguese language, circa 1912. Zenith translates with all the subtlety, finesse, and sheer poetic vigor that distinguish his two editions of *The Book of Disquiet[ude]*, from which a satisfyingly representative thirty pages are included here. If I had one quibble with these beautiful renderings, it would be regarding the occasional neutralization of the syntactic quirks that intensify the startling novelty of Soares's imagery. However, this infrequent dilution matters less in the context of Zenith's admirable preservation of the distinguishing qualities of the heteronyms' prose, which Pessoa himself confessed he struggled to achieve. Soares's meticulously constructed aphorisms and moody rhetoric remain distinct from the neo-classical rhythmic regularity of Reis's sentences, and Zenith revels in Campos's choppy cadences, lexical *épates* and scatological puns. Zenith is at his audacious best in the *Ultimatum*, serving up vivid assonantal flourishes that brilliantly compensate for those of the original that cannot survive translation. While Zenith offers footnote explanations of the "many possibly troublesome references" (71), even a reader unfamiliar with Anatole France will grasp the essence of Campos's manifesto from France's depiction as "Epicurus of homeopathic remedies […] wilted Renan tossed with Flaubert and served in a phony seventeenth-century salad bowl!" (72).

This is not the only passage Zenith includes that illustrates the oft-forgotten fact of Pessoa's broad and elaborate sense of humor. The author of the love letters revels in self-parody, re-inventing Álvaro de Campos as a comic-book baddie, not a literary and philosophical opposite number but something more like Dr. Evil to Pessoa's Austin Powers. At the same time, Pessoa's pen can bleed the lurid Sadeian satire of Jean Seul de Méluret's report from "France in 1950," where young girls are instructed in erotomania at the charitable "Institut Sans Hymen," and where "animal sperm as a beverage has fallen out of fashion" (232-3).

In this as in so many aspects, Zenith's anthology achieves his stated aim of attempting not to represent Pessoa's universe in microcosm, but rather to give "a sense of how far it reaches, and by what diverse paths" (xviii). The volume compels us to (re)consider Pessoa as urbane, spirited, socially engaged and able to wear his encyclopedic erudition surprisingly lightly. And Zenith's flair as translator and discretion as editor safeguard the thrill of discovering the full extent of Pessoa's diversity. This is an important, and highly attractive, publication. It vindicates Pessoa's prose output as a fascinating and distinguished corpus in itself, and adds to our appreciation of the poetical works. Over and above its significance for the reception of Pessoa in English, it sets an example for anthologies in any language of how to bring Pessoa's ideas and his writing to life.

Notes

[1] The list of the "100 best works of fiction of all time," as compiled from a vote by "100 noted writers from 54 countries," was released by the Norwegian Book Clubs in the first week of May 2002 (*The Guardian*, 8 May 2002).

[2] Zenith 2001, "General Introduction," xvii. All subsequent references to this volume are given, by page number only, in the main text.

Works Cited

Cabral Martins, Fernando. "O universo do ponto de vista literário." Review of Fernando Pessoa, *Crítica—artigos, ensaios, prefácios, entrevistas. A Phala* 91 (Jan-Mar, 2002): 134.

Lisboa, Eugênio, and Taylor. *A Centenary Pessoa.* Manchester: Carcanet, in association with the Calouste Gulbenkian Foundation, the Instituto Camões, and the Instituto da Biblioteca Nacional e do Livro, 1995.

Pessoa, Fernando. *The Book of Disquietude.* [1991]. Ed. and trans. Richard Zenith. Revised ed. Manchester: Carcanet, in association with the Calouste Gulbenkian Foundation, 1996.

———. *The Book of Disquiet.* Ed. and trans. Richard Zenith. London: Allen Lane, 2001.

Mark Sabine received his Ph.D. from the University of Manchester in September 2001 for his thesis "Form and Ideology in the Novels of José Saramago, 1980-1989." He was a Researcher at the Institute of Romance Studies, University of London, working as a member of the European Commission-funded CULTOS project, and has lectured on modern Portuguese cultural studies and on Portuguese and Luso-African literature at the Universities of Southampton and Manchester. In 2003 he lectured at the University of Oxford on Fernando Pessoa and Saramago. He has given conference papers and published articles on the work of these authors and of Eça de Queirós and Clarice Lispector, and has published (with Anna M. Klobucka) *Embodying Pessoa: Corporeality, Gender and Sexuality* (Toronto University Press). E-mail: mark.sabine@nottingham.ac.uk

Passos novos numa dança antiga

Sobre Paulina Chiziane
Niketche—*Uma Dança de Poligamia*. Lisboa: Caminho, 2002.
João de Mancelos

À superfície, *Niketche—Uma História de Poligamia*, de Paulina Chiziane, enquadra-se numa longa tradição literária de obras de amor e desamor, sexo e infidelidade, ciúme e vingança. Contudo, uma leitura atenta revela um romance complexo, onde se interroga e denuncia a sociedade patriarcal africana, influenciada por tradições tribais sexistas e por um pensamento europeu conservador—legado colonial que reitera o papel da mulher como ser passivo, insignificante e obediente.

Este meu texto pretende ser apenas um apontamento sobre a *margem*, e a figura que no romance a encarna—Rami. A protagonista, assumindo também a voz de narradora, é uma africana que reflecte e age sobre a sua condição de mulher negra, discriminada na sociedade, na família e no casamento. Rami busca a identidade ao equacionar e perceber a dinâmica dos binómios mulher/homem, esposa/amante, monogamia/poligamia, tradição/escolha individual, numa dança longa e custosa, ora feita a solo, ora em par, e pontuada por alguns passos em falso, várias hesitações, e muitas pisadelas.

O título da obra—*Niketche*—remete precisamente para a dança do amor, entre os zambianos e os nampules, que aqui emerge como uma metáfora menos para os percalços enfrentados por Rami quando descobre que o marido a engana com várias mulheres, e mais para um amor idealizado, e por isso mesmo impossivelmente perfeito:

> Niketche, a dança do sol e da lua, dança do vento e da chuva, dança da criação.
> Uma dança que mexe, que aquece. Que imobiliza o corpo e faz a alma voar. As
> raparigas aparecem de tangas e missangas. Movem o corpo com arte saudando
> o despertar de todas as primaveras. Ao primeiro toque do tambor, cada um sorri,
> celebrando o mistério da vida ao sabor do niketche. Os velhos recordam o amor

Portuguese Literary & Cultural Studies 7 (2008): 403-10.

que passou, a paixão que se viveu e se perdeu. As mulheres desamadas reencontram no espaço o príncipe encantado com quem cavalgam de mãos dadas no dorso da lua. Nos jovens, desperta a urgência de amar, porque o niketche é sensualidade perfeita, rainha de toda a sensualidade. Quando a dança termina, podem ouvir-se entre os assistentes suspiros de quem desperta de um sonho bom. (160)

A *niketche* de Rami passa, primeiro por se tentar vingar das amantes do marido, em número surpreendente e ameaçador—tantas que reconquistá-lo é improvável:

O coração do meu Tony é uma constelação de cinco pontos. Um pentágono. Eu, Rami, sou a primeira-dama, a rainha-mãe. Depois, vem Julieta, a enganada, ocupando o posto de segunda dama. Segue-se a Luísa, a desejada, no lugar de terceira dama. A Saly, a apetecida, é a quarta. Finalmente, a Manuá Sualé, a amada, a caçulinha, recém-adquirida. O nosso lar é um polígono de seis pontos. É polígamo. Um hexágono amoroso. (60)

O hexágono depressa se torna um octógono, com a chegada de duas novas amantes—Eva e Gaby. Os ajustes de contas entre Rami e estas mulheres resultam apenas em equizemas, esfoladelas e garrafadas na nuca. Rami pondera uma outra estratégia, que implica *compreender* as razões das amantes, no sentido duplo do termo: *perceber* e *abarcar*. Rami compadece-se da solidão das rivais e constata que estas transcendem o simplista arquétipo da *outra*: são seres carentes, que amam genuinamente Tony, e dele geraram vários filhos e ilusões. Nas palavras da narradora: "Tremo de piedade, de tristeza e de vergonha. Todas as mulheres são gémeas, solitárias, sem auroras nem primaveras. Buscamos o tesouro em minas já exploradas, esgotadas, e acabamos por ser fantasmas nas ruínas dos nossos sonhos" (28).

Por outro lado, Rami conquista as rivais para si mesma, não para as controlar, mas antes para as ter como aliadas, numa poligamia que se confunde com uma família alargada, onde Tony, o patriarca, cede paulatinamente a autoridade, perante a união, as conspirações e chantagens das mulheres, que desejam ser tratadas com a dignidade de esposas, e reclamam direitos que o marido / amante nunca pensara conceder.

O próprio estilo narrativo do romance evoca uma dança circular, feita de hesitações e digressões, monólogos e diálogos, a lembrar a forma como as histórias eram e são narradas entre os africanos. Reunidos ao redor da fogueira, os membros da tribo vão assumindo, um por um, a função de acrescentar detalhes ao enredo, fazendo progredir a acção, revisitando e mudando aspectos anteriormente referidos.

Também Rami medita ao longo do romance, recorrentemente, sobre questões como a poligamia, as diferenças entre a mulher do norte e a do sul, ou a solidão da mulher traída. De cada vez que regressa a um destes temas, fá-lo de forma *desigual*, caleidoscópica, revendo as suas ideias, confessando as dúvidas, meditando sobre as ambiguidades.

Um caso exemplar é a sua posição acerca da poligamia como instituição, um dos temas fulcrais do romance. No segundo capítulo, a narradora afirma: "Marido não é pão que se corta com faca de pão, uma fatia por cada mulher. Só o corpo de Cristo é que se espreme em gotas do tamanho do mundo para saciar o universo de crentes na comunhão do sangue" (21). Vinte páginas mais tarde, a opinião de Rami mantém-se inalterada: "Posso dar tudo, mas o meu homem não. Ele não é pão nem pastel. Não o partilho, sou egoísta" (41). No capítulo onze, o parecer é semelhante, mas é expresso de forma mais poética e conseguida, ao longo de cerca de cinco páginas: "Poligamia é um uivo solitário à lua cheia. Viver a madrugada na ansiedade ou no esquecimento. Abrir o peito com as mãos, amputar o coração. Drená-lo até se tornar sólido e seco como uma pedra, para matar o amor e extirpar a dor quando o teu homem dorme com outra, mesmo ao lado" (93). Sete capítulos mais tarde, a narradora encara a poligamia com alguma resignação: "Poligamia é isto mesmo. Encher a alma com um grão de amor. Segurar o fogo que emerge do corpo inteiro com mãos de palha. Estender lábios à brisa que passa e colher beijos na poeira do vento. Esperar" (128). No epílogo do romance, Rami e o leitor reconhecem a transitoriedade da poligamia, ela própria apenas um andamento na dança do amor, um afecto com dias contados, minado pelo desinteresse delas ou dele, e pela impossibilidade de partilhar *sempre*.

Outra das técnicas narrativas de Chiziane consiste em apropriar, reescrever e subverter mitos e elementos pertencentes à cultura ocidental, de forma criativa, irónica e, por vezes, bem-humorada. Ao transformar as rivais em amigas; ao despojar o homem de autoridade e ao investir a mulher com a soberania; ao reescrever o mito do marido enganado durante a ausência transformando-o no marido que trai e é *simultaneamente* traído; ao reinventar o significado do espelho, a autora provoca o leitor, desloca-o para longe da *terra cognita*, e desafia a sua capacidade interpretativa.

O espelho, por exemplo, é um elemento simbólico e frequente nos mitos, lendas e contos tradicionais europeus e asiáticos, tanto quanto a água—como superfície que reproduz uma imagem—o é nas Américas, em África e na Oceânia. No romance em análise, o espelho cumpre uma tripla função. Em primeiro lugar, *reflecte* no sentido de pensar, ou seja, é um conselheiro racional e afável, capaz de desdramatizar as situações e animar a narradora. No final do primeiro capítulo, perante a angústia de Rami, o espelho dança como que a dizer-lhe que a infidelidade é apenas um passo do *niketche*, a dança do amor.

A narradora procura, em vão, acompanhar o bailado dessa sua outra imagem, esse eu possível—se possível fosse a Rami tomar decisões racionais na circunstância de desespero, e perante uma situação inédita na sua vida conjugal, para a qual nada nem ninguém a preparara, apesar de ser relativamente comum na sociedade moçambicana, onde há apenas um homem para cada dez mulheres:

> Tento, com a minha mão, segurar a mão da minha companheira, para ir com ela na dança. Ela também me oferece a mão, mas não me consegue levar. Entre nós há uma barreira fria, gelada, vidrada. Fico angustiada e olho bem para ela. Aqueles olhos alegres têm os meus traços. As linhas do corpo fazem lembrar as minhas. Aquela força interior me faz lembrar a força que tive e perdi. Esta imagem não sou eu, mas aquilo que fui e queria voltar a ser. Esta imagem sou eu, sim, numa outra dimensão. (18)

Num segundo sentido, o espelho *reflecte,* isto é, reproduz a imagem: é uma consciência de Rami, que se interroga *a pari passu* sobre a sua condição de mulher casada, preterida por uma ou diversas amantes. No início do quarto capítulo, por exemplo, a narradora ultrapassou a fase da surpresa e da incredulidade perante o comportamento do marido, e passa à segunda etapa: a da auto-culpabilização:

> — Diz-me, espelho meu: serei eu feia? Serei eu mais azeda que a laranja-lima? Por que é que o meu marido procura outras e me deixa aqui? O que é que as outras têm que eu não tenho? [...] Diz-me, espelho meu, onde foi que eu errei? Serei feliz algum dia, com essas mulheres à volta do meu marido?

— Pensa bem, amiga minha: serão as outras mulheres culpadas desta situação? Serão os homens inocentes? (34-35)

Finalmente, o espelho *reflecte*, no sentido de devolver uma imagem *alterada*, invertida, ao remeter à narradora as suas próprias questões, para activar nela pensamentos e atitudes conducentes à mudança:

Vou ao quarto e dialogo com o meu espelho.

— Espelho meu, o que será de mim?

O espelho dá-me uma imagem de ternura e responde-me com a maior lucidez de sempre.

— Não serás a primeira a divorciar nem a última. Os divórcios acontecem todos os dias, como os nascimentos e as mortes, mas tranquiliza-te. Há uma grande diferença entre a vontade do homem e a vontade de Deus. O que Deus põe, o homem não dispõe.

— E qual é a tua vontade, gémea de mim? (171)

Ao responsabilizar Rami, o espelho está, concomitantemente, a investi-la do poder que a sociedade patriarcal e séculos de tradição persistiram em negar. Com o incentivo das amantes do marido, a narradora transita de mulher amordaçada para agente activo na luta pelo seu lugar de esposa principal, e aprende que quando uma mulher não pode mudar uma situação, tem de se mudar a si mesma.

Mas passará Rami para o outro lado do espelho? É aqui que o romance surpreende, ao contrariar o horizonte de expectativas do leitor. Este seria levado a crer que a protagonista, como personagem modelada, em constante reflexão e aprendizagem, tivesse o *bravado* de uma atitude lógica mas inesperada que conduzisse à sua libertação e à conquista da independência como mulher. Contudo, a autora prefere adiar o desenlace e aposta numa reviravolta irónica. São as circunstâncias externas, e não o comportamento da narradora que verdadeiramente conduzem o enredo. Tony voa para Paris, com vista a um fim-de-semana romântico com Gaby, a nova amante, sem informar a esposa nem dar qualquer tipo de justificação para a ausência. Entretanto, um acidente de automóvel faz uma vítima, difícil de identificar, o rosto esfacelado. À excepção da própria esposa, a mãe, família e os amigos acreditam—plausivelmente, diga-se—que o morto é o próprio Tony. De acordo com a tradição do *kutchinga*, uma semana depois do velório, os parentes invadem a casa de Rami, levam-lhe a mobília e demais haveres acumulados ao longo de uma vida de trabalho. Finalmente, o irmão do suposto viúvo segue os preceitos da tradição e possui a viúva.

Nestas circunstâncias, o regresso de Tony reescreve o mito do marido enganado, um tema comum na literatura, desde *A Odisseia* a *Frei Luís de Sousa*, e, ao mesmo tempo, subverte-o. Tony passa de traidor a traído, no quadro de um rito patriarcal e sexista, e torna-se alvo da chacota da vizinhança. Esta situação bizarra revolta-o e humilha-o, e leva-o a questionar a validade das tradições que, páginas atrás, subscrevia—porque eram o sustentáculo do seu poder como homem e figura autoritária na família e na sociedade, e lhe concediam toda a liberdade para enganar Rami:

> — Foi desumano o que fizeram contigo! Ah, cultura assassina!
> Ele entra em delírio. Diz que não sabia que a vida era má, nem imaginava que as mulheres sofriam tanto. Sempre achara que a sociedade estava bem estruturada e que as tradições eram boas, mas só agora percebia a crueldade do sistema.
> — Não condenes a tradição, Tony.
> — Rami, eu já morri assassinado pela tradição. Por isso assumo o risco de desafiar o mundo dos homens. Acabo de provar que dentro da humanidade vocês, mulheres, não são gente, são simples exiladas da vida, condenadas a viver às margens do mundo (228).

A epifania é de curta duração, talvez insincera, e não impede Tony de se apaixonar por uma sétima mulher: Eva. No entanto, e mau-grado o arrependimento de Tony ter sido aparente ou, pelo menos, momentâneo, constitui o primeiro comentário compadecido que este faz sobre a condição da mulher, e marca, também, o primeiro degrau numa escada que conduzirá à vingança de Rami, e que não revelarei, para preservar o segredo da obra. Até porque Chiziane utiliza a técnica do final semi-aberto, não apresentando uma solução definitiva para os conflitos enfrentados por Rami e Tony. O leitor fica com a ideia de que todas as histórias estão sempre em trânsito, sem um princípio nem um fim definidos, tendo o leitor apenas acesso a um fragmento inscrito entre a capa e a contra-capa. Perante a ambiguidade, quem lê ganha independência e espaço interpretativo suficientes para se envolver numa outra história—a que começa quando o livro acaba; a que se partilha, com outras leituras e experiências, *poligamicamente*.

O romance de Chiziane, pelo seu discurso poético e filosófico, e ao mesmo tempo pelo ouvido atento ao português oralizado, regional e gostoso de Moçambique, molda uma história *provável,* convertendo com talento o estranho em familiar e o familiar em estranho. Por outro lado, a autora interroga os valores, quebra o espelho dos costumes cristalizados, e esboça a consciência de uma *nova* mulher africana, capaz de inventar *novos* passos numa dança antiga. E quem melhor do que o artista, quando comprometido com a sua época e espaço, ao assumir-se como uma voz interventiva *e* criativa (não meramente panfletária), para reflectir sobre os destinos da tribo?

Niketche—Uma História de Poligamia não é um romance isento de falhas, e cabe-me, como crítico isento e construtivo, desde logo apontar duas. A primeira diz respeito à forma: ocasionalmente, Chiziane prolonga-se em meditações algo extensas e repetitivas, que distraem do enredo e desencorajam o leitor. Uma maior concisão nos solilóquios resolveria este problema, sem prejudicar a profundidade da obra. Por outro lado, se a personagem principal e o seu marido ultrapassam, graças ao engenho da autora, o estatuto de figuras tipificadas, ao evoluírem e entrarem em conflito consigo mesmas, com os outros e com a sociedade, o certo é que as várias mulheres de Tony parecem ser idênticas—não na idade ou aspecto, mas no papel, estatuto e aparente falta de uma personalidade que, de facto, as distinga umas das outras. São apenas duas irregularidades menores num romance quase perfeito, a remediar através de um trabalho de revisão cuidado.

Assistimos ao alvorecer da literatura moçambicana e a uma nova era no cânone literário. Cada vez mais, vozes autorais até aqui amordaçadas pelo racismo, sexismo e colonização são descobertas, estudadas e difundidas. Neste processo, os escritores marginais ou marginalizados aproximam-se do centro, o centro desdobra-se em centros, e a literatura torna-se polifónica. Na sociedade actual, enquanto as economias tendem para uma crescente globalização, a arte pluraliza-se através de uma visão abrangente e multicultural, em que o outro deixa de ser visto como o exótico distante, o Sexta-feira de *Robinson Crusoe,* e passa a habitar as estantes, cada vez mais ricas, da literatura escrita na língua de Camões, Jorge Amado, Mia Couto, Alda Espírito Santo, José Luís Cardoso ou Paulina Chiziane.

João de Mancelos é professor na Universidade Católica Portuguesa, mestre em Estudos Anglo-Americanos, e doutorado em literatura norte-americana. Investiga na área das literaturas norte-americana e portuguesa, debruçando-se em especial sobre obras de escritores étnicos que espelhem o relacionamento entre o ser humano e a terra. Neste âmbito, tem apresentado várias comunicações em Portugal e em diversos países europeus. Como escritor, publicou várias obras na área do conto e da poesia, entre as quais se destacam *As Fadas Não Usam Batom* (vídeo-livro do programa *Acontece*), *Serena* (publicado em Portugal e em Inglaterra), e *Línguas de Fogo*. Como declamador, gravou textos de Camões para um CD-Rom lançado pela Porto Editora e participou em diversos encontros nacionais e internacionais. E-mail: mancelos@oninet.pt

Provincetown's Portuguese

Frank X. Gaspar. *Leaving Pico*. Hanover, NH: University Press of New England, 1999.
George Monteiro

> When a mature writer creates a novel out of the stuff of his own childhood the results are masterpieces, such as *David Copperfield, Huckleberry Finn, La forja de un rebelde,* or this book, which takes us to the old part of Lisbon.
> Gerald M. Moser on José Rodrigues Miguéis's
> *A Escola do Paraíso* (1961)

> And how many times have you read in some review or other that a writer has finally found his 'voice'? Of course he has done no such thing. Instead, he has found a way of writing words down in a manner that creates the illusion of a voice.
> Margaret Atwood, *Negotiating with the Dead: A Writer On Writing* (2002)

Published by the University Press of New England in 1999, *Leaving Pico* is a poet-novelist's initiation book about a summer crucial to a boy's life in Provincetown about forty years ago. It is written as a first-person narrative from the boy-hero's point-of-view. It is that boy's voice that emanates from the pages of this first novel. It is also, paradoxically, the voice of the artist in mid-life who has discovered his "voice" (or at least one of them) or, rather, if we concur with Margaret Atwood, it is the "illusion of a voice." No one will insist, if he thinks for a moment, that Josie's words are exactly those that a boy his age would (or could) have spoken, anymore than anyone will think that Huck Finn's words and description are exactly recalled from pre-adolescent speech (whether Mark Twain's or his friend Tom Blankenship's) in mid-nineteenth-century Missouri. The magic lies in thinking that this must be the way such boys—Mark Twain's or Frank Gaspar's—spoke in their time. And more, we accept—when the illusion succeeds completely—that such voices are capable of carrying a credible narrative, whether or not we are asked to accept the notion that the boy-hero is a writer (as in Mark Twain's great novel, for instance).

Portuguese Literary & Cultural Studies 7 (2008): 411-15.
© University of Massachusetts Dartmouth.

Not all writers of such so-called boy's books have attempted the feat of narrating their tales in their boy-hero's own voice. At the beginning of the great American tradition of the boy's book, for instance, the New Englander Thomas Bailey Aldrich achieved a great success with *The Story of a Bad Boy*, an engaging narrative written from the omniscient vantage point of an adult looking back on (and judging) his childhood. It is precisely that inevitably judgmental perspective of the adult that the adult writers of *The Catcher in the Rye* and *The Adventures of Huckleberry Finn*, as well as *Leaving Pico*, strive and manage to evade.

From the earliest days of the genre, novelists have employed so-called interpolated tales. This device often takes the form of one character's giving the author a breather from his carrying on his major narrative by telling a story of his own. At their most cohesive, even when such tales shed thematic light on the main narrative (see, for instance, "The Town-Ho Story" in *Moby Dick*) such tales remain somewhat tangential to the main story. Gaspar avails himself of this device but makes a valiant and largely successful attempt to incorporate the tale of the great fifteenth-century Azorean Ancestor (Francisco Carvalho), whose monumental adventure—the discovery of America before Columbus—must be recovered, not through history books that do not mention him, but through the storytelling imagination of the boy Josie and his not entirely acculturated grandfather. With some indebtedness, I think, to Faulkner's dramatization of the story recovery and inventive efforts of Quentin and Shreve in Faulkner's *Absalom, Absalom!*, Gaspar's device is to dramatize the act of co-operative storytelling ("putting the ancestor together" [189]) in installments skillfully folded into the main action of the novel. If this novel strains, it may be when the boy attempts to recreate the voice of his grandfather as narrator. If the illusion of the boy's voice breaks occasionally, it is when John Joseph speaks about the Ancestor he would insert into his own revisionary history of Portuguese exploration and discovery.

At this point, permit me an interpolation of my own. The Grandfather's tale of the Ancestor's pre-Columbus discovery of the New World has at least one suggestive antecedent in John Fiske's *The Discovery of America*, his late nineteenth-century account of the King of Portugal's dealing with Columbus:

> King John was not in general disposed toward unfair and dishonest dealings, but on this occasion, after much parley, he was persuaded to sanction a proceeding quite unworthy of him. Having obtained Columbus's sailing plans, he sent out a

ship secretly, to carry some goods to the Cape Verde islands, and then to try the experiment of the westward voyage. If there should turn out to be anything profitable in the scheme, this would be safer and more frugal than to meet the exorbitant demands of this ambitious foreigner. So it was done; but the pilots, having no grand idea to urge them forward, lost heart before the stupendous expanse of waters that confronted them, and beat an ignominious retreat to Lisbon; whereupon Columbus, having been informed of the trick, departed in high dudgeon, to lay his proposals before the crown of Castile. (397-98)

Over the many decades, if not centuries, there has been a great deal written about Provincetown, most of it by visitors or temporary inhabitants. Some of that writing, for example, Henry David Thoreau's prose or Harry Kemp's poetry, has been distinguished. But there is little or no distinguished writing by a native worth singling out prior to the publication of *Leaving Pico*. Mary Oliver makes the point that while "over the years there has been a lot of talk about what the 'creative' people have added to the town," "none of us was born here. And no one, if you get my meaning," she continues, "ever considered the possibility of a Frank Gaspar" (xiii).

Leaving Pico will be misread or at least read reductively if it is approached as merely a local-color novel populated by quaint characters, exposing their quirky mores and odd customs. Something else is intended. If the novel is written from the inside by an insider, its energy comes from its empathy and sympathy for what once was in all its particulars and no longer is or what, at least, no longer is the same. It can be legitimately described, moreover, as an ethnic novel, if one recognizes that it is the view of Provincetown four decades ago available to the typical second-born generation Portuguese-American boy. Of course, the author of *Leaving Pico* is hardly typical, but his boy-hero Josie Carvalho is meant to be just that. At the least one can say that most of his experiences offer Portuguese-American readers shocks of recognition. But to say this is not enough, after all, for Frank Gaspar intends his narrative to typify his young hero's growing-up. In that sense it is the story of one summer in the village life of a child. Because his theme is as universal as can be imagined, the author writes about only what the boy sees, hears, thinks or imagines. The two men, who every summer rent the same rooms in Josie's house, therefore, are never "outed" in Josie's narrative, while the grandfather's women, rather comical bohemian types, are seen and commented on only in the context of the Portuguese-American community. It is what the boy sees and hears that matters. That the boy is observant, resourceful, even talented is shown to us in the way he can answer correctly the priest Father Santos's avid questions about the horrific deaths of the Church's martyrs. Only barely touched by his sanctimonious "Great Aunt Theophila," who has constructed a home shrine peopled by plaster figures of saints, he is a already a child of the sea, skilled at maintaining and sailing his grandfather's skiff grandiosely bearing the name of Caravella.

Frank Gaspar's achievement here is to have populated a highly credible historical town with realized characterizations. Without ceasing to contribute to the local color of a certain recent time in Provincetown, the neighbors and hangers-on—the kith and kin who speak and move and possess what may now be their only reality in the poems of *The Holyoke* or *Leaving Pico*—share, in their own way, the universality of those individuals who populate the best regional literature—the figures of Edwin Arlington Robinson's Tilbury Town, say, or the fence-menders and apple-pickers living north of Robert Frost's Boston. Provincetown's Carvalhos and the Portuguese in their orbit—islanders and "Lisbons" alike—have their niche in this New England literary company.

With an almost clerical focus, Frank Gaspar searches for the right word in the right place, the word that will move him forward in his quest for the immanent, in his search for what is meaningful, for what has import, in the characters and incidents stored away in memory. In short, as all writers worth reading must do, he searches for what must be written about, for what is most compelling to his artist's imagination, and not for what is merely the fancy of a passing moment.

Leaving Pico has earned Frank Gaspar a place at or close to the head of American fiction writers of Portuguese descent, a category that includes the redoubtable John Dos Passos. If Gaspar can be legitimately called a regional or ethnic writer—and those adjectives are not, in my lexicon, dismissive—he is also to be numbered, justly and primarily so, among those skilled and compelling artists whose interests are humanistic and whose themes are universal.

Works Cited

Fiske, John. *The Discovery of America*. Boston and New York: Houghton Mifflin, 1892.

Gaspar, Frank X. *Leaving Pico*. Hanover, NH: UP of New England, 1999.

Oliver, Mary. Introduction. *The Holyoke*. By Frank Gaspar. Boston: Northeastern UP, 1988. xi-xiii.

George Monteiro's most recent books are *The Presence of Camões* (1996), *The Presence of Pessoa* (1998), *Stephen Crane's Blue Badge of Courage* (2000), and *Fernando Pessoa and Nineteenth-Century Anglo-American Literature* (2000). Forthcoming are bilingual editions of Miguel Torga's *Poemas Ibéricos*, Pedro da Silveira's *Poemas Ausentes*, and *Selected Poems* by Jorge de Sena. He is currently at work on two other books, *The English Face of Fernando Pessoa* and *Elizabeth Bishop's Brazilian Beat*. "The Bureaucratic Tale of the Harbor-Master and the Collector of Customs," his translation of a story by José Saramago, appeared in *Portuguese Literary & Cultural Studies 6*. Email: georgemonteiro@prodigy.net

A Landscape Transformed: Narrative Shifts in Lídia Jorge's *O vento assobiando nas gruas*

Sobre Lídia Jorge
O vento assobiando nas gruas. Lisboa: Dom Quixote, 2002.
Ellen W. Sapega

Since her novelistic debut in 1980, Lídia Jorge has consistently used her fiction to develop an intricate portrait of contemporary Portuguese experience as it has developed in the aftermath of the 1974 revolution. Through the creation of characters who often reflect contradictions arising from abrupt and often unexpected changes in the nation's social fabric since the fall of the *Estado Novo* and Portugal's concomitant loss of empire, Jorge portrays a nation forced to reimagine itself and to reassess its past and present relationships with Europe and Africa. She is always conscious, however, of the limitations and dangers of using literary language to reflect collective experience. Her novels repeatedly deploy complex narrative strategies that at once condense and problematize traditional representational practices. In her continued investigations into the links between language and power, Lídia Jorge seeks, in effect, to call attention to unspoken cruelties and to the violence that frequently lurks just beneath the surface of order and method.

O Vento Assobiando nas Gruas, Jorge's eighth published novel and the winner of the *Grande Prémio* of the Portuguese Writer's Association (APE) for the year 2002, continues this project with the author's return to Valmares, a fictional district in the Algarve that was the setting of Jorge's previous novel, *O Vale da Paixão* (1998). The events of this more recent novel take place at a later date, though, and the characters are asked to play by the rules of a very different game. Revolving around an unlikely love story, the plot of *O Vento Assobiando nas Gruas* recounts the meeting of two very distinct and seemingly incomprehensible worlds. As a friendship and romance develops between Milene, the orphaned granddaughter of the local matriarch, and Antonino Mata, the second son of a large Cape Verdean family, Milene's aunts and uncles, heirs to a once thriving local industry, are thrust into a

Portuguese Literary & Cultural Studies 7 (2008): 417-22.
© University of Massachusetts Dartmouth.

series of unexpected situations that ultimately serve to reveal their many weaknesses, fears and prejudices.

Descended from José Joaquim Leandro, founder in 1908 of the family business, *Fábrica de Conservas Leandro,* the third generation of Leandros have made names for themselves in the fields of law, commerce, education and health care. They are leaders of the community and are active in local politics. Antonino's family, originally from the island of Santiago and proud of their heritage as *badios di pé ratchado,* are the de facto caretakers of the now defunct cannery. The Leandros disparagingly refer to the Matas as representatives of a third, and perhaps final, wave (*a terceira vaga*) in the history of their factory, which they privately refer to as the *diamante.* It is, of course, inconceivable to them that Antonino or any other members of this "third wave" should enter their private sphere or alter the course of their lives and fortunes.

The novel opens with a short section entitled "Cerimônia" in which Milene, waiting outside the factory, recalls the events put into motion by her grandmother's death five days earlier. It is August 1994 and, because the other members of Leandro family are all out of the country on vacation, Milene's grandmother, Avó Regina, had been entrusted to the care of a rest home. Her children's plan of assuring themselves tranquil, guilt-free vacations was to be ruined, nonetheless, for the old woman managed to disappear when an ambulance charged with returning her home stopped for directions at a busy gas station. Shortly thereafter, her body was found on the threshold of the *diamante,* leaving Milene to arrange for the funeral:

> Pelas ruas de Santa Maria de Valmares, deambulavam magotes de pessoas estrangeiras, com o olhar vagamente espantado sob as palas dos bonés, parando diante das fachadas das casas brancas, admirativas, como diante de um Nilo seco. De resto Milene ainda se havia cruzado com algumas pessoas simpáticas, que até lhe sorriam de passagem, mas nenhuma delas tinha a ver com a sua vida, muito menos com a vida dos seu tios. Não ia pedir-lhes que parassem no lancil para lhes contar o sucedido. (23)

After five days alone in a town as empty of family and neighbors as it is full of vaguely smiling foreign tourists, Milene is drawn to the space where her grandmother's life had ended. Finding herself unable to come up with an explanation of the events that might satisfy her aunts and uncles, she retreats from the world, hiding in the factory's inner courtyard behind several rows of laundry that the Matas had left out to dry.

The story that follows is comprised of some four hundred pages that bear the title "O Livro de Milene." When the Matas return from Lisbon, where they had gone to watch Antonino's brother, Janina, make his singing debut on national television, they find Milene and recognize her as their landlady's granddaughter. After spending several days in the Matas' care, Milene is finally reunited with her family. However, she is sent back to live in the now empty house where she receives only occasional visits from her two aunts: tia Ângela Margarida, whose husband, Rui Ludovice, is Valmares' recently elected mayor, and tia Gininha, the wife of a successful, if somewhat shady, businessman (for a bit on his past, see 190-196). The world inhabited by Regina Leandro's children is haunted by past mistakes and rivalries, making them incapable of caring for Milene and unwilling or unable to understand her needs. In the Mata household, on the other hand, Milene had caught a glimpse of the kindness and affection that she had earlier been denied or lost. It is inevitable that she be drawn to Antonino, her dependence on him evolving into an affection that leads to their mutual attraction and shared desire.

As Milene's relationship with Antonino develops, several parallel stories unfold. One of the novel's sub-plots follows Janina Mata King's ever more successful musical career, chronicling the various pressures and temptations that accompany his rapid rise to fame. In many respects, Janina's story complements that of Milene's two uncles by marriage, both of whom are local powerbrokers. While played out in very different worlds, the greed that threatens to corrupt Janina is no different than the rapacious acquisitiveness exhibited by Milene's tio Dom. (short for Domitílio) Silvestre, who runs a quarry that is aptly named *Indústria Extractiva, Explorações Dom. Silvestre*. Milene's other uncle, tio Rui Ludovice, executes a series of calculated bids to maintain political control at any cost. Despite his campaign slogan, "Outros só Fazem Gestos, Nós Somos a Acção," tio Rui Ludovice's lack of genuine interest in the well-being of his constituents, coupled with his obsession with maintaining his image as a man of action, neatly balances and supplements his brother-in-law's moral corruption, extending it to the political sphere.

The most important, overarching story of this novel is, however, the story of the *diamante* itself. During dinner with a Dutch developer who has plans to build a hotel on the land occupied by the cannery, Milene's tio Afonso explains that his use of the term *vaga* is really no more than a means of marking the different stages of the family's changing fortunes. In short, it refers to a perceived betrayal of the family heritage and patrimony. When Avó Regina signed the lease with the Mata family, her children saw her actions as inconceivable, even though the factory had long been inactive. By coining the phrase *terceira vaga*, tio Afonso likens the Matas' arrival at the cannery to an earlier wave that was also unexpected and unwanted. The *segunda vaga*, as it is retrospectively designated, took place at the time of the 1974 revolution, when Milene's father ceremoniously turned the keys of the factory over to a group of revolutionary workers: "o irmão havia concluído que não valia a pena lutar contra os ventos da História, e numa manhã de Setembro de setenta e cinco resolveu entregar as chaves da Fábrica aos novos responsáveis. Pior um pouco. O irmão José Carlos tinha tido a ideia de assumir o acto por inteiro, entregando as chaves aos operários sobre um almofada de veludo, onde se lia, em letras bordads, a palavra *Leandros*" (291).

The factory was eventually returned to the Leandros in early 1984, when the utopian project of a successful workers' cooperative had failed. No longer of use to the family as a productive business, the abandoned industrial space was then briefly taken over by Milene and her two cousins, who would thereafter refer to the adventures of that time as "o melhor Verão das nossas vidas." As the narrator recalls, however, "the best summer of our lives" was inevitably destined to come to an end, and the cousins, who had sworn to remain together forever, were eventually separated. By the time of Avó Regina's death, only Milene remains in Valmares, as both her cousins have left to study in the United States. While she calls one of them, João Paulo, almost every night, nobody is ever there, and Milene's only chance to "converse" with him comes through the messages she leaves on his answering machine.

The distance that has come between the cousins is emblematic of the times in which they live. Communication has been relegated to the impersonal realm of a machine that records words, but it is unclear whether anyone will ever hear them. In general, the five years that divide the second *vaga* from the third were marked by a loss of innocence and by the Leandro family's attendant entrance into the realm of self-interest. This is evident, above all, in the very words they use to make sense of history's uncontrollable upsurge and flow. While the term *vaga* may have been coined in an effort to command the past and dominate the present, it does little more than call attention to Milene's elders' shared disenchantment and their growing cynicism. By the time of the events narrated, the family has successfully turned the political and economic disappointments associated with revolution's aftermath (with its failure, if you will) to their financial and political advantage. The hostility implied in their seemingly innocent verbal exercise reminds us, nonetheless, of their collective moral bankruptcy.

The *gruas* (construction cranes) referred to in the novel's title are, of course, symbolic of the abrupt transitions that have occurred in Portugal in the decades following the revolution. Calling attention to the Algarve's many building projects, the image of the *gruas* framing the horizon stands as a constant reminder of the region's rapid geographical and economic transformation into a busy resort area. On a more terrestrial plane, the *gruas* also designate Antonino's job as a construction worker who often operates the crane at the Vila Camarga resort project. When seen from Milene's perspective, Antonino controls an enormous machine that is able to raise, lower and shift large objects that humans cannot move unaided. It may be true that the *gruas* are working a visible change on the landscape and that Antonino, from the top of his crane, has a wide-ranging view of the land below. Unfortunately, though, he is no more capable of controlling the hidden forces that determine the region's transformation than he is able to protect Milene from her aunt's possibly well-meaning, but terribly misguided, plans for her.

In her portrait of the Leandros and the Matas, and in the accompanying description of Valmares, Lídia Jorge succeeds in both reflecting and refracting certain easily identifiable elements of contemporary Portuguese society. Like the *Bairro dos Espelhos,* a clandestine neighborhood predominantly inhabited by Cape Verdeans that was once home to the Mata family, rays of light bounce off opaque and dust-covered surfaces in this novel, illuminating them in often unexpected ways. "O Bairro dos Espelhos não passava de um aglomerado raso, sem nome no mapa, e era assim chamado porque, a partir das cinco da tarde as chapas de alumínio e os vidros incrustados nas janelas uniam-se em milhares de reflexos, como se fossem lamelas duma estação orbital construída à semalhança dum olho de mosca" (45). While the characters' actions seem to logically arise in response to a unique, concrete situation, each individual is also so broadly delineated as to attain representative, symbolic dimensions. It is in the figure of Milene, above all, that this story's suggestive, almost allegorical, nature becomes apparent.

Possessing an innocence that her cousin describes in the end as a "sabedoria sem ciência" (527), Milene belongs neither to the world of the Leandros nor to that of the Matas. With her simple yet compelling behavior, she demonstrates a fundamental disregard for society's rules. A specific and logical explanation for Milene's conduct is given at a certain point in the narrative, but this clarification does little to account for her actions. Milene lives, in fact, outside of history and is free of its attendant nightmares. For this reason, her actions bring unspoken social tensions to the surface and call attention to the Matas' and the Leandros' many cultural misapprehensions. However, it is also Milene, in the final analysis, who has the potential to link the future of the two families, granting the Matas and the Leandros the possibility of reaching new heights. As the novel's closing image attests, one day they may be able to look back at themselves, as though from the top of a crane, only to realize that their differences have faded away:

> Milene e Antonino encaminharam-se na direção do portal. Os circunstantes voltaram a formar duas alas. Ali, rente ao chão, éramos cerca de quarenta, e ainda estávamos todos presentes. Para quem nos visse a partir da abóbada branca, seríamos todos parecidos. A partir da rotas dos pássaros, todos iguais. Existiríamos para a abóbada celeste? O padre fez um sinal de despedida sorrindo. Um raio de sol batia nele, fazendo brilhar a ramagem de ouro espalhada na sua capa. A voz prateada do coro, dirigido às alturas, ainda disse "—*Oh! Meu Senhor! Quando Te veremos?*"
>
> Lá fora, onde o grupo se formava, tiravam-se fotografias, sem cessar. (538)

Ellen Sapega is Professor in the Department of Spanish and Portuguese at the University of Wisconsin-Madison. She received her Ph.D. in Spanish and Portuguese from Vanderbilt University in 1987. A specialist in the Modernist movement in Portugal, she has published articles on Fernando Pessoa, Mário de Sá-Carneiro and José de Almada Negreiros, as well as on the contemporary Portuguese novel. She is the author of a book-length study on Almada Negreiros (*Ficções Modernistas: Um estudo da obra em prosa de José de Almada Negreiros* [Lisbon: ICALP, 1992]). Sapega is currently at work on a project that examines public memory and visual culture in Portugal during the 1930s and 40s. She is co-editor of the *Luso-Brazilian Review*. E-mail: ewsapega@facstaff.wisc.edu.

Forthcoming

António Lobo Antunes. The Art of the Novel.
Maria Alzira Seixo, Universidade de Lisboa

Portuguese Language Textbook Series

Francisco Cota Fagundes. *Um Passo Mais no Português Moderno: Gramática Avançada, Leituras, Composição e Conversação.*

Portuguese in the Americas Series

Portuguese-Americans and Contemporary Civic Culture in Massachusetts.
Edited by Clyde Barrow, Center for Policy Analysis,
University of Massachusetts Dartmouth
ISBN: 0-9722561-0-5

Through a Portagee Gate.
Charles Reis Felix
ISBN: 0-9722561-4-8

In Pursuit of Their Dreams: A History of Azorean Immigration to the United States.
Jerry R. Williams
ISBN: 0-9722561-6-4

Sixty Acres and a Barn: A Novel.
Alfred Lewis
ISBN: 0-9722561-5-6

Da Gama, Cary Grant, and the Election of 1934.
Charles Reis Felix
ISBN: 0-9722561-8-0

Distant Music
Julian Silva
ISBN: 0-9722561-9-9

The Representation of the Portuguese in American Literature
Reinaldo Silva
ISBN: 1-933227-18-4

The Holyoke
Frank X. Gaspar
ISBN: 1-933227-20-6

Two Portuguese-American Plays
Paulo Pereira and Patricia A. Thomas
ISBN: 1-933227-21-4

Forthcoming
The Complete Short Stories of Alfred Lewis
Alfred Lewis

Being "Azorean": Identity Politics in the United States and Brazil
João Leal

So Ends This Day: Portuguese and Cape Verdeans in the American Whaling Industry
Donald Warrin

The Complete Poetry of Alfred Lewis
Alfred Lewis

Fashioning Ethnic Culture: Portuguese-American Communities along the Eastern Seaboard
Edited by Kimberly da Costa Holton, Rutgers University, Newark and Andrea Klimt, University of Massachusetts Dartmouth